Legislation, Literature and Sociolinguistics: Northern Ireland, the Republic of Ireland, and Scotland

Edited by John M. Kirk and Dónall P. Ó Baoill

Cló Ollscoil na Banríona
Belfast 2005

First published in 2005
Cló Ollscoil na Banríona
Queen's University Belfast
Belfast, BT7 1NN

Belfast Studies in Language, Culture and Politics
www.bslcp.com

The publication of this volume has only been possible through the financial support of Foras na Gaeilge, tha Boord o Ulstèr-Scotch, and the Northern Ireland Community Relations Council, which aims to promote a pluralist society characterised by equity, respect for diversity and interdependence. The views expressed do not necessarily reflect those of the Council.

The cover photograph, 'Dawn over the Black Cuillin, Isle of Skye', was taken by Gareth McCormack and is reproduced with his kind permission.

British Library Cataloguing-in-Publication Data
A catalogue record for this book is available from the British Library.

ISBN 0 85389 874 X

Typeset by Nigel Craig and John Kirk in Granjon
Cover design by Colin Young
Printing by W. & G. Baird, Antrim

CONTENTS

The papers in this volume were first presented at the Fifth Language and Politics Symposium, "Taking Stock of the Literature, Sociolinguistics and Legislation of Minority or Regional Languages in Northern Ireland, the Republic of Ireland, and Scotland", held at Queen's University Belfast, 15-18 September 2004, as a constituent project of the Arts and Humanities Research Board Centre for Irish and Scottish Studies, for the Forum for Research on the Languages of Scotland and Ulster, which was supported by Foras na Gaeilge, and with additional funding from Iomairt Cholm Cille, the Seamus Heaney Centre for Poetry and Cló Ollscoil na Banríona.

CONTRIBUTORS

Ian Adamson, OBE is a graduate of Queen's University Belfast and for many years was registrar in pediatrics at the Royal Victoria Hospital, Belfast. He has been a member of Belfast City Council since 1989, was Lord Mayor of Belfast from 1996-97, and a Member of the Northern Ireland Assembly from 1999-2003. He is the founder chairman of the Somme Association and of the Ulster-Scots Language Society. In 1998 he was awarded the OBE for services to local politics. He is the author of numerous popular works, including *The Cruthin* (1974), *The Identity of Ulster* (1982), *The Ulster People: Ancient, Medieval and Modern* (1991), *1690: William and the Boyne* (1995) and *Dalariada: Kingdom of the Cruthin* (1998).

Gavin Falconer is a Parliamentary Reporter at the Houses of the Oireachtas in Dublin and was previously Sub-editor (English and Ulster-Scots) at the Northern Ireland Assembly. He is working on *The Bible in Plain Scots* with Dr. Ross G. Arthur of York University, Toronto. A native of Milngavie, he graduated in German and Irish Studies from the University of Liverpool; subsequently, he was awarded a PGCE by Queen's University Belfast, where is now engaged in postgraduate research on Scots.

Dr. Peter Gregson is Vice-Chancellor of Queen's University Belfast, a post he took up in September 2004. Previously he was Professor of Aeronautical Engineering and Deputy Vice-Chancellor at the University of Southampton. He was born in Dunfermline.

Michael Hance is a native of Morayshire but grew up in Aberdeen. He is a graduate in politics from the University of Edinburgh. He is a PR consultant and Director of his own company, Holyrood Connections Ltd. He is also Manager of the Scots Language Resource Centre, Director of the Saltire Society and Facilitator of the Scottish Parliament's Cross Party Group on the Scots Language.

Dr. Ivan Herbison is a native of Ballymena and a graduate of Queen's University Belfast. His PhD thesis is on Biblical narrative in Old English Poetry. His main research specialism is the literary tradition in Scots in Ulster, about which he is the author of numerous papers and pamphlets. He is currently preparing a monograph: *The Guid Scots Tongue: Aspects of the Literary Tradition in Ulster*.

Dr. John Kirk was born in Falkirk and is a graduate of the Universities of Edinburgh, Sheffield, where he did a PhD on Scots grammar, and Queen's University Belfast, where is currently a senior lecturer in English.

Dr. Will Lamb is an American by birth and a graduate from the University of Maryland in Psychology and from the University of Edinburgh in Celtic and also in Linguistics. He is currently a lecturer at the Benbecula Campus of Lews Castle College, part of the University of the Highlands and Islands. His PhD thesis *Speech and Writing in Scottish Gaelic: A Study of Register Variation in an Endangered Language* is awaiting publication. In 2001, he contributed the volume on Scottish Gaelic to the Languages of the World Materials series published by Lincom Europa in Munich.

Edna Longley is Professor Emerita in English at Queen's University Belfast, where she has spent her entire career. She is a leading literary critic. Her books include *Poetry in the Wars* (1986), *The Living Stream: Literature and Revisionism in Ireland* (1997), and *Poetry and Posterity* (2000).

Dr. Wilson McLeod is an American by birth and a graduate of Haverford College in Pennsylvania, Harvard University, where he studied law, and the University of Edinburgh, where he took his PhD in Celtic studies. His research interests are in language policy and planning issues in Scotland and internationally; language legislation and language rights; and the cultural politics of Irish and Scottish Gaelic literature from the late medieval period to the present day. His book *Divided Gaels: Gaelic Cultural Identities in Scotland and Ireland 1200-1650* appeared from OUP in 2004.

Dr. Michael Montgomery is a native of Knoxville, Tennessee and Distinguished Professor Emeritus of English at the University of South Carolina. He is Honorary President of the Ulster-Scots Language Society and Honorary President of the Forum for Research on the Languages of Scotland and Ulster. He has published extensively on Ulster Scots and on trans-Atlantic connections between American English and language varieties in Scotland and Ulster. In 2004, he published the *Dictionary of Smoky Mountain English*, a comprehensive historical dictionary of southern Appalachian English.

Dr. Dónall Ó Baoill is a native of West Donegal and a graduate of University College Galway and the University of Michigan. For 25 years, he worked at the ITÉ, Dublin. Since 1999, he has been Professor of Irish at Queen's University Belfast and, since 2002, Head of the School of Languages, Literature and Arts.

Dr. Conchúr Ó Giollagáin grew up in Dublin and now lives in the Ráth Chairn Gaeltacht in Co. Meath. He pursued his third level education in University College Dublin. He is a Lecturer at the Department of Irish, St. Patrick's College, Dublin City University, and is also a fellow of the National Institute for Regional and Spacial Analysis, the National University of Ireland, Maynooth. His doctoral thesis on the life history of Micil Chonraí, one of the first participants in the migration to Ráth Chairn in 1935, was published as *Stairsheanchas Mhicil Chonraí: Ón Máimín go Ráth Chairn, Cló Iar-Chonnachta*. He has published various articles on the linguistic anthropology and sociolinguistics of the contemporary Gaeltacht. He is a director of the research project commissioned by the Department of Community, Rural and Gaeltacht Affairs: 'A Comprehensive Linguistic Study of the Use of Irish in the Gaeltacht'.

Dr Pádraig Breandán Ó Laighin is a research associate at the Social Science Research Centre, University College Dublin. Formerly, he was Professor of Sociology and Head of the Department of Social Sciences at Vanier College, Montréal.

Ian James Parsley is a native of Groomsport and a graduate in Germanic Languages and Spanish from the University of Newcastle-upon-Tyne. In 1999, he launched the ULLANS-L email list and accompanying website, and since then he has founded the Ulster-Scots Research Centre and Ultonia. With the demise of the Northern Ireland Assembly, his career as a lobbyist became suspended, but his translation, editing and PR services continue unabated. He has been a consultant to the Ulster-Scots Agency, and a regular commentator on Ulster-Scots as well as general minority-language issues.

Alexander Pavlenko is a lecturer in foreign languages at Tagarog Institute of Technology. He is the author of previous articles on Scots and the Ukraine.

Dr. Jennifer Smith is a native of Buckie and a graduate in English Language and Linguistics from the Universities of Durham and York. She worked on the ESRC-funded project *Back to the Roots: The Legacy of British Dialects* from 2000-01. From 2001, she has been a lecturer at the

University of York. She is currently directing another ESRC-funded research project on *Caregiver, Community and Child in the Acquisition of Variable Dialect Features*. She has published results of her research on Scotland and Northern Ireland in *English World-wide* and *Language Variation and Change*.

Anne Smyth is a native of Ayrshire who has lived most of her adult life in Northern Ireland. She was an editorial assistant on the *Concise Ulster Dictionary* project at the Ulster Folk and Transport Museum, where she continues to look after the museum's extensive dialect archive. She is Chairman of the Ulster-Scots Language Society. She is co-editor (with Michael Montgomery) of *A Blad o Ulstèr-Scotch* (The Ullans Press, 2003) and (with Philip Robinson and Michael Montgomery) of *A Denkschrift for R.J. Gregg* (Ulster Folk and Transport Museum, forthcoming).

Dr. Alan Titley is a native of Cork and was educated there and in University College Dublin. He is the author of several novels including *An Fear Dána* (1993) based on the life of the Irish and Scottish poet Muireadhach Albanach Ó Dálaigh. He has also written dramatic works for the stage, for TV and for radio, including BBC and RTÉ. A selection of translations from his three collections of short stories will be published shortly by Lagan Press as *Parabolas*. His main scholarly work is *An tÚrscéal Gaeilge* (1991), a study of the Irish novel, and his selected essays appeared as *Chun Doirne* (1996). He is Head of the Irish Department at St. Patrick's College, Dublin City University, and he also contributes a weekly column to *The Irish Times*.

Dr. George Watson is a native of Armagh and a graduate of Queen's University Belfast. He is Professor of Irish Literature in English and Director of the Research Institute for Irish and Scottish Studies at the University of Aberdeen.

Dr. Christopher Whyte is a native of Glasgow and a graduate of the Universities of Cambridge, Perugia and Rome. He is currently a reader in Scottish Literature at the University of Glasgow. His critical works include the edited collection *Gendering the Nation: Studies in Modern Scottish Literature* (Edinburgh University Press, 1985) and *Modern Scottish Poetry* (Edinburgh University Press, 2004). He is an award-winning Gaelic poet and an extremely accomplished novelist: *Euphemia MacFarrigle and the Laughing Virgin* (1991), *The Warlock of Strathearn* (1997), *The Gay Decameron* (1998) and *The Cloud Machinery* (2000). His edition of Sorley MacLean's *Dàin do Eimhir* was joint winner of the National Library of Scotland / Saltire Society award for the most outstanding research publication of 2002.

Dr. Tomasz Wicherkiewicz is a lecturer in Linguistics and Minority Languages and Head of the Department of Language Policy and Minority Studies at the Adam Michiewicz University, Poznan. He is the President of the Polish Bureau for Lesser-used Languages and the author of *The Making of a Language: The Case of the Idiom of Wilamowice, Southern Poland* (Mouton de Gruyter, 2003).

Joe Zammit-Ciantar is a graduate of the University of Malta and is now a lecturer in Maltese at the University of Malta Junior College and also at the Istituto Universitario Orientale of Naples. As a representative of the Maltese Government, he was one of the drafters of the *European Charter for Regional or Minority Languages*. His most recent books are *A Benedictine's Notes on Seventeenth Century MALTA* (1997) and *The Placenames of the Coast of Gozo* (2000). In 2004, as editor, he launched two new journals: *Symposia Melitensia* and *Fora Melitensia*.

Legislation, Literature and Sociolinguistics: Northern Ireland, the Republic of Ireland, and Scotland

John M. Kirk and Dónall P. Ó Baoill

When we were planning a general conference on the languages of Scotland and Ireland in 2000, we came to realise that we had invited so many papers on language-political topics that they amounted to a separate event in their own right. In turn, those papers provided the material for the first volume of what was to become our series *Belfast Studies in Language, Culture and Politics*. A package of invited thematic papers and related proceedings thus provided the prototype, which was to continue as Project J of the AHRB Research Centre for Irish and Scottish Studies. Project J was initially funded for 2001-03, but additional funds were made available for a fourth year in 2004. An original motivation for these symposia lay with the *Belfast (Good Friday) Agreement* of 1998 and the subsequent legislative provision of the *North/South Co-operation (Implementation Bodies) (Northern Ireland) Order* of 1999, which consequently propelled the development of language policy in Northern Ireland centre stage through the creation of the Linguistic Diversity Branch within the Department of Culture, Arts and Leisure (DCAL) and two cross-border language agencies: Foras na Gaeilge and Tha Boord o Ulstèr-Scotch. Moreover, we immediately realised that policy for Irish and Scots in Northern Ireland could not be discussed in isolation, and that the policy and practice in the Republic of Ireland and in Scotland had to be considered at the same time. We were also aware that these policy issues were not topics to be left to academic researchers alone but needed input from all sides – Government ministers, politicians, civil servants and all their advisers, statutory and institutional practitioners, linguists, lawyers, educationalists, broadcasters, media people, journalists, economists, writers of all kinds, actors, producers, film-makers, activists and interested and informed individuals. And so evolved the formula for those symposia to provide and provoke critical reflection and discussion on language policy pertaining to the Gaeltacht and the Scotstacht in Northern Ireland, the Republic of Ireland and Scotland. After each symposium, a volume of edited papers has appeared. In 2000, *Language and Politics*,[1] in 2001, we published *Linguistic Politics*,[2] in 2002, *Language Planning and Education*,[3] in 2003 *Towards our Goals in Broadcasting, the Press, the Performing Arts and the Economy*[4] – each cumulatively informed by a previous symposium. During those three years, we produced position papers on each of the domains covered by the *European Charter for Regional or Minority Languages*: particularly 'education', 'judicial authorities',

[1] John M. Kirk and Dónall P. Ó Baoill, eds., *Language and Politics: Northern Ireland, the Republic of Ireland, and Scotland* (Belfast: Cló Ollscoil na Banríona, 2000).

[2] John M. Kirk and Dónall P. Ó Baoill, eds., *Linguistic Politics: Language Policies for Northern Ireland, the Republic of Ireland, and Scotland* (Belfast: Cló Ollscoil na Banríona, 2001).

[3] John M. Kirk and Dónall P. Ó Baoill, eds., *Language Planning and Education: Linguistic Issues in Northern Ireland, the Republic of Ireland, and Scotland* (Belfast: Cló Ollscoil na Banríona, 2002).

[4] John M. Kirk and Dónall P. Ó Baoill, eds., *Towards our Goals in Broadcasting, the Press, the Performing Arts and the Economy: Minority Languages in Northern Ireland, the Republic of Ireland, and Scotland* (Belfast: Cló Ollscoil na Banríona, 2003).

'administrative authorities and public services', 'media', 'cultural activities' and 'facilities, economic and social life'. In addition, we raised fresh questions on linguistic human rights and linguistic diversity in the European Union, and also provided fresh comparative studies between the linguistic situation of Irish and Scots and those of NyNorsk, Bokmal, Frisian, Low German, Swiss German, Meänkieli, Basque, and Walloon.

It was against this background that the AHRB Research Centre for Irish and Scottish Studies extended the symposium series with a fourth year of funding in 2004. All but two of the papers – now revised and edited for publication – are presented here.[5]

Legislation

The first article by **Pádraig Ó Laighin** addresses the linguistic and working status of Irish within the EU. It outlines the historical context in which Irish found itself and explains how people embarked on a recent campaign led by Stádas, an umbrella organization established in November 2003. The impetus for the campaign arose from a decision made to admit ten new countries and nine new official languages into the EU during Ireland's Presidency in the first six months of 2004. The political opportunity was seized in an attempt to secure official working status for Irish. As time progressed, a significant social and linguistic movement developed, resulting in the Government's decision in July 2004 to seek official recognition for Irish. A process of discussion was begun by the Dublin Government with EU institutions and Member States. Should this decision reach its logical conclusion, the exceptional status that Irish has held since 1971 will have come to an end and hence the historical distinction between treaty and official languages.[6] Irish citizens had the right since the Amsterdam Treaty of 1997 to write to the principal bodies and institutions within the EU in Irish and receive a reply in that language, but it was a right very few citizens exercised. As a new Constitution and Draft Treaty were drawn up, it afforded another opportunity for Member States to grant improved status to other languages spoken within their borders and the provision of relevant translations of those documents into other minority languages, including the Celtic languages. Irish has had an anomalous status as a treaty language but not an official working language for over 30 years.

A very useful comparison of the status of Irish *vis-à-vis* Luxemburgish and Catalan is duly outlined and discussed. Although Luxemburgish became a national language in 1984, it was not made a treaty or official language within the EU. This role was given to French and German, the two languages most used in education and as a literary medium. The case of Catalan has a different history; the language is not an official language of the EU and, indeed, has only limited rights within Spain itself. However, in an unusual move, the Spanish Government have now indicated that they would like to request that Basque, Catalan, Galician and Valencian be made official languages.[7] It is unclear at this point how this can be achieved as none of these

---

[5] We regret that the papers by Seán Ó Cuireáin and Brian Ó Curnáin were not submitted for publication.

[6] In June 2005, just before going to press, Irish received that recognition as an official language of the EU. The news was greatly welcomed across the country.

languages is a treaty language or likely to become one. Thus another anomaly would be created – languages having 'official status' but not being 'treaty languages' – the opposite of the Irish situation as it is at present.

Ó Laighin comments further on the advantages of having 'official status' for Irish. They include employment opportunities and the recognition of Europe's linguistic diversity. Legal documentation relating to all Member States must be made available in all official languages and since the implementation of the Official Languages Act 2003, the Irish Government must make all legal documentation available simultaneously in Irish and in English. All members will have the right to use Irish in the European Parliament and, with this new status, access to new linguistic projects such as LINGUA, SOCRATES and LEONARDOL will not have to be by special request or petition. This new status will have positive implications for learners and users of Irish throughout the world; it will enhance the linguistic development of the language due to its exposure to new domains of usage a huge increase in certain other domains. Exposure to different aspects of Irish heritage will add a distinctive dimension to the rich cultural mosaic which is Europe. The intrinsic and instrumental values of language will be much enhanced by its visibility and usefulness as a resource for its people as they go about their daily life.

With regard to Scotland, **Wilson McLeod** gives an extensive overall view of the significance of the revised *Gaelic Language (Scotland) Act*, which was placed before the Scottish Parliament in September 2004, shortly after the symposium. This was preceded by extensive public consultation, resulting in a drawn-out process of submission of written reports and recommendations, with the end result that the Bill had been strengthened in different ways although significant and substantial concerns still remain. On closer inspection of the Bill's content, it is obvious that it has benefited from the experience of those involved in the creation and publication of the *Welsh Language Act 1993* and the *Official Languages Act 2003* for Irish. The Scottish Bill, however, lacks the rigour and determination shown in the Irish and Welsh Bills. Bòrd na Gàidhlig, which has been designated the official language agency, is to be given greater powers. Much of the future success will depend on the successful implementation of these powers and the co-operation received from public bodies throughout Scotland in their endeavours to have practical and workable 'language plans' in operation. Gaelic has now for the first time achieved the status of an 'Official Language of Scotland'. This status, however, falls far short of what is required if Gaelic is to become a vigorous and revitalised language capable of dealing with the burden of having to extend into its utilising linguistic, economic and cultural domains, from which hitherto it had been excluded largely by prejudice and which it had not succeeded in penetrating with any great success. The Bill is very vague on many matters of relevance in terms of delivery – the content of language plans, the right to be educated through the medium of Gaelic at different levels of education, the right to engage with the public service and law courts through the medium of Gaelic, whether in writing or by means of oral communication, and the delivery of essential services through the language. Indeed, it would seem that no legally constituted body has any power to enforce any of these necessary changes. The rate at which language plans are expected to materialise is unrealistic in terms of having

---

[7] In June 2005, also just before going to press, Catalan - which since the declaration of the Valencian Language academy includes Valencian - received that recognition as a semi-official language of the EU. Basque and Galician were also granted semi-official status.

any impact on implementing whatever legislation is finally agreed. A fund is to be established by the Executive, which is expected to meet most of the costs of implementing Gaelic language plans. The derisory sums being mentioned cast serious doubts on the willingness of Government and indeed public bodies to take the matter of language planning seriously. The neglect shown in handling the fund for Gaelic Broadcasting should be a warning sign for us as to how Governments reduce the effectiveness of their policies through sheer inaction. Public debate is unlikely to assist a proper assessment of the Bill, whether that takes place in parliament or under the banner of unhelpful tabloid headlines. National language policies and strategies need to be developed and implemented with a sense of urgency if serious progress is to be made.[8]

In Northern Ireland, progress on language policy is slow, although, there took place on 9 September 2004 a public seminar on the proposed guidance to public sector bodies on the implementation of the European Charter for Regional or Minority Languages and its equality impact assessment, organised by the DCAL.[9] Mindful of the heated debate at the 2003 language and politics symposium,[10] we note with pleasure the release of £12m for use in the production of Irish-medium films. A matching £12m is earmarked for what was called in the *Hillsborough Joint Declaration* of 2002 "an Ulster-Scots Academy" in connection with which, although DCAL has consulted stakeholders in various ways, most notably in connection with a Business Plan conducted by DeLoitte Touche, there has been no genuine public discussion of such a use of public funds. Given that decisions are eagerly awaited, such discussion seems to us timely and important. There are many obvious questions: why an *Ulster-Scots* Academy and not a *Language* Academy, to include all languages, not just Ulster-Scots? Why an *Ulster-Scots* Academy and not a *Scots* Academy? If an Academy, in which university will it be located?

One issue which continues to exert more heat than any other is the question of the autonomy of Scots in Northern Ireland and its implications for Government and its agencies. With an acceptance that Scots has the potential to become language through *Ausbau* (use in all registers achieved through elaboration and the necessary codification into a standardised variety) – a language *de spe*, nor *de re*, **Gavin Falconer** provides the most comprehensive case to date for the bound-upness of Scots in Scotland and Ulster ('nature's social union' of his title); in so doing, he seriously challenges claims to the autonomy of Ulster Scots as a separate language. For the task, Falconer re-examines some well-known criteria: structure, apperception, and legislation. He rejects activists' self-definitions: 'Ulster Scots exists, and therefore it is a language', or 'Ulster Scots has existed for 400 years, and therefore it is a language'. Falconer rightly draws attention to the only legislative definition, that of the *North-South (Implementation Bodies) (Northern Ireland) Order 1999*, in which Ulster Scots is categorised as a 'variety of the Scots language'. That correct, descriptive categorisation should be at the centre of all policy-making and implementation activities – and these should, of course, involve Scotland, where the critical mass of speakers and expertise resides. Falconer goes on to problematise activists' pretence and obfuscation in experimenting with the creation of a language capable of

---

[8.] The Gaelic Language Bill was passed by the Scottish Parliament on 21 April 2005.

[9.] The main papers at that event were presented by Bryan Davis, Emyr Lewis and Dónall Ó Riagáin. Together with a note of the day's discussions, those papers are available on the DCAL website at www.dcalni.gov.uk/newsStory/default.asp?id=686 (accessed on 21 June 2005).

[10.] See footnote 4.

categorisation as a separate and autonomous system. What is offered as the written version in the form of translations into 'Ullans' is plain enough for all to see: a language that nae man iver spak.

With regard to apperception, or what Falconer considers 'democratisation', he finds that speakers are wiser than their advocates in perceiving that lack of autonomy and, ultimately and rightly, finding bound-upness only with the system of Scots, which for most remains part of English. Falconer finds a further argument against linguistic secession in the twin philosophies of 'cultural scepticism', which is inspired through religion, and 'regional scepticism', which sees economic and cultural emancipation through the United Kingdom.

Through his notion of politicisation, Falconer is able to explain two things: why so many Unionists are not supportive of Ulster Scots; and why those other self-styled Unionists intent upon separation view support for the maintenance of the natural link with Scotland as 'anti-Unionist'. In the Edmund plan, which underpins the proposals for an Academy discussed in the papers which follow, the suggestion that efforts should be made to help Scottish writers reach an Ulster audience could be interpreted as meaning that their works should be re-spelt in an 'Ullans' orthography – a self-defeating notion, as readers would automatically recognise the Scots of present-day Scottish writers as their own – a point, indeed, confirmed by recent empirical research. Besides, because of its outlandish spellings, few people can understand Ullans.

As Falconer points out, it all comes down to money and, seemingly, the 'he who pays the piper calls the tune' syndrome – Northern Ireland may enjoy the lion's share of funding for Scots – ironically enough, partly through its subvention from Great Britain – but the self-appointed advocates of its 2% of speakers are determined not to share it with the 98% of speakers and experts back in Scotland (an argument in itself for the Scottish Executive to provide at least matching funding and preferably *pro rata*).

Having dealt with status, Falconer profiles the practice of 'revivalist' written 'Ullans', with its rejection of traditional literary Scots of whatever provenance, its invention of the most outlandish orthography, neither mimetic nor symbolic, and its use of idiosyncratic and reductive vocabulary, showing how glaring the need for quality control is, particularly for public-sector publications, in which conventional norms of codification and expression are routinely rejected. Yet, bizarrely, it is just that egregious 'Ullans' which the Northern Ireland Government is supporting with generous funding, evidently unaware of its shortcomings or intent on some wider political goal. Falconer has grown to be an accomplished translator, with his version of *The Bible in Plain Scots* now completed. His criteria for the communicative value of translations merit widespread attention. This milestone article deserves the widest possible readership.

The issue of an Ulster-Scots Academy is addressed in the next three papers. In 1994, two years after its inception, the Ulster-Scots Language Society (USLS) decided to set up an Ulster-Scots Academy. **Anne Smyth**, USLS Chair, and **Michael Montgomery**, USLS Honorary President, write that the Academy consists of the USLS officers and some native speakers and has only linguistic goals: the promotion of the study of Ulster Scots, the recognition of its affinities with Scots in Scotland (the developmental consequences of which remain unelucidated), the pursuit of documentation, research and publication, the recovery of the literary tradition and the provision of access, and the encouragement of use and speaker confidence. They briefly set out the Academy's plans for a tape-recorded survey of present-day Ulster-Scots speech, already under way, an electronic text base of the written tradition, or *kist*, also already under way, the compilation of a dictionary programme, with an annotated bibliography already completed, a translation service, and a translation of the Bible. They also envisage a resource centre. Smyth and Montgomery look ahead with ambition and confidence, although the award of adequate taxpayer funding, for which the USLS has lobbied hard politically over a long period, must remain crucial to their plans.

The paper by Smyth and Montgomery shares much common ground (including the separate development of Ulster Scots) with the next paper by **Ian Adamson**, former MLA, USLS founding Chair, and more than anyone the person who initiated and has led the present Ulster-Scots movement, and who coined the controversial term 'Ullans'. In a brief historical overview, Adamson sets out what he considers to be the main developments in the study of Ulster Scots in general and the creation of an Academy in particular. As far as we can judge, although Smyth and Montgomery talk of an 'Ulster-Scots Academy' and Adamson of an 'Ullans Academy' and even of an 'Ullans (Ulster-Scots) Academy', they appear to be the same thing, facing the same funding needs and political and legislative challenges set out by Falconer.

Government inaction and ineffectiveness are the main focus of the paper by **Ian James Parsley**, former linguist with the Ulster-Scots Agency and now a free-lance language consultant and professional translator into Ulster-Scots. His paper is written in a Scots which most readers are likely to find accessible. His criticisms of Government are wide-ranging: conferences as smokescreens, broken promises, absence of translation policy, failure to consult or seek proper expert advice, delay after delay, deaf ears, and so on. In a succinct and pithy appeal, Parsley urges Government to talk directly to Scots speakers and academic experts about the way current public-sector translations – for which there is no demand from users – are ruining speaker pride, and pleads with it to avoid turning the speech variety into political football.

Taken together, these four presentations on Ulster Scots strikingly set out the parameters and oppositions of the debate about Scots in Northern Ireland between Government, language-society activists, scholarly experts and Scots speakers. It looks set to continue for a while to come, regardless of whether an Academy is funded.

The political climate with regard to Scots in Scotland could not be more different from that in Northern Ireland. Scotland has lacked the courage and vision of politicians such as Ian Adamson to take a lead and do something constructively for the language. A motivating factor in Northern Ireland has been the growing promotion and funding for the Irish language and the need to see fair play or, increasingly, 'parity' or 'equality' between the two sides – not generally an argument used in Scotland with regard to Gaelic and Scots. Promotion of Ulster-Scots has become inseparable from the wider cultural agenda about the recovery of Scottishness in Northern Ireland – such restoration and gainful cultural capital in Northern Ireland are not matched in Scotland, where many have been conditioned to view Scots and Scottish culture as backward and parochial. The rural background to traditional Ulster-Scots creates a certain shared classlessness about it, whereas much present-day spoken Scots in Scotland is regularly associated with the working-class, with which stigma the middle classes and even some working-class speakers themselves do not wish to be associated. Activism for Scots in Scotland in the latter half of the twentieth century has largely come from writers and readers of poetry in Scots, who regarded poetic Scots as a literary language, more than a match for English for all emotional and poetic uses and the expression of states of mind and feeling within the everyday Scot. It is to the Scots Language Society that the impetus for recognition of Scots under the European Charter is due. No doubt it served as a model for the Ulster-Scots Language Society, at least in its aspirations towards recognition for Scots, and the latter has in any case been highly political in its appeal for Academy funding, as mentioned above. Popular perceptions about Scots vary in both places; in Ulster, linguistic autonomy is accepted like an earnest of evangelical faith; in Scotland the myth of languageness is treated with a characteristic glint in the eye or viewed as the necessary first step in a process of refunctionalisation. Until the advent of the Scottish Parliament, no politician was prepared to take Scots on; some who were informed (such as the late First Minister, Donald Dewar) did not feel the need to do anything about it and urged *laissez-faire*. With its new electoral procedures, and with new fora for discussion and the generation of ideas, the Scottish Parliament's Cross-party Group on the Scots Language provides all concerned with Scots, as well as numerous individuals and a good cross-section of MSPs, with an unprecedented opportunity for advocacy and input on behalf of the language at the heart of the parliament.

One similarity between Scotland and Northern Ireland appears to be the inertia, inactivity and procrastination of Government, and the frustration thus engendered. **Michael Hance**, the cross-party group's resilient and indefatigable organiser, details parliamentary questions tabled to the Scottish Parliament in 2004 concerning action on Scots, particularly with regard to the criticism levied in the Committee of Experts' report against the Scottish Executive for its failures to meet its obligations under the European Charter. Much is answered in frustratingly generalised expressions of intent, and although reference is made to the Executive's National Cultural Strategy, it is far from clear what provision for Scots will be made, when, and with what funding. It is also clear that East-West co-operation at Government level is still pretty thin on the ground when they should be tackling the issue of the Scots language as a whole together, including standardisation and codification as well as funding and promotion.

Literature

Scots is renowned for its long historical canon of outstanding literary achievement, part of which is the development of that tradition in Ulster, although it is not so well known. A clear success of the Ulster-Scots movement has been the reawakening of popular interest in Ulster writers who both wrote and, in many cases, extended and adapted verse forms in Scots with considerable originality – the subject of the next paper by **Ivan Herbison**. Herbison's subject is traditional literature in Scots written in Ulster. In his careful and judicious overview, Herbison contrasts contemporary constructed terms such as 'Ulster-Scots' and 'Ullans' with those used by native speakers such as 'Scotch' or 'braid Scotch' or 'the guid Scotch tung'. For Herbison, Scotch in Ulster is a living tongue, presenting a case of survival, not revival, even although he also recognises that Scots has nowadays 'lost its position as a fully autonomous language' and that that loss of autonomy in the past has 'severely impeded the progress of Ulster Scots'. With erudite succinctness, ripe for expansion in a future monograph, Herbison contrasts the then revivalist poetry of Ulster and Scotland in the eighteenth and nineteenth centuries, showing literary as well linguistic tensions. He stresses the spectrum of Scots used in these poems in relation to genre, subject-matter, imagined audience, and persona. He draws political and legislative parallels between that earlier period and the present day. He also considers how language both then and now plays 'a vital role in establishing the boundaries of cultural identity'. In particular, he reports on the alienation felt by traditional speakers upon encountering the outlandish translations of public-service documents discussed above. Herbison applauds diversity and plurality, which he finds to be the traditional norm; he ends by wisely urging that standardisation and codification must neither exclude nor alienate native speakers.

Both Irish and Scottish Gaelic have had rich literary traditions, too. In the twentieth century, the Gaelic poet, Sorley MacLean (Somhairle Mac Gill-Eain 1921-1996), shone above all others. Sadly, it is only now, after his death, that his true achievement is beginning to emerge, in no small way through the edition of one of MacLean's major works, *Dàin do Eimhir*. **Christopher Whyte's** contribution to this volume examines the relationship between MacLean's poetry and literary modernism. White points to a strange anomaly about the body of criticism extant about Maclean's poetry, namely, that only a tiny percentage of it is written and discussed in the original language in which it was written. It is never clear, therefore, whether such criticisms are based on the originals or on the poet's own English translations of his poems. There is a danger of eliding the boundaries between the English and Gaelic versions that ought to be avoided. To view MacLean as modernist in relation to English, French or Russian writing within an almost identical historical period runs the risk of distorting the real picture by viewing him through a different critical framework applied mostly to English-language literature and where most of the analytical commentary is based not on the original Gaelic but on English translations. The basic question which needs to be answered is this: what is/are the appropriate context(s) within which MacLean's poetry should be read, and how useful is the modernism label in pursuing that goal? One of the main characteristics of modernist poetry in post-First War England is what is termed 'breakage' – a moving away from forms of poetry deployed at earlier times and now seemingly inaccessible. This led to further divisions between the poets and their readers. The existence of a shared body of knowledge both sides could draw on was not readily available, which in turn stifled any effective communication, opening up a gap between writers and their audience. New modes of writing were now required and others discarded. This led writers to look elsewhere for inspiration, and a return to previous myths was very much the order of the day, all in the hope of bringing new meaning and clarity to any contemporary perspectives.Similarly, with MacLean's poetry, it ceased to be of the lyrical type, and that in turn demanded that it be read rather than sung, which was an undeniable break with Gaelic tradition. It is probably fair to say that MacLean's access to the European symbolist and decadent poetry had been mediated by the works of his modernist forebears, a fact that also clearly distances him from it. MacLean's choice of Eimhir as a code name for two different women is shown by Whyte to hark back to one of the leading characters of the Ulster Cycle and the plight of Cúchulainn, the hero in much of that early Irish literature. MacLean's poetry is strikingly traditional in its presentation and contains a renewed simplicity which seems to possess both modern and ancient authenticity. In order to narrow the focus of discussion, the author goes on to discuss a specific characteristic of literary modernism under the term 'barrel organ', or perhaps in the English context, the term 'street piano' might be more appropriate. MacLean became familiar with the French literature of the second half of the nineteenth century, a poetry that led the way and heralded the transition towards modernity.

Whyte goes on to discuss in much detail the contents of MacLean's poem 'An Cuilithionn' ['The Cullins'] (depicted in the present volume's cover photograph) of which there exists a longer and an abridged version, the original appearing in 1939 and the abridged version in 1989. These show clearly how MacLean makes effective use of various and different fragments of Gaelic poetry. In this poem comparisons are made between the degrading, humiliating effect of 'castration' of an animal or pet dog and the disastrous effects of the clearances of ancestral lands belonging to Gaelic-speaking peasantry in eighteenth- and nineteenth-century Scotland. The poet's own voice is a solitary one, without an audience. The landscape he describes is an uninhabited countryside, which in his imagination he relates back to earlier historical betrayals among his own 'people' performed with the assistance and support of chieftains and of 'na bùirdeasaich' (the bourgeoisie) mentioned in the poem. The re-echoing of Iain Lom's song, used to such penetrating effect in the poem, announces the denunciation of the present state of things and demonstrates MacLean's genius in his rewording and recasting of the original, which he uses with devastating effect. Further examples of similar transfer of materials are used to exploit and give poignant effect to the bitter experiences which befell the wider Scottish Gaelic communities. The older, more attractive world has now disappeared and can be revived only in a weak and ineffective form.

Although MacLean's poetry, and particularly his *Dàin do Eimhir,* make it difficult to isolate biographical references from his use of lyrical outputs, they nevertheless offered a paradigm which allowed him to draw on his own and his people's literary background. The creation of a 'biographical legend' through 'conscious poetic art' and the possibility of further elaboration in literary form provided MacLean with a formula which future generations and a wider public within and beyond the English-speaking world could find relevant and informative in their own personal circumstances.

Alan Titley's paper begins with a survey of eighteenth- and nineteenth-century Irish writings and poses the question why anyone considered writing in Irish at any point throughout that period. Some wrote in English only, others in Irish only. The reasons for choosing to write in a particular language are personal, artistic or monetary in nature. Loyalty and local pride were the losers. Literacy in nineteenth-century Ireland came mostly with and through the English language, and those who learned to read and write Irish had poor provision in terms of reading material. Inevitably, as literacy was associated in the mind of the common people with Protestants, they became suspicious of the Bible societies active in many parts of Ireland. The Catholic clergy were also vehemently opposed to such proselytising activities.

With the coming of the Gaelic League, a sudden change in the negative thinking and attitudes that had left literacy in the Irish language in a very tenuous position was instilled in the Irish populus. An emphasis was placed on the development, extension and recreation of a native literature in order to affirm their self-esteem as a nation and a people. This new renaissance of literature was inextricably linked to many factors – political, economic, cultural – but also to the future worth and sustainability of a forward-looking and linguistically healthy community. One of the ways in which the gap between a mostly non-literate society and the creation of a vibrant Irish language was to be filled was through the provision of suitable reading materials for the new literate elite. This was done mostly through the ingenious translation scheme initiated by An Gúm, which had within a short period of ten years provided translations of some of the world's greatest literature. There was much debate about the purity of language used in the translations and the suitability of the subject-matter. The arrival of a superior author was eagerly awaited. Great strides were made by many writers to create a distinct literature in Irish, which compared with some of the best that was being produced in English or elsewhere in the non-English speaking world. They included bilingual writers in Irish and English and those who wrote in Irish only. Most of these authors, who have written significant works in the course of the last century, are for the most part unknown to a large percentage of the population. The works of Ireland's best prose authors have, by and large, not been translated into English and some of the translations that have been attempted are of poor linguistic quality due to overdependence on unsuitable registers of Irish English. Literature in Irish is now part of an extensive network or series of networks comprising cultural festivals, summer schools, radio and TV programmes, communities in the immediate environment of Irish-medium schools, poetry and prose readings and drama presentations. This is certain to enrich Irish people's understanding of themselves and to fashion the linguistic possibilities and creative integrity of the language as an instrument capable of sensitive interpretation and expression.

Sociolinguistics

Ulster-Scots activists have long pleaded for funds for a sociolinguistic survey of Ulster-Scots. There is growing desire in Scotland to re-do the linguistic survey of Scotland. Although language planners talk of sociolinguistics in the sense of language sociology – who speaks what languages when and where and how are they learned? – we take sociolinguistics in the current linguistic sense of social variation within a particular language, or how features of a language are indexical with features of social variation. In general, sociolinguistic surveys show that dialect knowledge and use are most frequent among lower social groups. In Scotland, however, studies have shown that knowledge and use of Scots lexis is most frequent among the middle classes, not least because of their knowledge of literature in Scots. It is also evangelical middle-classness which leads the revival of interest in Ulster-Scots.

The first paper deals with the current sociolinguistics of Scots. Behind **Jennifer Smith's** paper lie several general claims that spoken Scots is in attritional decline, with its forms increasingly being replaced by those of English 'moving inexorably towards the English pole'; and there is also a methodological concern about how to demonstrate the spoken language's present state. Born and bred in Buckie, a small fishing town in the north-East of Scotland and on the coastal boundary of a traditional Scots-speaking area, Smith was in an ideal position to tape-record the speech of family and friends whom she had known all her life. Smith reports on five salient phonological and morphological variables. She shows two variables to be in decline across three generations: the velar fricative /x/ to be in steady decline, and the past tense and past participle inflection –*it*, which is well recorded historically, in serious decline. She shows another variable to be erratic: the choice between Scots and English realisations for irregular verbs in their past tense and past participle realisations: *gaed* (for which other spellings are possible) is in cross-generational decline, whereas *sellt/tellt* are being cross-generationally maintained, indeed, increased. Smith shows that erosion is also bound up with diffusion – not every Scots word which meets the pattern is being substituted by the equivalent English form. This diffusional pattern also explains why the distal demonstratives *that*, *thon*, *them* and *those* do not change cross-generationally, but also why *that* (in that distal function) is maintained in each generation to a very high degree, whereas *them* and *those* (in that same function) are not at all realised in each generation. The final variable shows universally high maintenance cross-generationally: the North-East shibboleth of the substitution of /ʍ/ by /f/ in initial position. In seeking to explain these patterns of variation in linguistic change, Smith discounts external pressures. Rather, the choice of variable to maintain or lose is attributed to the community itself – the community evaluates each item for all sorts of social connotations or positive/negative value and decides which to keep or lose, only to be noticed over time.

Will Lamb's contribution on the sociolinguistics of contemporary spoken Scottish Gaelic (SG) outlines the future prospects of the community basis of Gaelic and concludes that the prognosis is far from promising. The inevitable death of many languages is a world-wide phenomenon and is likely to go unchecked unless radical changes and initiatives are put in place. Lamb's focus in his paper is on providing a corpus-based database for spoken SG. Research has shown that spontaneous speech differs radically from other varieties of language, particularly written discourse. The present study shows clearly that spoken SG diverges along several important parameters from other registers of the language, and the division is particularly acute in syntax. The author gives relevant and perceptive examples of how spoken language avoids tight-knit and lexically rich structures. Preference in the spoken register is for information to be spread over several clauses and great use is made of prosodic and pitch features to capture inter-clausal relations. Syntactic relations at conversational level are less overtly marked and less use is made of subordination structures and sequences. Code-switching has been found to be more productive in conversation and is characterised by the presence of unassimilated loans. Conversation has simpler morphological structures – absence of genitive marking on nouns, more use of pronominal forms and fewer complex NPs and instances of modifier use. Very little is known about the characteristics of spontaneous natural speech in SG and with the rapid contraction of linguistically socially-competent speakers, it is desirable that a response should be made to a wide range of needs in order to safeguard and archivise a sociolinguistic database for use by future generations. With the advent of adequate computer technology, this could be effectively managed and would offer access to resources currently lacking for detailed study of the language. Lamb's main proposal is to collate a large corpus-based database for SG, bearing in mind the unique situation and limitations within which SG survives. The collection should be of potential interest to a wide range of people. This should intensify an interest in SG linguistic study and lead to further applications in computer-based approaches to the language, including pedagogy. The provision of such basic resources is a prerequisite to further study and research possibilities.

As for Irish, **Conchúr Ó Giollagáin** has been studying language usage and change in differing Gaeltacht areas in Meath and Galway across different groups of speakers. Ó Giollagáin's paper brings to our attention some far-reaching and influential sociolinguistic outcomes related to the linguistic anthropology of language usage in a modern Irish-speaking community in West Galway, namely, the Ros Muc community. This is the second of a series of studies whose main aims are to gain some understanding of the sociolinguistic variables which determine language use and maintenance within the Gaeltacht, and particularly to identify the language's role as a dynamic cultural instrument within newly developed complex social networks. The study brings to our attention some significant sociolinguistic and socio-cultural changes which are ongoing within this community and which will have far-reaching implications for the self identity of Ros Muc as a vibrant linguistic community. The results delineating young people's linguistic preferences reveal that the Irish-speaking linguistic community in Ros Muc is about to cross a significant threshold, which will impact in a major way on the socio-cultural heritage of the area.

The study is based on a complete database of information relating to individuals and to families and family structure. Individuals are categorised according to their proficiency in Irish and the way in which they acquired their competency in the language. They include native speakers, the children of speakers who have acquired Irish but who are not native speakers, speakers raised in a mixed linguistic context, namely, where native Irish speakers speak English to their children while the children acquire their knowledge of Irish from the community and through the educational system. A fourth type is also identified and labelled 'comhchainteoir'. They are people who have learned Irish outside the home and as a result are able to participate in all community activities. They become fully competent in the use of Irish from age 8 onwards. The last category identified are English speakers with little or no knowledge of Irish. The distribution of these speakers, according to competence across nine different townlands, is shown by means of diagrams and charts. Their age and linguistic profiles are illustrated in a similar fashion. They give the reader a first glance synopsis of the bilingual make-up of the community. It is obvious from further detailed analysis of the facts that the community is facing serious socio-economic and demographic difficulties, whose end results can be seen in the use of language among the youngest age-cohort. What is disturbing is that 44% of the intake into the primary school are monoglot English speakers. These and similar facts lead to the conclusion that the future make-up of the Ros Muc community is a mixed one, where speakers will have various competencies in the Irish language, but where those with non-native competency are on the increase. The educational system thus far has succeeded in converting English speakers into competent users of Irish, but with the present sociolinguistic difficulties it is not easy to predict that this will continue. Proactive and secure language planning and co-ordinated supportive measures for teachers and educators must be undertaken by Government and other agencies immediately. The information made available through studies of this type provides a wider and very necessary framework which should inform discussion of all matters relating to intergenerational transmission of Irish amongst the native Irish-speaking population of the Gaeltacht. There is an urgent need to develop linguistically well-informed strategies in order to acculturate monoglot English speakers in a way that will ensure equal treatment and esteem for both languages before the normal major language/minority language relationship with regard to linguistic norms of behaviour emerge and take root. Certain linguistic dynamics arise due to social and personal conflicts among speakers who have acquired Irish in diverse contexts and domains. One is led to the conclusion that too many children are now dependent on acquiring their competency in and knowledge of Irish in an institutional context. This trend needs to be reversed if Ros Muc is to survive as a vibrant living linguistic community capable of transmitting Irish intergenerationally within the traditional family domain.

International Comparisons

When the symposium series was originally planned, as mentioned earlier, we decided to seek comparisons between the languages of the Gaeltacht and the Scotstacht and those elsewhere if a good case could be made. In this volume, we consider Kashubian, Ukrainian, and Maltese.

Tomasz Wickerkiewicz prefaces his profile of the Polish language of Kashubian with a short taxonomy of languages which are not the languages of nation states: such nation state languages used by a minority of speakers in another nation state; languages which are not related to that of a nation state; and languages which are linguistically related to a nation state language: regional languages, collateral languages (*langues collatérales*), *Ausbausprachen*, or as Pavlenko calls them, "closely cognate languages", the common features of which are listed, and of which Scots and Kashubian are examples. Kashubian is a West-Slavic language spoken in northern Poland on the southern coast of the Baltic Sea by the Kashubs, direct descendants of the Pomeranians, and which was revived in the nineteenth century. Regarded as a distinct dialect of Polish, but since 1989 upgraded in its linguistic status, 52,665 people indicated in the 2002 Census that they could speak Kashubian. Wickerkiewicz outlines the educational provision for Kashubian and regards the present number of speakers "an important indicator for language planners and educational activists".

Comparative linguistics has traditionally compared languages which are closely related to or quite separate from one another. To a growing set of comparisons between "closely cognate languages" or "typologically close languages", **Alexander Pavlenko** compares the Germanic languages of Scots and English with the Eastern-Slavonic languages of Ukrainian and Russian and draws illuminating parallels. Pavlenko shows how Scots and Ukrainian began their decline in the seventeenth century through unions with larger neighbours which led to quasi-voluntary Anglicisation and enforced Russification; how, in the eighteenth century, Scots and Ukrainian were revived as literary languages and in due course became associated with cultural nationalism; how in 1863 the Russian authorities banned all literature in Ukrainian, but how after the 1905 revolution that ban was lifted; how it is the literary language of the eighteenth century which forms the present-day national standard; how education is available nowadays in both Ukrainian and Russian but how, because of its utilitarian value, Russian is preferred.

Pavlenko then goes on to show the similarities and differences between Scots and Ukrainian. Similarities are rural dialects with literary traditions; separate philological treatment; no legal status; social-class connotations; and their status traditionally as 'threatened' or 'endangered' languages. Differences are extra-territorial use of Ukrainian leading to the existence of Ukrainian-speaking areas, and also the fact that Ukrainian is no longer endangered. In addition, Pavlenko considers the cultural gap between the Scots and English language communities and the role of language in the ideology of nationalism. He concludes that it is politics which shapes the fate and development of national languages. It is always refreshing to have the familiar facts about Scots reinterpreted through comparison with a superficially similar but actually very different situation elsewhere.

With the enlargement of Europe in 2004, many Irish people were shocked to see that Maltese, the language of only 350,00 people, had become an official language of the European Union. The case for official recognition for Irish was quickly established, as reported above, with the success of Maltese as a crucial plank of the argument. All the same, although the comparison was being made in the wider Irish community, little was known about Maltese. An account of the historical development of Maltese and its present-day uses and status is the subject of the paper by **Joe Zammit-Ciantar**. The history of language on Malta starts with Semitic Phoenician, which in due course became heavily influenced by Roman Latin and administrative Greek. Later Arabic (possibly Semitic Syrian) was brought to Malta by Arab Christians, who ruled Malta from the eighth to tenth centuries, and by Sicilian Arabs in the eleventh century. It is from this Sicilian Arabic that Maltese developed. In the centuries which followed, under conquering power, Maltese was in contact with Norman French, Tuscan, and English. Zammit-Ciantar provides specimens of early medieval texts and lots of examples from all levels of linguistic structure to illustrate the development of this heavily contact-induced, romanised Arabic tongue, now the country's national language. In the second part of this paper, Zammit-Ciantar provides an overview of Maltese in the present day. Fitting for one of the authors of the *European Charter for Regional or Minority Languages*, Zammit-Ciantar describes the Maltese alphabet and briefly sketches the functions of Maltese in administration, the law courts, religious worship, all levels of education, the media, signage and publications. Zammit-Ciantar concludes with the advent of language's official status in the EU in 2002. As Maltese has always been up against English and wider trends in globalisation through English in recent years, comparison with Irish is all the more pertinent.

Irish and Scottish Studies

The volume ends with three short statements about the importance of Irish and Scottish Studies to Queen's in general and of these language and politics symposia in particular, which were delivered as addresses at the symposium dinner in the magnificent Great Hall of Queen's University on 17 September 2004. As the symposium series is a project within the AHRB Research Centre for Irish and Scottish Studies, in which Queen's and Trinity College, Dublin are junior partners with the University of Aberdeen, and as the bid for Phase 2 funding from 2006-2010 has been successful, the present project looks set for continuation and development if suitable arrangements can be made. It is therefore opportune for that special Aberdeen-Queen's, East-West, Irish-Scottish relationship to be addressed by **Edna Longley,** who more than anyone has led the furtherance of interdisciplinary Irish-Scottish Studies at Queen's, by **George Watson**, a former Queen's graduate, now long-serving Professor of Irish Literature in English at Aberdeen and Director of Aberdeen's Research Institute for Irish and Scottish Studies, within which the AHRB Centre is based, and by Queen's new Vice-Chancellor, **Peter Gregson**, in what was only his third week of office. We are especially grateful to all three contributors for their permission to reproduce these addresses.

Stádas na Gaeilge i Réim Theangacha an Aontais Eorpaigh

Pádraig Breandán Ó Laighin

Réamhrá

Thosaigh an chomhghníomhaíocht is déanaí chun stádas a bhaint amach don Ghaeilge mar theanga oifigiúil oibre den Aontas Eorpach ag tús mhí na Samhna, 2003.[1] Ag amanna ar leith bíonn córais pholaitiúla oscailte do thionchar ó ghrúpaí dúshlánacha. Tharla go raibh Éire le dul i mbun Uachtaránacht an Aontais Eorpaigh ar an gcéad lá d'Eanáir 2004, agus níos tábhachtaí fós, go raibh cinneadh déanta roimh ré, ag leibhéal na hEorpa, go nglacfaí le deich dtír nua mar Bhallstáit, agus lena naoi dteanga nua mar theangacha oifigiúla oibre, le linn na hUachtaránachta céanna.[2] Tugadh suntas don neamhréir a bhí ann idir teangacha náisiún beag, mar Mháltais agus Eastóinis, a bheith á ligean isteach le stádas iomlán, agus gan an stádas céanna a bheith á iarraidh ag Rialtas na hÉireann do theanga náisiúnta agus príomhtheanga oifigiúil na hÉireann. Chomh maith lena stádas bunreachtúil agus dlíthiúil sa bhaile, tuigeadh d'Éireannaigh gur teanga ársa liteartha í an Ghaeilge ar thoise tábhachtach í den oidhreacht Eorpach le dhá mhíle bliain anuas, agus gur chóir, fiú ar an mbonn sin amháin, go mbeadh ról comhionann mura gradamach aici i measc theangacha oifigiúla na hEorpa. Ar ndóigh, bhí a lán cúiseanna pragmatacha ann arbh fhiú stádas oifigiúil a bhaint amach dá mbarr, cúiseanna a bhain le leas an phobail trí chéile agus le leas an Rialtais féin. Tapaíodh an deis pholaitiúil chun na cúiseanna sin a phlé go poiblí, chun eolas a scaipeadh, agus chun gníomhú d'fhonn is go n-iarrfadh an Rialtas stádas oifigiúil oibre don teanga. Ó fheachtas beag ar dtús, d'fhás mórghluaiseacht shóisialta. Ar 14 Iúil 2004, d'fhógair Rialtas na hÉireann go raibh cinneadh déanta acu stádas mar theanga oifigiúil oibre den Aontas Eorpach a iarraidh don Ghaeilge, ag comhlíonadh éileamh na gluaiseachta.[3] Déanfar brí agus impleachtaí an chinnidh sin a phlé sa pháipéar seo, i gcomhthéacs na reachtaíochta Eorpaí lena mbaineann sé.

Maidir leis an bhfeachtas féin, is féidir a rá go raibh sé iltaobhach, agus gur thug sé deis do phobal na Gaeilge agus d'Éireannaigh i gcoitinne a seasamh ar son stádais a thaispeáint. Is iomchuí go luafainn go raibh mé féin rannpháirteach sa chomhghníomhaíocht. Laistigh d'achar gairid, bhí an t-éileamh go n-iarrfaí stádas oifigiúil oibre don Ghaeilge ag teacht ón mbarr anuas agus ón mbun aníos. Tháinig daltaí ó Ghaelscoileanna, le hamhránaíocht is *joie de vivre*, chun cárta Nollag do Romano Prodi, Uachtarán an Choimisiúin, a sheachadadh ag Áras an Aontais Eorpaigh i mBaile Átha Cliath: d'iarr siad stádas oifigiúil air mar bhronntanas

---

[1] Bunaíodh an bhrateagraíocht *Stádas* ag cruinniú ar 10 Samhain 2003 i mBaile Átha Cliath. Rinne eagraíochtaí éagsúla iarrachtaí ó am go chéile roimhe sin tathant ar an Rialtas stádas oifigiúil a lorg, go háirithe Conradh na Gaeilge, Comhdháil Náisiúnta an Gaeilge, agus Institiúid Teangeolaíochta Éireann.

[2] Síníodh an *Conradh Aontachais leis an Aontas Eorpach* a shainigh na socruithe nua teanga ar 16 Aibreán 2003.

[3] Tógfaidh an próiseas plé tamall. Níl aon údar le ceapadh nach ngníomhóidh Comhairle na nAirí de réir thoil Rialtas na hÉireann ar an gceist thábhachtach seo.

Nollag. Tháinig píceadóirí ó Loch Garman chun seasamh ar aire ag Caisleán Bhaile Átha Cliath le linn don Fhóram Náisiúnta um an Eoraip a bheith ag plé na ceiste istigh i mí Eanáir 2004.[4] Thacaigh ionadaithe na bpáirtithe polaitiúla ar fad ag an bhFóram leis an éileamh.[5] Níos déanaí sa mhí chéanna, ritheadh rún uilepháirtí d'aon ghuth i Seanad Éireann ag moladh don Rialtas stádas a iarraidh. Ritheadh rún ar an dul céanna d'aon ghuth sa Dáil i mí Feabhra. Chuir an Rialtas Coiste Idir-Rannach ar bun chun scrúdú a dhéanamh ar an gceist. Rith formhór na gComhairlí Contae rún fabhrach. Tháinig tacaíocht ó cheardchumainn, ó chumainn agus eagrais den uile chineál, idir dheonach agus reachtúil, ó chomharchumainn, agus ó Éireannaigh as gach aird. Chuir cumainn Éireannacha san Airgintín agus i Meiriceá Thuaidh rúin fhoirmiúla faoi bhráid an Rialtais abhus. Tháinig buíon anall ó Shasana le hachainí a bhronnadh ar an Taoiseach. Mar bhuaic ag an bpointe sin, ghlac na sluaite páirt i mórshiúl ar shráideanna Bhaile Átha Cliath, agus lasmuigh den Dáil bhronn Panu Petteri Höglund ón bhFionlainn achainí idirlín le 80,000 ainm ar ionadaí an Taoisigh. Cuireadh an cheist os comhair an phobail le linn na dtoghchán Eorpach agus áitiúil, agus i measc na nÉireannach a toghadh mar Chomhaltaí de Pharlaimint na hEorpa, dheimhnigh a bhformhór roimh an toghchán go raibh siad i bhfabhar stádais. Sa deireadh thiar, rinne an Rialtas cinneadh an *status quo* lenar ghlac gach Rialtas Éireannach ó 1973 ar aghaidh a chur ar leataobh, agus tús a chur le próiseas plé le Ballstáit eile agus le hinstitiúidí an Aontais Eorpaigh d'fhonn stádas mar theanga oifigiúil oibre a bhaint amach don Ghaeilge.

Foinsí Réim Theangacha an Aontais Eorpaigh

Tá dhá fhoinse dhlíthiúla ag réim theangacha an Aontais Eorpaigh: na Conarthaí agus an reachtaíocht thánaisteach. Sna Conarthaí ar fad, tugtar liosta de theangacha barántúla nó údaracha, a mbíonn comhúdarás ag na téacsanna i ngach ceann díobh. Tugtar 'teangacha barántúla de na Conarthaí', nó 'teangacha conartha' orthu sin. Aon teanga chonartha is fiche atá ann, an Ghaeilge san áireamh. Is sa reachtaíocht thánaisteach, agus go sonrach i Rialachán 1, 1958, amhail leasaithe, a shainítear teangacha mar 'theangacha oifigiúla agus oibre le húsáid ag na hinstitiúidí Eorpacha'. Tugtar 'teangacha oifigiúla' gan agús na hoibre orthu sa Rialachán céanna, agus is mar sin a dhéantar cur síos orthu go hiondúil. Fiche teanga oifigiúil atá ann. San am i láthair, níl de dhifríocht idir liosta na dteangacha conartha agus liosta na dteangacha oifigiúla ach an Ghaeilge a bheith ar an gcéad liosta, agus gan a bheith ar an dara liosta. De bharr chinneadh Rialtas na hÉireann, cuirfear deireadh le stádas eisceachtúil na Gaeilge, agus beidh an dá liosta mar an gcéanna. Ní bheidh gá leis an idirdhealú idir teangacha conartha agus teangacha oifigiúla feasta.

Teangacha Conartha

Liostaítear na teangacha conartha in Airteagal 314 den *Chonradh ag Bunú an Chomhphobail Eorpaigh*, agus tugtar ann an bhuncháilíocht dhlíthiúil a bhaineann

---

[4] Thug an t-údar aitheasc thar a cheann féin agus thar ceann *Stádas* ag cruinniú iomlánach den Fhóram i gCaisleán Bhaile Átha Cliath ar 8 Eanáir 2004, agus leag sé aighneacht dá chuid féin os a gcomhair (Ó Laighin 2004).

[5] Féach Fóram Náisiúnta um an Eoraip 2004: 69–72.

leo, sé sin, go bhfuil comhúdarás ag na téacsanna i ngach ceann díobh. Ceithre theanga bharántúla a bhí ann nuair a síníodh Conradh na Róimhe sa bhliain 1957 – Fraincis, Gearmáinis, Iodáilis, agus Ollainnis – agus cuireadh leo de réir mar a tháinig tíortha nua isteach. Seo liosta na dteangacha conartha mar a luaitear iad i g*Conradh Aontachais 2003*, agus an fhoráil bharántúlachta mar chuid de:

> Déanfar an Conradh seo, arna tharraingt suas i scríbhinn bhunaidh amháin, sa Bhéarla, sa Danmhairgis, san Eastóinis, san Fhionlainnis, sa Fhraincis, sa Ghaeilge, sa Ghearmáinis, sa Ghréigis, san Iodáilis, sa Laitvis, sa Liotuáinis, sa Mháltais, san Ollainnis, sa Pholainnis, sa Phortaingéilis, sa tSeicis, sa tSlóivéinis, sa tSlóvaicis, sa Spáinnis, sa tSualainnis agus san Ungáiris, agus comhúdarás ag téacs gach teanga díobh, a thaisceadh i gcartlann Rialtas Phoblacht na hIodáile agus cuirfidh an Rialtas sin cóip dheimhnithe chuig Rialtas gach ceann eile de Stáit a shínithe.[6]

An bunsmaoineamh a bhí taobh thiar de phrionsabal chomhúdarás na dtéacsanna ná deimhneacht dhlíthiúil na gConarthaí sna Ballstáit ar fad, sé sin *la sécurité légale* nó *legal security*. Chaithfí a bheith in ann na Conarthaí a chur i bhfeidhm laistigh de chórais bhunreachtúla na dtíortha éagsúla, agus de réir riachtanais theangeolaíocha na gcóras sin. Nuair a tháinig an t-am le socruithe a dhéanamh maidir le hÉirinn sa bhliain 1971, d'iarr Rialtas na hÉireann an stádas ba lú don Ghaeilge a shásódh deimhneacht dhlíthiúil na gConarthaí, sé sin, go mbeadh na Conarthaí amháin le fáil i dtéacs barántúil Gaeilge. Is le drogall a ghlac Ballstáit Chomhphobal Eacnamaíochta na hEorpa le seasamh na hÉireann ag an am; bhí cuid díobh, go háirithe an Fhrainc, go láidir den tuairim go gcaithfeadh Éire glacadh le Gaeilge ní hamháin mar theanga bharántúil na gConarthaí, ach mar theanga oifigiúil agus oibre faoi Rialachán 1, 1958, chomh maith, de bharr stádas na Gaeilge mar phríomhtheanga oifigiúil na hÉireann.

Ó 1997 ar aghaidh, faoi leasuithe Chonradh Amstardam, tá ceart ag saoránaigh scríobh chuig príomhfhorais uile an Aontais in aon cheann de na teangacha conartha, an Ghaeilge san áireamh, agus freagra a fháil ar ais sa teanga chéanna.[7] Na forais atá i gceist ná Parlaimint na hEorpa, an tOmbudsman, Comhairle na nAirí, an Coimisiún, an Chúirt Bhreithiúnais, an Chúirt Iniúchóirí, an Coiste Eacnamaíoch agus Sóisialta, agus Coiste na Réigiún. Is ceart suntasach é seo, ach le fírinne is beag saoránach a bheadh á úsáid.

Tá na teangacha conartha céanna san áireamh sa *Dréachtchonradh* don Bhunreacht nua, maille le barántúlacht a dtéacsanna, agus an ceart comhfhreagrais agus freagra a fháil sa teanga chéanna. Ach cuireadh alt nua leis an Airteagal a thugann liosta na dteangacha sa *Dréachtchonradh* sular socraíodh an fhoclaíocht dheiridh le linn na hUachtaránachta Éireannaí. Thabharfadh an t-alt seo ceart do na Ballstáit aistriúcháin den Bhunreacht féin a chur fáil i dteangacha eile seachas na teangacha conartha agus oifigiúla. Ní bheadh na buntáistí a ghabhann le stádas mar

---

[6] Airteagal 3. Tá an liosta céanna agus an fhoráil bharántúlachta in Airteagal IV–10 den *Dréachtchonradh a bhunaíonn Bunreacht don Eoraip*.

[7] Airteagal 21 den *Chonradh ag bunú an Chomhphobail Eorpaigh*.

theanga chonartha ná le stádas mar theanga oifigiúil ag na teangacha seo dá bharr.[8] Níl ann ach go mbeadh aistriúchán den Bhunreacht ann a chuirfeadh an Ballstát féin ar fáil, agus gur dócha go mbeadh sé sin ina chabhair do mhuintir an Bhallstáit i gcúrsaí áirithe dlí. Seo a leanas foclaíocht an ailt nua:

> Féadfar an Conradh seo a aistriú freisin isteach i dteangacha eile ar bith mar a chinnfeadh Ballstáit as a measc siúd a bhfuil, de réir a n-eagair bhunreachtúil, stádas oifigiúil acu ar fud nó i bpáirt dá gcríoch. Déanfaidh na Ballstáit a bheadh i gceist cóipeanna deimhnithe d'aistriúcháin dá leithéid a chur ar fáil lena dtaisceadh i gcartlann na Comhairle.[9]

Is ar iarratas ó Rialtas na Spáinne, a gheall go ndéanfaidís iarracht ardú céime a shocrú don Chatalóinis, a tugadh an leasú seo ar an *Dréachtchonradh* isteach.[10] Catagóir nua i réim theangacha an Aontais Eorpaigh a bheadh i gceist, agus d'fhéadfaí stádas dá réir a bhaint amach do Ghàidhlig na hAlban, don Bhreatnais, don Bhascais, agus do theangacha eile, ach na rialtais cheannasacha a bheith sásta a chur in iúl do Chomhairle na nAirí gur mian leo aistriúcháin a chur ar fáil sa tslí seo sna teangacha sin.[11]

Teangacha Oifigiúla agus Oibre

Fágann an *Conradh ag bunú an Chomhphobail Eorpaigh* faoi Chomhairle na nAirí na rialacha i dtaobh theangacha institiúidí an Chomhphobail a chinneadh, ach amháin i gcás na Cúirte Breithiúnais, mar a leanas:

> Déanfaidh an Chomhairle, ag gníomhú di d'aon toil, na rialacha i dtaobh theangacha institiúidí an Chomhphobail a chinneadh, gan dochar do na forálacha atá i Reacht na Cúirte Breithiúnais.[12]

Is teanga oifigiúil í an Ghaeilge sa Chúirt Bhreithiúnais.[13] Faoin gcumhacht a tugadh dóibh, ba é an chéad rialachán lenar ghlac Comhairle na nAirí sa bhliain 1958 ná

---

[8] Athraíodh teideal an Airteagail ó "Teangacha" go "Téacsanna Barántúla agus Aistriúcháin" le go mbeadh an t-idirdhealú soiléir.

[9] Aistriúchán neamhoifigiúil d'Airteagal IV–10 (2). Níl leagan barántúil de na leasuithe ar an *Dréachtchonradh* le fáil fós i nGaeilge. Leagan oifigiúil Béarla: "*This Treaty may also be translated into any other languages as determined by Member States among those which, in accordance with their constitutional order, enjoy official status in all or part of their territory. A certified copy of such translations shall be provided by the Member States concerned to be deposited in the archives of the Council.*" CIG 76/04 (13 Bealtaine 2004), Uachtaránacht; CIG 81/04 (16 Meitheamh 2004), Uachtaránacht.

[10] Mar a fheicfear, tharla cor nua i scéal na Catalóinise níos déanaí.

[11] Tá molta go n-ainmneodh na Ballstáit na teangacha a bheadh i gceist laistigh de shé mhí ó dháta sínithe an chonartha nua.

[12] Airteagal 290.

[13] In Airteagal 223 den *Chonradh ag bunú an Chomhphobail Eorpaigh*, fágtar faoin gCúirt Bhreithiúnais féin na rialacha a bhaineann lena seirbhís a leagan síos.

Rialachán 1 a bhunaigh réim theangacha na n-institiúidí – a d'ainmnigh na teangacha oifigiúla agus oibre agus a shonraigh modh a n-úsáide.[14] De bhrí go mbaineann an Rialachán seo leis an reachtaíocht thánaisteach, ní bheidh gá le haon Chonradh a leasú chun stádas mar theanga oifigiúil agus oibre a shocrú don Ghaeilge. Beidh gá le comhaontacht Chomhairle na nAirí.

B'ionann na teangacha conartha agus na teangacha oifigiúla agus oibre i dtosach. De réir mar a tháinig tíortha nua isteach, rinneadh Rialachán 1 a leasú chun a dteangacha oifigiúla a ainmniú mar theangacha oifigiúla agus oibre de chuid an Aontais Eorpaigh. Tharla sin i ngach cás ach i gcás na hÉireann, agus mar atá ráite, ba iad Rialtas na hÉireann a d'iarr an socrú sin ag an am. Tugann réamhrá an Rialacháin bunús roghnaithe na dteangacha oifigiúla agus oibre: tá siad ann sa chéad áit mar theangacha barántúla an Chonartha, agus sa dara háit de bhrí go bhfuil siad aitheanta mar theangacha oifigiúla i gceann nó níos mó de Bhallstáit an Chomhphobail. Seo foclaíocht na coda sin den réamhrá mar a bhí ón tús:

> De bhrí go bhfuil gach ceann de na ceithre theanga ina bhfuil an Conradh dréachtaithe aitheanta mar theanga oifigiúil i gceann amháin nó níos mó de Bhallstáit an Chomhphobail;[15]

De bharr gur dhiúltaigh Éire glacadh le Gaeilge mar theanga oifigiúil agus oibre, rinneadh Airteagail áirithe den Rialachán féin a leasú chun na teangacha nua a thabhairt isteach, ach níor deineadh leasú ar an réamhrá. Tharla an próiseas céanna le gach fairsingiú ina dhiaidh sin. Níorbh fhéidir, agus ní féidir fós, an réamhrá a cheartú de bharr stádas eisceachtúil na Gaeilge. Ní féidir a rá anois, mar shampla, "De bhrí go bhfuil gach ceann den fhiche teanga ina bhfuil an Conradh dréachtaithe ...", mar go bhfuil an Conradh dréachtaithe in aon teanga is fiche, cé nach bhfuil ach fiche teanga oifigiúil agus oibre ann. Cloítear i gcónaí leis an bprionsabal go gcaithfidh teanga a bheith ina teanga bharántúil de na Conarthaí agus ina teanga oifigiúil i mBallstát amháin ar a laghad chun go n-aithneofaí í mar theanga oifigiúil agus oibre de chuid an Aontais Eorpaigh. Ó aontachas na hÉireann sa bhliain 1973, tá an Ghaeilge cáilithe faoin dá choinníoll sin.

Seo an téacs d'Airteagal 1 de Rialachán 1 mar a dheimhnigh Rialtas na hÉireann agus Rialtais na mBallstát eile é nuair a shínigh siad an conradh aontachais leis na tíortha nua sa bhliain 2003:

> Is iad Béarla, Danmhairgis, Eastóinis, Fionlainnis, Fraincis, Gearmáinis, Gréigis, Iodáilis, Laitvis, Liotuáinis, Máltais, Ollainnis, Polainnis, Portaingéilis, Seicis, Slóivéinis, Slóvaicis, Spáinnis, Sualainnis, agus

---

[14] 31958 R 0001: Rialachán Uimhir 1 ón gComhairle an 15 Aibreán 1958 ag cinneadh na dteangacha atá le húsáid ag Comhphobal Eacnamaíochta na hEorpa (IO 17 6/10/1958, lch. 385), agus Rialachán Uimhir 1 ón gComhairle an 15 Aibreán 1958 ag cinneadh na dteangacha atá le húsáid ag an gComhphobal Eorpach do Fhuinneamh Adamhach (IO 17 6/10/1958, lch. 401).

[15] Aistriúchán neamhoifigiúil. Leagan oifigiúil Béarla: *"Whereas each of the four languages in which the Treaty is drafted is recognised as an official language in one or more of the Member States of the Community."*

Ungáiris teangacha oifigiúla agus teangacha oibre institiúidí an Aontais.[16]

Cásanna na Lucsamburgaise agus na Catalóinise

Maidir leis na coinníollacha aitheantais do theangacha oifigiúla, is fiú féachaint ar chás na Lucsamburgaise, de bharr na mífhaisnéise faoi a scaipeadh le linn an fheachtais ar son na Gaeilge. Ní raibh aon stádas reachtúil ag Lucsamburgais sa bhaile nuair a bhunaigh Lucsamburg agus na tíortha eile Comhphobal Eacnamaíochta na hEorpa sa bhliain 1957. Is i bhfad níos déanaí, sa bhliain 1984, a rinneadh teanga náisiúnta den Lucsamburgais. Níor deineadh teanga oifigiúil de chuid an Stáit di, agus ar an ábhar sin bheadh amhras faoina hincháilitheacht i gcomhair stádais oifigiúil faoin Rialachán Eorpach. Is í an Fhraincis teanga aonair na reachtaíochta i Lucsamburg, cé go gceadaítear an Fhraincis, an Ghearmáinis, agus an Lucsamburgais a úsáid i gcúrsaí riaracháin. Is iondúil nach gcuirtear cáipéisí oifigiúla ar fáil sa Lucsamburgais. Ní fhoilsítear aon pháipéar laethúil ná seachtainiúil inti. Teanga labhartha í go príomha, ar leagan den Ghearmáinis í le meascadh láidir den Fhraincis. Ar aon nós, níor fheil sé riamh do phobal ná do Rialtas Lucsamburg go ndéanfaí teanga chonartha ná teanga oifigiúil agus oibre dá dteanga, agus níor éiligh siad riamh é. Bhí de bhua inmhaíte acu go raibh an dá theanga is mó a úsáideann siad i ngnóthaí oifigiúla, liteartha, agus oideachais sa bhaile, an Fhraincis agus an Ghearmáinis, ina dteangacha oifigiúla sa Chomhphobal ón tús.

Is teanga í an Chatalóinis a bhfuil líon lucht a labhartha i bhfad níos mó ná líon lucht labhartha cuid de na teangacha oifigiúla nua. Cé gur teanga oifigiúil sa Chatalóin agus sna hOileáin Bhailéaracha í, ní teanga oifigiúil de chuid na Spáinne í, agus is ag an Spáinn atá ballraíocht an Aontais Eorpaigh.[17] Ní hamháin nach teanga oifigiúil de chuid an Bhallstáit í, ach tá sí faoi mhíbhuntáiste ach amháin sna réigiúin ina bhfuil sí oifigiúil: ní ceadmhach de cheart, mar shampla, í a labhairt i bParlaimint na Spáinne. I gcasadh nua ar cheist na Catalóinise, tá iarrtha anois ag Rialtas na Spáinne go ndéanfaí "teangacha oifigiúla" de chuid an Aontais Eorpaigh den

---

[16] Aistriúchán neamhoifigiúil. Le bheith go hiomlán cruinn de réir dlí, tabharfaidh mé leagan den Airteagal i gceann de theangacha oifigiúla an Aontais: *"The official languages and the working languages of the institutions of the Union shall be Czech, Danish, Dutch, English, Estonian, Finnish, French, German, Greek, Hungarian, Italian, Latvian, Lithuanian, Maltese, Polish, Portuguese, Slovak, Slovenian, Spanish and Swedish."* Sna leaganacha Gaeilge de na conarthaí aontachais ar fad, ní thugtar aistriúchán Gaeilge ar fhoclaíocht leasaithe na nAirteagal ó Rialachán 1, 1958. Is i mBéarla a thugtar na téacsanna. Tá beagnach gach rud eile sna conarthaí aistrithe go Gaeilge, agus tá na mílte leathanach i gceist. Léiriú an-spéisiúil é seo ar an bhfíoras dlí nach teanga oifigiúil í an Ghaeilge san Aontas Eorpach. Is dócha nár ceadaíodh an t-aistriúchán sa chaoi is nach bhféadfadh aon duine a rá go raibh an Ghaeilge oifigiúil ar chuma éigin de bhrí go raibh Airteagail de Rialachán 1 aistrithe go Gaeilge.

[17] Is teanga oifigiúil í i réigiún uathrialach Valencia freisin, cé go dtugtar 'Valenciano' uirthi sa reacht uathrialach ansin. Tá cosaint áirithe ag an gCatalóinis i réigiún uathrialach na hAragóine. Deir Airteagal 3 de Bhunreacht na Spáinne gurb í an Chaistílis teanga oifigiúil Spáinneach an Stáit, agus go bhfuil teangacha eile oifigiúil freisin ina gcomhphobail uathrialacha faoi seach, de réir a reachtanna.

Bhascais *(el vasco)*, den Chatalóinis *(el catalán)*, den Ghailísis *(el gallego)*, agus den Vailéinsis *(el valenciano)* nuair a bheadh Rialachán 1 á leasú d'fhonn Gaeilge a chuimsiú ann.[18] Níl aon cheann de na teangacha sin i dteideal aitheantais mar theangacha oifigiúla faoi cheachtar den dá choinníoll, de réir mar a shainítear anois iad ar aon nós.[19] Le linn na hidirbheartaíochta ar an *Dréachtchonradh*, níor iarr an Spáinn go leasófaí an t-airteagal cuí chun go mbeadh na teangacha seo ina dteangacha conartha.[20] Tá comhaontaithe ag na Ballstáit, an Spáinn san áireamh, go síneofar an conradh sin níos déanaí i mbliana agus nach ndéanfar aon leasuithe eile air.[21] Ní fheicim ó thaobh dlí de go bhféadfadh teanga a bheith ina teanga oifigiúil agus oibre, agus na himpleachtaí ar fad a bhaineann leis sin, gan í a bheith freisin ina teanga bharántúil de na Conarthaí.[22] Gan leasú bunúsach a thabhairt i bhfeidhm i réim theangacha an Aontais Eorpaigh, rud a d'fhéadfaí a dhéanamh, níl ach dhá bhealach ann trína bhféadfadh muintir na Catalóine stádas iomlán Eorpach a bhaint amach dá dteanga: stát ceannasach neamhspleách a chur ar bun, teacht in aontachas mar Bhallstát ar leith, agus an stádas a iarraidh dá dteanga; nó go n-aithneodh an Spáinn an Chatalóinis mar theanga oifigiúil de chuid an Bhallstáit, agus go n-iarrfadh Rialtas na Spáinne stádas mar theanga chonartha agus mar theanga oifigiúil di.

Na Buntáistí a Bhaineann le Stádas Oifigiúil

Tá buntáistí díreacha le baint ag pobail agus ag Ballstáit as a dteangacha a bheith aitheanta mar theangacha oifigiúla agus oibre faoi Rialachán 1. Ar an gcéad dul síos, bronnann stádas oifigiúil buntáistí fostaíochta ar shaoránaigh na tíre atá i gceist. Tá sé mar bhunriachtanas i gcomhair gach poist a fhógraíonn an tAontas Eorpach go mbeadh dhá theanga oifigiúla ag na hiarrthóirí ar fad. Uaireanta iarrtar nó is ceadmhach cumas i dteangacha eile a lua de bhreis ar na teangacha a bheadh á n-úsáid i mbun an phoist féin; agus i gcásanna ina meastar iarrthóirí a bheith comhcháilithe, tugtar na postanna do na daoine a mbíonn na teangacha breise sin acu. Is bealach pragmatach é seo leis an urraim atá geallta do phrionsabal na héagsúlachta teanga a chur i ngníomh.[23] Ach tá an urraim srianta sa chás seo do réim

---

[18] I litir den 13 Meán Fómhair 2004 ó Miguel Ángel Moratinos, Aire Gnóthaí Eachtracha agus Comhoibrithe, chuig Bernard Bot, Aire Gnóthaí Eachtracha na hOllainne agus comharba láithreach Uachtaránacht Chomhairle na nAirí; cuireadh litir ar an dul céanna chuig Uachtarán an Choimisiúin, Romano Prodi.

[19] Cé go dtagraíonn réamhrá Rialachán 1 do theanga a bheith aitheanta "mar theanga oifigiúil i gceann amháin nó níos mó de Bhallstáit an Chomhphobail", tá glactha leis sa dlí-eolaíocht go dtí seo go gciallaíonn sé sin gur teanga oifigiúil de chuid an Bhallstáit í seachas teanga oifigiúil de chuid réigiúin den Bhallstát.

[20] Airteagal IV–10 (1).

[21] Tá an conradh le síniú ag na Ballstáit ar fad ag searmanas sa Róimh ar 29 Deireadh Fómhair 2004.

[22] Baineann deacrachtaí eile leis an liosta a chuir an Spáinn ar fáil: glactar leis go coitianta agus faoi dhlí na Spáinne gurb í an Chatalóinis a labhraítear i Valencia, ach, mar atá ráite, go dtugtar 'Valenciano' uirthi sa reacht uathrialach ann; agus tá na cosúlachtaí idir Gailísis agus Portaingéilis chomh cuimsitheach sin go bhfuil comhchaighdeán scríofa á phlé faoi láthair.

[23] Tá forálacha sa *Chonradh ag Bunú an Chomhphobail Eorpaigh* (Airteagal 151.1) agus sa *Dréachtchonradh a bhunaíonn Bunreacht don Eoraip* (Cuid I, Airteagal 3.3; Airteagal II–22) a chothaíonn iolrachas cultúrtha agus teanga.

theangacha an Aontais: ní cheadaítear ach teangacha oifigiúla a lua.[24] Úsáideann stáit a gcumhacht chun a dhearbhú go sainmhíneofaí na cumais theangeolaíochta atá leithleach dóibh féin mar chaipiteal i láthair an mhargaidh. Sainíonn Rialachán 1 an caipiteal teangeolaíoch don mhargadh Eorpach. Le stádas oifigiúil, beidh deireadh leis an íoróin leatromach a fhágann nach féidir an Ghaeilge a chur síos ar fhoirm iarratais i gcomhair poist san aon ghníomhaireacht de chuid an Aontais Eorpaigh atá lonnaithe in Éirinn – an *Foras Eorpach chun Dálaí Maireachtála agus Oibre a Fheabhsú*. Is é an Béarla teanga oibre an Fhorais sin, agus is féidir Liotuáinis nó Fraincis nó Máltais a chur síos mar theanga i dteannta an Bhéarla riachtanaigh chun post a fháil ann, ach ní féidir Gaeilge a chur síos leis an mBéarla.

Déantar an *Iris Oifigiúil* an Aontais Eorpaigh, a bhfuil fáil inti ar rialacháin, ar threoracha, agus ar cháipéisí tábhachtacha eile, a fhoilsiú i ngach ceann de na teangacha oifigiúla. Is é an bunphrionsabal a bhaineann leis seo ná go gcuirtear dlíthe na hEorpa i bhfeidhm go díreach sna Ballstáit, agus nár mhiste, chun a mbailíocht a dheimhniú, iad a chur ar fáil i dteangacha oifigiúla na mBallstát sin. Tagann breis is seachtó faoin gcéad den dlí a chuirtear i bhfeidhm in Éirinn ón Aontas Eorpach i bhfoirm rialachán. Déantar na rialacháin a shuíomh sa dlí Éireannach, agus tá dualgas bunreachtúil ar an Stát na dlíthe a chur ar fáil go i nGaeilge agus i mBéarla. Le teacht i bhfeidhm *Acht na dTeangacha Oifigiúla 2003*, beidh dualgas reachtúil ar an Stát na dlíthe a fhoilsiú go comhuaineach sa dá theanga. Leis an bhforbairt atá tagtha ar chumas an Aontais Eorpaigh i ndéanamh dlíthe ó 1973 i leith, agus leis an reachtaíocht nua teanga in Éirinn, ba dheacra go mór do Rialtas na hÉireann anois a áiteamh ar Bhallstáit eile, ná ar a saoránaigh féin, gur féidir na riachtanais maidir le deimhneacht dhlíthiúil a shásamh gan an Ghaeilge a bheith oifigiúil faoi Rialachán 1. Nuair a bheidh an Ghaeilge ina teanga oifigiúil Eorpach, tiocfaidh na rialacháin chun na tíre i mBéarla agus i nGaeilge, sé sin, i bhfoirm atá bailí, ar chostas an Aontais. Chosain réim theangacha an Aontais Eorpaigh timpeall dhá euro an saoránach don bhliain 2002: b'ionann an t-iomlán agus aon faoin gcéad de bhuiséad an Aontais. Íocfaidh Éireannaigh an dá euro sin an duine do na seirbhísí teanga, is cuma Gaeilge a bheith san áireamh nó as an áireamh. Leis an mbuiséad agus an daonra ag méadú i gcoibhneas a chéile, ní rabhthas ag súil go n-ardódh na costais mórán le fairsingiú. Sa bhliain 2003, bhí an fhéidearthacht fós ann gur deich dteanga nua a bheadh i gceist – an Turcais an deichiú ceann, don chuid sin den Chipir nár tháinig in aontachas sa deireadh.[25] Ní saor ó chostais a bheidh Éire sa ghnó seo. Beidh orthu an *acquis communautaire* – bailiúchán na gConarthaí agus na ndlíthe atá i bhfeidhm faoi láthair – a chur ar fáil in aistriúchán Gaeilge as a n-acmhainní féin.[26]

Cuirfidh an stádas nua ar chumas do Chomhaltaí Éireannacha a dteanga náisiúnta oifigiúil a úsáid i bParlaimint na hEorpa ar an mbonn céanna le cách, más rogha leo é. Féachtar ar chosaint an chirt seo i gcás an fiche teanga oifigiúil atá anois ann mar dhearbhchloch na cinnteoireachta daonlathaí. B'ionann Gaeilge a chur leo mar an t-aonú teanga is fiche agus an próiseas a láidriú, agus a shaibhriú freisin le léargas teanga Ceiltí.

Maoiníonn an tAontas Eorpach cláir éagsúla oideachais agus cultúir chun éagsúlacht teanga a chur chun cinn, ach is iondúil go mbíonn na cláir seo dírithe go heisiach ar na teangacha oifigiúla. Nuair a chomharthófar mar theanga oifigiúil í,

---

[24] Féach Ó Laighin 2004: 11–12.

[25] DN: MEMO/03/37 (19 Feabhra 2003), Coimisiún Eorpach.

[26] Tá na Conarthaí ar fad, agus ábhar áirithe eile, aistrithe go Gaeilge cheana.

beidh an Ghaeilge san áireamh do thograí nua teanga ar bhonn cothrom, gan aon ghá feasta le hiomarbhá chun stádas speisialta a lorg, mar ba ghá a dhéanamh i gcásanna LINGUA, SOCRATES, agus LEONARDO. Beidh an Ghaeilge ar liosta na dteangacha oifigiúla faoi Rialachán 1, agus dá bharr sin i dteideal maoinithe gan cheist gan achainí.

Seachas na buntáistí díreacha seo, bíonn impleachtaí eile i gceist: tionchar stádas idirnáisiúnta teanga ar lucht a labhartha agus a foghlama, agus an forás a thagann ar theangacha a bhíonn rannpháirteach in aistriúchán agus ateangaireacht, mar shampla.

Buntáistí móra d'Éireannaigh, thuaidh agus theas agus thar muir, na nithe seo. Ach is buntáiste freisin é do phobail na mBallstát eile go mbeidh an Ghaeilge ag glacadh a hionaid chuí mar cheann de na teangacha is ársa san Eoraip, leis an litríocht dúchais is sine i measc thíortha uile na hEorpa, ach amháin an Ghréig, lena saíocht, lena béaloideas, lena hamhráin, lena friotal laethúil – oidhreacht ar toise suaithinseach de shainmhíniú an Eorpachais í leis na cianta.

Socruithe Teanga na nInstitiúidí

Cé go dtugann Airteagal 1 de Rialachán 1, 1958, liosta na dteangacha oifigiúla agus oibre, ní hionann sin agus a rá go bhfuil cothromaíocht idir na teangacha sin maidir lena n-úsáid ag na hinstitiúidí. Go seachtrach, caithfear comhfhreagras i dteangacha conartha a fhreagairt sna teangacha sin; ach maidir le hobair inmheánach na n-institiúidí, tá an Béarla, an Fhraincis, agus an Ghearmáinis, go háirithe an chéad dá cheann, in uachtar ar fad. Ní bheidh aon mhaolú ar thionchar na mórtheangacha sin de bharr mhéadú líon na dteangacha oifigiúla. Glacadh le cinntí praiticiúla sa bhliain 2003, mar chuid den ullmhúchán don fhairsingiú, chun méid gnách an aistriúcháin agus na hateangaireachta a chiorrú go mór.[27] Tá sé seo go hiomlán dlíthiúil mar go dtugann Airteagal 6 den Rialachán cead do na hinstitiúidí a socruithe féin a dhéanamh maidir le húsáid inmheánach teangacha:

> Féadfaidh institiúidí an Chomhphobail a leagan amach ina rialacha nósanna imeachta féin cé acu de na teangacha atá le húsáid i gcásanna ar leith.[28]

Ar ábhar eile, de réir Airteagal 8 den Rialachán, tar éis don Ghaeilge a bheith ainmnithe mar theanga oifigiúil, ní bheidh dualgas ar Rialtas na hÉireann a gcleachtais chumarsáide leis an Aontas Eorpach a athrú: níl aon rud sa dlí go ginearálta ná in *Acht na dTeangacha Oifigiúla 2003* a d'éileodh a leithéid.[29] Beidh cead acu cáipéisí i nGaeilge a úsáid ó am go chéile, más mhian leo. Tá cosúlachtaí idir Éire

---

[27] DN: MEMO/03/37 (19 Feabhra 2003), An Coimisiún Eorpach.

[28] Aistriúchán neamhoifigiúil. Leagan oifigiúil Béarla: "*The institutions of the Community may stipulate in their rules of procedure which of the languages are to be used in specific cases.*"

[29] Airteagal 8 (Aistriúchán neamhoifigiúil): "Má tá níos mó ná aon teanga oifigiúil amháin ag Ballstát, beidh an teanga a úsáidfear, ar iarratas ó Stát dá leithéid, faoi rialú ag rialacha ginearálta a dhlí féin." Leagan oifigiúil Béarla: "*If a Member State has more than one official language, the language to be used shall, at the request of such State, be governed by the general rules of its law.*"

agus Málta sa chomhthéacs seo, le dhá theanga oifigiúla ag an dá thír, agus an Béarla coiteann eatarthu. Cé go bhfuil Máltais liostaithe mar theanga oifigiúil, bíonn an chumarsáid idir Málta agus na hinstitiúidí Eorpacha go hiomlán, beagnach, trí mheán an Bhéarla, díreach mar a bhí le linn a n-idirbheartaíochta um fhairsingiú.

Luachmhaireacht Teangacha

Ba mhaith liom tagairt a dhéanamh do ghearán amháin a rinneadh le linn an fheachtais ar son na Gaeilge – daoine a rá gurbh fhearr béim a leagan ar Ghaeilge sa bhaile seachas a bheith ag iarraidh stádas a bhaint amach di san Eoraip.[30] Is contrárthacht bhréagach atá i gceist anseo. Ní dhá rud scoite ó chéile iad stádas na Gaeilge san Eoraip agus stádas na Gaeilge in Éirinn. Baineann siad go dlúth le chéile. Cothóidh stádas oifigiúil oibre san Eoraip stádas agus úsáid na Gaeilge sa bhaile. Ní hamháin go méadaíonn stádas idirnáisiúnta stádas teanga sa bhaile, agus féinmhuinín lucht a labhartha, ach tabharfaidh stádas Eorpach le tuiscint do dhaoine óga gur teanga í seo a mb'fhiú dóibh a shealbhú agus a labhairt, teanga atá ní hamháin saibhir inti féin, ach atá úsáideach freisin maidir le dul chun cinn pearsanta, i mbaint amach rudaí sa saol mór.

Maireann teangacha de bhrí go bhfuil siad luachmhar iontu féin, a luach inmheánach, agus freisin de bhrí go bhfuil siad luachmhar go hionstraimeach chun spriocanna eile a bhaint amach, a luach seachtrach. Maidir le luach inmheánach na Gaeilge, tuigfear gur oidhreacht shaibhir í. Bíonn na cuspóirí seachtracha dá n-úsáidtear teanga an-tábhachtach do dhaoine: a húsáid i gcumarsáid le comhlachtaí poiblí, le seirbhísí sóisialta agus sláinte, mar shampla, os comhair cúirteanna, agus a húsáid i ngnóthú fostaíochta. An bealach is fearr le teanga a lagú, agus brú éifeachtach a chur ar dhaoine athrú ó theanga amháin go teanga eile, ná cumas na teanga i mbaint amach na gcuspóirí seachtracha sin a chur ó mhaith. Is féidir teanga a mhuirniú go bás mura ndéantar a hinfheictheacht, a feidhmiúlacht mar acmhainn sa ghnáthshaol, agus a ról i láthair an mhargaidh a dheimhniú in éineacht. Sin an fáth go mbaineann tábhacht as cuimse le feidhmiú éifeachtúil *Acht na dTeangacha Oifigiúla* agus le stádas oifigiúil oibre a bhaint amach don Ghaeilge san Aontas Eorpach araon: cuirfidh siad le hinmharthanacht na teanga. Labhróidh níos mó daoine an Ghaeilge dá mbarr.

Tagairtí

Fóram Náisiúnta um an Eoraip. 2004. *The Fourth Phase of Work of the National Forum on Europe: February 2003 to June 2004.* Baile Átha Cliath: Oifig an tSoláthair.

Ó Laighin, Pádraig Breandán. 2004. *I dTreo Aitheantais don Ghaeilge mar Theanga Oifigiúil Oibre den Aontas Eorpach: Aighneacht arna Leagan os Comhair an Fhóraim Náisiúnta um an Eoraip.* Baile Átha Cliath: Clódhanna Teoranta.

---

[30] Bhí sampla amháin den seasamh seo ina chuid den inspreagadh don mhionscrúdú a rinne mé ar chás na Lucsamburgaise. Tuairiscíodh san *Irish Times* (11 Márta 2004) gur mhol Viviane Reding, Coimisinéir Eorpach ó Lucsamburg, do mhuintir na hÉireann an Ghaeilge a labhairt sa bhaile in áit a bheith ag iarraidh stádas mar theanga oifigiúil oibre a bhaint amach di; dar léi, *"making it an official language doesn't bring you a thing".*

The Status of Irish in the Linguistic Regime of the European Union
(Author's Translation)

Pádraig Breandán Ó Laighin

Introduction

The most recent collective action to obtain status for Irish as an official working language of the European Union was set in motion at the beginning of November, 2003.[1] At certain times political systems are receptive to the influence of challenging groups. Ireland was embarking on the Presidency of the European Union on the 1st of January 2004, and more importantly, a decision had previously been made at the European level to admit ten new countries as Member States, and their nine new languages as official working languages, during the same Presidency.[2] The inconsistency between the languages of small nations such as Maltese and Estonian being admitted with full status, and the Irish Government not seeking the same status for the national and first official language of Ireland, became conspicuous. As well being aware its constitutional and legal status at home, Irish people understood Irish to be an ancient literary language which had been an important dimension of the European heritage for two thousand years, and which should, on that ground alone, be given a status of equality if not prestige among the official languages of Europe. There were, of course, many pragmatic reasons which would justify the achievement of official status – reasons which were in the interests of the people generally and of the Government itself. The political opportunity was seized to discuss these reasons publicly, to disseminate information, and to act so as to ensure that the Government would seek official working status for the language. From a small campaign at first, a significant social movement developed. On July 14, 2004, the Government of Ireland announced that they had decided to seek status as an official working language of the European Union for Irish, in fulfilment of the movement's demand.[3]

As to the campaign itself, it can be said that it was multifaceted, and that it gave an opportunity to Irish speakers and to Irish people in general to demonstrate their support for status. It is appropriate that I should mention that I was a participant in the collective action. Within a short period, the demand that official working status be sought for Irish was coming from the top down and from the bottom up. Children from *Gaelscoileanna* – Irish-medium elementary schools – arrived with song and *joie de vivre* to deliver a Christmas card for Romano Prodi, President of the Commission,

---

[1] *Stádas*, an umbrella organization, was formed at a meeting on November 10, 2003, in Dublin. Various organizations – especially *Conradh na Gaeilge, Comhdháil Náisiúnta na Gaeilge*, and *Institiúid Teangeolaíochta Éireann* – had previously attempted from time to time to convince the Government to seek official status.

[2] The *Treaty of Accession to the European Union 2003*, which specified the new language arrangements, was signed on April 16, 2003.

[3] The negotiation process will take some time. There is no reason to believe that the Council of Ministers will not act in accordance with the will of the Government of Ireland on this important question.

at the offices of the European Union in Dublin: they asked him for official status as a Christmas present. Pikemen and pikewomen from Wexford stood to attention at Dublin Castle while the National Forum on Europe was discussing the issue inside in January 2004.[4] Representatives of all of the political parties at the Forum supported the demand.[5] Later during the same month, an all-party motion was adopted by *Seanad Éireann* recommending that the Government seek status.[6] A similar motion was passed unanimously by the *Dáil* in February. The Government established an Inter-Departmental Committee to examine the question. A majority of the County Councils passed favourable motions. Support came from trade unions, from societies and organizations of all kinds, both voluntary and statutory, from cooperatives, and from Irish people everywhere. Irish organizations in Argentina and North America sent formal motions to the attention of the Government of Ireland. A group came from England to present a petition to the Taoiseach. As a climax at that point, thousands took part in a march on the streets of Dublin, and outside the *Dáil* Panu Petteri Höglund from Finland presented an internet petition with 80,000 names to a representative of the Taoiseach. The issue was put before the public during the European and local elections, and the majority of those Irish people who were elected as Members of the European Parliament had confirmed before the election that they supported status. In the end, the Government decided to set aside the status quo stance which every Irish Government since 1973 had adhered to, and to begin a process of discussions with other Member States and with the institutions of the European Union with a view to achieving official working status for Irish.

Sources of the Linguistic Regime of the European Union

The linguistic regime of the European Union has two legal sources: the Treaties and secondary legislation. All of the Treaties list the languages in which they are drawn up, and declare the texts in each of these languages to be equally authentic. These languages are referred to as 'authentic languages of the Treaties' or 'treaty languages'. There are twenty-one treaty languages, including Irish. It is in the secondary legislation, and specifically in Regulation 1, 1958, as amended, that languages are designated as 'official and working languages to be used by the European institutions'. These are referred to as 'official languages' without the 'working' appendage in the same Regulation, and that is the usual nomenclature. There are twenty official languages. At present, the only difference between the list of treaty languages and the list of official languages is the presence of Irish on the first list, and its absence from the second. Because of the Irish Government's recent decision, the exceptional status of Irish will end, and the two lists will be the same. There will be no further need for a distinction between treaty languages and official languages.

---

[4] The author, on his own behalf and on behalf of Stádas, addressed a plenary session of the National Forum on Europe in Dublin Castle on January 8, 2004; he also laid his own written brief before them (Ó Laighin 2004).

[5] See National Forum on Europe 2004: 69–72.

[6] Seanad Éireann is the upper house of the Irish parliament, and Dáil Éireann, or the Dáil, the lower house.

Treaty Languages

The treaty languages are listed in Article 314 of the *Treaty establishing the European Community*, and the basic principle pertaining to each of them is specified, namely, that the texts are equally authentic in each of the languages. There were four authentic languages when the Treaty of Rome was signed in 1957 – French, German, Italian, and Dutch – and these were added to as new countries were admitted. This is the list of languages as given in the *Treaty of Accession 2003*, and the associated authenticity provision:

> This Treaty, drawn up in a single original in the Czech, Danish, Dutch, English, Estonian, Finnish, French, German, Greek, Hungarian, Irish, Italian, Latvian, Lithuanian, Maltese, Polish, Portuguese, Slovak, Slovenian, Spanish and Swedish languages, the texts in each of these languages being equally authentic, shall be deposited in the archives of the Government of the Italian Republic, which will remit a certified copy to each of the Governments of the other Signatory States.[7]

The basic idea behind the principle of equal authenticity of the texts was the legal security of the Treaties in all of the Member States – *la sécurité légale*. It was necessary that the Treaties be capable of implementation within the constitutional systems of the various countries, and in accordance with the linguistic requirements of these systems. When the time came in 1971 to make arrangements for Ireland, the Irish Government requested the lowest possible status for Irish which would satisfy the legal security of the Treaties, namely, that only the Treaties themselves would be available in authentic Irish text. It was with reluctance that the Member States of the European Economic Community at the time accepted Ireland's position; some of them, especially France, were strongly of the opinion that Ireland should have to accept Irish not only as an authentic language of the Treaties, but as an official and working language under Regulation 1, 1958, also, because of the constitutional status of Irish as the first official language of Ireland.

From 1997 onwards, under Treaty of Amsterdam amendments, citizens have the right to write to the principal bodies of the Union in any of the treaty languages, Irish included, and to receive a reply in the same language.[8] The bodies in question are the European Parliament, the Ombudsman, the Council of Ministers, the Commission, the Court of Justice, the Court of Auditors, the Economic and Social Committee, and the Committee of the Regions. This is a significant right, though in reality few citizens choose to exercise it.

The same treaty languages are included in the *Draft Treaty* for the new Constitution, together with the authenticity of texts provision, and the right of correspondence and a reply in the same language. But a new paragraph was added to the Article which gives the list of languages in the *Draft Treaty* before the final wording was agreed during the Irish Presidency. This paragraph would give the right to Member States to provide translations of the Constitution in languages other than the treaty and official languages. Such languages would not as a consequence

---

[7] Article 3. The same list and authenticity provision are specified in Article IV–10 of the Draft Treaty establishing a Constitution for Europe.

[8] Article 21 of the *Treaty establishing the European Community*.

have the advantages which are associated with either the status of treaty language or the status of official language.[9] There would simply exist a translation of the Constitution which the Member State itself would provide, and which might be of assistance to citizens of the Member State in certain legal circumstances. The wording of the new paragraph is as follows:

> This Treaty may also be translated into any other languages as determined by Member States among those which, in accordance with their constitutional order, enjoy official status in all or part of their territory. A certified copy of such translations shall be provided by the Member States concerned to be deposited in the archives of the Council.[10]

This amendment to the *Draft Treaty* was introduced at the request of the Government of Spain, which had promised to seek an improved status for Catalan.[11] A new category in the linguistic regime of the European Union would be involved, and status in accordance with it could be achieved for Scottish Gaelic, Welsh, Basque, and other languages, if the sovereign governments were prepared to inform the Council of Ministers of their intention to provide the relevant translations in these languages.[12]

Official and Working Languages

The *Treaty establishing the European Community* authorizes the Council of Ministers to decide the rules governing the languages of the institutions, except in the case of the Court of Justice, as follows:

> The rules governing the languages of the institutions of the Community shall, without prejudice to the provisions contained in the Statute of the Court of Justice, be determined by the Council, acting unanimously.

Irish is an official language of the Court of Justice.[13] Under the power given to them, the first regulation adopted by the Council of Ministers in 1958 was Regulation 1 which established the language regime of the institutions – which named the official and working languages and specified the mode of their usage.[14] Because this

---

[9] The title of the Article was changed from "Languages" to "Authentic Texts and Translations" in order to clarify the distinction.

[10] Article IV–10 (2). CIG 76/04 (May 13, 2004), Presidency; CIG 81/04 (June 16, 2004), Presidency.

[11] As shall be seen, a new shift in the circumstances of Catalan occurred later.

[12] It is being recommended that Member States wishing to do so should nominate the languages concerned within six months of the date of signing of the new treaty.

[13] In Article 223 of the *Treaty establishing the European Community*, it is left to the Court of Justice to establish its own rules of procedure.

[14] 31958 R 0001: Regulation Number 1 from the Council of April 15, 1958, determining the languages to be used by the European Economic Community (IO 17 6/10/1958), and Regulation Number 1 from the Council of April 15, 1958, determining the languages to be used by the European Community for Nuclear Energy (IO 17 6/10/1958).

Regulation is part of secondary legislation, no treaty will need to be amended in order to confer the status of official and working language on Irish. The unanimous agreement of the Council of Ministers will be required.

At the beginning, the list of treaty languages was the same as the list of official and working languages. As other countries were admitted, Regulation 1 was amended to include their official languages as official and working languages of the European Union. That happened in the case of every country except Ireland, and, as previously stated, it was the Government of Ireland which sought that arrangement at the time. The preamble of the Regulation gives the basis of selection of languages as official and working languages: they are there in the first place as authentic languages of the Treaties, and in the second place because they are recognised as official languages in one or more of the Member States of the Community. This is the wording of that section of the preamble as it has been from the beginning:

> Whereas each of the four languages in which the Treaty is drafted is recognised as an official language in one or more of the Member States of the Community;

Because Ireland refused to accept Irish as an official and working language, various Articles of the Regulation were amended in order to include the new languages, but the preamble was not amended. The same process occurred with each subsequent enlargement. It was not possible, nor is it yet possible, to correct the preamble because of the anomalous status of Irish. It cannot be said, for example, "Whereas each of the twenty languages in which the Treaty is drafted ...," because the Treaty is drafted in twenty-one languages, though there are only twenty official and working languages. The principal that a language must be an authentic language of the Treaties and an official language of at least one of the Member States in order to be recognised as an official and working language of the European Union continues to apply. From the accession of Ireland in 1973, Irish has been eligible under both conditions.

The following is the text of Article 1 of Regulation 1 which the Government of Ireland and the Governments of the other Member States approved when they signed the treaty of accession with the new countries in 2003:

> The official languages and the working languages of the institutions of the Union shall be Czech, Danish, Dutch, English, Estonian, Finnish, French, German, Greek, Hungarian, Italian, Latvian, Lithuanian, Maltese, Polish, Portuguese, Slovak, Slovenian, Spanish and Swedish.[15]

---

[15] In the Irish versions of all of the accession treaties, Irish text is not given for the wording of amendments to Articles from Regulation 1, 1958. These texts are given in English. Almost everything else in these treaties has been translated to Irish, and this involves thousands of pages. This is a very interesting demonstration of the legal fact that Irish is not an official language of the European Union. It seems likely that the translation was not permitted so that nobody could infer from the existence of an Irish language version of Regulation 1 Articles that Irish was an official language.

The Cases of Luxemburgish and Catalan

Considering the conditions for recognizing languages as official, it may be worthwhile to look at the case of Luxemburgish, because of the disinformation about it which was disseminated during the campaign for Irish. Luxemburgish had no statutory standing at home when Luxemburg and the other countries founded the European Economic Community in 1957. It was much later, in 1984, that Luxemburgish became a national language. It was not made an official language of the State, and there would be doubt on that account as to its eligibility for official status under the European Regulation. French is the sole language of legislation in Luxemburg, though the use of French, German, and Luxemburgish is permitted in administrative affairs. Official documents are usually not provided in Luxemburgish. No daily or weekly newspapers are published in the language. A form of German, with a strong admixture of French, it is primarily a spoken language. In any case, it never suited the people or the Government of Luxemburg that their language be recognized as a treaty language or as an official and working language, and they never requested that it be so recognized. They had the enviable advantage of having the two languages which they themselves most often used in official, literary, and educational contexts at home, French and German, as official languages of the Community from the beginning.

Catalan is a language whose number of speakers far exceeds that of several of the new official languages. While it is an official language in Catalonia and in the Balearic Islands, it is not an official language of Spain, and it is Spain which holds membership of the European Union.[16] Not only is it not an official language of the Member State, but it is disadvantaged other than in the regions in which it is official: for example, it is not permitted as of right to speak it in the Spanish Parliament. In a new departure on the question of Catalan, the Government of Spain have now requested that Basque *(el vasco)*, Catalan *(el catalán)*, Galician *(el gallego)*, and Valencian *(el valenciano)* be made "official languages" when Regulation 1 is being amended to include Irish. None of these languages are entitled to recognition as official languages under either of the two conditions, at least as these are presently defined.[17] During negotiations on the *Draft Treaty*, Spain did not request that the relevant article be amended so that these languages might become treaty languages.[18] The Member States, including Spain, have unanimously agreed that that treaty will be signed later this year and that no further amendments will be permitted.[19] I cannot see from a legal perspective that a language could be made an official and working

---

[16] It is an official language of the autonomous region of Valencia also, though it is called *'Valenciano'* in the Statute of Autonomy there. Catalan has some protection also in the autonomous region of Aragon. Article 3 of the Constitution of Spain states that Castilian is the official Spanish language of the State, and that the other languages of Spain are also official in their respective autonomous communities, in accordance with their Statutes.

[17] In a letter dated September 13, 2004, from Miguel Ángel Moratinos, Minister of Foreign Affairs and Cooperation, to Bernard Bot, Dutch Minister of Foreign Affairs and current incumbent of the Presidency of the Council of Ministers; a letter along the same lines was sent to the President of the Commission, Romano Prodi.

[18] Article IV–10 (1).

[19] The treaty is to be signed by all of the Member States at a ceremony in Rome on October 29, 2004.

language, with all of the implications which that involves, without it also being an authentic language of the Treaties.[20] Without a fundamental revision of the linguistic regime of the European Union, which is a possibility, there are only two ways through which the people of Catalonia can achieve full official European status for their language: to establish an independent sovereign state, to accede to the European Union as a distinct Member State, and to request status for their language; or that Spain should recognize Catalan as an official language of the Member State, and that the Government of Spain should seek for it status as a treaty language and as an official language.

The Advantages of Official Status

Peoples and Member States derive direct advantages from having their languages recognized as official languages under Regulation 1. In the first place, official status confers employment advantages on the citizens of the country in question. It is a basic requirement for every position advertised by the European Union that all candidates must have two official languages. Sometimes it is requested or permitted that competence in languages other than those to be used in the conduct of the job itself be mentioned; and in circumstances in which candidates are deemed to be equally qualified, the positions are given to the people who have those additional languages. This is a pragmatic acknowledgement of Europe's formal commitment to linguistic diversity.[21] But the commitment is delimited in this case to the linguistic regime of the Union: only official languages may be mentioned.[22] States use their power to ensure that linguistic competencies peculiar to themselves are defined as capital in the marketplace. Regulation 1 specifies the linguistic capital for the European market. With official status, the partial irony inherent in the fact that Irish cannot be entered on an application form for a position in the only agency of the European Union situated in Ireland – the *European Foundation for the Improvement of Living and Working Conditions* – will be neutralized. English is the working language of that Foundation, and Lithuanian or French or Maltese may be entered on the application as the second language along with the compulsory English in order to get a job there, but Irish cannot be entered with English.

The *Official Journal* of the European Union, which contains regulations, directives, and other important documents, is published in each of the official languages. The basic principle underlying this is that European laws are directly enforced in the Member States, and that consequently, in order to ensure their validity, they must be made available in the official languages of those Member

---

[20] There are other difficulties with the list which Spain has presented: it is accepted generally and under Spanish law that it is Catalan which is spoken in Valencia, but, as has been said, the language is referred to as *'Valenciano'* in the Statute of Autonomy there; and the similarities between Galician and Portuguese are so comprehensive that a common written standard is being discussed at present.

[21] There are provisions in the *Treaty establishing the European Community* (Article 151.1) and in the *Draft Treaty establishing a Constitution for Europe* (Part I, Article 3.3; Article II–22) which promote cultural and linguistic diversity.

[22] See Ó Laighin 2004: 11–12.

States. More than seventy per cent of the law which is enforced in Ireland comes from the European Union in the form of regulations. The regulations are transposed into Irish law, and the State is constitutionally obliged to make that law available in Irish and English. With the implementation of the *Official Languages Act 2003*, there will be a statutory obligation on the State to publish the laws simultaneously in both languages. Considering the development of the capacity of the European Union to make laws since 1973, and the new language legislation in Ireland, the Government of Ireland would now have much greater difficulty in trying to convince other Member States, or their own citizens, that the requirements of legal security can be satisfied without Irish being an official language under Regulation 1. When Irish is an official European language, regulations will come to the country in English and Irish, that is, in valid form, at the expense of the Union. The language regime of the European Union cost approximately two euro per citizen for the year 2002: the total expenditure amounted to one per cent of the Union's budget. Irish people will pay the two euro per person for the language services whether Irish is included or excluded. With the budget and the population increasing proportionately, it was not anticipated that costs would increase significantly with enlargement. In 2003, the possibility was still there that ten new languages would be involved – Turkish the tenth, in respect of that part of Cyprus which did not accede at the end.[23] Ireland will not be free of costs in this enterprise. The State will have to provide an Irish translation of the *acquis communautaire* – the collection of Treaties and the laws in force at present – from its own resources.[24]

The new status will empower the Irish Members to use their national official language in the European Parliament on the same basis as others do, should they so choose. Protection of this right in the case of the current twenty official languages is viewed as the touchstone of democratic decision-making. Adding Irish as the twenty-first language can only enhance the process, and enrich it also with the discernment of a Celtic language.

The European Union funds various educational and cultural programmes designed to promote linguistic diversity, but these programs are usually directed exclusively towards the official languages. With Irish as an official language, new language projects will be equally accessible for Irish, without the need to struggle for special status as occurred with the LINGUA, SOCRATES, and LEONARDO programmes. Irish will be on the list of official languages under Regulation 1, and consequently entitled to funding without question or petition.

Besides these direct advantages, there are other implications involved: the influence of the international status of a language on its speakers and learners, and the development which languages themselves undergo through exposure to translation and interpretation, for example.

These are significant advantages to Irish people, north, south, and overseas. But it is an advantage also to peoples of the other Member States that Irish should take its due place as one of the oldest languages of Europe, with the oldest vernacular literature of all of the countries of Europe, except Greece, with its learning, its folklore, its songs, its daily expression – a heritage which has been a distinctive dimension of the definition of Europeanism for a long time.

---

[23] DN: MEMO/03/37 (February 19, 2003), European Commission.
[24] All of the Treaties, and some other material, have already been translated to Irish.

Language Arrangements of the Institutions

Though Article 1 of Regulation 1, 1958, gives the list of official and working languages, this does not mean that the languages are treated equally in their usage by institutions. External correspondence in treaty languages must be answered in the same languages; but with respect to the internal working of the institutions, English and French, and to a lesser extent German, are almost totally dominant. The increase in the number of official languages will have little effect on the dominance of these languages. Practical decisions were made in 2003, as part of the preparation for enlargement, to radically reduce the amount of translation and interpretation which would normally be provided.[25] These practices are completely legal, since Article 6 of the Regulation permits the institutions to make their own arrangements for the internal use of languages:

> The institutions of the Community may stipulate in their rules of procedure which of the languages are to be used in specific cases.

On another matter, according to Article 8 of the Regulation, subsequent to the naming of Irish as an official language, there will be no obligation on the Government of Ireland to change its communication practices with the European Union: there is nothing in the law in general, or in the *Official Languages Act 2003* which would require such change.[26] They would be entitled to use documents in Irish from time to time, should they so choose. There are similarities between Ireland and Malta in this context, both countries having two official languages, and with English in common. Though Maltese is listed as an official language, communication between Malta and the European institutions is conducted almost entirely through English, just as it was during the enlargement negotiations.

The Value of Languages

I would like to refer to one complaint which was made during the campaign for Irish – that it would be better to emphasize the use of Irish at home rather than trying to obtain status for it in Europe.[27] This is a false antinomy. The status of Irish in Europe and the status of Irish in Ireland are not two separate entities. They are inextricably intertwined. Official working status in Europe will promote the use of Irish at home. Not only does international status enhance a language's status at home, and the self-esteem of its speakers, but European status will bring to young people the understanding that this is a language which is worthwhile acquiring and speaking, a language which is not only rich in itself, but which is useful also in relation to personal advancement and the achievement of things in the wide world.

[25] DN: MEMO/03/37 (February 19, 2003), European Commission.

[26] Article 8: "If a Member State has more than one official language, the language to be used shall, at the request of such State, be governed by the general rules of its law."

[27] One example of this stance motivated in part my extended discussion of the situation of Luxemburgish. The *Irish Times* reported (11 March 2004) that Viviane Reding, the European Commissioner from Luxemburg, was recommending to the people of Ireland that they should speak Irish at home rather than attempting to obtain official working status for it; according to her, "making it an official language doesn't bring you a thing."

Languages survive because of their intrinsic value, their value in and of themselves, and also because of their instrumental value in the achievement of external goals. As to the intrinsic value of Irish, its rich heritage is well appreciated. The external goals of language use are of great importance to people: its use in communicating with public bodies, with social and health services, for example, before courts, and its use in obtaining employment. The best way to weaken a language and effectively force the adoption of another is to lessen its usefulness in the achievement of these external goals. You can love a language to death if you do not simultaneously ensure its visibility, its usefulness as a resource in everyday life, and its role in the marketplace. That is why the effective functioning of the *Official Languages Act* and the achievement of official status for Irish in the European Union are highly significant: they will both contribute to the viability of the language. More people will speak Irish as a consequence.

References

National Forum on Europe. 2004. *The Fourth Phase of Work of the National Forum on Europe: February 2003 to June 2004*. Dublin: Stationery Office.

Ó Laighin, Pádraig Breandán. 2004. *Towards the Recognition of Irish as an Official Working Language of the European Union: Brief Presented to the National Forum on Europe*. Dublin: Clódhanna Teoranta.

Bile na Gàidhlig: cothroman is cunnartan

Wilson McLeod

Air 27 Sultain 2004 chuir Riaghaltas na h-Alba dreachd choileanta de Bhile na Gàidhlig (Alba) fo chomhair Pàrlamaid na h-Alba. Tha luchd-iomairt na Gàidhlig a' dlùthachadh ri crìoch rathaid fhada — rathad a bha, gun teagamh, casta is creagach — agus chan eil ceann-ùidhe an turais seo buileach cinnteach fhathast.[1]

Thòisich an iomairt airson Achd Ghàidhlig grunn bhliadhnaichean air ais, ann am meadhan nan 1990an, nuair a mhothaich luchd na Gàidhlig nach robh an t-adhartas a rinneadh bho na 1980an air adhart a thaobh leasachadh na Gàidhlig, gu h-àraidh a thaobh solarachadh an fhoghlaim Ghàidhlig, daingeann no seasmhach — gu robh mì-chinnt phoilitigeach ag adhbharachadh cion misneachd am measg phàrantan agus luchd na Gàidhlig anns an fharsaingeachd. Air sàillibh na h-anfhoise seo chuir Comunn na Gàidhlig buidheann-obrach air dòigh agus b'e toradh a cuid obrach aithisg a chuireadh gu Oifis na h-Alba (mar a bha) anns an Dùbhlachd 1997, *Inbhe Thèarainte dhan Ghàidhlig: tagradh às leth coimhearsnachd na Gàidhlig* (CnaG 1997). Ann am meadhan 1999 dh'fhoillsich CnaG aithisg eile, *Dreach iùl airson Achd Gàidhlig* (CnaG 1999), a' togail air molaidhean farsaing na h-aithisg *Inbhe Thèarainte*, anns an do mhìnich iad na bhiodh a dhìth ann an Achd Ghàidhlig.

B'e 1997-99 mìos nam pòg (no bliadhnaichean nam pòg) aig na Làbaraich Ùra, agus tòrr fhuaimean binne rin cluinntinn bhuapa a thaobh na Gàidhlig. Bha a' choimhearsnachd Ghàidhlig an dùil gum freagradh an Riaghaltas na tagraidhean seo le reachdas cànain a bheireadh na molaidhean aig CnaG gu buil. Ach chan ann mar sin a thachair. An àite reachdais fhuaradh dàil, leisgeulan, dàil, buidhnean-obrach, dàil, barrachd bhuidhnean-obrach, agus barrachd dàlach. B'e 'loidhne' an Riaghaltais nach robh reachdas cànain a dhìth, nach biodh e gu mòran feum, agus gu robhas ag obair 'a dh'ionnsaigh' inbhe thèarainte don Ghàidhlig tro iomadach ceum is iomairt às leth na cànain (Dunbar 2003a, Dunbar 2003b).

Mu dheireadh thall, an dèidh foillseachadh aithisg na darna buidhne-obrach oifigeil, Aithisg Mheek (Buidheann Comhairleachaidh an Riaghaltais air Gàidhlig 2003), ann an 2003, rinn am Pàrtaidh Làbarach gealltanas anns a' mhanifesto taghaidh aca gun cuireadh iad Bile Gàidhlig fo chomhair na Pàrlamaid anns an ath Phàrlamaid. Choileanadh an gealltanas seo anns an Damhair 2003 nuair a dh'fhoillsicheadh a' chiad dreachd de Bhile na Gàidhlig agus a chuireadh co-comhairleachadh poblach air chois.

A' chiad dreachd Bhile agus na h-uireasbhaidhean aige

Bha a' chiad dreachd den Bhile — agus gu dearbh, an darna dreachd, a chuireadh fo chomhair na Pàrlamaid anns an t-Sultain 2004 — stèidhte, gu ìre mhòir, air Achd na Cuimris 1993. (Tha an aon seòrsa phrionnsabalan rim faicinn ann an Acht na dTeangacha Oifigiúla 2003 ann am Poblachd na h-Èireann). Mar sin, bha dà phrìomh amas aige: (1) stèidheachadh Bhòrd na Gàidhlig mar bhuidheann reachdail, agus soilleireachadh agus neartachadh a chuid cumhachdan, agus (2) leudachadh àite na Gàidhlig ann am beatha phoblach na h-Alba. Ged nach robh am Mìneachadh Poileasaidh a dh'fhoillsicheadh an cois a' Bhile a' cleachdadh cainnt an t-sòsio-chàn-

---

[1] Chaidh am Bile achdachadh air 21 Giblean 2005, gun atharrachaidhean susbainteach an dèidh ìre 2 den phròiseas phàrlamaideach.

anachais, faodar a ràdh gun cuireadh reachdas den t-seòrsa ri inbhe na Gàidhlig, ri cothroman cleachdaidh na Gàidhlig agus ri luach pragtaigeach/eaconamach na Gàidhlig, agus gun cuireadh na leasachaidhean seo ri misneachd luchd-labhairt na Gàidhlig, gum brosnaicheadh iad ionnsachadh na Gàidhlig, agus gun àrdaicheadh iad an ìre iarrtais airson foghlam tro mheadhan na Gàidhlig.

Fhuair an Riaghaltas còrr is 3,000 freagairt ris a' cho-chomhairleachadh air a' chiad dreachd den Bhile, a thàinig gu crìch anns an Fhaoilleach 2004. Gu ruige sin cha d'fhuair co-chomhairleachadh sam bith eile aig Riaghaltas na h-Alba uiread de fhreagairtean. Gu mì-fhortanach, is cinnteach nach b'e àgh is aoibhneas ach briseadh-dùil agus diomb a spreag mòran de na freagairtean seo: bha a' mhòr-mhòrchuid de na buidhnean Gàidhlig agus de luchd-labhairt na Gàidhlig anns an fharsaingeachd gu math mì-riaraichte leis an dreachd Bhile. An dèidh nam bliadhnaichean de dhàil bhathas an dùil gum biodh fada bharrachd brìgh anns a' Bhile nuair a thàinig e.

Ged a tha buidhnean poblach den t-seòrsa buailteach a bhith faiceallach agus stuama nuair a chuireas iad am beachdan an cèill gu poblach, bha fiù 's Bòrd na Gàidhlig gu math achmhasanach:

> . . . [Chan] eil am Bile làidir gu leòr. Tha an t-eòlas a tha againn fhìn mar bhuidheann agus an fhianais agus rannsachadh a chuir sinn air dòigh a' cur an cèill ma thèid am Bile a reachdachadh gun atharrachadh nach coilean e a chuid amasan . . . Gu mì-fhortanach cha tèid aig a' Bhile seo air crìonadh a' chànain a stad mar a tha e air a dhreachdachadh an-dràsta. (Bòrd na Gàidhlig 2003).

Rinn an t-ionad-rannsachaidh Lèirsinn sgrùdadh faiceallach air na freagairtean a chuireadh chun an Riaghaltais (Johnstone et al. 2004). Anns na freagairtean foirmeil, agus anns an deasbad phoblach air a' Bhile a chaidh air adhart aig an àm, chuireadh cuideam air grunn phuingean:

- nach robh de chumhachd agus de inbhe aig Bòrd na Gàidhlig airson buaidh a thoirt air buidhnean poblach na h-Alba;
- nach robh adhbhar a' Bhile soilleir gu leòr (cha robh an abairt shàr-chudromach 'cànain oifigeil' ga cleachdadh idir — dìreach gun aithnichte a' Ghàidhlig 'mar aon de chànain na h-Alba');
- nach robh uallach laghail air buidhnean poblach poileasaidhean Gàidhlig a dhealbhadh agus a chur an gnìomh (mar a bha ann an Achd na Cuimris 1993 a thaobh na Cuimris),[2] agus
- nach robh facal anns an dreachd mu fhoghlam Gàidhlig, ged a b'e uireasbhaidhean ann an siostam an fhoghlaim a spreag an iomairt airson inbhe thèarainte anns a' chiad dol-a-mach.

---

[2] An àite sin, seo na chuireadh an cèill ann an earrann 5 den dreachd Bhile:

> (1) Feumaidh a h-uile buidheann phoblach . . . taobh a-staigh na h-ùine air ainmeachadh ann am fo-earrann (2) —
>
> (a) co-dhùnadh, le spèis do na nithean air an ainmeachadh ann am fo-earrann (5), **a bheil e iomchaidh** plana-cànain Gàidhlig ullachadh agus fhoillseachadh, agus
>
> (b) ma cho-dhùineas buidheann gu bheil e iomchaidh sin a dhèanamh, am plana sin ullachadh agus fhoillseachadh.

Aig an aon àm, fhuaradh grunn bheachdan bho thaobh a-muigh saoghal na Gàidhlig a bha coma mu luach a' Bhile, agus fhuaradh beagan a bha gu tur diùltach no aibhisichte. Dh'agair a' bhuidheann *Universities Scotland* gun toireadh am Bile droch bhuaidh air farpaiseachd eadar-nàiseanta foghlam àrd-ìre na h-Alba, mar eisimpleir, agus dh'agair an Coimisean airson Co-ionnanachd Cinnidh gum bacadh am Bile iomairtean nan ùghdarrasan ionadail a thaobh co-ionnanachd cinnidh.[3] Anns an fharsaingeachd, ged-tà, cha chualas mòran ghearanan mun Bhile bho na comhairlean ionadail agus na buidhnean poblach eile; is dòcha gur e laigse agus fannachd na dreachd a chùm samhach iad.

An darna dreachd: dà cheum air aghaidh, ceum air ais?

Nuair a nochd an darna dreachd den Bhile anns an t-Sultain 2004 bha e follaiseach gun cuala an Riaghaltas gearanan coimhearsnachd na Gàidhlig agus tha grunn leasachaidhean rim faicinn anns an tionndadh ùr. Tha am Bile gu math nas treise na bha e; ach chan eil e idir cinnteach gun riaraich e dùil is dòchas nan Gàidheal. Aig an aon àm, is mathaid gun spreag bile a tha a-nis air a neartachadh barrachd connspaid agus diomb am measg nàimhdean na Gàidhlig agus luchd an aona-chànanais (cf. McLeod 2002).

Seo cuid de na leasachaidhean as cudromaiche a chithear anns an darna dreachd den Bhile:

- tha am Bile a-nis a' cur an cèill gum bi a' Ghàidhlig na 'cànain oifigeil an Alba' (ged nach eil am forail sin cho soilleir 's a dh'fhaodadh e bhith). Ged nach eil mòran brìgh laghail aig an fhògradh lom ud, tha eachdraidh na Cuimrigh a' nochdadh gun toireadh e buaidh air ìomhaigh phoblach na Gàidhlig (am measg chompanaidhean mòra agus bhuidhnean-carthannais, mar eisimpleir).
- bidh uallach laghail air buidhnean poblach poileasaidhean Gàidhlig a dhealbhadh agus a chur an gnìomh ma chuireas Bòrd na Gàidhlig brath thuca ag iarraidh orra sin a dhèanamh; agus tha barrachd cumhachd aig Bòrd na Gàidhlig a thaobh aontachadh agus coileanadh phoileasaidhean den t-seòrsa. A dh'aindeoin sin, tha cumhachdan Bhòrd na Gàidhlig fhathast gu math lag an coimeas ri Bòrd na Cuimris (air neo ris a' Choimisinéir Teanga ann am Poblachd na h-Èireann, a rèir cuid 4 de Acht na dTeangacha Oifigiúla 2003).
- tha leasachaidhean anns a' Bhile fhèin a thaobh foghlam Gàidhlig, a' toirt cumhachd do Bhòrd na Gàidhlig 'stiùireadh a thoirt a rèir an ullachaidh a thaobh foghlam Gàidhlig agus leasachadh an ullachaidh sin' (earrann 9(1)) agus a' toirt air na h-ùghdarrasan foghlaim feart a thoirt don stiùireadh sin. An co-cheangal ri foillseachadh Bhile na Gàidhlig, dh'fhoillsich an Riaghaltas fhèin stiùireadh ùr a thaobh foghlam Gàidhlig (fo sgèith Achd Inbhean ann an Sgoiltean na h-Alba msaa 2000), stiùireadh a chuir barrachd cuideim air na h-ùghdarrasan foghlaim a thaobh leasachadh agus leudachadh an t-solarachaidh aca.[4] Ach chan eil am Bile a' tighinn faisg air iarrtasan nam pàrant, a tha a' sireadh chòraichean deimhinne

---

[3] Gu fortanach, cha do ghabh an Riaghaltas ri beachd a' Choimisein idir: a rèir a' Mheòrachain Poileasaidh (paragraf 68), 'tha co-ionannachd chothroman aig cridhe a' Bhile seo agus tha an Riaghaltas airson Bile a thoirt a-steach a nì cinnteach gum bi tomhas de cho-ionannachd aig luchd-labhairt Gàidhlig'.

[4] Tha an stiùireadh seo, a tha na dhreachd fhathast, ri fhaighinn air an Eadar-lìon aig (http://www.scotland.gov.uk/about/ED/SACBranch2/00017909/page994361977.doc). Tha an

a thaobh foghlam Gàidhlig.

A dh'aindeoin nan leasachaidhean seo, tha beàrnan agus uireasbhaidhean gu leòr anns a' Bhile fhathast. Tha e gu math nas laige na Achd na Cuimris 1993, agus leis mar a tha e follaiseach gun deach an Achd sin a chleachdadh mar nàdar de mhodal do luchd-dealbhaidh a' Bhile, tha e soilleir gun deach a lagachadh a dh'aona ghnothaich — is e sin ri ràdh, nach robh Riaghaltas na h-Alba deònach an aon uiread de chumhachd a thoirt do Bhòrd na Gàidhlig 's a tha aig Bòrd na Cuimris, agus na h-aon bhuannachdan a thoirt do luchd na Gàidhlig 's a tha aig luchd na Cuimris.

Am measg nan uireasbhaidhean anns a' Bhile tha na leanas:

- chan eil guth air 'inbhe cho-ionnan' (*equal validity*) no 'co-ionnanachd meas' (*parity of esteem*). A rèir a' Mheòrachain Poileasaidh a dh'fhoillseachadh an cois a' Bhile, tha an Riaghaltas 'den bheachd nach eil e comasach no iomchaidh ceuman a chur sa Bhile a dh'fhaodadh leantainn gu ùghdarras poblach an àite sam bith an Alba air a chur fo dhleastanas laghail a bhith a' tabhann seirbheisean sa Ghàidhlig far a bheil iarrtas' (paragraf 15) agus gur e sin a' bhuaidh a bhiodh aig forail a chuireadh a' Ghàidhlig agus a' Bheurla air inbhe cho-ionnan (paragraf 50). Ged a bha abairt 'inbhe cho-ionnan' tuilleadh is draghail dhaibh, bha an Riaghaltas deònach an abairt 'spèis ionnan' (*'commanding equal respect'*) a chur anns a' Bhile, agus chaidh an t-atharrachadh seo a dhèanamh air earrann 1(3) den Bhile aig ìre 2 den phròiseas Phàrlamaideach. Chan eil ciall na h-abairt ùire seo buileach soilleir, ach tha follaiseach gu bheil an Riaghaltas riaraichte nach cuir e mòran cuideim air buidhnean poblach na h-Alba co-dhiù.
- ged a tha am Bile a' cur uallach air Bòrd na Gàidhlig 'Plana-cànain Nàiseanta Gàidhlig' a dhealbhachadh, chan eil e idir soilleir dè an inbhe a bhiodh aig a' phlana seo. Chaidh an Riaghaltas an aghaidh comhairle Bhòrd na Gàidhlig gum bu chòir cumhachan a chur ris a' Bhile a chuireadh dleastanasan co-èigneachail air Riaghaltas na h-Alba agus buidhnean poblach eile a thaobh coileanadh a' phlana-cànain nàiseanta. A rèir an Riaghaltais cha bhi anns a' phlana-cànain nàiseanta ach dòigh choileanta, 'cho-aontachail' airson 'leasachadh Gàidhlig a stiùireas ùghdarrasan poblach san dòigh-obrach aca a thaobh a' chànain' (Meòrachan Poileasaidh, paragrafan 32-33).
- ged a bhios uallach air buidhnean poblach poileasaidhean Gàidhlig a dhealbhadh ma dh'iarras Bòrd na Gàidhlig sin orra, tha grunn bheàrnan ann an structar a' Bhile, agus tha am Bile gu math doilleir an coimeas ri Achd na Cuimris 1993. Mar eisimpleir, chan eil e soilleir dè thachras mura freagair buidheann phoblach iarrtas foirmeil bho Bhòrd na Gàidhlig; ach tha earrann 14(2) de Achd na Cuimris a' toirt cumhachd do Bhòrd na Cuimris dèiligeadh ri fàilligeadh mar seo. Tha Achd na Cuimris (earrannan 17 agus 19) a' cur an cèill gum bi

---

stiùireadh ùr feumail, ach cha dòcha gun tig atharrachadh bunaiteach ri linn nan riaghailtean ùra seo, gu h-àraidh anns na 18 (a-mach à 32) sgìrean riaghaltais ionadail far nach eil a' Ghàidhlig ri faighinn (mar mheadhan teagaisg no mar chuspair) ann an sgoil sam bith an-dràsta. Mar eisimpleir, ged a bhios uallach air na h-ùghdarrasan foghlaim ionadail a bhith a' cur an cèill an ìre iarrtais a bhios a dhìth mus solaraich an t-ùghdarras foghlam Gàidhlig, is ann an urra ris na h-ùghdarrasan fhèin a bhios na co-dhùnaidhean seo. Chan eil e soilleir gum bacadh na riaghailtean seo ùghdarras a stèidhich ìre a tha mì-reusanta (can iarrtasan sgrìobhte às leth 50 sgoilear mus biodh foghlam Gàidhlig ga chur air dòigh).

cumhachd aig Bòrd na Cuimris rannsachadh a chur air dòigh gus dèanamh cinnteach gu bheil buidhnean a' coileanadh an cuid dhleastanasan, agus cumhachd toraidhean an rannsachaidh aca fhoillseachadh airson uireasbhaidhean bhuidhnean poblach a leigeil mu sgaoil (cumhachd 'ainmeachaidh agus nàrachaidh', mar gum b'eadh). Chan eil Bile na Gàidhlig, mar a tha e an-dràsta, a' toirt cumhachd den t-seòrsa do Bhòrd na Gàidhlig. A bharrachd air sin, tha Achd na Cuimris a' cur an cèill (ann an earrann 20(3)) gum faod Riaghaltas Sheanadh na Cuimrigh buidhnean nach eil a' coileanadh an cuid dhleastanasan a thoirt gu lagh, ach chan eil sin soilleir ann an dreachd Bhile na Gàidhlig.

- eu-coltach ri Acht na dTeangacha Oifigiúla (earrann 28), chan eil an dreachd Bhile a' cruthachadh chòraichean pearsanta a thaobh co-èigneachadh na h-Achd, .i. a' toirt cead don fheadhainn a dh'fhulaing ri linn cion coileanaidh poileasaidh Ghàidhlig cùis-lagha 'phrìobhaideach' a thogail. Is ann aig Bòrd na Gàidhlig agus Riaghaltas na h-Alba a-mhàin a tha an cumhachd a bhith a' sgrùdadh gnìomhan agus cion gnìomhan nam buidhnean poblach. Ann an dòigh chudromach, ma-thà, dh'fhaoidte a ràdh nach eil am Bile a' buntainn do luchd na Gàidhlig idir.

- chan eil dad anns a' Bhile mu chleachdadh na Gàidhlig anns na cùirtean. (Tha i, gu ìre mhòir, toirmisgte an-dràsta).[5] Ged a thig Seirbhis Cùirtean na h-Alba fo sgèith na h-Achd, agus bhiodh e ri shùileachadh gun nochdadh rudeigin ann am poileasaidh na Seirbhis (ma thig a leithid idir) mu chleachdadh na Gàidhlig anns na cùirtean, bhiodh e na b'iomchaidhe — agus na bu shàbhailte, gun teagamh — còraichean luchd na Gàidhlig a chur an cèill anns a' Bhile fhèin. Is ann mar sin a tha Achd na Cuimris 1993 a' dèiligeadh ris a' ghnothach: tha earrann 22 den Achd a' cur an cèill gu bheil e ceadaichte Cuimris a chleachdadh anns na cùirtean, agus gum bi na còraichean seo gan toirt gu buil le riaghailtean mionaideach nan cùirtean; tha sgeamaichean Cuimris nan seirbhisean chùirtean a-nis a' cur nam prionnsabalan seo an gnìomh (Dunbar 2003b: 150-51).

- chan eil am Bile a' mìneachadh dè dìreach a bu chòir a bhith ann am plana cànain, a bharrachd air a bhith a' cur an cèill gum bi na planaichean seo a' gabhail a-steach '(a) gnìomhan co-cheangailte ri modhan-obrachaidh, agus (b) ullachadh an ùghdarrais air seirbheisean sam bith don phoball' (earrann 10(3)). Bhiodh e na b'fheàrr buileach nam biodh liosta ghoirid de raointean gnìomha ga toirt seachad anns a' Bhile fhèin: poileasaidhean sgiobachd, fastaidh agus trèanaidh, ìomhaigh fhollaiseach agus phoblach, conaltradh poblach (an dà chuid sgrìobhte agus labhairteach), 7rl.[6] Bhiodh sin sònraichte luachmhor a chionn 's gu bheil cultar an

---

[5] A rèir co-dhùnadh na cùirte ann an *Taylor v. Haughney*, 1982 SCCR 360, chan fhaod tagraiche ann an cùis-lagha Gàidhlig a chleachdadh ma tha Beurla aige (feuch McLeod 1997: 99-100). Tha am prionnsabal farsaing sin fhathast an sàs ach tha riaghailtean cùirte a-nis a' ceadachadh cleachdadh na Gàidhlig ann an cùisean sìobhalta (ach chan ann an cùisean eucoireach) ann an cùirtean siorraim ann an trì siorramachdan ann an iar-thuath na h-Alba (Loch nam Madadh, Port Rìgh agus Steòrnabhagh).

[6] Bha liosta den t-seòrsa anns a' Bhile Buill a chuireadh fo chomhair na Pàrlamaid Albannaich le Michael Russell BPA ann an 2002; bhàsaich am Bile ud air sgàth cion ùine Pàrlamaidich. Chan eil mìneachadh foirmeil ga thoirt seachad ann an Achd na Cuimris 1993, ach tha e soilleir bhon Achd gum feum sgeamaichean Cuimris prionnsabal farsaing na co-ionnanachd chànanaich a chur an sàs.

aona-chànanais cho làidir is cho daingeann am measg bhuidhnean poblach na h-Alba (McLeod 2001, 2002). Chan eil eòlas sam bith aig a' mhòr-mhòrchuid aca air a bhith ag obair gu dà-chànanach agus a' tabhann sheirbhisean dà-chànanach. Ged a tha am Bile a' toirt cumhachd do Bhòrd na Gàidhlig a bhith a' dealbhadh stiùireadh mu shusbaint nam planaichean, is dòcha nach tuig mòran bhuidhnean gu bheileas (gu bheil tòrr Ghàidheal co-dhiù) a' sùileachadh phlanaichean farsaing a bheireadh atharrachadh air 'cultar obrachaidh' nam buidhnean. Tha 'poileasaidhean Gàidhlig' aig grunn bhuidhnean ann an Alba mar-thà, ach mar as trice cha ruig iad 'cultar obrachaidh' na buidhne; faodar a ràdh le tomhas de chinnt nach riaraicheadh gin aca Bòrd na Cuimris.

A bharrachd air na beàrnan agus an doilleireachd a chithear anns a' Bhile fhèin, tha mìneachaidhean agus rabhaidhean ann am Meòrachan Ionmhasail an Riaghaltais a tha car draghail. Mar eisimpleir:

- Tha paragraf 88 a' cur an cèill gu bheil 'an Riaghaltas a' sùileachadh gun iarr Bòrd na Gàidhlig cur ri chèile agus buileachadh mu 10 planaichean gach bliadhna'. Tha beagan cheudan de bhuidhnean poblach ann an Alba; aig an astar sin cha chuirte an Achd an sàs air feadh Alba airson 20 no 30 bliadhna! Ged a tha e cudromach nach bi uallach ro throm air Bòrd na Gàidhlig anns a' chiad dol-a-mach, bu chòir saorsa a bhith aige a bhith rud beag nas sgiobalta na sin. Bu chòir tomhas de cho-ionnanachd a bhith ann eadar poileasaidhean nan diofar bhuidhnean, agus gum bu chòir poileasaidhean a sgrùdadh agus a cheadachadh ann an dòigh a tha èifeachdach: carson a bhiodh mòran diofaran ann eadar poileasaidh Gàidhlig Comhairle Aonghais agus Comhairle Fìobha, mar eisimpleir, air neo na planaichean aig Coimiseanair Gnìomhachas an Uisge an Alba agus Buidheann Dìon Àrainneachd na h-Alba?
- Tha paragraf 92 ag ràdh nach 'eil an Riaghaltas a' sùileachadh gun cuir Bòrd na Gàidhlig brath gu ùghdarrasan poblach an Alba [ag iarraidh orra planaichean Gàidhlig a dhealbhadh] ann an sgìrean le beagan luchd-labhairt Gàidhlig sa chiad bhliadhnachan an dèidh achdachadh a' Bile'. Is dòcha gum bi am forail seo a' cuingealachadh a' Bhùird; agus tha cunnart ann gum biodh na h-abairtean neo-mhionaideach 'beagan luchd-labhairt Gàidhlig' agus 'sa chiad bhliadhnachan' gan cleachdadh an aghaidh obair a' Bhùird. An canadh Comhairle Dhùn Dè nach eil ach 'beagan luchd-labhairt Gàidhlig' anns an sgìre aice? An diùltadh Comhairle Chrìochan na h-Alba plana Gàidhlig a chur ri chèile còig no sia bliadhnaichean an dèidh achdachadh a' Bile?
- Tha paragraf 91 den Mheòrachan Ionmhasail a' cur an cèill gum 'bu chòir *a' chuid as motha* de ùghdarrasan poblach beachdachadh' air a bhith a' 'gealladh . . . ann an cur ri chèile plana a bhith a' toirt freagairt sa Ghàidhlig ri litrichean Gàidhlig'. Tha e cha mhòr do-chreidsinneach gum biodh Bòrd na Gàidhlig (air neo an Riaghaltas) a' beannachadh 'plana Gàidhlig' a bheireadh cead do bhuidheann phoblach a bhith a' diùltadh freagairt anns a' Ghàidhlig a thoirt do litir a bha sgrìobhte sa Ghàidhlig. Saoil am biodh e ceart gu leòr 'plana Gàidhlig' a chur ri chèile a rinn soilleir nach fhaigheadh litrichean sgrìobhte sa Ghàidhlig freagairt idir?
- Tha an clàr an cois paragraf 91 a' cumail a-mach gun cosgadh buidheann phoblach £0-£5,000 a bharrachd gach bliadhna mu choinneimh cosgaisean

trèanaidh air sgàth plana Gàidhlig. Tha an àireamh seo a' nochdadh nach eil an Riaghaltas a' sùileachadh gum biodh na planaichean seo ag obair a dh'ionnsaigh an dà-chànanais. Mar eisimpleir, chosgadh e co-dhiù £10,000 airson dìreach aon neach-obrach a chur air cùrsa-bogaidh Gàidhlig. Tha mu 7,000 neach-obrach aig Riaghaltas na h-Alba; tha an tuairmse seo ag innse dhuinn nach biodh an Riaghaltas fhèin a' cosg barrachd air 70 sgillinn an urra gach bliadhna a chum leasachadh sgilean Gàidhlig a chuid luchd-obrach!

• An rud as cunnartaiche buileach is e gu bheil an Riaghaltas a' cur maoin ùr mu seach (Maoin Leasachaidh Gàidhlig) a chum buileachadh phlanaichean Gàidhlig. A rèir coltais is ann bhon Mhaoin seo a thèid (cuid de?) cosgaisean cur an gnìomh nam planaichean a phàigheadh. Ach tha bagairt an lùib an structair seo, oir tha earrann 94 a' cur an cèill 'ann an iarraidh cur ri chèile agus buileachadh phlanaichean bheir am Bòrd aire don ìre cuideachaidh a gheibhear bhon Mhaoin Leasachaidh Gàidhlig'. A rèir coltais, mura robh airgead gu leòr air fhàgail anns an sporan, cha bhiodh e comasach do Bhòrd na Gàidhlig planaichean 'ro chosgail' a chur ri chèile (air neo dhiùltadh an Riaghaltas cead a thoirt do phlanaichean a' Bhùird). Mar sin, bhiodh e furasta gu leòr don Riaghaltas smachd a chumail air obair a' Bhùird tro bhith gearradh air ais air a' Mhaoin Leasachaidh. Tha eachdraidh thàmailteach maoineachadh Maoin Telebhisein Ghàidhlig (Comataidh Craolaidh Gàidhlig/Seirbhis nam Meadhanan Gàidhlig) a' nochdadh nan cunnartan an seo: tha luach na maoine ud air crìonadh gu mòr thairis air na beagan bhliadhnaichean a dh'fhalbh, a chionn 's nach do chuir an Riaghaltas airgead gu leòr rithe, rud a dh'adhbharaich gearraidhean mòra, sgriosail air an t-seirbhis. Nuair a stèidhicheadh a' Mhaoin ann an 1992, b'urrainnear mu 200 uair de thìde de phrògraman a dhèanamh gach bliadhna, ach tha an àireamh sin air tuiteam mu 25% a-nis air sgàth nan gearraidhean agus buaidh na h-atmhorachd. Ann an co-theacs na Maoine Leasachaidh Ghàidhlig, is dòcha gum biodh e comasach do bhuidheann phoblach tagradh a dhèanamh an aghaidh molaidhean Bhòrd na Gàidhlig, ag argamaid nach biodh airgead gu leòr anns a' Mhaoin airson coileanadh molaidhean a' Bhùird — molaidhean a bhiodh, uime sin, 'mì-reusanta'.[7]

Cunnartan poilitigeach air fàire?

A bharrachd air uireasbhaidhean a' Bhile fhèin, dh'fhaoidte gum faighear cunnartan

---

[7] Tha beàrn chudromach eile anns a' Bhile: chan eil meòir Riaghaltas Westminster fo a sgèith idir, agus mar sin cha bhi ùghdarras aig Bòrd na Gàidhlig iarraidh (gu foirmeil) air buidhnean a tha stèidhte ann an Lunnainn planaichean Gàidhlig a chur ri chèile. Tha a h-uile buidheann phoblach anns a' Chuimrigh — a' gabhail a-steach meòir Riaghaltas Westminster — fo sgèith Achd na Cuimris 1993, ged-tà. Is e as coireach dha seo gun deach Achd na Cuimris 1993 achdachadh le Pàrlamaid Westminster, aig a bheil ùghdarras air na buidhnean seo, ach cha bhiodh e ceadaichte (a rèir Achd na h-Alba 1998, a chuir siostam tiomnadh chumhachdan an gnìomh) do Phàrlamaid na h-Alba reachdas cho leathann achdachadh. Tha còmhraidhean oifigeil air a bhith a' dol air a' cheist seo ach chan fhacas mòran adhartais gu ruige seo. Bhiodh e na chall mura faigheadh fuasgladh don duilgheadas seo; chan eil e ciallach idir gum biodh, can, Dualchas Nàdair na h-Alba agus bùird slàinte fo uallach a bhith a' tabhann sheirbhisean dà-chànanach ach gum biodh Oifis a' Phuist agus Oifis na Cìse Nàiseanta saor a bhith a' diùltadh dad den t-seòrsa a dhèanamh.

de dhiofar sheòrsaichean fhad 's a bhios am Bile a' dol tron Phàrlamaid:

- A' chiad trioblaid is e na Buill Pàrlamaid fhèin. Tha cuid dhiubh taiceil don Ghàidhlig (agus beagan dhiubh nan sàr-chàirdean); tha cuid eile nan nàimhdean; agus tha tòrr a bharrachd aig nach eil mòran ùidh no eòlais idir. Tha a' Ghàidhlig air iomall poileataigs na h-Alba agus air iomall an iomaill bho shealladh an dream a tha ga stiùireadh, .i. luchd-poileataigs a' Chrios Mheadhanaich (McLeod 2001, 2004). Mar sin tha tomhas de mhì-chinnt ann oir chan eil eachdraidh shoilleir no beachdan deimhinne aig a' mhòrchuid, agus is dòcha nach tuig iad na ceistean mòra, gun caith iad cus ùine air gnothaichean neo-chudromach, agus gun gabh iad ri argamaidean suarach no gòrach.
- Trioblaid den aon t-seòrsa is e ròl nam meadhanan Beurla, gu h-àraidh na *tabloids*. Anns an fharsaingeachd, chan ann idir tric a bhios poileataigs na Gàidhlig a' tighinn air aire nam pàipearan-naidheachd Beurla (McLeod 2001, 2004), agus sin mar a bha a thaobh na dreachd Bhile Gàidhlig: ged a bha deasbad teann is connspaid a' dol air adhart ann an saoghal na Gàidhlig, is e glè glè bheag dheth a ràinig na meadhanan Beurla. Ach is dòcha gun nochd ceist a' Bhile air na sgàilein ràdair aca a-nis, rud nach bi feumail do chùis na Gàidhlig, oir gu ìre mhòir chan eil anns a' Ghàidhlig ach cùis-bhùirt bho shealladh nam meadhanan Beurla. Gu dearbh tha beagan airteagalan nimheil air nochdadh mar-thà.
- Ged a bha cuid de na freagairtean ris a' cho-chomhairleachadh air an dreachd Bhile dubhach gu leòr, uile gu lèir cha robh buidhnean poblach na h-Alba ro ghearanach. Tha cunnart ann gun atharraich sin a-nis, agus am Bile air a neartachadh gu ìre, agus uallach nas truime gu bhith ga chur air na buidhnean poblach a thaobh dealbhadh phlanaichean Gàidhlig. B'e ceistean ionmhais am prìomh adhbhar-iomagain rè a' cho-chomhairleachaidh, agus is dòcha gum maothaich cruthachadh Maoin Leasachaidh Gàidhlig an iomagain ud. Ach chan eil gràin-chànain agus 'mì-rùn mòr nan Gall' daonnan reusanta no pragtaigeach, agus tha teans ann gun toir luchd a' mhì-rùin buaidh air an deasbad fhathast.
- Ceist thoinnte is e an dàimh eadar a' Ghàidhlig agus na cànainean eile a tha gam bruidhinn an Alba, gu h-àraidh a' Bheurla Ghallda agus 'cànainean coimhearsnachd' leithid Cantonais, Panjabi agus Urdu. Ma tha Bòrd na Gàidhlig gu bhith ann, chanadh cuid, carson nach stèidhich an Riaghaltas Bòrd na Beurla Gallda agus Bòrd na h-Urdu a dh'iarras air buidhnean poblach na h-Alba planaichean Beurla Gallda agus Urdu a dhealbhadh? Ceist chonnspaideach, a gheibh iomadach seòrsa freagairt, is dòcha. Is e beachd an Riaghaltais — beachd a tha stèidhte, tha e coltach, air an aithisg thoirteil aig Joe Lo Bianco air cànainean agus litearrachd an Alba (Lo Bianco 2001) — gu bheil reachdas sònraichte às leth na Gàidhlig a dhìth air sgàth suidheachadh èiginneach na cànain:

> Tha an Riaghaltas den bheachd às aonais na h-obrach shònraichte air a mìneachadh sa Bhile seo gum bi a' Ghàidhlig ann am fìor chunnart agus mar sin tha e a' leantainn eisimpleir dhùthchannan eile ann a bhith a' toirt ceuman gus inbhe aon de na cànainean aice a chur air stèidh thèarainte. (Meòrachan Poileasaidh, paragraf 67).

Aig an aon àm, ann an Aonta Com-pàirteachais Riaghaltas na h-Alba (an t-aonta co-bhanntachd a rinneadh eadar am Pàrtaidh Làbarach agus am Pàrtaidh

Libearalach Deamocratach an dèidh an taghaidh mu dheireadh), tha an Riaghaltas air gealltainn 'gun cuir e ri chèile ro-innleachd cànain coileanta a chuireas aghaidh air feuman a h-uile cànan an Alba, a' gabhail a-staigh Scots [a' Bheurla Ghallda], cànainean coimhearsnachd agus Cànain Soighnidh Bhreatainn' (Meòrachan Poileasaidh, paragraf 67). Cha chualas guth air an ro-innleachd seo gu ruige seo, ged-tà.

- Duilgheadas mòr an seo is e gu bheil 'an t-ioma-chànanas breugach' na chleas cumanta ann am poileataigs cànain na h-Alba. Is e sin ri ràdh, gum bi cuid de dhaoine a' leigeil orra gu bheil iad airson a' Bheurla Ghallda, air neo an Urdu, adhartachadh maille ris a' Ghàidhlig, no an àite na Gàidhlig; ach an da-rìribh, cha bhi mòran diù aca don Bheurla Ghallda no don Urdu agus is e am fìor amas aca a bhith a' dìon uachdranachd na Beurla agus an *status quo* aona-chànanaich. Is dòcha gum bi cuid de Bhuill Pàrlamaid buailteach gabhail ri argamaidean den t-seòrsa, ged-tà, agus iad cho neochiontach mu chùisean poileataigs cànain is poileasaidh cànain (mar a mhìneachadh gu h-àrd).

Co-dhùnadh

Rud nach fhaicear anns a' Bhile is e spiorad na 'tairgse gnìomhaich' — is e sin ri ràdh, nach bi uallach air buidhnean poblach na h-Alba Gàidhlig adhartachadh, a leasachadh, a bhrosnachadh. Bidh aca ri iarrtasan airson seirbhisean Gàidhlig a fhreagairt, ach chan eil e idir soilleir gum bi aca ri luchd na Gàidhlig a mhisneachadh agus cleachdadh na Gàidhlig a leudachadh. An àite spiorad na gnìomhachd, gheibhear spiorad na fulangachd. Mar eisimpleir, a rèir earrann 3(5) den Bhile, nuair a bhios buidheann phoblach ag ullachadh plana-cànain Gàidhlig, feumaidh i spèis a thoirt don 'ìre [a tha] a' Ghàidhlig air a cleachdadh leis an t-sluagh ris a bheil gnìomhan an ùghdarrais a' buntainn'. Chanadh cuid gur e cleachdaidhean deireannach, aona-chànanach an Riaghaltais agus nan ùghdarrasan eile a rinn an ìre sin ìosal sa chiad dol-a-mach. Air an làimh eile, chuireadh atharrachadh feumail ris a' Bhile aig ìre 2 den phròiseas Phàrlamaideach: feumaidh plana-cànain buidhne poblaich aire a thoirt don 'c[h]omas a tha ann cleachdadh cànan na Gàidhlig a leasachadh co-cheangailte ri coilionadh [gnìomhan na buidhne]'. Tha fhios gur mòr an comas sin.

Is e an trioblaid, mar a mhìneachadh gu h-àrd, nach eil buidhnean poblach na h-Alba idir cleachdte ri no eòlach air an dà-chànanas. Cha bhiodh e furasta dhaibh gluasad a dh'ionnsaigh an dà-chànanais, fiù 's nam biodh deagh rùn aca, rud nach eil idir cinnteach. Trioblaid mhòr eile is e gu bheil luchd-labhairt na Gàidhlig cho fìor ghann: dìreach 1.25% den t-sluagh nàiseanta. Ann an iomadach sgìre, Glaschu is Dùn Èideann nam measg, tha an ìre nas ìsle na 1%. Dè tha reusanta agus pragtaigeach anns an t-suidheachadh seo a thaobh cleachdadh agus brosnachadh na Gàidhlig? Dè an seòrsa dà-chànanais a ghabhas togail an da-rìribh?

Tha e follaiseach bho theacsa a' Bhile fhèin agus bhon mhìneachadh a gheibhear anns na Meòrachain Poileasaidh agus Ionmhasail nach eil an Riaghaltas idir airson còraichean deimhinne, co-èigneachail a thoirt do luchd na Gàidhlig, ach gu bheil iad airson siostam 'sùbailte', stèidhte air 'còmhradh' agus 'co-aonta' a chur an sàs. Mar a tha Robert Dunbar a' rabhadh, chan eil an tuigse agus an dòigh-obrach seo freagarrach do shuidheachadh na Gàidhlig:

Acceptance in the civil service and in local government of the need for language planning and promotion is not nearly as widespread in Scotland [as in Wales]. In this context, an approach which relies heavily on administrative accommodation may leave too much power in the hands of people who are wholly indifferent and, in some cases, actively hostile to the needs of Gaelic language users and of the Gaelic language community as a whole. While a planning model is essential, the creation of at least some enforceable individual language rights in this context may be very important, both symbolically and practically, in giving the significantly more marginalized Gaelic language community a tool with which to demand the attention from public bodies which they may not otherwise be able to command. (Dunbar 2003b: 163).

Mura tèid am Bile a leasachadh agus a neartachadh, ged-tà, tha cunnart mòr ann gu bi beachd Bhòrd na Gàidhlig air a' chiad dhreachd a cheart cho fìor mun darna dreachd: nach tèid aige air crìonadh na cànain a stad.[8]

Iomraidhean

Bòrd na Gàidhlig (2003). 'Geàrr-Chunntas Gnìomha de Fhreagairt Bòrd na Gàidhlig gu Pàipear Co-chomhairleachaidh Bile na Gàidhlig'. Inbhir Nis: Bòrd na Gàidhlig.

Buidheann Comhairleachaidh an Riaghaltais air Gàidhlig / Ministerial Advisory Group on Gaelic (2002). *Cothrom Ùr don Ghàidhlig / A Fresh Start for Gaelic*. Dùn Èideann: Riaghaltas na h-Alba.

Comunn na Gàidhlig (1997). *Inbhe Thèarainte dhan Ghàidhlig / Secure Status for Gaelic*. Inbhir Nis: Comunn na Gàidhlig.

Comunn na Gàidhlig (1999). *Dreach iùl airson Achd Gàidhlig / Draft brief for a Gaelic Language Act*. Inbhir Nis: Comunn na Gàidhlig.

Dunbar, Robert (2003a). 'Bile Gàidhlig, Mu Dheireadh Thall — Ach am Bile a tha Bhuainn?' *Gath*, 2, 4-8.

Dunbar, Robert (2003b). 'Legislating for Language: Facing the Challenges in Scotland and Wales', ann an *Language and Law in Northern Ireland*, deas. le Dónall Ó Riagáin, 138-63. Béal Feirste: Cló Ollscoil na Banríona.

Johnstone, Richard et al. (2004). *Draft Gaelic Language Bill: Consultation Analysis*. Slèite: Lèirsinn.

Lo Bianco, Joseph (2001). *Language and Literacy Policy in Scotland*. Sruighlea: Scottish CILT (ri fhaighinn air an Eadar-lìon aig http://www.scilt.stir.ac.uk/pubs.htm#083).

McLeod, Wilson (1997). 'Official Status for Gaelic: Prospects and Problems', *Scottish Affairs*, 14 (1997), 95-118 (ri fhaighinn air an Eadar-lìon aig http://www.arts.ed.ac.uk/celtic/papers/officialstatus.html).

McLeod, Wilson (2001). 'Gaelic in the New Scotland: Politics, Rhetoric and Public Discourse', *Journal on Ethnopolitics and Minority Issues in Europe*, an t-Iuchar 2001 (ri fhaighinn air an Eadar-lìon aig http://www.ecmi.de/jemie/download/JEMIE02 MacLeod28-11-01.pdf).

McLeod, Wilson (2002). 'Alba: Luchd an Aona-Chànanais agus Buaidh na Cairt

---

[8] Tha mi buidheach de Joan NicDhòmhnaill agus de Rob Dunbar airson na comhairle a thug iad dhomh an lùib deasachadh na h-aiste seo.

Eòrpaich', ann an *Language Planning and Education: Linguistic Issues in Northern Ireland, the Republic of Ireland, and Scotland*, deas le. John M. Kirk and Dónall P. Ó Baoill, 284-89. Béal Feirste: Cló Ollscoil na Banríona.

McLeod, Wilson (2004). 'Securing the Future of Gaelic'. *Scottish Left Review*, 20 (2004),   12-13   (ri   fhaighinn   air   an   Eadar-lìon   aig http://www.scottishleftreview.org/ Pastissues/SLRI20.pdf).

Abstract: The Gaelic Bill: opportunities and threats

Following a drawn-out process of recommendations and reports, and an extensive public consultation on an initial draft, the revised Gaelic Language (Scotland) Act was placed before the Scottish Parliament in September 2004. The Bill is rather stronger than the consultation draft, which was perceived in the Gaelic community as being much too weak, but significant problems and concerns remain.[9]

The Bill is based to some extent on the Welsh Language Act 1993 and bears some resemblance to the Official Languages Act 2003 in the Republic of Ireland, but is distinctly less vigorous. The official language agency, Bòrd na Gàidhlig, is to be given additional powers and public bodies in Scotland will be required to produce Gaelic language plans if formally asked to do so, while Gaelic is now designated an 'official language of Scotland'.

Gaelic is not being granted equal validity or parity of esteem with English, however, and the Scottish Executive has made clear it is not willing to require genuine bilingual provision in Scotland. Bòrd na Gàidhlig is charged with producing a National Gaelic Language Plan, but this Plan will not be enforceable and may end up gathering dust on a shelf. The Bill does not specify what language plans should consist of, and it is possible that some bodies might contemplate merely tokenistic schemes that do not involve the delivery of any Gaelic services. Bòrd na Gàidhlig's powers of enforcement are weak in comparison to those given to comparable agencies/offices in Wales and Ireland. There is nothing in the Bill concerning rights to receive Gaelic education or use Gaelic in the courts; indeed, the Bill creates no language rights at all.

Above and beyond these shortcomings in the Bill itself, there are a number of worrisome provisions in the Financial Memorandum that accompanies the Bill. For example, the Executive states that it expects Bòrd na Gàidhlig to produce about ten language plans per year; given that there are several hundred public bodies in Scotland, full implementation of the legislation would take decades. The Executive also suggests that the Bòrd should not require bodies in areas with 'few' Gaelic speakers to produce plans 'in the years immediately after the enactment of the Bill'. There is much potential for abuse here given the historic disregard for Gaelic in areas outwith the traditional *Gàidhealtachd*.

The Financial Memorandum suggests that annual staff training costs for a public body's Gaelic Language Plan would amount to no more than £5,000 a year. Given that some public bodies in Scotland (e.g. Glasgow City Council and the Scottish

---

[9] The Bill was enacted on 21 April 2005, without significant amendment after stage 2 of the parliamentary process.

Executive itself) have several thousand employees, it is difficult to conclude that meaningful language plans are being contemplated here. Most worrisome of all, the Financial Memorandum indicates that a Gaelic Language Development Fund established by the Executive is to meet most of the costs of implementing Gaelic language plans. Ominously, the Bòrd is required to consider the extent of funding available from this source before it can request the development and implementation of language plans. As such, by ungenerous funding of this Development Fund, the Executive can effectively choke off the Bòrd's work and ensure that language plans are largely tokenistic. The shameful history of the Gaelic Broadcasting Fund, whose value has been whittled away over the years by inflation and neglect, gives an object lesson here.

In addition to these problems involving the legislation itself, there are several potential complications lying ahead. The MSPs themselves will of course assess and debate the Bill, but few of them have any real understanding of Gaelic issues and language policy generally, and they cannot be relied upon effectively to scrutinise and improve the Bill. The English-language media, especially the aggressive tabloids for whom Gaelic serves only as a joke and an irritant, may also play an unhelpful role. The public bodies affected by the legislation, whose response to the initial draft of the Bill was fairly muted, probably because it was so extraordinarily weak, may now seek to have the revised Bill watered down once again. Finally, there are issues involving language policy in Scotland more generally: what will be done to promote Scots and community languages? The Executive promises that the Gaelic Bill, which it rightly views as an immediate priority given the fragile state of Gaelic, will be followed by a national language strategy, but this has yet to appear.

Absent from the Bill is of any sense of the principle of 'active offer'. The prevailing spirit is one of passivity and sufferance. Developing a meaningful role for Gaelic now will certainly be a difficult and complex task given the very low density of Gaelic speakers in Scotland (just 1.25% of the national population). Dedicated and focused action will be necessary if serious progress is to be achieved. The spirit and substance of the current draft of the Gaelic Language Bill seem plainly inadequate for this task; a more robust, rights-based model would be more appropriate in the Scottish context.

Breaking Nature's Social Union — the Autonomy of Scots in Ulster

Gavin Falconer

The last decade or so has seen a massive expansion in the number of minority languages recognised in Europe, a change driven by the European Bureau for Lesser Used Languages and the Council of Europe Charter for Regional or Minority Languages. While in part the increase has been due to an admission that *Abstand* languages exist in states which had previously been loath to acknowledge the national minorities within their borders — some of whom speak idioms similar or identical to those of neighbouring states and are of consequent significance in border disputes — a large proportion of the new languages owe their newly won status to a relaxation in the rules constituting languageness itself. One such language is Scots, which, while generally functioning as a dialect of English, has the obvious potential to be developed as an independent language. The shift that took place in the 1990s was to recognise that the dialectal status of Scots was both a symptom of language death and an excuse for official inaction regarding minority language promotion.

While a moderate relaxation in the criteria for languageness, particularly for those idioms which formerly enjoyed language status, might be expected to have a positive impact on linguistic diversity, a wholesale shift to activist self-definition might well achieve the opposite effect, increasing the number of languages at the expense of a reduction in their speech communities, raising costs and rendering economies of scale difficult. In some cases it might even deprive the idiom to be promoted of the critical intellectual mass necessary for the task. Carruthers (2003: 306) mentions one report on the linguistic situation in France which delineated 75 languages, an astonishing figure when one considers that, for those idioms derived from Latin — the majority of those identified — a high degree of mutual intelligibility could be expected. Clearly, such galloping inflation in what constitutes languageness has the potential to render the language versus dialect debate meaningless, not only semantically but numerically, since soon there will be no dialects left. In the *Passport to Pimlico* world of linguistic secession, not only has Pimlico become Burgundy; Burgundy has become Pimlico.

The Scots language too has been the subject of such controversy, through the claim that the Ulster dialect represents an independent linguistic system. Ulster Scots has been classified as a "variety of the Scots language" in the North/South Co-operation (Implementation Bodies) (Northern Ireland) Order 1999, which seems explicit enough. Despite that, the question of status has been the subject of vigorous debate. The claim of languageness for Ulster Scots can have three possible justifications: structural; legal; and democratic.

Structural claims of languageness for Ulster Scots seem the weakest. Although there are differences in phonology, lexis and syntax, only the distinctive accent of Ulster Scots is always present in unselfconscious use, something naturally enough not always visible in writing. The phonological system is clearly Scots, and the differences are at the level of articulation within a single linguistic system; people from other parts of Ireland often have trouble distinguishing between Northern and Scottish accents.

The uncertain geographical reach of Ulster Scots renders it difficult to judge its lexis, but Kirk (1999) has calculated that 61.6% of the non-standard lexis collected in the *Concise Ulster Dictionary* is either uniquely Scots or shared by Scots and northern English, despite the fact that Scots-speaking areas account for only a small part of the historic province. Moreover, many non-Scots lexical items are not part of the core vocabulary and reflect distinctive cultural practices, many of them now moribund. A document issued by the Ulster-Scots Language Society entitled 'Quhit wud Ulstèr-Scotch be?' lists over 60 words typical for the contemporary dialect, only a very small number of which differ at all from mainstream Scots, even in spelling, and most of the spelling differences are due to contemporary innovation.

The syntax of Ulster Scots seems most distinctive, being shared in large measure with Hiberno-English. However, the fact that there is no groundswell of opinion that Hiberno-English is a language separate from English considerably weakens the case for Hiberno-Scots — as the Ulster variety of the language, under different political circumstances, might well have become known. The two idioms differ from their parent dialects in much the same way, but Hiberno-English has the stronger case, being by and large the product of language shift within a single speech community, allowing considerably more opportunity for interference from its Irish substratum. In contrast, Hiberno-Scots is on the whole the product of language contact between two speech communities, the Irish element being not a substratum but an adstratum. Neither is Ulster the only area influenced by contact with Goidelic languages, and many of the observations made on Ulster syntax could also be made of western Scotland. Moreover, much more research is necessary on the syntax of Scots as a whole. For example, Murray (1873: 222) records the sentence structure used in the question "Hae ye yer wark duin?" in southern Scotland, referring to it as the "analytical perfect"[1] and believing it a marker of Scots *vis-à-vis* English. Typically Irish features in Ulster Scots such as the lack of *do*-fronting in *have* questions are also features of conservative Anglic speakers everywhere. One need only think of Mr. Justice Caulfield's rhetorical description of Mary Archer during the 1987 libel case instigated by her husband: "Has she elegance? Has she fragrance?" The present writer's own father would be surprised to discover that the word order of the phrase "A'm gey auld gettin" had been claimed as something distinctively Ulster-Scots, having used it all his life as a native of Forfar and not having set foot in Ulster until his 70s. Perhaps the best argument against syntax-based claims to languageness is that, in addition to forms which set Irish English and Ulster Scots apart, speakers of both varieties also dispose over the mainstream syntactic structures, and often use the alternative forms not as the default but determined by semantic and pragmatic considerations.

The legal case for Ulster Scots being separate rests on the interpretation of the European Charter for Regional or Minority Languages, which was signed by the UK Government for Scots in Scotland and, separately, for Ulster Scots in 1999. An NIO press release dated 4 June 1999 read as follows.

> The Government has decided that Ulster-Scots in Northern Ireland will be recognised as a regional or minority language for purposes of Part II of the Council of Europe Charter for Regional or Minority Languages. This will bring Ulster-Scots into line with the treatment of the Scots language in Scotland.

---

[1] In contemporary linguistic terminology, it is more commonly known as the "medial object" or "resultative" perfect.

This indeed sounds like Ulster Scots has been recognised as a separate language. However, it is only a press release. The text of the European Charter itself is somewhat different.

> b) The United Kingdom declares, in accordance with Article 2, paragraph 1 of the Charter that it recognises that Scots and Ulster Scots meet the Charter's definition of a regional or minority language for the purposes of Part II of the Charter.

It is to be noted that "language" is here in the singular. Moreover, interpreting the charter as recognition of Ulster Scots as a separate idiom seems problematic for several reasons.

The charter specifically excludes dialects, presumably because of the negative impact on linguistic diversity of their recognition as languages, something discussed in the opening paragraphs of this paper. The UK Government recognising Ulster Scots as an independent linguistic system could therefore be challenged on structural grounds.

Articles 33 and 34 of the explanatory report to the charter specify a geographical field of application, suggesting that the separate provision is connected with the separate jurisdictions of Scotland and Northern Ireland, which might not necessarily be able to deliver on the same sections of the charter.

The charter is a purely aspirational document with no legal status, while the implementation bodies legislation quoted above has the status of an international treaty, one which the UK Government has no power to amend unilaterally. Moreover, it is the definition in the implementation bodies legislation that forms the remit of the Ulster-Scots Agency, on which the main burden of linguistic promotion falls.

As suggested above, recognition of Hiberno-Scots as separate could lead to pressure to recognise Hiberno-English, something complicated by the fact that users of the former are mainly Protestant and users of the latter mainly Catholic.

If Scots were split in two, it is also possible that there would be enough Scots-born speakers of Scots resident in Northern Ireland to demand their own provision, potentially doubling DCAL's costs.

Another reason not to recognise Ulster Scots as separate from Scots is the obviously and grossly discriminatory effect that it would have in curbing access to jobs and services on the part of those Scots-born residents of Northern Ireland who by overwhelming academic and popular consensus speak what is transparently the same language, something bad not merely for them but for the very survival chances of Scots in Ireland.[2] Even if the UK Government were to declare Ulster Scots separate, the decision would be open to legal review. If it were found to be both scientifically inaccurate and discriminatory in its outworking — as would surely be the case — it would have to be reversed. At times the opacity of DCAL's current

---

[2] According to the 2001 census, the total number of NI residents born in Scotland is 16,772. If there is the same proportion of Scots-speakers among them as believed in Scotland itself by the General Register Office, i.e. 30%, the number of Scots-born Scots-speakers is 5,031. Assuming an Ulster-Scots population of 30,000 based on the 1999 Northern Ireland Life and Times Survey, this would make those born in Scotland around 14% of Scots-speakers in the jurisdiction. The statistics are available from NISRA at http://www.nisra.gov.uk/census/Excel/commissioned_output/EXT20030910C.xls.

policy leads one to suspect deliberate obfuscation on the issue of status founded in a desire to neutralise a political "hot potato" and keep everyone happy, but one assumes that the general rule is of "one language, two names".[3]

In the present writer's view even the two-names policy is unsatisfactory and ultimately untenable owing on the one hand to the degree of ignorance surrounding the nature of Scots everywhere and the relationships of its various dialects, even among native users, and on the other to the politically inspired campaigns of influential Northern Ireland figures, many of them current or former board or staff members of the Ulster-Scots Agency, either to have Ulster Scots declared independent or to pretend that such a declaration has already been made.[4] Ironically, the largest group thus discriminated against consists of Lowland Scots soldiers stationed in Northern Ireland. That there are Unionist politicians willing, for the relatively frivolous purpose of winning vicarious status for the wider Protestant community, to discriminate against people risking their lives for their sake must be especially disappointing for those concerned. Occasionally — one hopes, unintentionally — DCAL itself follows suit, for example, in a news release dated 10 August 2004.[5]

> Anyone with an interest in the Ulster-Scots or Irish languages is invited to the Stormont Hotel, Dundonald, on Thursday 9 September, to a conference DCAL are organising on the European Charter.

From the above one deduces that the presence of Scots-born Scots-speakers resident in Northern Ireland is not desired at the conference and that their views are not valued or considered relevant.

The democratic case for according language status to Ulster Scots has been argued perhaps most eloquently by Michael Montgomery. However, Montgomery (1999: 91-2) too details the scholarly consensus that Ulster Scots is structurally a form of Scots, also admitting (1999: 103) that "No research has examined how the Ulster Scots speech community views itself and its speech". This would seem to place the recognition of Ulster Scots on apperceptional grounds in the realm of hypothesis. It is of course one of the ironies of the present revival that many of the most strident supporters of the separateness of the Ulster variety are themselves not habitual users. The present writer finds it unlikely that a majority of ordinary people in the core Ulster-Scots areas as defined by Gregg would see Ulster Scots as separate from Scots or even from English, and those who view Ulster Scots as an English dialect could be expected to view all other varieties of Scots in the same light, in which case Scots on the two sides of the Straits of Moyle would still be part of one linguistic system, albeit one called "English" rather than "Scots".

The possibility exists that a high degree of politicisation could bring Protestant Scots-speakers to believe that the languageness of Ulster Scots was an issue related to the existential crisis of Northern Ireland, allowing them to be mobilised in support of the claim. Recent years have seen debates on such matters as the Israel-Palestine

---

[3] When delivered on 16 September 2004, the paper contained the following at this point. "Perhaps there is a DCAL representative present ready to take the microphone at the end of the presentation and tell us whether Ulster Scots is a language or a variety of Scots; it certainly cannot be both." None of the eight DCAL staff members in attendance took up the invitation.
[4] The agency website provides many instances of the latter.
[5] Downloaded from .http://www.dcalni.gov.uk/newsStory/default.asp?id=645.

conflict and the retention of grammar schools divide on sectarian lines, though neither has any real connection with communal politics. However, according to the 1999 Northern Ireland Life and Times Survey, 25% of Ulster-Scots users stating a religion were Catholic. If those stating no religion are removed from the statistics, the proportion of Protestant to Catholic speakers is closer to 2:1 than 3:1. Indeed, the ratio of self-identified Unionists to Nationalists is exactly 2:1, raising serious questions about the confessional neutrality of the way in which the idiom has been promoted hitherto. Since the claim that Ulster Scots is an independent language is generally limited to Ulster Protestants, an overwhelming majority would have to be achieved among them to overcome the views of Catholic speakers, who generally class Ulster Scots as a Hibernic variety of English or Scots. However, persuading so many Protestant speakers of the separateness of Ulster Scots would be a difficult task because of two well-established tendencies in both Scotland and Ulster, which one might term "cultural scepticism" and "regional scepticism".

Cultural scepticism is connected with the revolutionary reshaping of culture of the Scottish Reformation that viewed the traditions built up by the Catholic Church as a distortion of biblical truth and a barrier between contemporary Christians and their forebears. More extreme versions of the philosophy see novels as lies and the tradition of western visual art as compromised by associations with idolatry, paganism and pornography. The biblical literalism of some adherents can also mean a literal attitude to the story of the tower of Babel as a source of discord and division among God's people. The uncompromising logic used to justify Christian purity on the one hand and the economic exploitation of creation on the other leaves little room for culture, which falls between two stools. The great diversity of the world's 6,000 languages in place of the utilitarian and presumably God-inspired universal language before Babel may also be seen as suspect, being the creation, at least latterly, of mankind rather than the deity. Although such views may now be uncommon in Scotland, Presbyterianism in Ulster is much more traditional. The political symbolism of the King James Bible as a unifying force among Protestants is also not to be underestimated.

Regional scepticism is common both in Scotland and among Ulster Protestants. In simple terms, its supporters view the existence of the United Kingdom as economically and culturally emancipating. Although they may agree with some of the utilitarian and cost arguments against linguistic diversity used by cultural sceptics, their real rejection is of what they perceive as parochial, backward or limiting. It goes without saying that English, which has superseded Scots in so many functions, can provide not only better economic opportunities but a cultural life of greater scope and diversity. In Scotland, such views are common among both Protestants and Catholics, and while the logical extreme of such thinking is to become a member of what one Scottish Nationalist once described to me as the *asimilado* class, most adherents will not be speakers of RP, and some may be people of working-class origin who owe their embourgeoisement in part to their command of Standard English. Northern Ireland Unionists allied themselves with such ideas when they rejected independence with the rest of Ireland, which they saw as having an undeveloped economy and conservative social attitudes. Today, those whose mind-set most closely resembles that of their counterparts in Great Britain often apply the same reasoning to Northern Ireland itself, since, paradoxically, many of the most emblematic cultural manifestations of Protestantism and Unionism in the province also underline the acontemporaneity and otherness of Northern Ireland *vis-*

à-vis the rest of the United Kingdom. The stereotypical regional sceptic in Northern Ireland might be a middle-class resident of north Down, politically either professing liberal *ennui* or supporting the Alliance Party or the more moderate wing of the UUP, but the group would also include at least some who view the politics of group identity as a barrier to the politics of class — and who may even have an ideological motivation for linguistic unity similar to that of the cultural sceptics.

A third reason for scepticism towards Ulster Scots among Protestants and Unionists is the fact that economic and utilitarian arguments against state support for Irish have been rehearsed by them almost since the foundation of the state and may well have been internalised. Some of the above factors may have influenced the paper on the economic value of language given by Esmond Birnie and Steven King (2003) at last year's symposium.

It is sometimes claimed — almost invariably by non-linguists — that the status of Ulster Scots *vis-à-vis* Scots in Scotland is a matter of little importance. For example, consultees whose views informed the Edmund plan for the promotion of the idiom are reported as follows.

> Generating recognition and acceptance of Ulster-Scots outside its core community has, it is said, been hindered by a politicised argument (largely irrelevant to the mass of the population) about whether Ulster-Scots is a language or a dialect of Scots or of English. It is perceived by some that this has been fuelled by anti-Unionist sentiment, by the broadcast media's search for controversy and an attempt to deny the Ulster-Scots language community the benefits of minority language recognition.

One wonders why maintaining the existing linguistic bond with Scots in Scotland should be seen as anti-Unionist. The actions of those Ulster-Scots activists arguing for separate development within the same state stand in stark contrast to those of their Irish-language counterparts, who have adopted all-island policies for their language despite the existence of two jurisdictions. By the same token, where is the denial of recognition in stating that Ulster's Scots-speakers share a language with Robert Burns? The academic Philip Hobsbawm stated on *Newsnight Scotland* on 22 January 2001 that Scots as a whole, though in his view a dialect, had been the vehicle of great literary achievement. However, he was not aware of any literature of the same standing having been written in the Ulster variety specifically.

Edmund's consultees recognise that the contemporary lack of writers in Ulster constitutes a barrier to linguistic development, suggesting that the problem be circumvented by "facilitating writers in Scots to reach an Ulster audience" (28). One possible interpretation is that money would be spent on persuading writers from Scotland to adopt a non-traditional orthography in order to impose that orthography on local writers, who would otherwise have written very largely like the Scots. If that was what they were suggesting, it would be an astonishing use of public funds, since promotion of Scots in Ulster, given a head start, might ultimately become self-funding if its products remained acceptable to the Scottish market.[6] The proposal also fails to acknowledge the fact that the lack of writers in Ulster, like the atypicality and divergence of its revived forms, is ultimately a symptom not of lack of development but of a numerically weak community of speakers. Horsbroch (2000: 135) sums up the situation as follows.

The Scots speaker in Ulster buckles his belt his ain gait an haes the scowth tae dae it. Becis sae monie fowk in Scotlan[d] speak the leid ilka day — the feck o thaim no even thinkin aboot it — it's no affa easy tae fouter aboot an experiment wi it. In [i]ther wurds, ye'll no get awa wi muckle. But in Ulster, whaur the'r no monie speakers, an whaur the leitratur is, we can airgue, less, a bodie can get awa wi mair in the wey o langage plannin.

As MacDiarmid might have said had he lived to consider the contemporary revival of Scots in Ulster, "He canna Ulster see wha yet/Canna see it's leemitit."

There is also the pragmatic argument for separate development in Northern Ireland that granting linguistic autonomy to the local dialect will enable it to access funds without the lack of similar interest across the Straits of Moyle acting as a brake. The disappointment in Scotland at such an approach is not difficult to imagine. As *Scots Tung Wittins* 73 opined, "It's aye guid tae see a wee bairn weel fendit for but whit kinna fowk wad juist gaun by an leave its mither tae sterve?" However, the developmental framework of the implementation bodies legislation states that there is only one Scots language, albeit with more than one name, indicating that the UK Government has not used any such linguistic fig-leaf to justify discriminatory treatment. Moreover, a language's autonomy or lack thereof is a matter of linguistic observation rather than political fiat. Public funds spent on developing an idiom can encourage or facilitate only those able and willing to use it. The outcome is decided by forces of nature, with status important only to the extent that it can help build capacity. It is hard to conceive how the capacity of Scots in Northern Ireland could be boosted far enough to balance out the deleterious effects of reducing the number of its speakers by up to 98%.[6] Far from being "weel fendit for", the "wee bairn" of Ulster Scots, if developed separately, would be stranded on a linguistic island, and declaring it King of the Blaskets would do little to improve its chances in such a hostile environment.

Evidence of the damaging effects of breaking up an existing linguistic continuum by the imposition of an untraditional orthography is provided by the case of Manx, an idiom which varies little from Antrim Irish and the Gaelic of south-west Scotland but whose written form presents profound difficulties for speakers of the other Goidelic languages because of its spelling, also failing to equip users to read Irish or Scottish Gaelic, despite the fact that the spoken language, being intermediate between the two, has a high degree of mutual intelligibility with both. Writing in the preface to his dictionary, Fargher (1979: vi) says, "My own view, shared by many respected and authoritative speakers of the language, is that this system is a historical abomination, separating, as it does, Mann from the rest of Gaeldom, and thus destroying the linguistic unity of the Gaels without replacing it with anything better

---

[6] This truth appears not to have escaped all players. Staff of the Ulster-Scots curriculum project at Stranmillis University College have argued both that the idiom is separate from Scots in Scotland; and therefore best promoted using their local expertise; and that their teaching aids are in Scots and thus suitable for purchase by Scottish schools.

[7] The percentage is based on there being c. 30,000 speakers in Northern Ireland (almost 29% over 65), according to the 1999 Northern Ireland Life and Times Survey, and c. 1·5 million in Scotland, according to the 1996 estimate of the General Register Office for Scotland. These are the only official figures available.

in the way of a truly phonetic orthography". Sebba (1998) suggests that the orthography both hastened the demise of the spoken language and maintains its independence from the other Gaelic languages and thus its symbolic value, a view shared by Adams (1986: 16), who says, "In the Isle of Man, where classical Irish was probably little known or cultivated, the adoption of a hybrid Anglo-Welsh orthography for the local dialect cut it off from its relatives and doubtless hastened its extinction as a spoken vernacular in the present century." The notion of money being spent on translating Scots texts from Scotland into "Ullans" may sound far-fetched; yet that is just the situation in which Manx activists find themselves today *vis-à-vis* Irish and Scottish Gaelic. The reason that the deviant orthographies adopted for Manx and Ulster Scots have been so damaging is that they were selected on grounds external rather than internal to the idioms in question. In the case of Mann, the reason was to facilitate proselytism by Anglophone clerics without their needing to learn Manx. With Scots in Ulster, the reason is to differentiate the dialect from both English and Scots in Scotland and increase its identificational, symbolic value for Ulster Protestants to something approaching that of Irish for Ulster Catholics. Such differentiation is necessary precisely because the structural, legal and democratic arguments for the autonomy of the Ulster dialect are so unconvincing.

It might be useful to consider some examples of revivalist "Ullans" and the degree to which they accord with the legal frameworks both for promoting Scots in Northern Ireland and for preventing discrimination. Since, in Klossian terms, Scots is a potential *Ausbau* (i.e. through elaboration and codification) rather than *Abstand* (i.e. through structural divergence) language, it is reasonable to assume that the definition of Ulster Scots as a "variety of the Scots language" contained in the implementation bodies legislation prescribes a shared written standard for formal and communicative purposes, with the local Hiberno-Scots dialect being promoted in oral and creative use, i.e. in those fields where it is already plausibly used. If one has more than one standard written form, one has more than one *Ausbau* language.

The following is from an "Ulster-Scots" summary of a document issued by the Office of the First Minister and the Deputy First Minister.[8]

A Yinsum Jonick Bäll fur Norlin Airlann

A Scrow fur Collogue anent walins fur a Bäll furtae compluther, mak modrèn an eik, quhaniver it's effeirin, tha laas agane steekin fowk oot an adae wi jonick in Norlin Airlann.

Whatever feelings the translator may have for such pre-revival Ulster-Scots writers as Orr, Porter and Thomson, it is clear that he or she rejects them absolutely as literary models. One also suspects that the person responsible views his or her role as that of one empowered to undertake major structural reform rather than as a synthesiser or mediator of attested practice. Two innovations unknown in traditional Scots literature anywhere strike one immediately: the respelling of the definite article as *tha*; and the presence of diacritics. According to the *Dictionary of the Scots Language*, *tha* was used in Older Scots for Modern Scots *thae* ('those') and 'they'. The definite article has never been rendered *tha* in any mainstream form of Scots, whether in Scotland or in Ulster, making the change both ahistorical and confusing — especially for those acquainted with the traditional language.

---

[8] Downloaded from http://www.ofmdfmni.gov.uk/equality/seb/ulsterscotssummary.pdf

The *Umlaut* is borrowed from the IPA to show the Ulster lowering of /ɪ/, but is applied only to the word *Bäll*, which would otherwise be identical with its English equivalent, and not, for example, to the word *yinsum*, tempting one to believe that, regardless of the philosophical justification, in practical use its purpose is not phoneticisation but differentiation from English and more mainstream forms of Scots.

The grave accent on *modrèn* is intended to show the interdental quality of the <d>. However, the interdentalisation is environmentally conditioned — and arguably adequately marked — by the following <r>. The fact that diacritics over vowels usually refer either to the quality of the vowel itself or to the stress of the sentence also renders it doubtful whether the generality of people would understand the intent, particularly since the grave accent on *modrèn* refers to a phenomenon two letters before. The clumsiness of the innovation is indicated by the fact that only a minority of the words exhibiting such interdentalisation in the word list discussed above — produced by no less a group than the Ulster-Scots Language Society — are marked with a grave, suggesting that its application is too difficult even for its most enthusiastic advocates.[9]

Both the vowel lowering and the interdentalisation would be arrived at automatically by native speakers and are panlectal in much of the province, also being present in Mid Ulster English. Furthermore, users of Ulster Scots exhibit them when speaking, though not writing, Standard English. One wonders why written Scots should be treated any differently.

From the above we can conclude that the orthographic practices in question not only differ considerably from any attested form of literary Scots, of whatever provenance, but contain diacritics borrowed from phonetic notation for the specific purpose of giving minor articulatory differences at the level of accent a presence in the written form of the idiom, i.e. of turning a spoken dialect into a written one. If the diacritics have any legitimacy at all, it is as crutches for learners; they have no place in a communicative text aimed at native speakers, whom they are likely merely to confuse.

Using the definition of Ulster Scots from the implementation bodies legislation, it is reasonable to assume that quality assurance work on such translations would be carried out by at least one professional linguist from both Scotland and Ulster to maintain the Government policy of a single written form. Quite obviously, such quality assurance is not taking place, and justifying inaction with the excuse that an authoritative language planning body has not yet been officially established is plausible only if DCAL intends an Ulster-Scots Academy employing academicians rather than academics. Moreover, since the texts in question contain so many innovations, in both orthography and lexis, intended to boost the case of Ulster Scots as an *Abstand* language structurally different from conventional Scots, their communicative value for native users of the Ulster variety is also severely diminished, as traditional Scots writing from Scotland and Ulster cannot always easily be distinguished. The weaver poets exhibited the same loyalty to pandialectal Scots as their Scottish counterparts, and their concessions were no greater. Orr, Porter, Thomson and Burns all wrote the number one as *ane* but pronounced it with an initial glide. At a time when the Plain English Society is advising UK Government Departments on the communicative value of forms and correspondence, the

---

[9] *Cootèr* and *shoodèr* are marked, while *founder*, *scunner* and *oxter* are unmarked.

readiness of Northern Ireland officialdom to consign taxpayers' money to a black hole of translations incomprehensible to ordinary users is worrying.

Perhaps the greatest problem with the text discussed above is not its spelling but the idiosyncrasy and reductiveness of its vocabulary. Does *jonick* really mean 'equality' or just 'fair play'? The problem is widespread. For example, the July edition of the *Ulster-Scot* newspaper informed readers that *kist o scrievins* meant 'treasury of literature', disregarding the Scots alternatives *thesaur* and *leeteratur*. The present writer would translate it as 'chest of scribblings'. Revivalist errors often arise through treating Scots words as one-to-one equivalents of English ones. While it is plausible for the blessing *fair faw ye* to be used in welcome, one wonders whether saying "Fair faw ye tae the meetin hoose" is any more correct than saying "God bless you to church". One suspects that the Scots word *walcome* is being shunned because it is not different enough from the English. In October 2003 an advertisement placed in the main Northern Ireland newspapers by the Ulster-Scots Agency translated 'finance and administration manager' as *offis heid*, a description one is tempted to apply to the translator. The director of the Ulster-Scots Heritage Council has been referred to as *heid yin*, a generic term unsuited to an individual title and usually ironic or subversive in native discourse. The same name has been adopted for the chairman of the Ulster-Scots Agency, in apparent ignorance of the suitable Scots alternatives *preses* and *convener*, both of which would surely have been known to the more educated of the original Planters. A third meaning, 'administrator', is recorded in a Belfast City Council leaflet discussed in Kirk (2000). It will be clear that the co-ordination of translation effort is — to carry on the literary reference of the paper's title — "aft a-gley".

While academic linguists are careful to distinguish between something that is wrong linguistically and something that is merely non-mainstream, the diffuseness of knowledge of Scots may mean that there is in some cases a connection between the correctness of a text and its approximation to a standard, even where that standard itself displays a marked degree of flexibility. In other words, if one does not talk to people, one learns neither what is right nor how to communicate with ease. In that regard, it is interesting to consider whether, in addition to failing to dispose over the relevant critical mass of speakers, an independent Ulster Scots might not also lack the relevant intellectual community able to drive on development; the number of individuals in Northern Ireland academically qualified for the task is certainly very small, and even those few have been marginalised by non-linguists.

To test the communicative value of translated texts, one might suggest the following criteria.

- Will readers be able to access the information in the text drawing on a familiarity with traditional Ulster-Scots literature?
- Since so many users, even of full Ulster Scots, are literate only in English, will readers be able to access the information in the text drawing on a familiarity with the orthographic practices of that language?
- Is the spelling of the text logical and consistent?
- Is all the information in the English text given in the Scots translation?
- Are the translations used for individual terms consistent, including across different translations, or are they being coined on an *ad hoc* basis?
- Would a back translation into English produce something close to the original, in a comparable register and without excessive paraphrase?

Perhaps a philosophical question regarding the translator's understanding of what constitutes good Ulster Scots might also be posed. Is it defined positively and in its own terms as an authentic representation and continuation of the native speech and literary tradition, or as an anti-English, anti-Scots or quasi-Irish? Is a linguacentric approach based on the primacy of the idiom itself being taken, or are external concerns paramount? The present writer has no wish to anticipate the result of an academic review. However, there are serious questions about the ability of such translations — and, by extension, those who produce them — to communicate the information intended to a broad audience of Ulster-Scots users. As the intention behind commissioning them is presumably to disseminate information to the public more widely and prevent the exclusion of linguistic minorities, they disappoint even in the terms in which they are conceived. If the commission has been inspired by the terms of an equality scheme, the failure to assess the result may well constitute a breach. Indeed, the fact that the work is of such low quality and doubtful communicative value probably precisely because of external political concerns, yet is commissioned nonetheless, may even constitute political discrimination against other potential providers without the patronage of elected representatives. If, however, the intention is to show an accommodating attitude to Ulster Protestants by providing space for what has been described as their own "gibberish", the assignment is easier to explain. Given the obvious difficulty of communicating information textually in an overwhelmingly oral and unstandardised idiom whose users write only in English, one also wonders why more use is not made of radio.

As present trends, if allowed to continue, are likely to result in the creation of a separate, if obscure, standard for Scots in Ulster, it is interesting to consider the reaction of native users over the perhaps one or two generations then left for the dialect. For example, if there were separate questions regarding the two Scots standards in the next Northern Ireland census, would there be a large cohort of people who could speak Ulster Scots but read only texts produced in Scotland — ostensibly in a foreign language? Such possibilities seem not have been considered.

Bertold Brecht, writing about the petulant reaction of the East German regime to the uprising of 1953, said, "The people have lost the faith of the government. Perhaps the government should dissolve the people and elect a new one." The revival of Ulster Scots has seen just such an attitude adopted, in full seriousness and with the tacit backing of the state, which has itself discriminated against Scots-born Scots-speakers by geographically qualifying the word "Scots" when advertising services and devised structures for the promotion of Scots in Ulster bound to result in its ethnic stereotyping and the alienation and effective exclusion of Catholic users. Though aware, through its representatives' attendance at these symposia, of the overwhelming academic consensus regarding the status of the Ulster variety as part of the same linguistic system as Scots in Scotland and the unacceptably low quality and communicative value of contemporary translations, DCAL itself commonly refers to Scots in Ulster as a language in its own right and commissions translations apparently without applying any objective quality criteria, so that one wonders whether success might not instead be based on the acceptability of the person of the translator to "the movement".

From being an archipelagic language spoken by mixed populations, Scots in Northern Ireland has seen its appeal deliberately reduced as part of an ethnic crusade aimed at establishing exactly conterminous political and speech communities. To counteract that, urgent remedial activities must be undertaken to maintain the unity of Scots, preserve the intellectual basis of its promotion, and rebuild its community of users. To that end, one might suggest accepting as a guiding principle the slogan adopted in the 1950s by the West German Chancellor Ludwig Erhard, a man who had witnessed at first hand the grave effects of ideology on the civilisation and standing of his country: "No experiments".

References

Adams, G. B. (1986) 'Language and Man in Ireland' in *The English Dialects of Ulster: an anthology of articles on Ulster speech by G. B. Adams*. Cultra: Ulster Folk and Transport Museum. 1-32.

Birnie, E. and King, S. (2003) 'Not Such a Big Deal? The Economy-Language Interaction' in Kirk, J. M. and Ó Baoill, D. (eds.) *Towards Our Goals in Broadcasting, the Press, the Performing Arts and the Economy: Minority Languages in Northern Ireland, the Republic of Ireland, and Scotland*. Belfast: Cló Ollscoil na Banríona. 224-228.

Carruthers, J. (2003) 'The Walloon-Scots Comparison: Are There Further Parallels with Other *Langues d'Oïl?*' in Kirk, J. M. and Ó Baoill, D. (eds.) *Towards Our Goals in Broadcasting, the Press, the Performing Arts and the Economy: Minority Languages in Northern Ireland, the Republic of Ireland, and Scotland*. Belfast: Cló Ollscoil na Banríona. 303-308.

Fargher, D. C. (1979) *Fargher's English-Manx Dictionary* [by] Douglas C. Fargher; edited by Brian Stowell and Ian Faulds. Douglas: Shearwater Press.

Horsbroch, D. (2000) '*Mair as a Sheuch Atween Scotland an Ulster*: Twa Policie for the Scots Leid?' in Kirk, J. M. and Ó Baoill, D. (eds.) *Language and Politics: Northern Ireland, the Republic of Ireland, and Scotland*. Belfast: Cló Ollscoil na Banríona. 133-141.

Kirk, J. M. (1999) 'The Dialect Vocabulary of Ulster' in *Cuadernos de Filología Inglesa* 8. 305-334.

Kirk, J. M. (2000) 'The new written Scots dialect in present-day Northern Ireland' in Magnus Ljung (ed.) *Language Structure and Variation. A Festschrift for Gunnel Melchers*, Acta Universitatis Stockholmiensis, *Stockholm Studies in English 92*, Stockholm: Almqvist and Wiksell International. 121-138.

Kloss, H. (1952, 1978) *Die Entwicklung neuer germanischer Kultursprachen (erweiterte Auflage)* Düsseldorf: Pädagogischer Verlag Schwann.

Montgomery, M. (1999) 'The position of Ulster Scots' in *Ulster Folklife* 45: 86-107.

Murray, J. A. H. (1873) *The Dialect of the Southern Counties of Scotland*. London: Asher and Co. on behalf of the Philological Society.

Sebba, M. (1998) 'Orthography as Practice and Ideology: the case of Manx'. Lancaster: Lancaster University Department of Linguistics and Modern English Language. Downloaded from http://www.ling.lancs.ac.uk/pubs/clsl/clsl102.pdf.

The Ulster-Scots Academy

Anne Smyth and Michael Montgomery

The Ulster-Scots Academy is now ten years old. Founded in 1994 and incorporated as a Registered Company in April 2003, for most of its history it has functioned as a voluntary, community-based organisation with occasional modest grant aid from Government sources. Its parent organisation, the Ulster-Scots Language Society, has been engaged in language development work since 1992 and now has a dues-paying membership of approximately three hundred. The Academy consists mainly of officers of the Society along with native speakers, some of whom comprise advisory groups for specific projects.

From its beginning the Ulster-Scots Academy has been guided by principled goals. Claims that these are motivated by politics are both unfounded and unfortunate because they have been used as a smokescreen in the cultural politics of Northern Ireland. The Ulster-Scots Academy and Language Society are part of no political movement or cause; both are non-political and non-sectarian.

Among the goals of the Academy are the following five:

1. to elevate the linguistic study of Ulster-Scots to that of a living European language in its own right, that is, as an entity worthy of study as an autonomous academic subject, a step achieved by Lowland Scots several decades ago in Scottish universities. For over a century, linguists have accepted that language varieties should he described in terms of themselves, not within the framework of other languages. Its status as a language or dialect or otherwise is immaterial to whether Ulster Scots can be treated as an academic subject in its own right.
2. to recognise that the closest affinities of Ulster-Scots are to Lowland Scots. The Ulster-Scots Language Society and Ulster-Scots Academy have pressed this argument for over a decade in various forums in Northern Ireland. It counters the view of nearly the entire Northern Ireland academic establishment that Ulster-Scots is a local variety of Irish English, a view that is not shared by Scottish academics.
3. to accomplish the first two goals through documentation, research and publication programmes of the highest academic standard, and to serve as a bridge between researchers and the native-speaking community. To date, two major reference works have appeared under Academy auspices: a comprehensive dictionary of traditional County Antrim Ulster-Scots, *The Hamely Tongue* (1995), by James Fenton, a third revised. edition of which is ready for the press, and Dr. Philip Robinson's Ulster-Scots Grammar (1997). This latter work has been hailed on its cover by Dr. John Kirk of Queen's University as "a quite superb masterpiece" Other volumes are in progress, including a comprehensive historical dictionary.
4. to recover the Ulster-Scots literary tradition through its collection and study, and to provide public access to it in electronic and print forms. For a history of this literature, see Michael Montgomery and Robert J Gregg, in *The Edinburgh History of the Scots Language*, edited by Charles Jones (Edinburgh University Press, 1997), which is currently being expanded.
5. to encourage the use of Ulster-Scots and increase the confidence of its speakers and writers. With the Ulster-Scots literary tradition being confined mainly to the 18th

and 19th century, Ulster-Scots does not have a modern codified form, although Robinson's grammar made an attempt to provide guidelines for codification. The Academy can help encourage speakers and writers to express themselves in terms that are most natural to them.

These goals and the inter-related programmes and projects to meet them, five of which we shall briefly examine, have been formulated through long-term consultation between native-speakers and the Ulster-Scots Language Society. The Society is the only body established to study, conserve, promote and develop Ulster-Scots.

The Academy's projects have been progressed with the aid of voluntary workers When fully resourced it will serve native speakers (on whom itwill continue to rely for much of its work), academic specialists, and others by providing expertise and access to its resources and collections.

1. Tape-Recorded Survey

Soon after its founding, it became clear that the Academy should with urgency undertake a programme recording older native speakers on topics of community or family interest, in order to make a permanent record and to serve as a baseline for researchers. Like most regional or minority language varieties in Europe, Ulster-Scots has long experienced low status, and its native speakers are rarely unguarded in interaction with outsiders. For these reasons, native speakers have been carrying out the Academy's interviewing. The more than fifty interviews recorded since 2002 in Counties Antrim, Down, and Donegal are only a fraction of what will be collected, transcribed, and used for the Academy's dictionaries. Perhaps the surest measure of the value of interviews is the enthusiasm they have generated within Ulster-Scots areas. With its many contacts, the Academy has had no difficulty in enlisting native speakers willing to conduct the interviews.

The recorded interviews are being transcribed according to established protocols and conventions. These involve two levels of revision and cheeks, including by the native-speaking interviewers. Transcripts are becoming part of the electronic text base. Among other things, the material gathered in a permanent, recorded form will establish how Scottish cultural and linguistic influence in Ulster has evolved into the 21st century.

2. Electronic Text Base

Since the publication in 1974 of John Hewitt's ground-breaking study, *The Rhyming Weavers and Other Country Poets of Antrim and Down* researchers have become increasingly aware of the innumerable poems and songs written between the late eighteenth century and the middle of the nineteenth, as well as other, largely forgotten, traditions of writing in Ulster-Scots over the past four hundred years. This documentary legacy extends from correspondence and legal records from the Ulster Plantation days of the early-17th century, down to the present.

As in the case of the tape-recorded survey, the Academy is in a natural and strategic position to produce this resource. Language Society members have uncovered a great deal of Ulster-Scots literature in recent years. Many texts appeared originally in local ephemeral publications, while others have existed only within local oral tradition. Relying on members from local Ulster-Scots areas to identify and retrieve such texts has proven both necessary and invaluable, because it is local citizens, not academic researchers, who usually know where appropriate texts - both historical and contemporary - are to be found.

Once identified, texts are evaluated for inclusion according to linguistic and geographical criteria. The text base of Ulster-Scots differs fundamentally from a linguistic "corpus" such as the Helsinki Corpus of English, in that the latter is usually constructed for linguistic purposes that require equivalent text portions from various historical periods, etc.

The immediate goal of the electronic text base is to prepare as much raw material as possible on which the analysis and definition of forms in the Academy's dictionary programme will be based. But the larger value of a corpus of Ulster-Scots material for a range of scholarly initiatives and fields is easy to see. More than five hundred texts have already been keyed and proofed comprising in excess of a quarter of a million words.

3. Dictionary Programme

The Academy's dictionary programme has several related strands, all of which make use of material compiled by the tape-recorded survey and electronic text base just discussed. Recent lexicographical works such as Fenton's *The Hamely Tongue* (1995/2000) and Macafee's *Concise Ulster Dictionary* (1996) represent major additions to the knowledge about language varieties in Ulster, but they provide little historical information and insufficient illustrative content to meet the needs of scholars or the Ulster-Scots community at large. For its dictionary programme the Academy sees the on-going work of Scottish Language Dictionaries Limited as its model and natural partner. It has in a variety of ways been laying the groundwork for several related dictionaries and glossaries. Because the heart of a dictionary programme is its citation bank the assembling of this material in a full manner has represented the major lexicographical thrust of the Academy's work to date.

In further establishing the foundations for a comprehensive, historical dictionary of Ulster-Scots, the Academy has compiled and annotated a bibliography of items on Ulster-Scots language, encompassing the entire range of scholarly literature.

4. Translation Service

A fourth Academy initiative is a formal partnership with the Language Society to progress development of translation and spelling standards and guidelines. Prevalent forms will emerge as a natural outcome of the other programmes and feed into the dictionary programme, as historical texts are studied alongside the contemporary writing and work in progress. However, the process involves much more than simply spelling. It involves agreed new terminologies, acceptable revivalisms of historic forms, and agreed grammar and syntax. All of these have been, or are in the process of being, provisionally codified by the Academy and the Language Society, but it has to be emphasized that this is at present a process rather than a product. Out of this process standards for benchmarking translations will be provided. The Academy is the only - and can be the only - ultimate authority on the language that is acceptable both academically and in community terms.

5. Bible Translation

Progress is being made on a collective translation exercise by native speakers themselves. The Academy has begun holding workshops chaired by professional translators to translate the Bible into authentic Ulster-Scots. While this project has status-building potential for Ulster-Scots, it has great merit on many other accounts as well. As community representatives join in an extended translation exercise, they and those they represent will find an increasing sense of ownership of the language. The dynamics of the process will suggest alternative ways of expressing ideas or points and provide considerable raw material and insights for the dictionary programme. Development of more authoritative translation and spelling and standards or guidelines will he a natural outcome.

Looking Ahead

A decade ago members of the Ulster-Scots Language Society had the vision to bring Ulster-Scots and awareness of it into the mainstream of the cultural life of Ireland. They sought those who could assist in fulfilling this vision in the proper place - the native-speaking community. Today the work of an early outgrowth of that vision, the Ulster-Scots Academy, has already done much to involve and revitalise the Ulster-Scots community and to ensure that research and public information about Ulster-Scots is based on sound scholarship and readily available materials. When fully resourced, it will serve native speakers, academic specialists and others, by providing expertise and access to its resources and collections. Through its intertwined projects, it is laying the foundation upon which scholars from many fields, language planners, and other interested parties can build for years to come.

Virtually from its inception, all those involved in the Ulster-Scots Academy have wished to model it on the Frisian Academy in the Netherlands. That body is much more advanced in development but the demographics in Friesland parallel those in Ulster. Frisian and Ulster-Scots are both closely related to national languages in their respective states.

While it has made a good start, the Ulster-Scots Academy is also consulting with other language academics to fine tune its articulation of programmes. It is neither a closed shop nor a small band of enthusiasts uninterested in being informed by the experience and practice of other European regional languages. It stands ready to help the Government fulfil the Belfast Good Friday Agreement commitment to linguistic diversity and provisions of the European Charter for Regional and Minority Languages, international agreements which the United Kingdom has ratified.

Finally, this paper gives a partial overview of Academy work and plans for a coherent strategy to document, conserve and develop Ulster-Scots. We do not suggest that the Ulster-Scots Academy has yet identified, much less gauged, all the needs or desires of Ulster-Scots or various clienteles. Nor has it refined or initiated all the programmes that should be undertaken.

We have said not nothing here, for instance, about a Resource Centre that will ensure availability of language knowledge and expertise to all, without prejudice, and will help people to access their own cultural and Linguistic heritage. It will house, conserve, and provide public access to the unique oral and text archives collected by the Academy, along with other rescarch materials, reference works and necessary resources. It will operate as a research base and a reading room with public access. It should be an integral part of the day-to-day core funded premises of the Academy, because its workers will use this facility constantly, and it will provide a secure and dedicated environment in which they can make the latest version of their on-going work accessible to both the public and scholars, develop (and possibly test) instructional materials, co-ordinate the work of translation, build the text base, and so on. The Centre will be a bottom-up operation to encourage the public to participate in Academy collection programmes and contribute data to its archives.

These activities will be possible only if the Academy is not perceived as an ivory tower. It must never lose sight of the principle that has, throughout its existence, been at the forefront of all its work – that the speakers of any language are its most important resource. Our strategy will continue to evolve, but experience and consultation over several years have shown what most of the major programmes should be.

References

Fenton, J. 2000. *The Hamely Tongue: A Personal Record of Ulster-Scots in County Antrim Speech*. Second Edition. [Belfast]: The Ullans Press.

Montgomery, M.B. and R.J. Gregg. 1997.'The Scots Language in Ulster'. In ed. Jones, C. *The Edinburgh History of the Scots Language*. Edinburgh: Edinburgh University Press. 569-622.

Robinson, P. 1997. *Ulster-Scots: A Grammar of the Traditional Written and Spoken Language*. [Belfast]: The Ullans Press.

The Ullans Academy

Ian Adamson[1]

The roots of the Academy go back to the establishment of the Ulster Dialect Archive established at Cultra Manor, the headquarters of the Ulster Folk Museum and to the pioneer work of G. B. Adams, J. Braidwood, P. L. Henry and R. J. Gregg. Following a visit to the Friesian Academy in 1978 with a group of community activists, I used their book *Ulster Dialects* (1964) to form the basis of the chapter "The Language of Ulster" in my *Identity of Ulster* (1981). I followed this up throughout the 1980's through the creation of the Farset organisation. I liased with the Ulster Folk Museum and the Institute of Irish Studies at Queen's University Belfast in order to develop an interest in language and oral history in the local community. This work was supervised by René Frechét, Professor of Irish Studies, Université de Paris III, Sorbonne Nouvelle. The intended object was the creation of an Ulster-Scots Academy at Cultra Manor. The Ullans (Ulster-Scots) Academy was eventually founded in July 1992 following a meeting in Vancouver, British Columbia, Canada between Professor R J Gregg and myself. In December of that year the Ulster-Scots Language Society (USLS) was founded in Craigavon House with myself as Chairman. Since then, the Academy has continued to exist as a community-based voluntary organisation. Despite its close links with the USLS, it has always been represented separately on the Executive of the Ulster-Scots Heritage Council. Its prime aims were to campaign for academic research into Ulster-Scots and for equality of status as a European "Lesser-Used" or regional language as well as to establish Craigavon House as the centre of excellence for Ulster-Scots studies in Ireland.

Craigavon House was the former home of James Craig, JP, MP, who became Lord Craigavon, the first Prime Minister of Northern Ireland and has been associated historically with the beginning of the Northern Ireland State. Apart from Parliament Buildings, Stormont, it is perhaps the most important heritage site from a Unionist standpoint in Northern Ireland. Craig also thought of himself as an Ulster Scot in the broad sense and, as an indigenous Ulster person, was conscious of his Ulidian heritage deeply rooted in Ireland. Craigavon House is presently owned under lease by the Somme Association, of which I am also the founder Chairman. This Association grew out of Farset, following a Press Conference arranged by Rev Dr Ian Paisley on 1 July 1986.

In 1992, I published under my imprint, Pretani Press, the *Folk Poets of Ulster* series to bring before the public some of the finest pieces of literature in the Ulster-Scots language by James Orr, Hugh Porter and Samuel Thompson. In February 1994, I asked Mr Jim Nicholson, MEP, to raise the issue of an Ullans Academy in the European Parliament at Strasbourg. This was followed up by Mr David Trimble MP. In December 1995, I also asked my friend, Rev Dr Ian Paisley, to arrange for members of the USLS including myself to meet the NIO Minister, Michael Ancram, to put forward a comprehensive proposal for a core-funded Academy. The costed and itemised proposal then included details for a language development programme

---

[1] I am grateful to Dr John Kirk for the opportunity to outline the origins of the Ullans or Ulster-Scots Academy and to provide an insight into its development.

and an Ulster-Scots Language Resource Centre. Without any funding being awarded, the Academy managed to complete some aspects on a purely voluntary basis. These outputs included a regional Dictionary, *The Hamely Tongue* (Fenton, 1995), which is the most important record yet produced of current Ulster-Scots speech. In association with the USLS, numerous contemporary Ulster-Scots writings and re-prints of traditional literature have also been published, including an Ulster-Scots Grammar book (Robinson, 1997).

My progress in promoting the Ulster-Scots Academy is fully documented in press reports and correspondence throughout 1993 to 1997. (*East Belfast Herald and Post*, 22 July 1993 (Helen Carson); *Irish News*, 25 January 1994 (Conor McCauley); *Belfast Telegraph* 10 February 1994 (Vincent Kearney). On 9 November 1998, I raised the issue in the New Northern Ireland Assembly (*Official Report Hansard*, Vol. 1, p. 235).

In 1998-9, Government funded the USLS to produce a development plan for the Ulster-Scots Language. The "Edmund Report" was produced in July 2000 by a consultant, John Edmund, *Strategic Plan for the Promotion of the Ulster-Scots Language* (see also Edmund 2002). It provided an updated, detailed language development proposal as a model for the work of the Ullans Academy. This Report again provided detailed costings for a core-funded Academy. The language development proposals in the Edmund Report re-emphasised the following priorities:

- Progress a tape-recorded survey of native speakers by native speakers (long identified as the most urgent priority).
- Create an electronic text base of Ulster-Scots literature.
- Develop a comprehensive two-way Ulster-Scots/English dictionary programme.
- Develop a process for agreeing standardised spellings and an accredited translation service (including a translation of the Authorised Version of the Bible).
- Set up an Ulster-Scots Language Resource Centre.
- Develop Ulster-Scots Language courses and classes.
- Conduct research programmes.
- Publish and broadcast in Ulster-Scots.

With the establishment of the Ulster-Scots Agency and *the Noarth/Sooth Boord o Leid* under the Belfast Agreement of 1998, and the formal recognition of Ulster-Scots as a European Regional Language by the UK government in 1999, the implementation of the Academy's Language Development Plan has become a government imperative.

The resourcing of the critical elements of the Academy's Language Development Plan was agreed by government and approved in the 2000-2003 Corporate Plan for the Ulster-Scots Agency. However, after three years operation of the North/South Body, none of the agreed £1,500,000 expenditure on the language plan has been processed.

In September 2002, the Agency held its first formal meeting with the Ullans Academy. It was agreed that the Academy would re-constitute itself as a Company Limited by Guarantee, in order that the existing voluntary programme of the Academy and USLS could be properly resourced and established.

In October 2002, the Minister for Culture, Arts and Leisure, Michael

McGimpsey, responded to the repeated representations from the Ulster-Scots community for resolute action by government to promote Ulster-Scots more effectively. His Department (DCAL) organised a three-day "Future Search" conference to agree the way forward between statutory bodies, government and the Ulster-Scots community. A number of language-centred policies were signed up to by all present, including:

- Full and immediate implementation of the Edmund Report recommendations for strategic development of the Ulster-Scots language.
- The establishment of a fully functioning Ullans (Ulster-Scots) Academy.
- Equality of Resourcing, Respect, Recognition and Representation for the Ulster-Scots and Irish languages throughout both jurisdictions in the island of Ireland.
- Measures to be taken by government to ensure Stage 3 status and ratification for Ulster-Scots under the terms of the *European Charter for Regional or Minority Languages*, within 3-5 years.

The purpose of the Ullans Academy therefore was to conserve, develop and promote the Ulster-Scots language in the context of its attendant history, culture and moral philosophy.

The Ullans Academy would be capable of delivering:
- A regulation and standardisation of the language for modern usage. These standards will be agreed by and for the Ulster-Scots community, and be academically sound.
- The previously agreed but delayed language development programme.
- Progress to stage 3 for Ullans (Ulster-Scots) under the terms of the *European Charter for Regional or Minority Languages*.
- Equality of status and respect with the Irish language.
- An Ulster-Scots Resource Centre to make Ulster-Scots materials accessible to researchers and the community.
- Accredited language classes and courses for speakers and non-speakers.
- Status-building measures for the language.
- Expert advice and an authoritative linguistic service to the Ulster-Scots Agency, Government and Statutory Bodies.

In the context of Ulster-Scots as a recognised "European Regional and Minority Language", the Ullans Academy is modelled on the Friesian Academy in the Netherlands. However it will also promote the interrelationships between Ulster-Scots, Ulster English, including Belfast English, and Ulster Gaelic as well as the study of Northumbrian English in general. The Academy's research interests will also extend beyond language and literature – to historical, cultural and moral philosophical themes such as the life and works of Francis Hutcheson and C S Lewis, and studies in the history of Ulidia in general, especially Dalriada, Dalaradia, Dal Fiatach and Galloway. The Scotch-Irish Diaspora also provides a particular focus on the American dimension, but emigration studies will also be necessary for the countries of the Commonwealth and other countries.

The Academy is closely associated with the "*Heirskip Bilfawst*" project, which is a proposal to reconstruct a living history and traditional crafts centre based on the

18th century Ulster-Scots town of Belfast at the time of the American war of independence. This project has many parallels with the leading American attraction at Colonial Williamsburg. It is significant that another philosophical model for the Academy is the College of William and Mary at Williamsburg, Virginia (founded 1693).

Finally, in 2003, the Joint Declaration of the British and Irish Governments indicated that the British Government would take steps to encourage support to be made available for an Ulster-Scots Academy.

References

Adamson, I. 1982. *The Identity of Ulster*. Bangor: Pretani Press.

Edmund, J. 2002. 'Ulster-Scots Language and Culture'. In ed. John M. Kirk and Dónall P. Ó Baoill. *Language Planning and Education: Linguistic Issues in northern Ireland, the Republic of Ireland, and Scotland*. Belfast: Cló Ollscoil na Banríona. 175-182.

Fenton, J. 1995. *The Hamely Tongue: A Personal Record of Ulster-Scots in County Antrim Speech*. [Newtownards]: The Ulster-Scots Academic Press.

Robinson, P. 1997. *Ulster-Scots: A Grammar of the Traditional Written and Spoken Language*. [Belfast]: The Ullans Press.

The Ulster Scots – A New Wey Foreairt

Ian James Parsley

It wad be gey guid bean here thedey sayan ma warnins frae fernyeir is efter a-heedan an fowk is nou gan the richt wey wi the forder o the Braid Scotch Tongue in Norlin Airlan. Unfortunatlik, A canna dae siclyke acause it isna sae. Theyeir, but, A will pit fore twathree nories o ma ain for fowk tae mak a kirk or a mill o.

Last news

The war a muckle collogue twal mond syne anent the upset o an Ulster-Scots or Ullans Academie. Thar a muckle collogue thenou anent the upset o an Ulster-Scots or Ullans Academie. A guarantee twal mond frae nou thar will be a muckle collogue anent the upset o an Ulster-Scots or Ullans Academie. But thar will be nae Academie! Siclyke is juist a smokescreen for tae hap the fact thar nae policie anent Ulster Scots an nae ploys for ane, an onie o us yet leevean! The Govrenment canna tell us whit research shaws sicna Academie bes a-needan, whan siclyke cud be sat up, or whitwey hit cud be managed. It is nae wunner fowk taks a sair hairt, an dealan wi a government at maks promises hit canna hauld tae (thaim as bes waitan yet for reception o TG4 in Norlin Airlan will ken richtlie the intent o ma discourse!)

The war a muckle collogue twal mond syne, 24 mond syne, 36 mond syne an 48 mond syne anent the want o ken anent the Braid Scots Tongue amang thaim as taks responsibilitie for policie anent it; anent the want o onie discourse ava wi fowk as taaks it forordinar (an no juist thaim as allous, wi nae pruif ava, at thay represents thaim ein whaur thay canna pit a bodie foreairt as taaks the tongue for onie comatee or siclyke a-dae wi the forder o the leid); an anent the scunnersom qualitie o translations put owre intae sae-cryed 'Ulster Scots' frae feed fowk wi nae qualitie assurance process. Fowk cud maybe guess thon is the case yet anaa!

Thar nae dout ava it juist isna guid eneuch for the govrenment a promise wi nae ettle at hauldan tae it.

It is waur yet at govrenment taks nae tent o the basic need for tae bring on real expertise anent the issues an the leid itssel, as taakit frae its ain uisears.

It is waur yet at the govrenment haes a deliberat policie o no takan onie tent ava o thaim as taaks the leid forordinar, an taakan lane wi curns as canna provide an aefauld hamelie tongue taakar or linguistic qualification amang thaim.

Maist scunnersom o aa, is the ongan want o onie qualitie assurance process ava a-dae wi Ulster-Scots translations – A wad challenge onie official frae DCAL tae pruive at A cudna juist pit in a translation in Esperanto, cry it 'Ulster Scots', an thay wad be gart pey me for it. A am thinkan ilka aefauld bodie as gies owre thair cesses tae the govrenment sud ken at the govrenment gies siller out for sairvices, wi nae road ava for pruiwan, wad thon sairvice cum tae ein the maist basic qualitie staunarts. Thay wad maybe explain tae thaim as taaks Ulster Scots forordinar, deyandeilie, whitwey sic scunnersom wants fits thair needs unner onie 'agenda o coequalitie'! A bodie cudna say but thaim as richtlie taaks the tongue is bean discriminate agin wi thair ain ordinar wey a taakin a-uisean an a-abuisean in sicna manner.

Nae mair can govrenment allou this is aa for a want o tyme. Sax yeir efter the Greement an fyve yeir efter the upset o the Ulster-Scots Agentrie onie attempts at allouan thay ar heiran tae whit linguists an, mair important, taakars is sayan is richtlie faan tae deif ears. The farce maun awa.

Foreairt tae the futur

For aa thair 'Academie Ploys' an 'Futuresearches', the Govrenment haes nae ettle at settan furth a SMART[1] policie anent Ulster Scots. Hit wad be best juist admittan it!

The solution isna sweir. The Govrenment sud bring on a policie an taakan wi thaim as haes richt linguistic qualifications an, mair important, thaim as taaks the leid forordinar. Nae ither bodie haes the richt tae represent sic fowk. The Govrenment maun get awa upkintra an taak direct wi thaim as uises the tongue.

Here juist twathree things thay wad maybe finnd, an sae daean:

- thar nae caa frae taakars thairsels for onie translations o govrenment screeds!
- ill-daen translations juist taaks the pride out o the tongue – direct agin the statet aim o the govrenment!
- the notion o onie Bible translation isna juist ridiculous sae earlie in the oncum o the tongue, it is richt scunnersom tae a wheen fowk.
- thar nae caa for fowks wey o taakin tae cum a political fitbaa in direct opposition tae the Earse Gaelic – for the maist fek o thaim, the Gaelic isna thair problem!
- fowk taks pride in the oral tradition an fowk poetrie (i.e. screeds made in the Braid Tongue, no put owre intae it).

But whitwey cud the Auld Tongue leeve on, an takan thon pad? Maybe fowk cud speir at the Swiss Germans, as wisna daean sae bad on ma last visit just last mond!

For thaim ats interest is for the Tongue an no political fitbaas, thar a braw vision o the futur at cud learn us aa twathree things anent richt linguistic oncum. Meantyme, A am juist howpan A haena run out o weys o sayan the ae thing owre the twalmond cuman!

---

[1] SMART: Specific, Measurable, Achievable, Relevant, Timebound.

The Development of Scots Language Policy in Scotland since Devolution

Michael Hance

Since devolution the Scottish Executive has come under increasing pressure to develop a national language strategy and to give proper recognition and support to the country's indigenous languages. Agitation for change has come in particular from language activists and the small number of MSPs who have an interest in the promotion of the Gaelic and Scots languages. The most notable of these in the case of Scots has been Irene McGugan. The Executive has responded in a variety of ways to this pressure and has made differing levels of commitment to change. The most significant and obvious difference in its approach to indigenous languages has been its comparative willingness to improve the situation for Gaelic and its continued resistance to making any progress in developing a policy on Scots that extends beyond the most token recognition of the language.

It would not be unreasonable to argue that the main characteristics of the Executive's language policy are inconsistency and incoherence. Policy is inconsistent because the government has taken entirely different approaches towards funding and supporting Gaelic and Scots. The extract from an internal Scottish Executive memo which is reproduced below reveals that the Government and its civil servants recognise that there there are no rational or logical arguments for not according Scots the same level of support as Gaelic.

> Supporters of other languages, in particular of Scots. will be quick to seek to gain an equivalence of treatment and other than reference to the danger of extinction there is little in linguistic grounds to defend a different approach top Scots. This will have to be addressed during the Bill's passage - the long title proposed would preclude any reference to anything other than Gaelic in the Bill. Wider consultation is needed on how to approach the wider language commitment and we shall discuss with Ministers how best to approach this at an early opportunity. (Scottish Executive internal memo to Peter Peacock, MSP, Minister for Education, 28 May 2003)

I would suggest that the Executive's policy towards Scots is incoherent because there appears from the outside at least to be no clear framework within which policy is developed. Instead, policy appears to be developed "on the hoof" often in reaction to external pressure. Policy on Scots is not underpinned by any clear reference to wider political priorities like, for example, social justice or cultural rights, although this may change as a result of the recommendations which the newly established cultural commission may make.

The Executive's policies on all matters within its areas of competence are underpinned by the so-called Partnership Agreement. This document represents the outcome of the discussions to establish a governing coalition which took place between the Scottish Labour Party and the Scottish Liberal Democrats after the 2003 election. It replaces the agreement which was drawn up between the same parties after the first Scottish general election in 1999. The partnership agreement outlines the intended general thrust of the government's legislative and policy development programme over the period during which it holds office and covers the full range of devolved matters including culture. In the section dealing with culture and the arts, the Executive outlines its language policy in the following ways.

A Partnership for a Better Scotland: Partnership Agreement

We will develop a plan to support our traditional and other languages
We will develop a new focus for Scotland's languages recognising both
  our heritage and diversity
We will develop a new focus for Scotland's languages recognising both
  our heritage and our diversity
We will legislate to provide secure status for Gaelic through a Gaelic
  Language Bill. We will introduce a national language strategy to
  guide the development and support of Scotland's languages,
  including British Sign Language and ethnic minority community
  languages. We will give local authorities and other public bodies a
  responsibility to draw up a languages plan which reflects the
  communities they serve.

We can see here in this statement that the Executive has committed itself to supporting Gaelic through legislative measures. The government is indicating that it views Gaelic as a serious subject, and that it is determined to be seen, at the very least, as supportive of the language and interested in improving its status. Indeed, it is the case that the Executive in the early months of the present Parliament drew up a draft Gaelic Bill which it subsequently put out for consultation. A legislative timetable has been established and a Gaelic Bill will be presented to Parliament in September 2004 (see further Wilson McLeod, in this volume). Scots, on the other hand, is not even accorded the dignity of a name in this document. Instead, it is described as a traditional (or perhaps, other) language. This is in line with the usual Executive approach to Scots, which is to avoid naming the language if at all possible.

This approach of the Executive is in line with the (un)official policy which the various arms of the United Kingdom state have applied to the language throughout the twentieth century and before that, too. It is principally characterised by an unwillingness to recognise that a language called Scots exists. It should be obvious to anyone that such a position presents a major impediment to the development and implementation of policies designed to support, encourage and promote the language, and that until this view is successfully challenged progress of the sort hoped for by language activists remains unlikely. However, while the outlook remains rather bleak in totality, there are some glimmers of hope that suggest that some improvement in the situation for Scots and its various dialects may be possible in the not too distant future.

The most significant recent development has been the adoption by the UK government of the *European Charter for Regional or Minority Languages*. The UK has agreed to apply the various parts of the Charter to the languages other than English which are indigenous to its geographical territory. These are Welsh, Cornish, Irish Gaelic, Scots Gaelic, Ulster-Scots and Scots. The UK has also signed the charter on behalf of the Isle of Man government in relation to Manx. The various devolved territorial governments have been given the responsibility of acting on behalf of the UK in implementing the provisions of the Charter in the geographical and legislative areas over which they have competence. This means that the Scottish Executive is responsible for this matter in Scotland. At international level, then, Scots has achieved a degree of recognition and status which it has signally failed to do at home.

So, has this recognition made a difference to the ways in which the Scottish Executive has approached questions relating to the status of Scots, the provision of resources for those who wish to use and learn the language, and the level to which it is funded by central government? The depressing answer to all these questions is that nothing much seems to have changed, and that there seems to be little more understanding of the issues now than there was before the Charter was signed. The level of support given to a language depends on which parts of the Charter the signatories agree to apply to it. Scots and Ulster-Scots are covered by Part II of the Charter, the lower of the two levels of commitment available to signatories. While this is the less demanding of the options, it still obliges the signatory to carry out a number of actions and provide a specified level of practical support to the language, the particulars of which are outlined in considerable detail in the Charter itself.

So far the Executive has failed to apply any of the provisions as they relate to Scots. In fact, in its response to an inquiry into the application of the Charter by a European Union Committee of Experts, the Executive did not even attempt to answer many of the questions that were asked of it and, where it did respond, it gave oblique and often (deliberately?) meaningless answers. In the sessions of the enquiry held by the Committee of Experts in Edinburgh, the Executive failed even to send its culture minister to answer questions and was represented instead by a (recently appointed) civil servant whose job is to head up the *Gaelic Unit* in the Education Department. The purpose of dealing with this matter in such a fashion remains unclear, but it is not unreasonable to suppose that is informed by the approach described above. That is that resistance to the notion of Scots as a language remains the principle which underpins the Executive's attitude to Scots even when, absurdly, it is being asked for information about the ways in which it has applied the provisions of an international Charter to which it (indirectly) is a signatory and which not only recognises Scots as a language but has as its main purpose the protection and promotion of that and other minority languages.

The report from the Committee of Experts did not contain the damning criticism of the Executive that many Scots activists had hoped for (and which the Executive undoubtedly deserved). This was a disappointment to those who have felt frustrated at the Government's continued inaction and had hoped that the Executive would finally be shamed into taking its obligations to the language seriously. However, it may be that the remit and style of reporting of such committees has been misunderstood. It seems that the Committee may have steered clear of an overly critical approach in order to avoid provoking a hostile response from the Executive and has instead sought to help the Government find ways of improving its record. We can only hope that this is indeed the outcome but, if it is not, there seems to be little that can be done to force the Executive's hand. The Charter does not place legal obligations on signatories and so far the Executive appears to be largely unmoved by any sense of moral responsibility either. The question of obligation has been explored recently by Donald Gorrie, MSP, the Liberal Democrats' arts and culture spokesperson, who wrote during the summer of 2004 to the Parliament's information centre to ask for clarification of the legal standing of the Charter. The response from a Parliamentary official follows:

> The Executive haes telt me that they taen legal advice anent the maitter an that Cooncil o Europe Chairters disnae hae ony legal wecht at aw. In ither words, they hiv nae legal staundin in ony European Coort. In effect, they're juist a statement o intent or guid-will. There nae sanctions associated wi sic Chairters apairt frae the sair publicity associated wi no cairryin oot whit wis signed up for if thon shuid be the case. (Stephen Herbert, Scottish Parliament Information Centre; owerset bi Bob Fairnie)

While this advice seems to put the Executive in the clear as far as the Charter is concerned pressure may be building from another direction. The Liberal Democrats, the junior party in the Government coalition, passed a strongly pro-Scots motion at their annual Scottish conference in Dundee, 26-28 March 2004.

Scottish Liberal Democrats on the Scots Language
Conference recongises the importance of Scotland's two heritage
languages of Gaelic and Scots. It approves the support already
given to Gaelic by the Scottish Executive and welcomes the
commitment to establish secure status for the language. It regrets,
however, the Executive's failure to give comparable support to
Scots.
Conference therefore calls on the Scottish Executive to:
meet its present commitments to Scots set out in the European
Charter for Minority Languages and ensure that the status of
Scots is raised from Part II of that Charter to Part III;
establish a Ministeral Advisory Committee on Scots (modeled on
the Advisory Committee on Gaelic);
examine the current position of Scots and bring forward proposals
to enhance its use, increase its status and safeguard its future;
establish an Institute for the Languages of Scotland;
respond to the Parliament's Education, culture and sports
Committee's call for the preparation of a comprehensive
language policy for Scotland.
Conference also calls for the appointment of a party spokesperson on
Scots.

The motion indicates a change of view from the Liberal Democrats – previously the party had largely ignored the language. It is worth noting that the motion was opposed by the party leadership, and there is a school of thought which believes that it was supported by the membership in order to indicate general displeasure with the Lib Dems approach to coalition government rather than as a means of indicating a clear change of policy direction on language. However, it is now party policy and an internal working group has been established to look at the implications of the policy and how it might be implemented in the future.

Other questions asked during the summer of 2004 have at last provided answers to the some of the most vexing questions about Scots and the Scottish Executive. For instance, we now know that the Culture Minister, at the time Frank McAveety, is the member of the Government with responsibility for Scots. Consider the following Written Answer by Frank McAveety on 26 August 2004:

> **Chris Ballance (South of Scotland) (Green):**
> To ask the Scottish Executive which minister has responsibility for ensuring that it meets its obligations in respect of the Charter for Regional or Minority Languages as these relate to Scots. (S2W-09841)
> **Mr Frank McAveety:**
> I have lead Ministerial responsibility within the Scottish Executive for matters relating to the Scots language.

We also know that the Executive still intends to develop a national language strategy, although when exactly this will happen remains unclear. Consider the following Written Answer by Frank McAveety also on 26 August 2004:

> **Chris Ballance (South of Scotland] (Green):**
> To ask the Scottish Executive, further to the answer to question S2W-8183 by Mr Frank McAveety on 25 May 2004, what specific initiatives it has taken in response to the recommendations of the Council of Europe Committee of Experts' report into the Charter for Regional or Minority Languages, as they relate to Scots. (S2W–09840)
> **Mr Frank McAveety:**
> Action in relation to the recommendation of the Committee of Experts and the Charter undertakings for Scots are for a range of bodies and institutions. A wide range of Scots initiatives is being taken forward throughout Scotland. The Executive will also consider these matters within the context of the Partnership commitment to develop a National Language Strategy.

Euan Robson, MSP, the Deputy Minister for Education and Young People, provided more information about the Executive's plans when, in an Oral Question and Answer session on 24 June 2004 on Schools (Scots Language Teaching), he provided the following answer to a question about teaching Scots in schools which was asked in Parliament by Rob Gibson, MSP, the Convener of the Cross Party Group on the Scots language.

> **Rob Gibson (Highlands and Islands) (SNP):**
> To ask the Scottish Executive what innovative measures it is taking in schools regarding the teaching of the Scots language. (S20-2822)
> **Euan Robson:**
> I recognise the member's interest in the subject and thank him for his question ... as a result of the report of March 2004 by the Committee of Experts on the Charter [*European Charter for*

Regional or Minority Languages], officials have embarked on discussions with the academic community on the production of a Scots language strategy. I understand that the Scottish centre for information on language teaching and research in Sterling is in active discussion with Executive officials on that point. We hope to produce a strategy by, optimistically, later this year, more realistically, early next year. The matter is of considerable interest to the Executive and we will pursue it. As I said, I am grateful to the member for highlighting the issue.

It iseems reasonable to conclude that pressure is building on the Executive to develop a clear policy on Scots. The number of questions asked on the subject by MSPs from all parties and the debate which is taking place at a popular and more sophisticated level about the language question in newspapers and on television and radio demonstrates that Scots is a matter of interest to large numbers of people. The Executive's stated desire to improve the status of Gaelic (some would say driven to a great extent by political self-interest) has exposed the inequity of their position on Scots and has put them under increasing pressure to develop a broader language strategy.

However, the faint glimmers of hope from the Executive need to be set against a continuing aversion by the Executive's agencies to take the language seriously. Only during the present summer of 2004, the newly appointed Cultural Commission, set up by the Executive to investigate the provision of cultural services in Scotland, failed in typical style to mention Scots in its outline policy statement. Consider the following extract from the Commission/Executive's outline policy statement:

> **1.12** The Commission's findings will be informed by the diverse cultural and linguistic communities within Scotland, with particular regard to Gaelic language and culture. (Cultural Policy Statement, April 2004)

There may be soime hope of a more enlightened attitude developing inthe Commission. In recent statements, the Commission indicates that it would like those makingsubmissions to it to consider questions of esteem and even suggests as an example that people may wish to ask for "parity of esteem for the Scots and Gaelic languages". This early capitulation on the question of Scots suggests that questions have already been raised about the absence of any reference to the language in the outline statement. It may also reveal thatat least one of the Government's agencies is prepared to accept such an omission is no longer acceptable. It is to be hoped that such an approach becomes the Executive's usual rather than exceptional manner of dealing with the Scots language.

The Revival of Scots in Ulster: Why Literary History Matters

Ivan Herbison

Introduction

This paper offers some preliminary observations on recent developments in relation to Ulster-Scots language. My title, 'The Revival of Scots in Ulster', should not be interpreted as implying any reservations about the status of Ulster Scots. Rather, it points to an attempt to relate linguistic and literary expression in Ulster to the wider literary-historical perspective of Scots as a whole. I am aware of the sensitivities attached to terminology. There is no wholly satisfactory term for the variety of Scots found in the north of Ireland. 'Ulster Scots' and 'Ullans' are both constructed terms, exogenous rather than endogenous. Historically, native speakers have used the term 'Scotch', sometimes further qualified as 'the guid Scotch tung' or 'braid Scotch'.[1]

However, 'Scotch' has the capacity to irritate some speakers of Scots in Scotland, where, since the nineteenth century, Scotch has become restricted in its reference to whisky, broth, oats, and a few other specialised usages.[2] Among Ulster Scots it has retained its former primacy, and it is in this context that I will use the term. The word 'Scotch' has thus become emblematic of the continuities and discontinuities between the Scots in Scotland and the Scots in Ulster. It is both a bridge and a boundary, simultaneously proclaiming a shared linguistic identity and demarcating a boundary of linguistic difference. It is a shibboleth which is at the same time inclusive and exclusive. [3] The title refers to the phenomenon of revival. This term too is problematic, since it implies both continuity and discontinuity. What does it mean to speak of the 'revival' of Ulster Scots? What is being revived, and from what state or condition? This issue I will explore through a personal reflection.

My paternal grandmother, Sarah McCaughey, was born in 1867 in the townland of the Clougher, and grew up in Killyfleugh, near Ballymena. She lived well into her nineties, and spoke a pure and unselfconscious form of the 'braid Scotch'. My maternal grandmother, Helena McFetridge, was born in the townland of the Eglish, near Clough, County Antrim in 1885. She too was a speaker of the traditional language, which she handed on to her children, growing up on the family farm in the townland of Galgorm Parks, near Ballymena. As I grew up, I heard Ulster Scots spoken, and I also became aware of the literary tradition of Ulster-Scots poetry, through the work of my forebear David Herbison, the Bard of Dunclug.[4] Thus my personal experience convinces me that the traditional Scotch is a living tongue: it is a case of survival rather than revival.

---

[1] James Orr, 'The Irish Cottier's Death and Burial' in P. Robinson, ed. and intro., *The Country Rhymes of James Orr, The Bard of Ballycarry 1770-1816* (Bangor, 1992), p.30.
[2] M. Robinson, ed., *Concise Scots Dictionary* (Edinburgh, 1999), s.v. Scots.
[3] For the concept of shibboleth, see J. Corbett, 'Literary Language and Scottish Identity', Association for Scottish Literary Studies Conference, 13 May 2000, accessed at http://www.arts.gla.ac.uk/ScotLit/ASLS/NoFrames/JCorbett2.html on 10/09/2004.
[4] See I. Herbison, *David Herbison, The Bard of Dunclug: a poet and his community, 1800-1880* (Ballymena, 1988).

Clearly, if a traditional language is not handed on, it will not survive. Elsewhere I have examined the social, educational and political pressures which have contributed to the decline of Ulster Scots. [5] Yet, however reduced, that traditional language is still to be heard in my native mid-Antrim in a form which would have been familiar to my grandmothers. This leads me to question the meaning and impact of revival in connection with a traditional language.

The title also refers to literary history. This is a term which I interpret in its widest sense. I am not concerned here with the construction of a canon, but with the historical development of the written forms of Scots. What insights can be gained from a consideration of processes of revival in the past? How might such insights help us to understand the present challenges facing Ulster Scots? I am convinced that a literary-historical perspective will facilitate a clearer assessment of the choices confronting Ulster Scots today.

Scots and Literary History: Origins

Scotland has always been a linguistically diverse region. Bede (d. 735), in his *Historia Ecclesiastica Gentis Anglorum*, identifies five languages spoken in the island of Britain in the seventh century: British (by which Bede meant Welsh); Pictish; Scots (by which Bede meant Irish); English (by which Bede meant various dialects of Old English); and Latin. [6] All of Bede's linguistic communities had a presence in Scotland: P-Celtic was the language of Strathclyde; Pictish, of the north of the region; Q-Celtic, of parts of the south; a variety of the Northumbrian dialect of Old English was spoken in the south-east; Latin was the language of the Church and scholarship. After Bede's time, to these five were added Old Norse, in parts of the north and west, and French, the language of the Norman aristocracy. However, by the eleventh century, Pictish and Strathclyde Welsh had disappeared. [7]

Old English has had a significant presence in Scotland since the seventh century. Indeed, the earliest text of an Old English poem, a Northumbian version of part of *The Dream of the Rood*, is inscribed in runes on the Ruthwell Cross, dated to between 650 and 700. [8] The Ruthwell Cross poem implies the presence of a linguistic community. The term Inglis, by which it came to be known in the later medieval period, reflects its origin as the most northerly exemplar of the Anglian variety of Old English. A southern variety of Anglian was the ancestor of Present-day English. Inglis came to be the dominant language in the South of Scotland, and may be regarded as the ancestor of Scots.

[5] I. Herbison, ' "The Rest is Silence": Some Remarks on the Disappearance of Ulster-Scots Poetry' in *Cultural Traditions in Northern Ireland: Varieties of Scottishness, Exploring the Ulster-Scots Connection*, ed. J Erskine and G. Lucy (Belfast, 1997), pp. 129-47.

[6] B. Colgrave and R.A.B. Mynors, ed. and trans. *Bede's Ecclesiastical History of the English People* (Oxford, 1969), Book I, Ch. 1; he mentions four languages (excluding Latin) in Book III, Ch. 6.

[7] For a discussion of the linguistic situation in early Scotland, see J. Corbett, *Written in the Language of the Scottish Nation: A History of Literary Translation into Scots* (Clevedon, 1999), Chapter 2, pp. 13-27.

[8] See M.J. Swanton, ed., *The Dream of the Rood* (Manchester, 1970); B. Cassidy, *The Ruthwell Cross: Papers from the Collegium sponsored by the Index of Christian Art, Princeton University, 8 December 1989* (Princeton, NJ, 1992).

Scots, however, never achieved linguistic hegemony. It was in competition with the higher status languages of Latin and French. It was also in competition with Gaelic as a vernacular. From the sixteenth century onwards, and especially from the Union of the Crowns (1603), Scots was in competition with Suddron, the southern variety of English. The linguistic competition often involved cultural and religious factors. William Dunbar in his 'Flyting of Dunbar and Kennedy' delights in depicting Kennedy's Gaelic as Irish and hence foreign.[9] John Knox's use of 'Southeroun' in preference to 'auld plane Scottish' attracted scorn and criticism from his religious opponents.[10] Nevertheless, in the classic writing of Middle Scots writers such as William Dunbar and Robert Henryson, Scots achieved a considerable measure of acceptance in all registers: as a high status language, used for courtly poetry and tragedy (Henryson's *The Testament of Cresseid*); in the plain style, used for moral and didactic works (Henryson's *The Morall Fabillis of Esope the Phrygian*); and in the low style, used for satire, polemic and invective (Dunbar's *Tretis of the Tua Mariit Wemen and the Wedo*).[11]

Ulster Scots shares the multilingual context of Scots but has encountered more disadvantages and obstacles. It has had to compete with both Irish and English as vernaculars, but the dominance of English in most areas of public life has denied it any official status. Scots was, albeit briefly, the language of a politically independent nation; Ulster Scots has not until recent times had any recognition.[12] The fact that Scots lost its position as a fully autonomous language severely impeded the progress of Ulster Scots. Both were subject to a process of Anglicisation.[13] If, as a consequence, Scots is sometimes considered a *Halbsprache*,[14] then Ulster Scots is perhaps a *Viertelsprache* or what Kirk (2003: 344) calls a *farlleid*.

Scots and Literary History: Vernacular Revivals

The vernacular revival of the eighteenth and early nineteenth centuries marks a new direction and a new beginning for literature in Scots. The work of Allan Ramsay (1684-1758), Robert Fergusson (1750-74) and their followers involved discontinuity and the elision of many of the traditions of Middle Scots. The semi-standardised orthographic practices of Middle Scots were abandoned, to be replaced by a symbolic orthography, more semiotic than phonetic. The orthography of the revival was much closer to Standard English, but marked difference through frequent use of apostrophes and non-standard spellings. These served as signs to remind readers that the language was Scots rather than English. There was also a contraction of style and

---

[9] See C. I. Macafee and C. Ó Baoill, 'Why Scots is not a Celtic English' in H.L.C Tristram, ed., *The Celtic Englishes*, Anglistische Forschungen 247 (Heidelberg, 1997), pp. 245-86 (pp. 251-2).

[10] Corbett, *Written in the Language of the Scottish Nation*, p. 59.

[11] J. Kinsley, ed., *The Poems of William Dunbar* (Oxford, 1979), pp. 42-59 ; D. Fox, ed., *The Poems of Robert Henryson* (Oxford, 1981), pp. 1-131.

[12] The Belfast Agreement mentions Ulster Scots as 'a variety of Scots' and Ulster Scots has been recognised under Section II of the *European Charter for Regional or Minority Languages* since July 2001.

[13] M. Montgomery, 'The Anglicisation of Scots in Early Seventeenth-Century Ulster', *Studies in Scottish Literature*, 26 (1992), 50-64.

[14] See M. Görlach, 'Ulster Scots: A Language?', in J. M. Kirk and D. P. Ó Baoill, eds., *Language and Politics: Northern Ireland, the Republic of Ireland, and Scotland* (Belfast, 2000), pp. 13-32.

vocabulary. The high register Middle Scots, with its predilection for aureation, was lost. The lexis of Scots was no longer enriched by independent borrowings from Latin and French. These losses were to some extent compensated for by borrowings from the folk tradition. This was justified by an appeal to classical precedent, the use of the Doric dialect in Theocritus. This, combined with an eighteenth-century appeal to decorum, provided the poets of the revival with a rationale for using both English and Scots in their works, according to criteria of subject-matter and style.

It is highly significant that the first known Ulster-Scots poet is closely associated with Allan Ramsay. William Starrat of Strabane exchanged poetical epistles with Allan Ramsay. Starrat's 'A Pastoral in Praise of Allan Ramsay', dated 1722, was published as a broadsheet in 1725.[15] This suggests a close connection between the vernacular revival in Scotland and in Ulster, an impression further confirmed by the popularity of the works of Ramsay in the north of Ireland. Nine editions of Ramsay's *The Gentle Shepherd* were printed in Ulster between 1743 and 1792 (five in Belfast, three in Newry and one in Strabane).[16]

However, it was Robert Burns (1759-96) who was the strongest influence on the Ulster-Scots poets, becoming a model for their own revival movement. Burns employed a rich spectrum of linguistic variation. Building on the achievement of Ramsay, he created a heightened literary Scots, with a more extensive use of distinctive vocabulary. As a collector and recorder of the folk tradition, he enriched and augmented literary Scots through the use of local dialect. Yet he continued to employ the conventions of English poetic diction, to highlight and contrast with his vernacular voice. These techniques were enthusiastically employed by the Ulster poets. It is significant that none of the Ulster poets chose Ulster Scots as an exclusive medium. All follow the practices of the Scots revival in modulating the density of their use of Scotch according to subject-matter, style and form. The Scots vernacular revival also provided the Ulster poets with their characteristic verse forms, such as Standard Habbie and the Holy Fair stanza. As with their use of revival orthography, the verse forms came to acquire a symbolic or semiotic significance, and became a visual representation of revival Scots.

There are frequent intertextual references and allusions to Burns in the work of the Ulster poets. James Campbell's 'The Epicure's Address to Bacon' refers to Burns's 'Address to a Haggis':[17]

> Though poet Burns did oft declare
> A haggis he would still prefer
> To ought within his bill of fare,
> For inside oils;
> When I do light on't like a bear,
> My stomach spoils.[18]

---

[15] P. Robinson, 'William Starrat of Strabane: The First Ulster-Scots Poet', *Ullans*, 5 (1997), 30-39.

[16] See J. R. R. Adams, *The printed word and the common man: popular culture in Ulster 1700-1900* (Belfast, 1987), Appendix 1: Ulster publications, 1699-1800, pp. 175-81.

[17] A. Noble and P. S. Hogg, eds., *The Canongate Burns* (Edinburgh, 2001), pp. 212-13.

[18] *The Poems and Songs of James Campbell of Ballynure* (Ballyclare, 1870), pp. 61-6 (p. 64).

James Orr's 'The Irish Cottier's Death and Burial' clearly alludes to Burn's 'The Cotter's Saturday Night' [19] Samuel Thomson's 'To a Hedgehog' owes something of its inspiration to Burns's 'To a Mouse'.[20] Such was the admiration of the Ulster poets for Burns that they were among the first to elevate him to iconic status.[21] Samuel Thomson visited him in 1794:

> O Yes, Hibernians, I beheld the Bard,
> Old Scotia's jewel, and the muse's darling,
> Whose matchless lays, despite of wasting time,
> Shall to the last of earthly generations,
> Remain old Nature's boast and Scotia's pride.
> ('A Jonsonian Fragment, Occasioned by a Visit to Mr Burns, in Spring, 1794'[22])

After his death in 1796 Ulster poets continued to pay homage at his grave.[23]

The Ulster poets saw in Burn's achievement a validation for their own linguistic and cultural identity. His model of Bardic Nationalism provided them with a model of identity that did not exclude Englishness. Burns's use of folk traditions and popular song not only broadened his appeal. It drew on a shared cultural inheritance. The rural bards of the 'Rhyming Weaver' tradition saw themselves as co-heirs with Burns of the Scots vernacular revival.[24]

Just as there is a linguistic tension between Scots and Ulster Scots, so there is a corresponding tension between the two literary traditions. Geographically and politically separated from Scotland, Ulster Scots have had to cope with feelings of exile and alienation, and anxieties about national identity. Even the legacy of Burns has proved ambiguous. On the one hand, as we have seen, the poets of the Ulster-Scots revival rushed to claim Burns as one of their own. On the other hand, they grew to resent the constant comparisons which living under his shadow inevitably entailed. Thomas Beggs (1789-1847) and Robert Huddleston (1814-87) complain of accusations of imitation of Scots and of Burns in particular.[25] Their affinity with Burns led to denials of their own cultural authenticity.

Socio-economic change, the introduction of an educational system promoting a British imperial identity through National Schools, and the political repercussions of the Home Rule crisis all conspired to silence the poets of the Ulster-Scots revival. By the beginning of the twentieth century they had all but disappeared.[26]

---

[19] P. Robinson, ed. and intro., *The Country Rhymes of James Orr, The Bard of Ballycarry 1770-1816* (Bangor, 1992), pp. 29-33.

[20] E. M. Scott and P. Robinson, ed. and intro., *The Country Rhymes of Samuel Thomson, The Bard of Carngranny 1766-1818* (Bangor, 1992), pp. 1-2.

[21] See L. McIlvanney, *Burns the Radical: Poetry and Politics in Late Eighteenth-Century Scotland* (East Linton, 2002), Chapter 9, ' "On Irish Ground": Burns and the Ulster-Scots Radical Poets', pp. 220-40.

[22] *The Country Rhymes of Samuel Thomson*, p. 46.

[23] See I. Herbison, *David Herbison The Bard of Dunclug: a poet and his community, 1800-1880* (Ballymena, 1988), p. 10.

[24] See J. Hewitt, *Rhyming Weavers and other country poets of Antrim and Down*, introduced by T. Paulin (1974; new ed. Belfast, 2004).

[25] I. Herbison, ' "The Rest is Silence" ', pp. 139-40.

Conclusions

What conclusions can be drawn from the literary history of the Scots and Ulster-Scots revivals? Revivals mark endings as well as beginnings. Traditional language and traditional literary genres may be under threat from the establishment of newer vernacular forms. The effect of the Scots revival and its Ulster counterpart was to introduce a spectrum of language use, ranging from a dense, demotic 'braid Scotch' to a lightly Scotticised English. No single form of Scots achieved dominance. This new spectrum allowed the poets of the revival the maximum degree of freedom in experimenting with different styles and voices. The revival also entrenched the principle of decorum as a feature of the literary tradition. A writer's choice of language or register could be varied according to genre, subject-matter, imagined audience, or persona.

The literary history of the revival also underlines the connections between cultural and political history. Just as the eighteenth-century revivals were in some sense related to losses of political and legislative independence resulting from the Unions of 1707 and 1800, so the cultural and linguistic revival of Ulster Scots which has taken place since the 1980s is a response to the loss of Stormont in 1972 and the subsequent political alienation of Unionism from a series of British governments. While the sense of Britishness still functions as a political identity, it is no longer sufficiently cohesive or distinctive to sustain allegiance as a cultural identity. The dissolution of Britishness is further exacerbated by the collapse of the Imperial British identity, the growth of multi-culturalism, and the renascence of Englishness. In this context, the revival of Ulster-Scots identity can become a new focus for those questioning traditional allegiances.

In the twenty-first century, as well in the nineteenth, language plays a vital role in establishing the boundaries of cultural identity. The rediscovery of the linguistic and literary heritage of Ulster Scots has helped to consolidate a new sense of belonging. There have been many positive consequences of the recovery of an Ulster-Scots identity, not the least of which is a revival of the literary language. Perhaps for the first time since the demise of the weaver poets, Ulster-Scots poetry is exploring new forms and finding a distinctive voice. James Fenton experiments with innovative poetic structures as well as traditional verse-forms such as Standard Habbie, but his work continues to explore themes of place, belonging, change and loss.[27] Other poets such as Charlie Gillen and Charlie Reynolds demonstrate the continuing potential of traditional verse forms.[28] Philip Robinson has made innovative use of Ulster-Scots prose in his novels: *Wake the Tribe o Dan* and *The Back Streets o the Claw* employ a variety of voices to explore an Ulster-Scots community in a rural and urban environment.[29]

It is a pity that these examples of literary Ulster Scots are not the most visible forms of the written language. The revival has also seen a new variety of Ulster Scots, which appears in translations of official documents. These translations have aroused

---

[26] I. Herbison, *Presbyterianism, Politics and Poetry in Nineteenth-Century Ulster: Aspects of an Ulster-Scots Literary Tradition* (Belfast, 2000), pp. 20-23.

[27] J. Fenton, *Thonner An Thon: An Ulster-Scots Collection* (Belfast, 2000).

[28] M. Montgomery and A Smyth, eds., *A Blad o Ulstèr-Scotch frae 'Ullans': Ulster-Scots culture, language and literature* (Belfast, 2003).

[29] P. Robinson, *Wake the Tribe o Dan* (Belfast, 1998); *The Back Streets of the Claw* (Belfast, 2000).

strong reactions and have left many traditional speakers puzzled by their choice of vocabulary, use of a restricted register, and inconsistent choice of orthography.[30] Traditional speakers feel alienated from this new variety, which is driven by a bureaucratic rather than a literary agenda. There is a real danger of creating diglossia and an artificial division between Scots and Ulster Scots.[31]

There has never been a standard form of Ulster Scots, and the literary history of revivals suggests that any attempt to impose a standard on Ulster Scots is likely to fail, because of the determined resistance of those voices excluded by standardisation. What would be the advantage of substituting one hegemony (that of Standard English) for another? In a situation of linguistic diversity, the imposition of any single form will meet with resistance from those who do not feel that the approved form expresses their identity or addresses their cultural needs. In the context of Northern Ireland, there is no alternative to recognising linguistic diversity both within and among the different language communities. Recognising diversity means respecting difference and accepting plurality. In the context of Ulster Scots it means that we should expect to encounter a range of voices, styles and registers from the Ulster-Scots community. Ways must be found of developing and extending the styles and registers of Ulster Scots which do not exclude or alienate traditional speakers. I look forward to the development of a form of Ulster Scots which my grandmothers would still recognise as their ain native tung.

References

Adams, J. R. R., *The printed word and the common man: popular culture in Ulster 1700-1900* (Belfast: Institute of Irish Studies, The Queen's University of Belfast, 1987)

Campbell, James, *The Poems and Songs of James Campbell of Ballynure* (Ballyclare: S. Corry, 1870)

Cassidy, B., *The Ruthwell Cross: Papers from the Collegium sponsored by the Index of Christian Art, Princeton University, 8 December 1989* (Princeton, NJ: Princeton University Press, 1992)

Colgrave, Bertram, and R.A.B. Mynors, ed. and trans., *Bede's Ecclesiastical History of the English People* (Oxford: Clarendon Press, 1969)

Corbett, John, *Written in the Language of the Scottish Nation: A History of Literary Translation into Scots*, Topics in Translation 14 (Clevedon: Multilingual Matters, 1999)

Corbett, John, 'Literary Language and Scottish Identity', Association for Scottish Literary Studies Conference, 13 May 2000, accessed at http://www.arts.gla.ac.uk/ScotLit/ASLS/NoFrames/JCorbett2.html

---

[30] See I. J. Parsley, 'Twa Ulster Scotses: Authentic versus Synthetic' in J. M. Kirk and D. P. Ó Baoill, eds., *Language Planning and Education: Linguistic Issues in Northern Ireland, the Republic of Ireland, and Scotland* (Belfast, 2002), pp. 183-185; G. Falconer, 'Commercial Scots Translation; A Northern Ireland Perspective' in *Doonsin' Emerauds: New Scrieves anent Scots an Gaelic/New Studies in Scots and Gaelic*, ed. J.D. McClure (Belfast, 2004), pp. 68-79 (pp. 72-73).

[31] See G. Falconer, 'Breaking Nature's Social Union: The Autonomy of Scots in Ulster' in this volume.

Erskine, John and Gordon Lucy, eds., *Cultural Traditions in Northern Ireland: Varieties of Scottishness, Exploring the Ulster-Scots Connection* (Belfast: Institute of Irish Studies, The Queen's University of Belfast, 1997)

Falconer, Gavin, 'Commercial Scots Translation; A Northern Ireland Perspective', in McClure, J. Derrick, ed., *Doonsin' Emerauds: New Scrieves anent Scots an Gaelic/New Studies in Scots and Gaelic*, Belfast Studies in Language, Culture and Politics 12 (Belfast: Cló Ollscoil na Banríona, 2004), pp. 68-79

Falconer, Gavin, 'Breaking Nature's Social Union: The Autonomy of Scots in Ulster', in the present volume

Fenton, James, *Thonner An Thon: An Ulster-Scots Collection* (Belfast: Ullans Press, 2000)

Fox, Denton, ed., *The Poems of Robert Henryson* (Oxford: Clarendon Press, 1981)

Görlach, Manfred, 'Ulster Scots: A Language?', in Kirk, John M. and Dónall P. Ó Baoill, eds., *Language and Politics: Northern Ireland, the Republic of Ireland, and Scotland*, Belfast Studies in Language, Culture and Politics 1 (Belfast: Cló Ollscoil na Banríona, 2000), pp. 13-32

Herbison, Ivan, *David Herbison, The Bard of Dunclug: a poet and his community, 1800-1880* (Ballymena: Dunclug Press, 1988)

Herbison, Ivan, ' "The Rest is Silence": Some Remarks on the Disappearance of Ulster-Scots Poetry', in *Cultural Traditions in Northern Ireland: Varieties of Scottishness, Exploring the Ulster-Scots Connection*, eds. John Erskine and Gordon Lucy (Belfast: Institute of Irish Studies, The Queen's University of Belfast, 1997), pp. 129-47

Herbison, Ivan, *Presbyterianism, Politics and Poetry in Nineteenth-Century Ulster: Aspects of an Ulster-Scots Literary Tradition* (Belfast: Institute of Irish Studies, The Queen's University of Belfast, 2000)

Hewitt, John, *Rhyming Weavers and other country poets of Antrim and Down*, introduced by Tom Paulin (1974; new ed. Belfast: Blackstaff Press, 2004)

Kinsley, James, ed., *The Poems of William Dunbar* (Oxford: Clarendon Press, 1979)

Kirk, John M. 'Archipelagic Glotto-Politics: the Scotstacht', in *The Celtic Englishes III*, ed. Hildegard L.C. Tristram (Heidelberg: Winter, 2003), pp. 339-356

Kirk, John M. and Dónall P. Ó Baoill, eds., *Language and Politics: Northern Ireland, the Republic of Ireland, and Scotland*, Belfast Studies in Language, Culture and Politics 1 (Belfast: Cló Ollscoil na Banríona, 2000)

Kirk, John M. and Dónall P. Ó Baoill, eds., *Language Planning and Education: Linguistic Issues in Northern Ireland, the Republic of Ireland, and Scotland*, Belfast Studies in Language, Culture and Politics 6 (Belfast: Cló Ollscoil na Banríona, 2002)

Macafee, Caroline I. and Colm Ó Baoill, 'Why Scots is not a Celtic English', in *The Celtic Englishes*, ed. Hildegard L.C. Tristram (Heidelberg: Winter, 1997), pp. 245-86

McClure, J. Derrick, ed., *Doonsin' Emerauds: New Scrieves anent Scots an Gaelic/New Studies in Scots and Gaelic*, Belfast Studies in Language, Culture and Politics 12 (Belfast: Cló Ollscoil na Banríona, 2004)

McIlvanney, Liam, *Burns the Radical: Poetry and Politics in Late Eighteenth-Century Scotland* (East Linton: Tuckwell Press, 2002)

Montgomery, Michael, 'The Anglicisation of Scots in Early Seventeenth-Century Ulster', *Studies in Scottish Literature*, 26 (1992), pp. 50-64

Montgomery, Michael, and Anne Smyth, eds., *A Blad o Ulstèr-Scotch frae 'Ullans':
Ulster-Scots culture, language and literature* (Belfast: Ullans Press, 2003)

Noble, Andrew, and Patrick Scott Hogg, eds., *The Canongate Burns: The Complete
Poems and Songs of Robert Burns* (Edinburgh: Canongate, 2001)

Parsley, Ian J., 'Twa Ulster Scotses: Authentic versus Synthetic', in Kirk, John M.
and Dónall P. Ó Baoill, eds., *Language Planning and Education: Linguistic Issues
in Northern Ireland, the Republic of Ireland, and Scotland*, Belfast Studies in
Language, Culture and Politics 6 (Belfast: Cló Ollscoil na Banríona, 2002), pp.
183-85

Robinson, Mairi. ed., *Concise Scots Dictionary* (1985; Edinburgh: Polygon, 1999)

Robinson, Philip, ed. and intro., *The Country Rhymes of James Orr, The Bard of
Ballycarry 1770-1816* (Bangor: Pretani Press, 1992)

Robinson, Philip, 'William Starrat of Strabane: The First Ulster-Scots Poet', *Ullans*,
5 (1997), 30-39

Robinson, Philip, *Wake the Tribe o Dan* (Belfast: Ullans Press, 1998)

Robinson, Philip, *The Back Streets of the Claw* (Belfast: Ullans Press, 2000)

Scott, Ernest McA. and Philip Robinson, ed. and intro., *The Country Rhymes of
Samuel Thomson, The Bard of Carngranny 1766-1818* (Bangor: Pretani Press,
1992)

Swanton, Michael J. ed., *The Dream of the Rood* (Manchester: Manchester University
Press, 1970)

Tristram, Hildegard L.C. ed., *The Celtic Englishes*, Anglistische Forschungen 247
(Heidelberg: Winter, 1997)

Tristram, Hildegard L.C. ed., *The Celtic Englishes III*, Anglistische Forschungen 324
(Heidelberg: Winter, 2003)

Maclean and Modernism: "Remembered Harmonies"

Christopher Whyte

[1]

The relationship of Gaelic poet Sorley MacLean (Somhairle MacGill-Eain) (1911-1996) to literary Modernism is a question both of context and perspective, of the setting in which we view his work and the particular interpretive tools which we bring to it. It is therefore relevant to pause for a moment and reflect on more general peculiarities concerning the reception and criticism of MacLean's poetry. It may sound like a truism to say that poetry is generally approached, by a majority of its readers, in the language in which it was originally written, and that the language in which it will be discussed, both when talking and when writing, will be the language of the text itself. Yet this is no truism where MacLean is concerned. If his poetry undoubtedly enjoys a wide audience beyond the specific community of those who speak and read Scottish Gaelic, this has largely been due to the availability of translations into English which are overwhelmingly (one further peculiarity) the work of the poet himself. Though the poetry is written in Gaelic, only a small proportion of the now considerable critical literature on MacLean is not in English. In what relation does this place us to him? Are we "foreign" readers of MacLean, as we might consider ourselves to be when discussing a French, German or Italian author? This description, though, fails to match, because each of these would be assumed already to possess a sizeable readership in their own language, as well as disposing of a body of criticism in that language likely to outweigh anything that might be done in English.

The anomaly deserves attention because it can produce a further, and more dangerous anomaly, namely that, when dealing with MacLean's work, it is not universally clear what is in fact being discussed, the Gaelic originals, or the poet's own translations of these into English. A sizeable volume of critical essays, published in 1986 and edited by Raymond Ross and Joy Hendry, marked a watershed in substantive criticism of MacLean's poetry.[1] In a note at the start of the volume, five of its sixteen contributors are described as 'a native speaker of Gaelic'. No attempt is made to clarify the competence in the language of the remaining eleven, though throughout the volume, quotations from MacLean's work are printed in the same format, with Gaelic and English side by side. The danger of a slippage here, of reaching a point where it does not really matter what one's views are based on, MacLean's English translations or the Gaelic poems he in fact wrote, is evident, and clearly must be avoided at all costs. The point is not that valid conclusions cannot be drawn from a study based exclusively on the English versions.[2] This is, however, not the same as an examination of the Gaelic originals. To elide the boundary between

---

[1] Raymond Ross and Joy Hendry eds. *Sorley MacLean: Critical Essays* (Edinburgh, Scottish Academic Press 1986).

[2] MacLean himself has declared that 'Gaelic poetry that is published with English translations cannot be assessed on its translation alone even by the most honest and perceptive of critics who do not know Gaelic.' See William Gillies ed. *Ris a' Bhruthaich: the Criticism and Prose Writings of Sorley MacLean* (Acair, Stornoway 1985) p.14.

the two can be in no-one's interest.

These preliminary considerations are also relevant to the question which prompted this essay, namely the extent to which it is useful to look on MacLean as a Modernist poet. Modernism is a term whose relevance to English language literature and within the English language critical tradition cannot really be matched if one turns to French, or Italian, or Russian literature. And conversely, terms such as Decadent, Symbolist, Futurist, Neoclassical have only been marginally deployed where English-language literature of the period from 1850 to 1930 is concerned. They retain a foreign ring and require careful definition if they are to be imported into discussion of such texts. In casting MacLean as a Modernist do we run the risk, not just of occluding the actual language of his poetry, but also of viewing him through a distorting prism drawn from a different, if related, literary culture?

For present purposes, I will argue that the term Modernism is useful because it draws our attention to a range of features common to literary texts published in English, though not always in the British Isles, during the decade which followed the end of the First World War.[3] It would be foolish to assume that all texts published at this time in English, or in languages other than English, whether these are spoken in the British Isles or not, will exhibit the same characteristics. The work of Paul Valéry (1871-1945), for example, represents a reaction against the perceived excesses of the Romantics and the *poètes maudits* who had preceded him. He prefers traditional metrical patterns, and his work exhibits its own brand of Neoclassicism, one which has a specific contemporaneity in the context of the 1920s. The Prague-born, German language poet Rainer Maria Rilke (1875-1926), an enthusiastic translator of Valéry, shows a clear continuity with German Romanticism in his tendency to idealise a classical Greek past (a trait the two poets shared) and in the central role ascribed to the figure of Orpheus. His use of the hexameter, while linking him to Goethe and Hölderlin, is also symptomatic of a rather different brand of Neoclassicism.

On what basis could we assume that the characteristics of Modernism will be any more relevant to MacLean's work than to that of these two continental European poets? If it cannot be reduced to a mere choice of language, to a reified Gaelic otherness, what do we expect the substance of MacLean's difference to consist in? Given that the main body of his poetry dates from the years 1939 and 1940, in wishing to relate him to Modernism, is there a danger of our making unthinking assumptions, according to which writers in a peripheralised and colonised cultural milieu such as that of Scottish Gaelic will 'naturally' lag behind the centre by a decade or two, reproducing its templates in a watered down, localised form?

[2]

Like so many others, the question about MacLean and Modernism is useful not so much for the answers it leads to as for the additional questions it raises, first and foremost about the appropriate context or contexts within which to read MacLean's poetry.

---

[3] A useful bibliography can be found on pp. 213-219 of Peter Childs *Modernism* (London & New York: Routledge, 2000). For the Scottish situation, Margery Palmer McCulloch, ed., *Modernism and Nationalism: Literature and Society in Scotland 1918-1939: Source Documents for the Scottish Renaissance* (Glasgow: Association for Scottish Literary Studies, 2004) is particularly helpful.

At this point, it will be helpful to outline as specifically as possible what the characteristics of literary Modernism might be. Like any such 'identikit', this one will be partial, fallible, needy of completion and open to discussion, and will undoubtedly reflect some idiosyncracies of its deviser. I should perhaps add that I see Modernism, in the English language context, as strongly conditioned by the horrors of the First World War, the struggle to digest and come to terms with that carnage, and by the beginning of the end of the British Empire.

In the aftermath of those four traumatic years, Victorian and Edwardian culture inevitably became stigmatised because of what they had made possible, the conflict they had preceded. This meant that any tranquil continuity with previous literary artefacts was out of the question. Modernist writing is characterised by breakage. The diction and the forms of poetry deployed by the preceding generation were now out of bounds. Such inaccessibility could even provoke a sense of nostalgia when looking back, of something lost and never to be recovered. This is a point I will return to.

If there was no longer general agreement about how poetry should be written, neither was it possible for writer and reader to count on a shared body of reading and understanding, a cultural humus to which both could refer, and which could be used for effective communication, even just at the level of passing allusions. The canon was redefined. The point of the enormous, overwhelming and at times wearying display of erudition in the texts of Eliot, Joyce and Pound is not that readers should feel guilty at being unable to match it, but rather that there is no way they could possibly be expected to have read all of these books. A gap opened up between the writer and his audience, with elitism, aggressive highbrowism and a sense of talking down as its consequences. Readers had to work extraordinarily hard to understand these texts, and writers refused to compromise, taking no prisoners. This is a literature which, while conscious of its greatness, stubbornly refuses to be popular. At the same time, redefinition of the canon allowed an injection of new energy from an impressive range of sources, not just Verlaine and Wagner, but the Provençal troubadour poets, the *dolcestilnovisti* and Dante himself.

The gap opening up between writers and their public was a symptom of cultural collapse. The old currency no longer had value. Previous forms and modes of writing were discarded and stowed away, not unlike old banknotes in a country where several zeros have been lopped off at the end. One might retain a sneaking, lingering attachment to them, but there is little likelihood of their being of use in the future. Against this background, writers reverted to earlier myths, to what could be seen as "founding" narratives of western culture, so as to provide large scale structures for their work and to reinject meaning where meaning had been lost. Such loss of confidence cannot be restricted to the British Isles or to the period immediately following the First World War. A return to founding myths lies at the core of Wagner's Ring tetralogy, and goes some way towards explaining the fascination Wagner exerted on both Eliot and Thomas Mann.

The troubadours and the Italian poets of the late thirteenth century could be seen as standing at the "beginning" of the western lyric. Joyce's *Ulysses* uses Homeric epic to underpin its construction, offering its own particular brand of Neoclassicism. There is no need to underline the risks this approach brought with it, in terms of obscurity and pedantry, as well as the difficulty, seen from our contemporary perspective, of coming up with any valid 'beginning', from which a 'new start' might be possible.

Modernist writers tended not to come from the old charmed circle of the cultivated classes of the Empire. Eliot, Pound, Joyce, Woolf, MacDiarmid and even Lawrence were each in their own way outsiders, thanks to gender, class or geographical origin. The tendency, too, at least in the immediate postwar period, was for these writers to avoid explicit political affiliation, even though the attraction of totalitarian, authoritarian ideologies (situated both to right and left of centre) proved harder and harder to shake off, especially in the wake of the 1929 Wall Street crash.

Where technique is concerned, Modernist writing frequently deploys a hugely inflated subjectivitity in the interests of achieving greater objectivity. This formulation reflects the paradoxical nature of the approach adopted. The self became identified with discourse, with self-talk, with the 'stream of consciousness', as if its essence lay in a constant recounting to oneself of perceptions and sensations. Thus the self could be lodged in linear time in a fashion peculiarly suitable for rendering in verbal texts, thanks to the link established between existence and discourse. The placing of a self so conceived at the centre of the world was inherently unstable and problematic.

[3]

It would be feasible, and arguably helpful, to take each of the above characteristics singly and examine its usefulness to our understanding of the work of Sorley MacLean.

A break with tradition is undeniable, in so far as MacLean's work marks the point at which Gaelic poetry (in its most prestigious manifestations, rather than in the undervalued work of the 'village poets' now in course of reassessment[4]) leaves music definitely behind, ceases to be lyric in the strict sense of the word, and demands to be read rather than sung. The poet's brother John, incidentally a Gaelic translator of Homer, on seeing Sorley's poems in April 1942 'roundly denied they were Gaelic poetry at all' and proposed 'a series of utterly idiotic academic would-be emendations.' The words are Douglas Young's.[5] His epithet 'academic' suggests John's wish to pull MacLean's work back towards a previously obtaining and now, in Young's view, obsolescent poetics with which it clamorously breaks.

In the English class at Edinburgh University MacLean had Herbert Grierson as his teacher. Though he himself was not 'half as pro-Donne as his undergraduate admirers', MacLean studied in an environment where 'it would have been blatant heresy to suggest that Milton was as great a poet as Donne or Yeats as great a poet as Eliot.'[6] The redefinition of the English canon brought about by Eliot had already become orthodoxy. Poem XIII in the Eimhir sequence suggests that, if not his access to, then at least MacLean's perceptions of the work of the troubadours were strongly influenced by Pound's free versions from the Provençal originals.[7] The case of the

---

[4] One of the merits of *An Tuil: Anthology of 20th Century Scottish Gaelic Verse* ed. Ronald I. M. Black (Edinburgh, Polygon 1999) is that it offers integrated coverage of both strands during the modern period.

[5] Letter to MacLean dated April 2nd 1943. See National Library of Scotland Acc. 11572/6.

[6] See *Ris a' Bhruthaich* pp. 10-11.

[7] See Christopher Whyte 'A note on *Dàin do Eimhir* XIII' in *Scottish Gaelic Studies* XVII *Fèill-Sgrìbhinn do Ruaraidh MacThòmais* (1996) pp. 383-392 and the notes in Somhairle MacGill-Eain/ Sorley MacLean *Dàin do Eimhir* ed. Christopher Whyte (Glasgow, Association for

Russian symbolist poet Alexander Blok (1880-1921) is still more striking. Here MacLean's knowledge was almost certainly derived from MacDiarmid, who included two of Blok's lyrics, in Scots versions, in his long poem *A Drunk Man Looks at the Thistle*.[8] In other words, MacLean's relationship to European Symbolist and Decadent poetry was mediated by his Modernist forebears, a fact that links him to Modernism while at the same time distancing him from it.

Redefinition of the canon, then, was a *fait accompli* by the time MacLean reached maturity as a poet. This change was the work of the preceding generation yet one he espoused with undisguised enthusiasm. By championing Gaelic lyricist William Ross (Uilleam Ros) (1762-1791), whose iconic presence in MacLean's love sequence, both as model and as *alter ego*, leaves no room for either Alexander Macdonald (Alasdair Mac Mhaighstir Alasdair) (c.1695-c.1770) or Duncan Bàn MacIntyre (Donnchadh Bàn Mac an t-Saoir) (1724-1812), MacLean was enacting, within the Gaelic tradition, the kind of reversal or revaluation Eliot had already achieved within the English one.[9]

His choice of Eimhir as a code name for two different women does indeed hark back to the Ulster Cycle in early Irish literature, where Eimhir is the wife of the hero Cuchulainn.[10] Poem XIII in the sequence compares the beloved to Deirdre, the tragic heroine of that cycle and, though the poem's treatment is heavily indebted to Pound's version of the Provençal poet Bertran de Born (1150-c.1215), it offers a roll call of celebrated lovers from Scottish and Irish tradition. Whether these tales are exploited as 'founding' narratives, however, is a different question. One would be hard put to it to see MacLean's other major achievement of 1939 and 1940, the long poem 'An Cuilithionn' ('The Cuillin') as having recourse to earlier mythic or 'founding' texts.[11]

The self presented in the love sequence tends to the traditional in its unquestioning, unproblematic nature. An indication of this traditional approach is the fact that cleavage, disunity, self-division is consistently presented as lamentable, undesirable, 'unnatural'.[12] Whatever one may think about the actual relationship between the material of the love sequence and MacLean's biography, it is a tactic of many poems to present themselves as immediate, spontaneous annotations made under the effect of events possessing an almost documentary authenticity. The development of the speaker's love affair goes hand in hand with the slide towards total war on the European continent. Whether the seeming lack of artifice is an indication of a higher kind of artifice or not is a point meriting extended discussion.

Scottish Literary Studies 2002) pp. 186ff. This is the edition from which poems in the sequence are quoted.

[8] See Hugh MacDiarmid *A Drunk Man Looks at the Thistle*, an annotated edition by Kenneth Buthlay (Edinburgh: Scottish Academic Press, 1987), pp. 16-21 (lines 169-220) and 22-23 (lines 241-252).

[9] Entries plus bibliographical indications concerning all three poets can be found in Derick Thomson ed. *The Companion to Gaelic Scotland* (Oxford, Blackwell 1983).

[10] For more information about Eimhir see *Dàin do Eimhir* p.154.

[11] 'An Cuilithionn' forms the second section of Somhairle MacGill-Eain/ Sorley MacLean *O Choille gu Bearradh: Dàin Chruinnichte/ From Wood to Ridge: Collected Poems* (Manchester and Edinburgh, Carcanet and Birlinn 1999). The collected edition first appeared in 1989. The relationship between the 1989 'An Cuilithionn' and the earlier 1939 version is discussed later in this essay.

[12] See, among others, poems XVIII and XXII.

The contemporary references are accompanied by a bewitchingly old-fashioned quality, as if Petrarch or Ronsard or even the Yeats of the Maud Gonne love poems could be revived against the background of autumn 1939 and the following winter.[13] Rather than talking of pastiche, it could be helpful to posit a specific brand of Neoclassicism on MacLean's part here, a renewed simplicity which has the attraction of seeming ancient and modern at one and the same time.

The issue about outsiders coming to occupy central positions in the production of English language literature is hardly relevant to MacLean, whose choice of language assured for him, until the 1980s and beyond, a position of excentricity which even the observable slippage between his Gaelic originals and his own English versions, mentioned above, has not succeeded in dissolving. Where political affiliation is concerned, comparing MacLean with the Modernists is a complex undertaking indeed. 'An Cuilithionn' reads in sections like a tract for international socialism. Urging MacLean to write something which might 'compel the attention of the Gaels', Young was uncertain whether 'the Communist Manifesto would come home to their business' but felt that perhaps 'the Coolin will, given the chance.'[14] A major element in the love sequence is the conflict between passion and political commitment. If by its close the latter has unequivocally yielded to the former, even in circumstances where any appeasement of that passion through the formation of a relationship, sexual or otherwise, has become impossible, one could nonetheless argue that the compelling, almost compulsory quality of this predicament sets MacLean at a considerable distance from his Modernist predecessors. That sense of external events forcing upon each individual the necessity of adopting a stance, while willed detachment itself amounts to a political choice, definitely belongs to the later 1930s.

[4]

Each of these aspects could provide material for an essay of its own, where MacLean's relationship to Modernism could be plotted with some precision, but probably leading to equivocal conclusions. In the interests of narrowing the focus of discussion, and also of introducing close examination of his texts, I would like to turn to a specific characteristic of literary Modernism which has not yet been listed, and in doing so to introduce the barrel organ.

Strictly speaking, the term to use would be 'street piano', as barrel organs, at least in the British Isles, were conceived for use in church services. Mechanical means allowed these instruments to dispense with a player, indeed, with any human intervention beyond the turning of a crank. They could accurately reproduce popular tunes as well as hymns. The accuracy nonetheless brought with it a degree of distortion, precisely because of the mechanical nature of the execution. This is where

---

[13] MacLean told Douglas Young, in a letter dated September 11th 1941, that 'I did not read Yeats at the university at all and only read him in bulk about 1936, and it is only in the last two years that his poetry has become one of my obsessions. I now read and re-read him.' The relationship between MacLean and Yeats awaits adequate critical investigation. A preliminary treatment can be found in *Dàin do Eimhir* pp. 27-29. MacLean's letters to Young, our most valuable source for information about the poet in the years from 1940 to 1943, are deposited in the National Library of Scotland Acc.6419 Box 38b.

[14] Letter dated June 17th 1943.

the notion of 'remembered harmonies' is helpful, of hearing a melody one already knows but which has somehow lost its original purity and spontaneity. One is reminded of the anecdote concerning Giuseppe Verdi, said to have paid all the owners of barrel organs within earshot to lay off work because he was so irritated by hearing their contraptions mangle his own melodies.

Jules Laforgue (1860-1887), whose experiments with free verse offered such a useful stimulus to Eliot, wrote not one but two poems about barrel organs. For him these were 'Barbary' organs ('orgue de Barbarie'), suggesting a link not just to the north African coast but also to 'barbarian' practice, as if cultural difference could explain the mangled music of these 'complaintes'. In the first he addresses the instrument as a poor old nag in pain ('ma pauvre rosse endolorie'), and as a 'scie', which could mean anything from a saw to a nuisance to the catch-phrase of a comic song. The second poem continues the horse metaphor ('orgue au galop') and introduces declassed liturgical language such as weeping candles ('larmes de cierges') and a price-list of alleluias ('tarifs d'alléluias').[15]

The Italian Decadent poet (the accepted term is 'crepuscolare' or 'twilight') Sergio Corazzini (1885-1907) is more explicit, and more comprehensible, in his 'Per organo di Barberia':

> Elemosina triste
> di vecchie arie sperdute,
> vanità di un'offerta
> che nessuno raccoglie!
> [...]
> Sfogli la tua tristezza
> monotona davanti
> alla piccola casa
> provinciale che dorme;

('Sad charity/ of old airs gone astray,/ uselessness of an offer/ no-one takes up! [...] Shedding your monotonous/ sadness in front of/ the little house/ sleeping in the provinces').[16] In this quotation, the melodies have wandered far from their original source. Nobody pays any attention to the barrel organ's offering, which is impregnated with an unchanging sadness.

Corazzini lived barely past his twentieth, and Laforgue did not see his thirtieth year, both falling victim to tuberculosis. An atmosphere of doom hangs over them, and not just retrospectively. MacLean was barely thirty when he departed for active service in North Africa, and there is reason to believe that he saw himself as similarly doomed. As published in 1943, when it appeared as one of the 'Dàin eile' or 'Other songs', poem VI in the Eimhir sequence begins 'A dh'aindeoin ùpraid marbhaidh/ anns a' Ghearmailt no san Fhraing' ('In spite of the uproar of killing/ in Germany or in France'). The passage had originally read 'Gus an tèid mo mharbhadh/ anns a' Ghearmailt no san Fhraing' ('Until I am killed/ in Germany or in France').[17] He

[15] See *Poems of Jules Laforgue* translated and introduced by Peter Dale (London, Anvil Press 1986) pp. 56 and 86. Translations here are my own.

[16] Sergio Corazzini *Poesie edite e inedite* a cura di Stefano Jacomuzzi (Torino, Einaudi 1968) p.129. My translation.

[17] Manuscript reading conserved in Aberdeen University Library Special Collections MS 2864.

clearly thought the odds were against him ever returning home alive. What made possible the revolution the Modernists brought about in English language poetry was their reading of the French Decadent and Symbolist poets. Both Eliot and Pound would come to realise that, while Queen Victoria reigned, the future of European poetry was being decided not in London, but in Paris. Joyce had read Flaubert. Virginia Woolf was familiar with the work of Proust. After mentioning the 'completely magical breath-taking poetry' of MacDiarmid's early lyrics (and the transition may not be accidental), MacLean told Douglas Young that 'I liked Verlaine very much but I fancy that in one or two places Baudelaire has influenced me stylistically, the "sous la griffe effroyable de Dieu" manner'.[18] The quotation is not quite accurate, and comes from the close of 'Les petites vieilles', poem XCI in *Les Fleurs du Mal*, where the speaker asks 'Où serez-vous demain, Èves octogenaires,/ sur qui pèse la griffe effroyable de Dieu?'[19] Despite the gulf separating MacLean, with his Free Presbyterian upbringing, and the French poet's post Catholic angst, he can sympathise with what may be termed a sense of existential emergency pervading Baudelaire's work. Like Eliot or Pound, MacLean had made himself familiar, in this case without obvious mediation, with the literature which, more than any other, heralded the transition towards modernity in the second half of the nineteenth century, namely French literature.

The grim revisiting of the *carpe diem* topic at the close of poem XIX in the Eimhir sequence is an anachronism in one very precise sense. The news that the poem's dedicatee is to be married in Ireland precludes any prospect of her giving herself to the speaker, therefore rendering the reasoning behind the topic ('we are all going to die, so why not enjoy all the pleasure that comes your way') pointless. The range of echoes here goes from Horace not just to Shakespeare's Sonnets (18, 18 and 107 are all relevant) and Marvell but on to the Baudelaire of 'La Charogne', poem XXIX in *Les Fleurs du Mal*.[20] That combination indicates how evocation of the past goes hand in hand with a recognition of its unavailability. If the topic is still sustainable, and credible, in Marvell's poem, the male addressee of Shakespeare's sequence problematises traditional roles.[21]

'Craobh nan Teud' ('The Tree of Strings'), an extended poem written in late 1939 or early 1940 and dedicated to George Campbell Hay, published in 1943 and included, in a shortened version, in MacLean's 1989 collected volume,[22] contains two references to Baudelaire. Beneath the shadow of the tree of the title, the 'little old decrepit prostitutes' seen by 'Baudelaire in his loneliness' walk 'luminously' down the Paris streets ('a' coiseachd sràidean Pharais gu lòghmhor/ na seann siùrsaichean beaga breòite/ a chunnaic Baudelaire 'na ònrachd.') The city prostitute is of course a crucial figure in the imagery of European Decadentism, often brought into perilous

---

My essay on the Aberdeen manuscripts is to appear as 'Sorley MacLean's *Dàin do Eimhir*: New Light from the Aberdeen Holdings' in the proceedings of the second Rannsachadh na Gàidhlig conference, held in Glasgow in 2002.

[18] See the 'Autobiographical Sketch' quoted in *Dàin do Eimhir* p.148.

[19] See *Dàin do Eimhir* p.217.

[20] For a more detailed account of these references see the annotations in *Dàin do Eimhir* pp. 212ff.

[21] In 'Craobh nan Teud' MacLean speaks of Shakespeare as 'struggling in the strife of his nature' ('geur an gleac a nàduir') (*O Choille gu Bearradh/ From Wood to Ridge* pp. 54-55).

[22] See *O Choille gu Bearradh/ From Wood to Ridge* pp. 48-57.

proximity with the beloved. Blok's poem 'Neznakomka' ('The Stranger'), one of the two translated into Scots by MacDiarmid and mentioned above, is supposed to have been inspired by the vision of a prostitute in a sordid station restaurant. In four quatrains published in 1946 but never subsequently reprinted, which undoubtedly concern the addressee of a majority of the Eimhir poems, MacLean's vituperation more or less conflates the two figures:

'N dèidh t' adhaltranais 's do ghille-mirein
a shaobh thu le airgead blàth
's ann a chuireadh do bhriag ealamh
cleòc air salchar do chàs.[23]

('After your adultery and Nancy-boy/ who misled you with his warm money,/ your ready lie would put/ a cloak over the sordidness of your vicissitudes.') The second mention of Baudelaire in 'Craobh nan Teud' interestingly pairs him with William Ross ('Ros is Baudelaire an cràdhlot', 'Ross and Baudelaire in misery'), as if the Gaelic lyricist could be promoted to the company of the Decadents and even given an urban setting. Ross is said to have died of tuberculosis, and to have been betrayed by the woman who gave him her troth, bringing her into line with the corrupted heroines of both Baudelaire and MacLean.[24]

[5]

The 'barrel organ' effect outlined earlier typifies passages in Eliot's *The Waste Land* like the one beginning 'The chair she sat in, like a burnished throne'.[25] One has the impression that, were one only to rub one's eyes, or tune the receiver more precisely into the correct frequency, then one could indeed be listening to Shakespeare. But it is never quite possible to locate him, to get 'back to the original'. MacLean, as we shall see, does very much the same with fragments from Gaelic tradition.

The version of 'An Cuilithionn' published in his 1989 collected volume is effectively an abridgement of the original, 1939 draft, which can be consulted in manuscript in Aberdeen University Library and in typescript, in a fluctuating textual condition, in the National Library of Scotland.[26] The 1939 version is one third as long again as that eventually published. I argue elsewhere that the most fruitful critical approach, at least in the immediate future, may well be to look on the two as separate,

---

[23] See 'Do Bhoirionnach Briagach Coirbte' (with English translation) in *Poetry Scotland* 3 (Glasgow, William Maclellan 1946) pp. 32-33.

[24] Traditions concerning Ross are resumed in the 'Short Memoir of the Life of William Ross' in George Calder ed. *Gaelic Songs by William Ross* (Edinburgh and London, Oliver and Boyd 1937) pp. xix-xxix.

[25] The opening lines of Part II 'A Game of Chess'. See T.S. Eliot, *Selected Poems* (London: Faber & Faber, 2002), p. 44.

[26] A manuscript version offering the earliest surviving version of the poem can be found in Aberdeen MS 2864. Gaelic typescripts, with annotations from MacLean's and other hands, which represent a later version or versions are in the National Library of Scotland Ms 29558. Ms 29559 in the same library contains a typed version of MacLean's English translation of the poem.

distinct poems, each possessed of its own distinctive logic and consistency, each eloquent of a stage in the poet's development and his changing view of his own work.[27]

In both versions, the poem consists of seven parts or 'earrainn', in the third of which the bourgeoisie and their bailiffs, the landlords and their slaves geld the heroic stallion identified with a cliff in Vaternish on the island of Skye. A footnote to the English version of 'An Cuilithionn' which MacLean produced for private circulation in the early 1940s tells us that the following passage, absent from the published text, parodies the chorus of a well known Gaelic song, 'They put out poor Pilot's eye', Pilot being the name of a dog:

> Thug iad a bhrìgh bhon ainmhidh bhochd,
> thug iad a bhrìgh bhon ainmhidh;
> thug iad a bhrìgh bhon ainmhidh bhochd,
> 's bha fhios air an lochd a rinn iad.

('They have taken his virtue from the poor beast,/ they have taken his virtue from the poor beast,/ they have taken his virtue from the poor beast,/ and they knew the evil they did.')[28] Here the text being echoed mirrors the degrading, humiliating effect of the treatment to which the stallion has been subjected. The issue is, not the loss of an eye, but castration, and the victim not a pet but a figure whose symbolic status within the poem as a whole is really only overshadowed by that of the mountains from which it gets its title.

Twelve lines further on, in the 1939 version, MacLean echoes a very different text. Iain Lom, or John MacDonald of Keppoch (c.1625-post 1707), celebrates in the song 'Là Inbhir Lochaidh' the Royalist victory at the Battle of Inverlochy, fought on Sunday February 2nd 1645. The poet was a descendant of the first Lords of the Isles, a supporter of Charles I and later an inveterate enemy of the Protestant succession. In this, one of his earliest dated works, he takes a very personal delight in the defeat of the Campbells at the hands of Clan Donald. The first three stanzas are as follows:

> 'N cuala sibhse 'n tionndadh duineil
> thug an camp bha 'n Cille Chuimein?
> 'S fada chaidh ainm air an iomairt,
> thug iad as an naimhdean iomain.
> Dhìrich mi moch madainn Dòmhnaich
> gu bràigh caisteil Inbhir Lochaidh;
> chunnaic mi 'n t-arm dol an òrdugh,
> 's bha buaidh a' bhlàir le Clann Dòmhnaill.

---

[27] See my essays 'Sorley MacLean's "An Cuilithionn": a critical assessment' in *Studies in Scottish Literature* XXXIV (forthcoming) and 'Sorley MacLean's "An Cuilithionn": the emergence of the text', to appear in the proceedings of the third Rannsachadh na Gàidhlig conference, held in Edinburgh in 2004.

[28] See National Library of Scotland Mss 29558 (f79) and 29559 (f16). Dr John McInnes kindly informs me that 'Thug iad an t-sùil o Pilot bochd' was composed by John MacDougall, whose father Duncan MacDougall was the first Baptist minister on the island of Tiree and himself the author of a number of Gaelic hymns.

Dìreadh a mach glùn Chùil Eachaidh,
dh'aithnich mi oirbh sùrd bhur tapaidh;
ged bha mo dhùthaich 'na lasair,
's èirig air a' chùis mar thachair.

('Have you heard of the heroic countermarch made by the army that was at Kilcumin? Far has gone the fame of their play - they drove their enemies before them.// Early on Sunday morning I climbed the brae above the castle of Inverlochy. I saw the army arraying for battle, and victory on the field was with Clan Donald.// When you were ascending the spur of Culachy I perceived in you the enthusiasm your bravery inspired; although my country was in flames what has happened is compensation.')[29] MacLean omitted the first of his four stanzas in the printed version, possibly because its opening is duplicated in the fourth:

An cuala sibhse 'n obair dhuineil
a rinn na bùirdeasaich dhuinne?
'S fada chaidh ainm air an iomairt;
thug iad bhon ainmhidh a bhunait.

Dhìrich mi moch madainn Dòmhnaich
gu mullaichean nam baideal ceòthar:
chunnaic mi na Bùirdeasaich an òrdugh,
Dòmhnallaich gun bhuaidh, is Leòdaich.

Dìreadh a mach glùn Choir-Each
dh'aithnich mi bhur sùrd 's bhur dreach:
ged bha mo dhùthaich 'na fàsaich,
cha b' èirig air a' chùis an tràth ud.

An cuala sibh an sgeul salach
mar rinneadh air an Aigeach Dhalach?
Beag siod dhen gnìomharan trùillich,
obair uachdaran 's am fùidsean.

('Have you heard of the manly work/ done for us by the bourgeoisie?/ Far went the name of their exercise:/ they took from the animal his substance.// I went up one Sunday morning/ to the summits of the misty pinnacles,/ I saw the bourgeois in battle-order,/ MacDonalds without victory, and MacLeods.// Going up the spur of Coir-each,/ I knew your mood and your aspect:/ though my country was a desert,/ that hour was no reparation.// Have you heard the filthy tale/ of what was done to the Glendale Stallion?/ That's little of their base deeds,/ work of landlords and their coward slaves.')[30] Iain Lom's song had celebrated, with a bloodthirsty glee that is at times disturbing, a significant victory won by his clan at a time when Gaelic-speaking Scotland was still capable of offering military resistance to those perceived as its enemies on the British front, and to their allies. MacLean's poem focuses on the disastrous effects of the clearance of the Gaelic peasantry from their ancestral lands

---

[29] See Annie M. Mackenzie ed. *Òrain Iain Luim: Songs of John MacDonald Bard of Keppoch* (Edinburgh 1964, Scottish Academic Press for the Scottish Gaelic Texts Society) pp. 20-21.

in the eighteenth and above all the nineteenth centuries, at the hands or with the connivance of their chiefs. In the world of the poem, his is a solitary voice without an audience among his own people. The landscape through which he moves is deserted, populated in his imagination only by the grotesque perpetrators of this betrayal. Given such a background, the precise echoing of Iain Lom's song has the effect of a bitter denunciation of the present, irreversible state of things. Though he sometimes goes no further than substituting one single word, MacLean's recasting of the original is devastating. The mention of Clan Donald at the end of the second stanza, now the enemies rather than the champions of their people, and the rewording of the last line of the third, where the notion of 'compensation' is retained but turned on its head, are especially telling. His first stanza establishes a link with the earlier quotation of the Pilot song through the bathos of its concluding line, the English 'his substance' being a euphemistic rendering of what the Gaelic original clearly indicates.

Part VI of 'An Cuilithionn' opens with a monologue from the Gesto girl, a half mythical figure said to have been kidnapped, along with nearly one hundred others, and shipped to the New World on 'Long nan Daoine', the Slave Ship,[31] from where she is thought of as looking back to her beloved homeland. After 40 lines (of which four are eliminated in the 1989 version) there is a striking change of rhythm which heralds a further redeployment by MacLean of an earlier text. The poignant effect of loss, presence and distortion which I have summed up in the image of the barrel organ is powerfully moving:

> agus chan fhaic mi an Cuilithionn cràcach
> ag èirigh thar Minginis mo shàth-ghaoil.

> Mo shàth-ghal goirt
> mar a tha mi 'nochd
> is dàl nam bochd ri m' ùidh.

> Cha bhàs nan triath
> a chràidh mi riamh,
> ach càs is dìol luchd rùin.

('... and I may not see the horned Cuillin/ rising above Minginish of my full love.// My sore fullness of grief/ how I am tonight/ and the dispensation of the poor in my mind./ It is not the death of chiefs/ that ever pained me/ but the hard lot of those I loved.')[32] The song echoed here is by a woman who stands at the fountainhead of Scottish Gaelic vernacular verse, Màiri Nighean Alasdair Ruaidh (Mary MacLeod) (c.1615-c.1707). Born into an aristocratic family in Rodel, Harris, she was associated with the house of MacLeod of Dunvegan, though tradition connects her more strongly with Berneray, Harris, where the croft given to her by the chief is still pointed out. Her 'Cumha do Shir Tormod Mac Leoid' ('Lament for Sir Norman MacLeod') opens as follows:

---

[30] The first stanza is quoted from NLS Ms29558 f79, and its translation from Ms 29559 f16. For the other three see *O Choille gu Bearradh/ From Wood to Ridge* pp. 88-89.

[31] For more information see two articles by Norrie Maclennan in the *West Highland Free Press* dated 12th and 19th May 1989 as well as *Dàin do Eimhir* pp. 168-169.

[32] See *O Choille gu Bearradh/ From Wood to Ridge* pp. 106-107.

Mo chràdhghal bochd
mar a thà mi nochd
is mi gun tàmh gun fhois gun sunnd.

('Sad and heart-sore my weeping, for I find myself tonight without rest, without peace, without cheer'). This is the standard text. The version printed in 1911 in *The MacDonald Collection of Gaelic Poetry*, recorded by Francis Tolmie in Ebost, Skye, in 1861, has a first line identical to MacLean's: 'Mo shàthghal goirt'.[33] Here, as in the previous instance, material is transferred from a heroic to an unheroic world, to the expulsion and cultural collapse which was the bitter experience of the Gesto girl and of many of her generation. The exploitation of earlier material offers a context for what later befell the wider community of those who spoke Scottish Gaelic. The older world has vanished and can only now be evoked in a distorted and weakened form.

Heard at this point, as 'An Cuilithionn' draws to its close, the metre of Màiri Nighean Alasdair Ruaidh's song has a powerfully anachronistic ring, all the more poignant because it belongs to an irretrievable past. MacLean offers an extraordinarily subtle phonetic foreshadowing, as 'shàth-ghaoil' ('full love') gives place to 'shàth-ghal' ('fullness of grief'). A phrase like 'bàs nan triath' ('the death of chiefs') is part of the earlier poet's repertory, not of his, so that the effect is at one and the same time tenderly nostalgic and a denunciation of the changes that have taken place. Those very chiefs whose death provoked a lament from their leading poets are now accomplices in the destruction of a culture and the dismembering of the society which nurtured it.

These three instances from 'An Cuilithionn' exemplify the mournful, plangent tone which is only one of the poem's modes. Seen as a whole, it draws the 'microworld' of Skye and the Hebrides into relation with the 'macroworld' of international socialism, of a universal struggle against oppression and injustice conceived in heroic terms which recognise no boundaries of nation, creed or language. Despite the grimness of many passages, the poem envisages a final victory of these positive forces, identified with the rising of the Cuillins on the horizon and the rugged, overwhelming strength of that geological formation. Its overall message is therefore one of dogged hopefulness rather than despair.

My final instance of the 'barrel organ' effect comes from the Eimhir sequence. The poem in question, XL, though written in or around March 1940, was not published for thirty years. MacLean most likely withheld it because of the sensitive nature of the subject matter. It is, however, an item of considerable importance, not just because in it the 'wounded Eimhir' makes her first appearance before the reader. The manuscript redaction of the cycle preserved in Aberdeen stops at this point, or rather with a brief pendant, XLI, followed by a 'Dimitto' in the style of Ezra Pound. In other words, shortly after its composition, MacLean may have looked on XL as a point of arrival for the sequence, even though he was careful to snip it out (or have this done by Douglas Young) from the manuscript copy. The song he reworks here, 'Mo rùn geal, dìleas', is still a popular favourite today. The relevant stanza is quoted in the version printed in Archibald Sinclair's *An t-Òranaiche* (*The Gaelic Songster*) in 1879:

---

[33] See J. Carmichael Watson ed. *Gaelic Songs of Mary MacLeod* (Edinburgh, Oliver and Boyd for the Scottish Gaelic Texts Society 1965) pp. 96ff. for the standard text and pp. 141-142 for Miss Tolmie's version.

Cha bhi mi 'strìth ris a' chraoibh nach lùb leam,
ged chinneadh ùbhlan air bhàrr gach gèig;
mo shoraidh slàn leat ma rinn thu m' fhàgail,
cha d' thàinig tràigh gun mhuir-làn 'na dèigh.

('I will not strive with the tree that will not bend for me,/ though apples should grow on top of each branch;/ my farewell to you if you have left me,/ ebb never came without a floodtide after it.')[34] The speaker, rejected by the woman he loves, and whom he pictures as an apple tree laden with fruit, with evident but sensitive erotic colouring, expresses a kind of gentle resilience. He will survive the rejection, because a turn for the better will follow as surely as the ebb-tide is followed by a flow, in accordance with inalterable natural cycles. MacLean's poem has two stanzas, of which the first is as follows:

Chan eil mi strì ris a' chraoibh nach lùb rium
's cha chinn na h-ùbhlan air gèig seach geug:
cha shoraidh slàn leat, cha d' rinn thu m' fhàgail:
's e tràigh a' bhàis i gun mhuir-làn 'na dèidh.

('I am not striving with the tree that will not bend for me,/ and the apples will not grow on any branch;/ it is not farewell to you; you have not left me./ It is the ebb of death with no floodtide after it.') As had happened with the Iain Lom stanzas, minimal changes in wording keep the original in the reader's mind while instigating a devastating change of direction. The profuse apples of the song no longer grow. Here there has been no rejection of the lover by his beloved. This ebbing away is a deadly one, without any prospect of subsequent balancing or recuperation.

MacLean's second stanza gives the imagery of the song a specifically anatomical application which, though not indecent, is profoundly shocking. Though one must be wary of bringing in biographical evidence too glibly, it would appear that at this stage MacLean believed the woman who inspired the poem to be incapable of having physical relations with a man, most probably as the result of an illegal abortion which had been incompetently performed.[35]

Marbh-shruth na conntraigh nad chom ciùrrte
nach lìon ri gealaich ùir no làin,
anns nach tig reothairt mhòr an t-sùgraidh -
ach sìoladh dùbailt gu muir-tràigh.

('Dead stream of neap in your tortured body,/ which will not flow at new moon or at full,/ in which the great springtide of love will not come -/ but a double subsidence to lowest ebb.') This stanza is thoroughly modern, not just in its imagery, but in its tone of utter hopelessness. Yet it would be unthinkable without the song as a basis. MacLean's last line takes two words from the last line of the song stanza ('tràigh' and 'muir'), reverses their order, puts them together in a compound, and places them in final position, emphasising both his dependence on the song and the utterly different conclusion which his version of it reaches.

---

[34] Archibald Sinclair ed. *An t-Òranaiche / The Gaelic Songster* (Glasgow, Archibald Sinclair 1879) p.264 (my translation).
[35] See *Dàin do Eimhir* p.13.

One of the many riddles connected with MacLean's *Dàin do Eimhir* love sequence is that, while the title encourages us to read it as dedicated to a single woman, what we know about the circumstances of its composition, along with elements in the texts themselves, suggests the existence of two distinct addressees. When he allowed the *Dàin do Eimhir* to be published in 1943, in incomplete form, one reason behind the omission of certain poems may have been the desire, on MacLean's part, to disguise the existence of two Eimhirs, conferring on the sequence a unity it did not possess as actually written. The shifting of poem VI, for example, to the 'Dàin eile' section, could have been motivated by the way its second stanza sets the two Eimhirs unequivocally side by side:

Am bliadhna roghainn na h-Albann,
an nighean ruadh, clàr na grèine;
's a' bhon-uiridh an nighean bhàn,
roghainn àlainn na h-Èireann.

('This year the choice of Scotland,/ the red-haired girl, sun forehead;/ and the year before last the fair-haired girl, the beautiful choice of Ireland.') The identity of the Irishwoman was widely known during the poet's lifetime. She could be named, and appears to have deserved in considerable measure the idealisation MacLean subjected her to. He never declared his passion, so the idealisation retained a dreamlike, even oneiric quality which allowed him to continue dedicating poems to her after the second woman, the Scottish Eimhir, known to him from when she had been a girl, re-entered his life in spring 1939.

Not just the physical mutilation she claimed to have suffered, but also her conduct towards the poet made it hard to turn the Scottish woman into an idealised figure. The gap between what the speaker in the sequence feels towards her, his idealisation of these feelings, and what he subsequently learnt renders her a very different figure, almost a counterpart, to the Irishwoman. MacLean would in fact apologise to the latter, in 'A' Mhalairt Bhreugach' ('The False Exchange'), for transferring twelve poems to the ambiguous figure of the Scottish woman,[36] whose initials 'A.M.' were at one point intended to appear as a dedication to the published cycle.

MacLean had ready widely within the tradition of the European love lyric. He was aware, then, of the caesura marked by Baudelaire's love poetry, where a semi-masochistic relationship to the beloved combines idealisation with vituperation. How far we have come from Petrarch! The beloved is no longer an unavailable, virtuous, even saintly figure who can in the end point the poet towards heavenly things, to her own transcendence in Mary the Mother of God, virgin and mother at one and the same time. Though this new figure may engage in a sexual relationship with the poet, or with another man, she is corrupted and contaminated by the circumambient world. All effective transcendence, except for that limited to an impossible dream on the part of the poet, is denied her.

The Scottish woman is the overwhelming presence in MacLean's love sequence. If, as would seem likely, poem I evokes a memory of her as an adolescent (in which case the poet's 'ten years of labour' ('mo dheich bliadhna saothrach'), specifically

---

[36] 'Gabh mo leisgeal, a luaidh,/ gun tug mi uair do 'n téile/ an dà dhàn dhiag a rinn mi dhutsa' ('Accept my excuse, dear,/ that once I gave to another/ the twelve poems I made for you'). See *O Choille gu Bearradh/ From Wood to Ridge* pp. 192-193.

poetic labour, should be taken in a literal sense),[37] she precedes the appearance of the Irish woman with poem IV, returns at V, and definitively ousts her from poem XXIII onwards. MacLean wrote the love sequence as his country prepared to engage in the Second World War. Conscious as he was of the inheritance of European Decadentism, both directly and as mediated by Modernism, it was peculiarly appropriate that a figure like the Scottish woman should come to dominate.

Discussing the *Requiem* sequence, which Russian poet Anna Akhmatova was prompted to write by the arrest, in the course of the Stalinist purges, of both her second husband the art historian Punin and her son by her first marriage, Lev Gumilyev, Joseph Brodsky draws our attention to the fact that writing can never be a simplistic transcription of first-hand biographical experience:

> Akhmatova is describing the state of the poet who is looking at everything that is happening to her as if she were standing off to one side. For the poet, the writing of this is no less an event than the event she is describing. [...] You start cursing yourself horribly: what kind of monster are you if you can be seeing this whole horror and nightmare as if it had nothing to do with you? [...] When someone is weeping, that is the weeper's private affair. When someone writing weeps, when he is suffering, he actually gains something from the fact that he's suffering. The writer can suffer his grief in a genuine way, but the description of this grief is not genuine tears or gray hair. It is only an approximation of a genuine reaction, and the awareness of this detachment creates a truly insane situation. [...] The rationality of the creative process assumes a certain rationality of emotion, a hardened heart. That is what drives the author mad.[38]

Though MacLean's situation was not quite as dramatic as Akhmatova's, he did write to Young on September 11th 1941 that:

> before I ever met you, actually just when I finished 'The Cuillin' about New Year 1940 I had an experience which has nearly driven me mad and not until July of this year did I become anything like normal, and even yet I have very frequent moods that approach the suicidal, though the real cause of those moods has been removed.

Whatever the respective intensities of the two poets' predicaments, Brodsky's argument retains its relevance, and supports the point with which this essay will conclude. Douglas Young had already touched on it in a letter to MacLean dated December 8th 1941, where he lists the dominant elements in the sequence as follows:

> of course the infatuation with the face of Eimhir, and as a second thought the feeling of revolution; as a third thought the self-consciousness of being a poet ...[39]

---

[37] See *Dàin do Eimhir* pp. 110-111.

[38] Solmon Volkov *Conversations with Joseph Brodsky* translated by Marian Schwarts (The Free Press, New York 1998) p.227.

[39] A typed copy of this letter will be found in National Library of Scotland Acc. 6419, Box 38b, along with MacLean's letters to Young.

Unsettling as it may be to raise such issues with a writer like MacLean, for whom biography and lyric output are so closely intertwined, it is undeniable that the Scottish woman, as presented in the cycle and in several ancillary poems, offered a paradigm which, if it corresponded to his actual experience, was also appropriate and fitting in terms of the literary background within which he wrote.

Thus our initial problem of terminology, an issue of a specifically, almost drily literary nature, has in the end brought us face to face with a crucial and all too often neglected aspect of MacLean's work, the extent to which conscious poetic art and artifice led him to model his experience into a 'biographical legend'.[40] That legend had to be capable of being elaborated in a literary form which would speak cogently to generations beyond his own, and to a broad public, not just English-speaking, which might otherwise never have learned of the existence of the marvellous, imperilled tongue in which he wrote.

---

[40] The term comes from Russian Formalist critic Boris Tomashevsky. See *Dàin do Eimhir* p.10.

Irish and its Expectations

Alan Titley

Discussions of Irish literature like to plumb the depths and to examine the shadows. Given the longevity of tradition it is never surprising when tradition comes back to control the present. But since the Irish language and its traditions have been under siege from memorial time, I may be forgiven for posing a question that must seem absurd for most people of cosmopolitan speech and reach. It may well be asked why anyone wrote in Irish at all, at all, in the late eighteenth and for all of the nineteenth century. This may seem like a stupid question, particularly when most of the people were Irish speakers and a considerable number monoglot Irish speakers, and when Irish was the language of the community over the largest swathes of territory from the fatfields of Meath to the rocky outcrops of the barren Burren of Clare. It may seem obvious why Máire Bhuí Ní Laoghaire (1774-1849) wrote her songs in Irish on the cusp of the outcrop of Céim an Fhia in West Cork in the years before the famine, or why Raftery voiced his lyrics between scraping his fiddle in East Galway around the same time. They wrote their verses in Irish because it was the language of their community and it was for them that they wrote, apart altogether from the fact that it was the only language they knew. On the other hand, a contemporary of theirs, the scribe and writer Dáibhí de Barra lived only a few miles from Cork city, and could just as easily have written in English as he did in Irish. Indeed, it might be argued that if he wished to make any small amount of money he should have done so, as there was very little to be had from his subsistence farm and the bit of scribal activity he engaged in for his own purposes.

Others chose the other route. William Carleton, who was equally fluent in both languages, simply never dreamed of writing his novels in Irish because it was as unthinkable as some of his plots. There was nothing in it for him and it would not bring him beyond the County of Cavan. There was no novel in Irish, and he was not going to invent it. Charles Macklin (1697?-1797), born Cathal Mac Lochlainn on the Inishowen peninsula, needed to be a dramatist. He went to London and carved out a good existence as a playwright with cheering and laughing audiences which he would never have got in the haggards above Malin.

There is, therefore, almost always a personal, or artistic, or monetary reason for people to choose one language over another when they speak more than one. The number of novelists from the Indian subcontinent who write in English is continually growing, and while there are many more who write in their native tongues we hear nothing about them. The might of Mammon and of international recognition win out over any kind of local pride, or loyalty to their first community. The same is true in Africa, where the call of the wide world leads to English and to French, and to a lesser extent Portuguese. He who used to be known as James Ngugi, and is now again Ngugi Wa' Th'iongo, and who has 'reverted' to writing in his native Kikuyu is remarkable

---

[1] This figure is much disputed but we can get a picture from other sources. David Greene in an essay entitled 'The founding of the Gaelic League' records that in Donegal in 1874 'that only about a thousand people, out of an Irish-speaking population of well over seventy thousand, could read Irish.' In Seán Ó Tuama *The Gaelic League Idea* (Cork 1972) p. 14.

because he is exceptional. But, as he has often explained, he did so for commendable ideological and cultural reasons. Like the writer in Irish, he has done so out of a hard choice.

In early and mid-nineteenth century Ireland there was only a minimal literary public in Irish. It was a literacy often furtively learned in well-hidden schools of poetry, or in hedge-schools where the teacher happened to want to impart the skill of reading in Irish. But when reading was learned, the question was raised as to what people would read. The perusal of manuscripts is a labour of love for those interested in literary tradition, and a crabbed hand or a torn parchment can deflect the young eager mind especially when cheap chap books are easily available in another language. The fact is that literacy largely came with the English language, and that even when a native speaker in a fully unholed Irish-speaking area learned to read in Irish it was so much easier to avail of English language material. This is in some contrast to Scotland and to Wales where literacy strengthened the language and provided material for reading, even if that reading was not always for frivolous pleasure.

There was also a certain suspicion of literacy in Irish among the population, because literacy in the language, particularly literacy of the printed word as distinct from manuscript literacy, was associated with Protestants and who were not always looked on with the most loving Christian charity by the Catholic population. The activities of the Bible Societies in the nineteenth century added to this suspicion. Their remit was to spread the word of God in the language of the people so that they would be able to read the Bible and to fear the Lord. To this end, they had to teach the reading of the Irish language, and in such a way did literacy in Irish become associated with Protestantism. These Bible societies were particularly active in West Munster, in Connaught and in that swathe of territory that stretches from Cavan to South Armagh. Many people refused to learn to read Irish in the dread terror that they would be forced to read the Bible; and the Catholic clergy were vehement in their opposition to the activities of the 'Bíoblóirí', or 'Bibulists' as one mispronunciation had it. Literacy in the language had become so tenuous that Tadhg Ó Donnchadha, who later became Professor of Irish in Cork, reckoned that only about fifty people were literate in the language at the time of the foundation of the Gaelic League in 1893.[1] While this is undoubtedly a gross misunderestimation, as George W. Bush might say, it does show that if there were many thousands who could read and write the language, they were unwilling to admit it, and hid it like a kind of secret shame.

After the 1880s, during the highnoon and bright day of the Irish revival, a massive change was brought about in this negative and shamefaced thinking. The main aims of the Gaelic League were on the one hand to preserve and extend the spoken language, but also wished fervently for the creation of a new literature whether original or translated. The thinking behind this was clear. A literature is a badge of honour, a mark of maturity, a sign of worth. To have a literature of your own is a bugle for the world and an affirmation of self-esteem. What would be the point of learning a language if it was only going to be a mere patois, the blabbering and slavering of peasants who were beneath contempt? If that was all it was going to be, then it would reinforce the viewpoint of the conqueror that it was a tongue that deserved to be plucked out and cast to perdition as it had nothing to say. One of the major points of the revival is that the Irish had something to say, and something to sing, and something to hold forth about.

---

[2] Philip O'Leary *Gaelic Prose in the Irish Free State 1922-1939* (Dublin 2004) p. 1.

It was because of this that a huge and massive and unrealistic emotional investment was made in literature, an investment which might never have been able to yield the results expected of it. The new literature was meant to bind up the wounds of yesteryear, hail the present moment and point to the peaks of the future. This literature would also, of course, act as a support, a source and a saviour of the language because of its prestige and its prowess. I had a teacher in secondary school who seriously opined that if Yeats had written in Irish then the entire country would be Irish-speaking by now. Even though at that young age I had not yet quite honed my crap-detector I felt the stirrings of something deep down that was not quite right in the bowels of things. Even though Yeats believed in fairies and of ectoplasm seeping out of the cracks in Anima Mundi it was not necessary for his readers to believe in the farther reaches of improbability.

This was, however, the period of high literacy. Literature rather than video was the unchallenged primary discourse. The hopes of society were reflected in it, and the writer was the pop-star of the age. Charles Dickens, only a short few years before, packed concert halls with his readings at a time when the attention-span of his listeners went beyond the sharp short gasp of an imagistic lyric. High literature was seen as an index of civilisation, and the higher the literature the richer the civilisation. While Drake was winning seas for England and we sailed in puddles of the past, Shakespeare was penning the glories of the English tongue even though it was of little reach. A facile connection was made between the butchery of conquest and the wonder of the word, and the wonder of the word was made another general in the march of progress. Lord Macauley has been oft quoted as saying that one shelf of English literature was worth a whole library of Indian literature, although this calculation may have been made more through the lens of a gin and tonic than through the thumbing of books. The comment revealed, however, that literature was more than literature and that words were more than words.

But, for most of us, literature is literature in the first place. Looking back beyond these hundred years it is difficult to grasp the ferment and the sense of discovery that accompanied the years of the 'Revival'. Irish was 'the Rip Van Winkle of languages' awoken and shaking its locks after years of being shorn and shaved and silenced. For the first time in more than two hundred years the Irish speaker was recognised as a human being, somebody who might not necessarily have to apostate and convert to the new dispensation in order to live a normal life in his or her own country. This is an imaginative leap that would have been difficult for any Irish person to make in the year 1700, and it is an imaginative leap backwards which very few Irish people can make now in the year 2004. At the very beginning of Philip O'Leary's new and invaluable book *Gaelic Prose in the Irish Free State 1922-1939*, he asks us to make such an imaginative journey:

---

[3] ibid. p. 1.

[4] ibid. p. 3.

[5] ibid. p. 9.

[6] ibid. p. 9.

[7] ibid p 10. I have been generous in my use of this book for the purposes of part of this essay because I had just obtained a copy of it before the time of writing. Up until now we have all been indebted to Muiris Ó Droighneáin's *Taighde i gComhair Stair Litridheachta na Nua-Ghaedhilge ó 1882 Anuas* (Dublin 1936) for discussion of these cultural debates, but a great deal of research has been done since then, as this book exemplifies.

Had an early Gaelic Leaguer suddenly found himself transported to the mid-1930s, he would have been astounded at how many of his dreams had come true. He would see twenty-six of Ireland's thirty-two counties under native rule; his former movement colleagues in positions of authority in all brances of government from chief executive down; an educational system dedicated to re-Gaelicising the nation through the schools, schools in which all children took Irish as a major subject; and an entire state agency devoted exlusively to the publishing of books in what was now the country's first official language.[2]

The blunt point being that the world had turned outside in and that a great psychic wrong was on the way to being righted. Liam Ó Rinn, a man of cosmopolitan and classical tastes, but wholly subscribing to the Irish revival predicted in the early 1930s that in a few decades time nobody would be amazed or surprised by the language, because it would be as natural as the unpolluted air that we breathed.[3] What was true of the language it was supposed would be true of the literature also. It was like eidelweiss to bloom and grow and bloom and grow forever:

The seed planted in the spring does not bloom until the heat of summer comes. That is how it is with literature in Irish. We are gradually approaching the summer of the literature, and it is a good omen for that season that there are so many good writers in the field who encourage us all that there will be a good heavy harvest ahead.[4]

It seemed that them hard times they were a'comin' again no more, and the broad sunny uplands beckoned the writer and the reader. This renaissance was inextricably linked to the future of the language, as if the literature itself be great then the tongue must needs be great also. The earlier years of the revival made this connection explicit, and Aodh de Blácam who himself wrote a fine and spirited book on the Gaelic literatures of Ireland and Scotland warned that it would be 'a work in vain' to revive Irish merely as a backward patois of mountainy men and women scraping their knuckles on the barren rocks, if this was to be a mere gabble of words without literature and without learning. 'Unless we intend to create a fine majestic literature in modern Irish, it would be far better for us to give up the business and take up English and all the intellectual wealth to be found in it.'[5] Or again, Tomás Ó Máille, scholar and professor:

It is said that the teachers are the soldiers of the Irish language. If so, writers are the chieftains. If the writers choose to give direction to the Gaels, those with Irish will follow them. If the writers pay attention to their business and if they give direction and insight and pleasure to their readers as the writers of every languge give their readers, the Irish

---

[8] *Bliainiris 2003.* (Rath Cairn 2004) Ruairí Ó hUiginn, Liam Mac Cóil (eds). See in particular two essays which deal with two writers experience of An Gúm. 'Máirtín Ó Cadhain agus Sally Kavanagh' Uí Laighléis, Gearóidín; and 'Padraic Ó Conaire agus An Gúm' Ó Cathasaigh, Aindrias.

[9] 'Súil soir – léargais ar Albain' Ruaraidh Mac Thòmais (Derick Thomson). *Comhar* Aibreán 1980.

language will not disappear. If the writers of Irish want, it will be dominant in Ireland.[6]

And Cearbhall Ó Dálaigh, later to become President of Ireland:

It is this lack of literature that causes people to ignore Irish; it is what causes the laziness and the lack of earnestness, and the apathy that have taken hold in people. If we were developing a great and important literature, you would be amazed how quickly the English-speakers of the country would take up Irish at once![7]

This was a common understanding re-inforced by the central place of literature in the schools and by the linking of a superior canon with superior cultural gunfire. While this may have been understandable not many of the millions and millions who learn English throughout the world today do so in order to read the intricacies of Shakespeare's sonnets, or to fathom the mysterious proprieties of Jane Austen's dishumourous comedies, or even to savour and enjoy the latest bestseller from Maeve Binchy. For it is a truth universally acknowledged that languages grow and flourish for reasons of commerce and of social prestige and for getting one's hand in the grubby till, and not for reaching the foothills of the outreaches of Parnassus.

So, if Irish literature was called upon to illuminate the past, reflect the present and to guide the future, this may have been a sandbank too far. In its own terms, however, a great deal had been achieved. Even by the middle of the twentieth century there had been more Irish literature written and published than in all the previous centuries put together and wrapped up in one pile. The lid was lifted off a society that had been dumped in silence deep, and words were wrestled with that would otherwise have breathed their last gasp in extreme dudgeon. And yet, for all that, this was not always a literature that pointed the way to the future.

A great classic such as Tomás Ó Criomhthain's *An tOileánach*, hard, spare, precise, with each phrase drawn with the clarity of a scalpel, penned by a singular man without any doubt about his selfworth and dignity, was nonetheless a book which celebrated the bad old times and the woes of yesteryear. It was not warm towards the rising sun. It showed up the stark contradiction between the life of expression or the passion of a driven personality against the bleakness of the social idea which it bore. For all that you might admire Tomás Ó Criomhthain, the life he lived was a life that had to be escaped from. The great discovery of the Gaeltacht and the celebration of the goodnesses of that life was in stark contrast to the ships with white sails upon a painted ocean going westward to fall over the ends of the Irish earth. Ireland wanted prosperity now, and the 'Gaelic' rural past did not help point the way.

One of the ways in which the gap between the failed society and the vibrant language could be bridged was through translation. Here you could have the rich

---

[10] *An Odaisé*. Pádraig de Brún a d'aistrigh. Ciarán Ó Coigligh (ed) (Dublin 1990); *An Choiméide Dhiaga*. Pádraig de Brún a d'aistrigh. Ciarán Ó Coigligh (ed) (Dublin 1997).
[11] Philip O'Leary. *The Prose Literature of the Gaelic Revival 1881-1921: ideology and innovation*. (Pennsylvania 1994) pp. 32, 50.
[12] O'Leary (2004) p. 58.
[13] ibid. p. 62.
[14] see Tadhg Ó Dúshláine's edition of *Fánaí* (Maynooth 1989).

idiomatic tongue without the peasant society. The Irish government set up An Gúm in 1927 in order to provide reading material for the new literate society in the making and quickly invited leading writers to work on translations for this purpose.[8] Although often snotted upon in later years by many of these writers it was nonetheless a revolutionary scheme. Its primary aim was simply to provide books for reading, but it also had the secondary purpose of providing practice in writing for authors. Derick Thomson later argued that one of the reasons why imaginative prose in Scottish Gaelic was so slow in developing in the twentieth century was precisely because of the lack of this kind of scheme.[9]

Within a few short years Irish writers had provided versions of some of the world's greatest literature. Aeschylus, Euripedes, Dickens, Chekov, Tolstoi, Maupassant as well as some household Irish authors such as Canon Sheehan, William Carleton and Charles J.Kickham had all been 'Gaelicised' in a language as clear and as idiomatic as the pure water from the twelve bens. And outside the scheme Dante's *Divine Comedy* and Homer's *Odyssey* had been rendered into Kerry Irish by Monsignor Pádraig de Brún bringing Florence to Dún Chaoin and Attica to Ard na Caithne1[10] Despite this excellent work, the scheme was not a roaring success, particularly as a commercial enterprise. It was never likely that a fine translation of *The Hound of the Baskervilles* or of *Dracula* would command the same readership when they were readily available in English.

Other strains and threads and wisps and strands needed to be drawn apart in the debate on Irish literature. It was also seen as a bulwark or as a defence against the outside world, and indeed Yeats called it to his side in his battle against the 'filty modern tide'[11] He did, in all seriousness propose that only Irish and Greek should be taught to the youth of Ireland as a basis for their knowledge and civilisation, but he failed to take his own advice in the matter. Much of this bulwark stuff was a defence of the 'purity' of Ireland, and while it was not always specifically Catholic, a great deal of it came from this legion. Again and again we read of 'imported, denationalising filth', 'feasts of filth and unashamed parades of profligacy,' 'dirty rotten things that give off a foul stench', 'poisonous literary rubbish imported from abroad', 'the rubbish and filth of a foreign tongue' ('dramhaíl agus salachar teangan iasachta')[12] This was braodcast with such gusto that it may well have induced the less salubrious to run out and buy. In *Irisleabhar Muighe Nuadhat* one writer summed this attitude up by declaring that 'The Irish language is the only protective shield we have, the only rampart against the enemy. Even America, however great its power, is part of the English empire.'[13] There are many today who might put it the other way around.

This idea of the language as being a prophylactic against the diseases of the world was quite endemic and found its way into literary criticism. The great Donegal writer Séamas Ó Grianna in one of his early stories recounts the tale of a 'spoiled priest' and was criticised for showing the less savoury side of Irish catholicism where heartbreak and isolation can often haunt a broken ideal. Ó Grianna replied that a priest had told him he should write nothing that he would be ashamed of his mother reading, advice

---

[15] See for example, Kevin Casey's sour review of the translation of Breandán Ó hEithir's *Lig Sinn i gCathú,* 'Paddywhackery' in *Hibernia,* 5 October 1978.

[16] See Anthony Cronin's *No Laughing Matter* (London 1989) p.131; and Breandán Ó Conaire's *Myles na Gaeilge* (Dublin 1986).

[17] There is the exception of the novels of Pádraig Standún, who has translated his own work, very often shortly on the heels of the Irish original.

which he said he took to heart. One wag was heard to say that this meant that his mother became the arbiter, not only of matters of morals and of faith, but also of literary excellence. When Seán Óg Ó Caomhánaigh published *Fánaí* in 1927, it was quickly withdrawn as scenes most subtley set which would easily make the pre-nine o'clock television watershed even for the most touchy and litigious parents were objected to.[14]

Beyond the purity of the tongue and the subject matter, however, the Irish-reading public craved for a big name. If only we could have one great author, it was argued, we would be able to hold our heads up high and look at the world with equal eyes. This 'great author' argument, of course, prompts the question as to how such a being could be recognised if he or she came along. There is no stick with which to measure the arts comparison in the race, there is no easy football league promotion and demotion between writers. Irish-speakers will boast of their boys, and English-speakers of the meaner sort will scoff with derision.[15] The only neutral ground might well be to glance at the bilingual writers, those who wrote in both tongues, and achieved something thereby. Thus, for example, Flann O'Brien who was a native speaker of Irish and who didn't go to school until he was about twelve years of age and had read just about everything by that stage, gained international acclaim with his novels and his columns in the *Irish Times*. But he himself thought his best work was his Irish novel *An Béal Bocht*, and dismissed with disdain those works such as *At Swim-Two-Birds* which are often seen as important.[16] Likewise Liam O'Flaherty is often recognised as one of our most important short-story writers, as well as being a novelist of distinction. His first language was Irish, and his collection *Dúil* is seen as a classic. Michael Hartnett began his poetic career in English and then turned to Irish, making poetry of at least an equal standard with what he had done before. Breandán Ó hEithir, although primarily seen as a journalist, wrote one of the finest books on the GAA *Over the Bar*, which is indeed mere memory and anecdote compared with his novels in Irish. Brendan Behan wrote his poetry in Irish, as well as some of his dramatic works including *An Giall* before it became transmogrified and transmusichalled into *The Hostage* for the gawping London stage.

The crude point here is that, even for those with no knowledge of the language or its literature, there is an *ipso facto* case for saying that, at the very least, fine and significant works were written in Irish in the twentieth century. Within the Irish community itself, however, these writers are not seen as the real biggies, the heavy gang, the first division. A writer such as Máirtín Ó Cadhain in prose, or Seán Ó Ríordáin in poetry would more fit the bill for Irish speakers and readers, with others on their tails not very far behind. The question then is posed, and you can see it coming from afar: 'Then, why don't we know more about them?' And the answer is that we don't know very much about them because they are not translated, and when they are translated they doth lose their savour. And they are not translated for the same reason as when we walk into our local bookstore we don't find too many translations from the Arabic, or the Portuguese, or the Urdu which are three massive world languages, not to mention the smaller voices of Bulgarian or Polish or Finnish. English itself spreads

[18] *The Field Day Anthology of Irish Writing Vol 111*. Seamus Deane (general editor) (Derry 1991) pp. 857, 859.

[19] Percy Bysshe Shelley, *A Defence of Poetry* (London 1824) p. 37.

[20] See Guglelmo Cavallo and Roger Chartier *A History of Reading in the West* (Cambridge 1999) p. 4. See also Chapter 12. pp. 313-344.

its wings upon every tide and deposits its parcels all over the universe; it doesn't, however, suck too many other literatures into its maw, and where it does they only live by happenstance and provide a tiny itch. I am only aware of about five novels that have been translated from Irish into English[17], but the most typical prose works that have been made available are versions of the Gaeltacht autobiographies usually rendered in a mingle-mangle or gallimaufry of subhuman peasant chatter which turn these flesh and blood men and women into primitives beyond salvation. There is a Slovakian proverb which states that 'with every new language you acquire a new soul', but sometimes the metampsychosis into another tongue can be raw and painful.

There is an impossibility inherent in translation that is often mentioned but quickly passed over. The difficulties that lurk in the first sentence of Máirtín Ó Cadhain's *Cré na Cille* are legion. 'Ní mé an ar Áit an Phuint nó na Cúig Déag atá mé curtha? D'imigh an diabhal orthu dhá mba in Áit na Lethghine a chaithfidís mé, th'éis ar chuir mé d'fhainiceachaí orthu ....' The entire book has been translated by Eibhlín Ní Allúráin and Maitiú Ó Néill but only excerpts have appeared. They make this sentence thus: 'Now I wonder is it in the Pound Plot or the Fifteen Shillings Plot they have me buried. They went to the devil entirely if it's in the Ten Shilling Place they threw me after all the warnings I gave them .....'[18] The problem is that the Irish is rich and idiomatic, the English is Syngesprach. Only broken communites ever spoke that crude lingo, and Ó Cadhain's *Cré na Cille* is a community in full possession of all its linguistic faculties. On the other hand to render it into 'standard English' would emasculate and emaciate a speech that is fierce and loud and bitter and beautiful. The problem is entirely intractable. Shelley in his *A Defence of Poetry* speaks of 'The vanity of translation: it were as wise to cast a violet into a crucible that you might discover the formal principal of its colour and odour, as to seek to transfuse from one language to another the creation of a poet.'[19] And there we have it all. It is all about 'colour and odour' and taste and tang, the ineluctable, irreducible magic, the emanation, of one language rather than another. It is about the deep wells and the echo chambers, the ghosts in the grammar. If this were not the case, then one language would be the same as another, which it patently is not. It is this dirty, messy, sloppy integrity that makes literature so important to language. A government document does not have too many echoes, although it may raise the fear of God in somebody, but literature it isn't.

The literature, then, is not so much an expression of nationalism in competition with others, or a bulwark against the tides of change, or a statement of purity, or a quest for a great writersaviour, but much more an expression of itself. It can, of course, be called upon to do lots of other things depending on the community of users it has, but it is none of these things in itself. Irish literature has its 'communities of interpretation'[20] like every other discourse, and these will be reflected in the interests of the time along the road.

This is not to argue that literature does not have a 'social function', but it is not one in the old simple sense. It may, or may not be, an expression of that society. In the Irish-language community, I prefer to see it as one of the building-blocks, one of the bricks, part of the glue and plaster that holds us together. For Irish speakers form a very scattered community even in the different Gaeltachtaí. Outside of the traditional strongholds of the language they live through a series of networks or songlines that often comprise, for example, Irish-speaking schools, cultural festivals, summer organisations, literary readings, Raidió na Gaeltachta, TV programmes and beyond.

The importance of the literature is that it is part of this network, it is one of the ways in which we speak to ourselves, and hopefully to others. It certainly also challenges the language itself, often enriching and stretching and pushing it around. But mostly it binds us together, and that enriches the community's sense of itself and what it is capable of.

The Sociolinguistics of Contemporary Scots: Insights from one Community

Jennifer Smith

1. Introduction

One of the main aims of sociolinguistic research is to discover the external and internal pressures that bring about variation and change in any given language or dialect. The case of written Scots provides a clear case study of how external forces are implicated in the rise of one variety to the detriment of another: its decline can largely be attributed to historical events, including the Union of the Crowns in 1603 and the Union of Parliament in 1707, which resulted in the adoption of southern English forms in writing north of the border. The replacement of 'diagnostic' Scots forms (e.g. Meurman-Solin 1993, Devitt 1989) with 'English' equivalents in the period 1450 to 1700 gives rise to the present day situation where Scots is, on the whole, not used by institutionalised bodies such as government, school and the law.

It is generally assumed that a language or dialect lacking a written standard must be in decline (e.g. Corbett et al 2003: 13) – so what of spoken Scots? Although the rapid obsolescence of *written* Scots was not replicated in speech in this time period, even the very briefest of overviews of the situation suggests that present day *spoken* Scots may indeed now be following this pathway of change towards anglicisation. Macafee (1997: 546), for example, states that 'Scots is already a long way along a trajectory which is taking it towards integration with English as the continuum between the two shrinks, apparently inexorably, towards the English pole'. Murison (1977: 1) asserts that present day Scots is 'rapidly losing its historic forms and structure'.

As with written Scots, this change in speech is also attributed to external forces: Corbett (2003: 252-3) for example, states, this is not 'the result simply of 'natural' linguistic evolution' but 'overt and covert 'language engineering' in which standard varieties of English have, for generations, been mythologised as the correct forms'. This situation has led to cries for reformation of the current legislative system and recognition of Scots as a bona fide language in its own right (see e.g. Hance, in this volume, Corbett 2003, Macafee 1996) in order to stop, or at least decelerate, the attrition of Scots.

However, even the most superficial observation on the ground will reveal people still using Scots and sounding Scottish. At the same time, undoubtedly there are pressures at work on spoken Scots from a variety of sources, but how deep is their impact? While we have clear evidence from the written historical record of the loss of peculiarly Scottish forms - it's there in black and white - the spoken language remains more elusive. This is in part due to lack of empirical data on the current state of spoken Scots, summed up in a quotation from the Mini-Guide to the Lesser-Used Languages of the E.C. entry on Scots: 'there is very little information on the use and spread of the Scots language which is spoken south and east of the Highlands' (quoted in Macafee 1997: 515).

So how do we go about establishing the current state of the Scots language and inextricably linked to this, the sociolinguistics of contemporary Scots?

One way of obtaining such information is through census data: actually asking speakers about their use of the Scots language (e.g. Murdoch 1995). These types of data give us an insight not only into how many people describe themselves as speakers of 'Scots', but also how they perceive 'the Scots language'. These data provide not only essential statistical data for government bodies but on a broader level, can be instrumental in ascertaining attitudes to Scots, and hence an invaluable tool in assessing the status of the Scots language amongst the speakers themselves.[1]

The second way to establish the state of the Scots language is to actually listen to the Scots language in use through large scale sociolinguistic studies (Labov 1984). Research of this kind has been undertaken in, for example, Glasgow (Macafee 1983, Stuart-Smith 1999), south-west Scotland (Macaulay 1991), and Edinburgh (Johnston 1983). Most report erosion of historically Scots forms.

But what of more insular rural areas? Macafee's (1997: 546) survey of the sociolinguistic situation in Scotland leads her to conclude that 'it seems likely that broad dialects of Scots will survive only in communities that have some degree of immunity to hegemonic external forces, which usually means rural communities with sufficient economic resources to prevent massive migration of the younger generation and sufficient self-assurance to absorb and nativise incomers. The north-east, Orkney and Shetland are the places that best fulfil these criteria.'

However, the loss of Scots forms may be all encompassing, as 'the state of Scots in urban areas … probably indicates the likely future of language in general' (Macafee 1994: 69). Wilson (1993: 111) suggests that even in traditionally relic areas such as the north east, the language is 'in danger of extinction, due to pressures towards conformity with Standard English'. Marshall's (2004) study of Huntly, a rural, agricultural community in north east Scotland certainly lends support to these statements. He finds obsolescence in a number of diagnostic Scots forms across four age groups of speakers.

This brief overview of the literature makes for pessimistic reading on the future of Scots. However, the motivations for language change are notoriously complex and what may be the case in one community might not apply in another. Moreover, is there wholesale attrition of all Scots forms within the linguistic inventory, whether morphosyntactic, lexical or phonetic, or is the situation more complicated?

In this paper, I seek to address these questions by examining the dialect used in a fishing community in the north east of Scotland, Buckie. Does this variety 'retain a degree of immunity to hegemonic external forces' or is it moving 'inexorably towards the English pole'? The answer to this may shed further light on the current state of the Scots language more generally, and its sociolinguistic status within the communities who use it.

2. Data and methods

2.1 The community
Buckie is a small fishing town on the north east coast of Scotland (popn. 8000), as shown in Figure 1. It was settled in the 17th century and in the 20th century grew to be the second largest fishing port in Britain (Thompson, Wailey and Lummis 1983). In recent years, the fishing industry has declined, but alternative work is found on

---

[1] Unfortunately, there have been few studies of this kind to date (e.g. Macafee 1997: 514, Corbett 2003: 265).

the oilrigs. Thus, unlike similar rural areas, Buckie has not suffered from depopulation and, remarkably in these present times, a strong tradition of endogamy exists (see detail in Smith 2000). Economic self sufficiency, coupled with geographic isolation and a sense of local pride has resulted in the community remaining relatively immune to more mainstream developments. This is reflected in the speakers' language behaviour, as this area more generally is described as 'well preserved and highly differentiated' (McClure 1979: 29).

Figure 1: Map showing location of Buckie

2.2 The speakers
The speakers in the sample (see Table 1) are all Buckie born and bred and can be considered working class in sociolinguistic terms. In fact, a class stratified study of this community in traditional sociolinguistic terms would be in appropriate due to the 'vertical integration' (Macafee 1997: 546) of the community, where 'strict class-tying is lacking' (Johnston 1997: 445).

Table 1: Speaker sample

Age	Male	Female
22-31	8	8
50-60	7	7
80+	4	5

Each speaker was recorded for 1-2 hours using standard sociolinguistic methodology (Labov 1984). Given the constraints of the sociolinguistic interview, the speech is highly vernacular in nature, due to the fact that I am an in-group member and most speakers are known personally to me.

2.3 The data

The data amount to approximately 40 hours of tape-recorded speech. The corpus has been fully transcribed and consists of over 300,000 words. To give a flavour of the dialect, included is an extract from Bess, a former fish gutter, who is 84 years old at the time of recording. Here she discusses a relative's wedding.

> That 's a special one. Crikey! Just about foonert. And then of course, aifter that, it was the telegrams and a' that, you ken fit I mean. Telegrams, afore they were a' read and a'l the rest o' it. And a' the toasts and athing. And you ken the kin' o' that Aiberdeen crowd. Every one wi' the kilt on. Gordon had on the kilt, you see. And that Aiberdeen crowd was atween hez and the top table. We was hine up, you see. And her brother was just across fae hez, you-see. That crowd fae Aiberdeen, I thocht they were Brechin and I says to Isla aifterhine, I says 'Hey thon mob' I says 'that was aside hez,' I says 'What a noisy crowd. Is thon fae Brechin?' 'No, Bess' she says 'thon 's a' Aberdeen.' Oh me, what a nicht they had! However, fin a' that's gan by, ken this, it was twenty past seven. Afore we was deen of eatin and the dance - the dance was starting at eicht. A quarter to eight or eight.

Bess has many forms in her speech that can be considered to be markedly Scots or north eastern Scots and thus function as diagnostics in the use of Scots or the incoming 'English' forms. For example, use of the velar fricative /x/ in *nicht*, *gan* for *going* and *ƙen* for *ƙnow*.

But the key point about these forms is that they are **variable**: notice that Bess uses the traditional Scots form *eicht* then the anglicised *eight* at another.

It is such variability that can give us an insight into how the language is changing: utilising the apparent time method (e.g. Bailey 2001) the quantitative patterns of use across the three generations in the Buckie sample can shed light on the processes of obsolescence, innovation or stability over time. Specifically, which of the competing forms – Scots or more standardised English - are 'winning out' over time?

I now turn to an analysis of the forms: velar fricatives, past tense *–it* ending, regularised verbs, distal demonstratives and /ʍ/ > /f/ alternation.

3. The Variables

3.1 Velar fricatives

The consonant /x/, as in *nicht*, is an excellent diagnostic of Scots as it is not generally found in 'southern accents of English English' (Stuart-Smith 2003: 124). Meurman-Solin (1993: 157-160) finds a dramatic decrease in use in the *ch* spelling variant (representing the velar fricative), as in (1-4) in favour of *gh* in the historical record in the period 1470-1700.

1. He **thoucht** to virk with **slicht**. (1375, Barbour, Bruce v. 488)
2. He may **nocht fecht** apon e burges.(c1400, Burgh Laws, xii Sc. Stat. 1)
3. Off Februar the fyiftene **nycht**...I lay in till a trance. (1500-20, Dunbar, Poems Xxvi)
4. Wische me the **richt** way till Sanct-Androes. (1535, Lyndesay, Satyre 1929)

In present day urban varieties, the velar fricative may be reaching extinction: Macafee (1994: 74) reports no uses at all in over 40 hours of data from Glasgow and Stuart-Smith observes loss of this consonant from such fossilised lexical items as *loch* in her adolescent speakers also from Glasgow. This trend is spreading to more rural areas as well. Marshall (2004: 132), reports '/x/ suffering attrition very rapidly' in Huntly.

For the present analysis, a qualitative view of the Buckie data might lead us to suspect that this variant has not suffered the same fate as it can be found in older, middle aged and younger speakers, as in (5-7):

5. a. I gied aie up wi' him, every time that he **soucht** me.
    b. She **thought** she was dick! (Bess, 84, fish gutter)

6. a. They **boucht** this al' croft hoosie.
    b. That 's fit he kind-of **bought** it for. (Willy, 59, Fisherman)

7. a. I **thoucht** 'Och, I'm nae getting' intae that again'.
    b. Finn I was aboot **eighteen** I was gan oot wi' this quine.
        (Scott, 30. Oil rig worker)

However, the quantitative view of the data presents an altogether different story. Figure 2 shows the use of the velar fricative across the three generations of speakers.

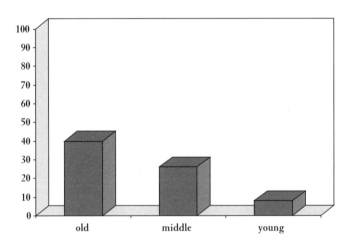

Figure 2: Velar fricatives by age

Figure 2 shows a steady decline in use of the Scottish form in the Buckie data. These results, coupled with the findings in other areas, both rural and urban, lead to the conclusion that this particularly Scottish form is becoming obsolete and may in fact have disappeared altogether in the next generation or two.

3.2 Past tense –*it*
One of the main distinguishing features of Scots is the use of past tense irregular verb

inflection (e.g. Devitt 1989, Meurman-Solin 1993). In present day standard English, preterit and past participle regular verbs are formed by adding the suffix *–ed* which undergoes certain euphoric changes in accordance with the preceding letter or syllable. This was also the case in the historical record. In contrast, 'In old Scotch the past tense and past participle were formed by adding *it*, or *yt* to all verbs of [the regular] class.' (Murray 1873: 99). This suffix was circumscribed to the set of regular verbs, which, in the bare form, end in a stop, e.g. /p/, /k/, as in (8-9):

8.   ... fe cawe e mouth of stane **stopyt** wele. (*c*1375. *Sc. Leg. Saints* xxiii, *Seven Sleepers*)
9.   Be that it drew to the nicht, The King **lykit** ill. (*c*1475, *Rauf Coilear* 39)

Meurman-Solin (1993: 126) shows the loss of the spelling variant *–it/–yt* in favour of the English variant *–ed* in a number of Scots texts from 1450-1700. In these 250 years, we see the use of the standard variant take over: from almost no use at all to near categorical use.

Although its use continues in modern day Scots dialects (e.g. Dieth, 1932: 139, Macafee 1983: 49, Miller 1993: 106), the trajectory of change in writing may be emulated in speech. Marshall (1994: 143) finds a drop from around 80% to 20% use of *–it* across the generations in his Huntly data.

In the Buckie data, all age groups use the form, as in (10-12).

10. a.   I aie **likit** to ging to the kirk .
    b.   The dog never **barked** at me. (Nancy, 84, fish gutter)

11 a.   You're **chokit**, eatin' it.
   b.   We **stopped** at Macduff. (Elsie, 59, housewife)

12. a.   That mannie wi' the **checkit** shirt.
    b.   She's aie **worked** at the scampi since. (Pauline, 28, shop assistant)

Figure 3 shows its use across these three generations of speakers.

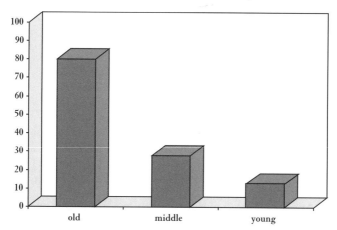

Figure 3: Past tense *–it* by age

The results in Buckie mirror those found in Huntly: 80% use of *–it* in the older speakers but less than 20% use with the younger speakers.[2]

Thus, the first two variables would seem to confirm the predictions regarding the future of Scots. These markedly Scots forms are fast becoming obsolete even in the most rural areas.

3.3 'Regularised' irregular verbs

Past tense verbs have gone through many changes in the past 800 years and most of these have been shared by both Scots and English south of the border (e.g. Krygier 1994, Jespersen 1954). However, 'few verbs which retain in English the strong form have in Scotch adopted a new weak one' (Murray 1873: 203), namely *go*, *sell* and *tell*.

Go had the Old English preterit *eode*. However, in Modern English it was replaced by the suppletive form *went* (e.g. Jespersen, 1954: 75). The form maintained the strong form in Older Scots, but from the 18th century, a weak inflection *gied* is attested (e.g. Görlach, 1994; King, 1997), as in (13-14):

13. Bonnye Kilmeny **gede** up the glen. (1813, Hogg, *Queen's Wake*)
14. The third, that **gaed** a wee a-back. (1786, Burns, *Holy Fair*)

Tell and *sell* originally belonged to the strong class of verbs with the vowel alternation in the preterit form *tauld/sauld*. However, from the 16th century onwards the vowel of the stem form was leveled to the preterite, resulting in the weak form *tell/selt* (CSD s.v. *tell/sell*) as in (15-16):

15. It will be **sell'd** the morn to the highest bidder. (1815 Scott,*Guy Mannering* xii)
16. In a' thae wee bits o' ways I ha'e **tell't** ye. (1881, Scott *Heart of Midlothian,* Intro.)

These forms continue to exist in present day Scots (e.g. Macaulay 1991: 109) and are also used in Buckie, as in (17-19):

17. a.   Doctor Paterson **telt** him right up, right oot.
    b.   So Doctor Paterson **told** her it was multiple sclerosis. (Ruth, 84, fish gutter)

18. a.   We **gied** across atween Christmas and New Year.
    b.   We picked her up in Glasgow and **went** across and bade there. (Jean, 59, housewife)

19. a.   I **selt** it a few year ago to the rowp man.
    b.   He was expectin' a hunner-thoosan' dollars if he **sold** it. (Alex, fisherman, 86)

---

[2] This alternation makes up a much wider set of variation where *–it* or *–t* can occur (see e.g. Beal 1997: 351-354). In this case, only those verbs which ended in /k/ or /p/ were included as these are maximally different in auditory terms from standard English.

Figure 4 shows the use of these forms across the three generations.

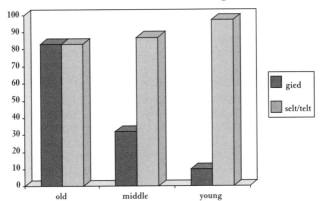

Figure 4: 'Regularised' irregular verbs by age

The graph shows that there is severe erosion of the regularised form with *gied*, but in sharp contrast, maintenance, or even increased use of *selt/telt*. Thus it is not the case that there is wholesale attrition of these verb forms. The individual lexical verbs are doing something quite different across apparent time.

Taking into account these variables, the picture on the demise of Scots forms starts to look more complex. We now turn to the fourth variable form in the analysis.

3.4 Plural distal demonstratives

The system of demonstrative use has gone through a number of changes since old English (e.g. Quirk and Wrenn 1960: 70, Strang 1970: 269). With plural distal demonstratives from the Middle English period onward, the most common form in the historical record is *those*, as in (20). However, a number of other forms existed: *them* as in (21), *yon/thon*, as in (22), *that* as in (23) and *thae* as in (24).

20. A fig for **those** by law protected! (1785, Burns, 'The Jolly Beggars')
21. **Them** are the women I meant. (1825, Forby, *Voc E*, Intro 141)
22. I mind aye the drink o'milk ye gae me **yon** day. (1818, Scott, *Heart of Midlothian*)
23. To see his wife with **that black clouts** dangling at their lugs. (1772, *Lyon in Mourning*, S.H.S)
24. Now Tam, O Tam! had **thae** been queans. (1790. Burns, 'Tam O' Shanter': 151)

With (23) and (24), Beattie (1788: 92-93) remarks that 'They who speak any dialects of the South of Scotland will be pleased to observe that *these* is of the same import with Scotch *thir* and *those* with Scotch *thai*. In the North of Scotland *thai* and *thir* are not used; and the vulgar say, *this things* and *that things,* as if *this* and *that* had no plural form.'

Beattie's comments hold today: in Buckie, *they* (*thai*) is not used, but *that* is, as in (25a), alongside three other competing forms *them* (26a), *thon/yon*, (25b, 26b, 27b) and *those* (27a).[3]

---

[3] Murray (1872: 186) states '*thon* is probably a corruption of *yon*, developed by analogy of *this*, *that* to render it more significantly demonstrative'.

25. a.   Nae acquant with any of **that north areas**, lyke.
    b.   Saw **thon little birdies** dashin' aboot the bushes. (Donald, 27, fisherman)

26. a.   **Them** days they used to have the choir.
    b.   It was **thon** old fashioned grid iron **beds**. (Mary, fish gutter, 87)

27. a.   Cleverness in **those** days was a' rote learnin'.
    b.   Ken **thon flat things** you smooth cement with? (Jock, 60, caretaker)

Figure 5 shows the use of these four variants across the three generations.

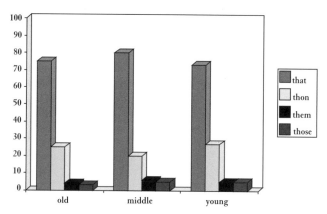

Figure 5: Plural distal demonstratives by age

Figure 5 shows that distal demonstratives show no change in apparent time. The pan-dialectal form *them* is almost non-existent, as is the standard form *those*. Instead the peculiarly north east form *that* exists alongside the older *thon/yon* form. Thus not only is there little influence from standard or supra-local forms, but there is also no change across time in the use of the two predominant variants *that* and *thon*.

I now turn to the last variable under scrutiny.

3.5 /ʍ/ > /f/

The alternation between /ʍ/ and /f/ in initial position or orthographically *wh-* and *f-* as in (28-30) is described as a 'well marked peculiarity of the N.E.' (Dieth 1932: 120).[4]

28. Yon stoot chap wi' the **fite fuskers**. (1871, Alexander, Johnny Gibb of Gushetneuk)
29. Ye'll see **faur** ye'll lan' some day wi' that **fuskey** makin' (1880, Robbie, Glendornie)
30. **Fa** kens **fat** may be in store for oorsel's. (1887, Philip, *Covedale*)
    Marshall (2004: 126) finds that the /f/ form 'is being lost' in Huntly. In Buckie, it

---

[4] However, it may not apply in every context as '*wheel* ... is never recorded with *f*, possibly as the change seems to have taken place in the fifteenth century before wheeled carts were used in n. Scot.' (*Scottish National Dictionary*, s.v. *w*)

appears to be robust, most conspicuously in *wh-* question words: *what/fit, when/far, where/far, who/fa, whose/fas*, as in (31-33):

31. a.   She wasna long in it **finn** Irene packit in.
    b.   Oh well, it a' depends **where** you're fishin'. (John, 87, fisherman)

32. a.   **Finn** you put them in the machine…
    b.   Cos **when** Mark used to come home fae the school…(Jessie, 58, housewife)

33. a.   Is that **farr** you're gan next week?
    b.   **Farr** you stayin' **finn** you're here? (Karen, 26, housewife)

Figure 6 plots the rates of use across the three generations.

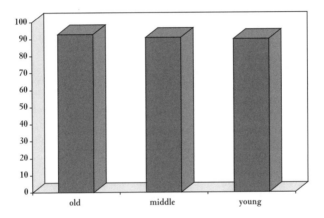

Figure 6: /ʍ/ > /f/ by age

In line with the results for distal demonstratives, there is stability across time in the use of /f/ for /ʍ/ with virtually no evidence of encroaching anglicisation with this variant. Indeed, the speakers can be described as near categorical in their use of the local form.

4. Conclusion

In sum, we have considered six different morphosyntactic and phonetic variables in Buckie which are peculiar to Scots or the north east. The use of competing forms across three generations of speakers allows us to view the effects of standardisation and/or anglicisation in apparent time. Velar fricatives and past tense *–it* marking are rapidly following a trajectory of change towards the standard form. The regularised irregular verb *gied* is also being lost in favour of the standard *went*. However, the two other regularised verbs *selt* and *telt* remain stable across the three age groups. With plural distal demonstratives, neither the standard form *those* nor the pan-dialectal form *them* have made any inroads at all in the system: competition between the older form *thon/yon* and north eastern form *that* remains unchanged over the three generations. Likewise, *wh- > f-* alternation showed hardly any impact at all from the standard form: all ages showed near categorical use of the local form. Thus in the variables considered here, three are fast approaching obsolescence, with the anglicised forms winning over the diagnostic Scots forms, but three remain robust and stable across time despite pressures from prescriptive norms.

5. Disucussion

So what are we to make of this snapshot of Scots as viewed through its use in one small, rural community? What are the pressures that operate to bring about language change (or not) in Buckie and can they be applied elsewhere?

Given the demise of the written standard in Scots in the historical record, coupled with the results for other speech communities in Scotland, we might have expected to find that standard English variants would be increasing to the detriment of these Scots forms in Buckie. But the results are not so black and white. There is no wholesale attrition of Scots forms within the linguistic inventory but instead a mixture of obsolescence and stability. Moreover, what stays and what goes seems to be entirely **random**. Why for example, are velar fricatives hardly ever used by younger speakers, but the variants *fit, farr, fan* etc are used robustly? Why is one regularised verb on the way out, but not others? In the case of written Scots, standardisation due to external pressures was undoubtedly the cause of its demise, and this may be true with other synchronic varieties of Scots which have been studied. However, in Buckie, while some non-standard forms are being replaced by their English equivalents, others are not, thus standardisation simply does not work as a global explanation for the forms analysed in this study.

It might be argued that it is the most highly localised forms that are being retained i.e. *that* in distal demonstratives, and the *wh-/f-* alternation. But this would not account for the maintenance of *selt/telt*, for example, nor the use of the older form *thon* in demonstratives: these forms are not peculiar to the north east but instead have used throughout Scotland. Moreover, if we look beyond the present analysis, maintenance of localised forms does not apply in Huntly, a community very similar to Buckie in socio-ecomomic terms, where *wh-* to f- is obsolescing (see Section 3.5). It could simply be that Huntly is further along the trajectory of change towards the English pole when compared to Buckie, but this account does not explain why some forms show the same distributions across time, but others are radically different: in contrast to *wh-* > *f-*, velar fricatives and *–it* past tense marking in Buckie actually mirrors the Huntly results.

Thus, the explanation for these patterns of use cannot lie solely with external pressures: standardisation has not had an impact on all Scots variants in the Buckie data as it did in the written language. Nor can it lie in the opposition between highly local and more generally Scots forms, both within the community itself or when compared to similar communities.

Instead of looking to external pressures, we must turn to the community members themselves. The differential language behaviour demonstrated in this analysis can be explicated in terms of how the actual users of the Scots language evaluate these forms. These evaluations, whether conscious or subconscious, are revealed through the quantitative patterns of language use. For example, the obsolesence of /x/, but maintenance of *selt/telt*, strongly suggest that the younger speakers have no problem saying, '*Have you selt onythin' the night?*' but avoid '*Have you sold anythin' the nicht?*'. We can hardly claim that the velar fricative is rejected because it is Scots, and Scots forms are less highly valued than their English counterpart, when *selt* is retained. It seems more likely that the velar fricative (or the past tense *–it* marker, or *gied*) is rejected for community-internal reasons: it is associated negatively with older speakers, and non-velar accents are thus marked not as 'English' but as 'young'. On the other hand, *selt/telt*, (or *that/thon* demonstrative or *wh- > f-*) have no such connotations in this community.

Thus, while there may be external pressures to reject or embrace a form, whether Scots, English or anything else, it is finally the speakers who will decide what is 'good', 'bad', 'in' or 'out' in their variety. Moreover, the maintenance of one form and loss of another can provide an insight into the the speakers' attitudes towards these forms and hence their sociolinguistic status within community norms.[5]

Undoubtedly, 'denigration of vernacular varieties plays a role in dialect loss' (Trudgill 2002: 29) and 'linguists are in a particularly strong position to oppose this discrimination' (ibid). In other words, we should seek not only to describe dialects, but also to take some responsibility for their preservation. While this is true, the overriding factor in choice of the local form or the standard form, at least in Buckie, seems to lie at the heart of the community itself.

References

Bailey, G. (2001). 'Real and apparent time'. In Chambers, J.K., Trudgill, P., and Schilling-Estes, N. eds., *The Handbook of Language Variation and Change*, Oxford: Blackwell. 312-332.

Bayley, R. (2002). 'The Quantitative Paradigm'. In Trudgill, P., Chambers, J., and Schilling-Estes, N, eds., *Handbook of Language Variation and Change*. Oxford: Basil Blackwell. 117-141.

Beal, J. (1997). 'Syntax and Morphology'. In C. Jones ed., Edinburgh History of the Scots Langauge. Edinburgh: Edinburgh University Press. 355-377.

Beattie, J. (1788/1968). *The theory of language*. Menston, England: Scolar Press.

Corbett, J. (2003). 'Language Planning and Modern Scots'. In Corbett, J., McClure, J.D. and Stuart-Smith, J. eds., *The Edinburgh Companion to Scots*. Edinburgh: Edinbugh University Press. 251-272.

Corbett, J., McClure, J.D. and Stuart-Smith, J. (2003). 'A Brief History of Scots'. In Corbett, J., McClure, J.D. and Stuart-Smith, J. eds., *The Edinburgh Companion to Scots*. Edinburgh: Edinbugh University Press. 1-16.

Devitt, A. J. (1989). *Standardising Written English: Diffusion in the case of Scotland 1520-1659*. Cambridge: Cambridge University Press.

Dieth, E. (1932). *A grammar of the Buchan dialect*. Cambridge: Heffer.

Görlach, M. (1994). 'Morphological standardization: The strong verbs in Scots'. In D. Britton, ed., *English Historical Linguistics 1994: Papers from the 8th International Conference on English Historical Linguistics*. Amsterdam and Philadelphia: John Benjamins. 161-181.

Grant, W. and Murison, D. D., eds., (1931-76). *The Scottish National Dictionary*. Aberdeen: Aberdeen University Press.

---

[5] Of course, a very different picture may have emerged if another set of variables were examined. These may all have shown loss of the local forms or indeed may all have shown stability across apparent time. (see Smith 2001, 2001, 2004 for further analysis of more variables).

Jespersen, O. H. (1954). *A modern English grammar on historical principles. Part VI: Morphology*. London: George Allen and Unwin.

Johnston, P. (1983). *A Sociolinguistic Investigation of Edinburgh Speech*. Social Science Research Council end of grant report.

Johnston, P. (1997b). 'Regional variation'. In C. Jones ed., *The Edinburgh history of the Scots language*. Edinburgh: Edinburgh University Press. 433-513.

King, A. (1997). 'The inflectional morphology of older Scots'. In C. Jones ed., *The Edinburgh history of the Scots language*. Edinburgh: Edinburgh University Press. 112-55.

Krygier, M. (1994). *The disintegration of the English strong verb system*. Frankfurt: Lang.

Labov, W. (1984). 'Field methods of the project on linguistic change and variation'. In J. Baugh and J. Sherzer ed., *Language in Use: Readings in Sociolinguistics*. Englewood Cliffs, N.J.: Prentice-Hall. 28-54.

Macafee, C. (1994). 'Dialect erosion with special reference to urban Scots'. In Fenton, A. and MacDonald, D. A. eds., *Studies in Scots and Gaelic: Proceedings of the Third International Conference on the Languages of Scotland*. Edinburgh: Canongate Academic. 111-117

Macafee. C. (1996). 'The case for Scots in the 2001 census'. Unpublished paper submitted to the General Register Office (Scotland) and the Scottish Office [www.abdn.ac.uk/scots/slin/soct-bib.htm]

Macafee, C. (1997). 'Ongoing change in Modern Scots: The Social Dimension'. In Jones, C. ed., *The Edinburgh History of the Scots Language*. Edinburgh: Edinburgh University Press.

Macaulay, R. K. S. (1991). *Locating dialect in discourse: The language of honest men and bonnie lasses in Ayr*. Oxford: Oxford University Press.

Marshall, J. (2004). *Language Change and Sociolinguistics: Rethinking Social Networks*. London: Palgrave

McClure, J.D. (1979) 'Scots: Its Range of Uses'. In Aitken, A.J. and T. McArthur, eds., *Languages of Scotland* Edinburgh: Chambers. 26-48

Meurman-Solin, A. (1993). *Variation and Change in Early Scottish Prose: Studies based on the Helsinki Corpus of Older Scots*. Helskinki: Suomalainen Tiedeakatemia

Miller, J. (1993). 'The grammar of Scottish English'. In Milroy, J. and Milroy, L. eds., *Real English: The grammar of English dialects in the British Isles*. New York: Longman. 99-138.

Murdoch, S. (1995). *Language Politics in Scotland*. Aiberdenn Univairsitie Scots Leid Quorum.

Murison, D. (1977). *The Guid Scots Tongue*. Edinburgh:Blackwood.

Murray, J. A. H. (1873). *The dialect of the Southern Counties of Scotland: Its pronunciation, grammar and historical relations*. London: Philological Society.

Quirk, R. and Wrenn, C. L. (1960). *An Old English grammar*. London: Methuen and Company Ltd.

Thompson, P., Wailey, T. and Lummis, T. (1983). *Living the fishing*. London: Routledge.

Smith, J. (2000). *Synchrony and diachrony in the evolution of English: evidence from Scotland*. PhD disseration, University of York.

Smith, J. (2001). 'Negative concord in the Old and new World: Evidence from Scotland'. *Language Variation and Change* 13:2. 109-134.

Smith, J. (2001). '*Ye Ø na hear that kind o' things:* Negative *do* in Buckie'. *English World Wide*, 21/2: 231-259

Smith. J. (2004) 'Accounting for vernacular features in a Scottish dialect: relic, innovation, analogy and drift'. In Kay, C., Horobin, S. and Smith, J. eds., *New perspectives on English Historical Linguistics*. Selected papers from 12 ICEHL, Glasgow, 21-26 August, 2002. Volume 1: Syntax and Morphology. Amsterdam: John Benjamins

Strang, B. M. H. (1970). *A history of English*. London: Methuen and Co. Ltd.

Stuart-Smith, J. (1999). 'Glasgow: accent and voice quality'. In Foulkes, P. and Docherty, G. eds., *Urban Voices: Accent Studies in the British Isles*. London: Arnold. 181-204

Stuart-Smith, J. (2003). 'The Phonology of Modern Urban Scots'. In Corbett, J., McClure, J.D. and Stuart-Smith, J. eds., *The Edinburgh Companion to Scots*. Edinburgh: Edinbugh University Press. 110-137.

Trudgill, P. (2002). *Sociolinguistic Variation and Change*. Edinburgh: Edinburgh University Press.

Wilson, W. (1993). *Speak o' the North East*. Aberdeen: NES publication.

Toward A Corpus of Spontaneous Spoken Scottish Gaelic

William Lamb

Sociolinguistic Background

> With [endangered languages] there is a limited time frame within which
> data can be recorded and preserved before the extinction of the
> language. Even where textual data can be found to represent the
> language, the imperative to record the spoken form of these languages is
> very strong... such recordings may form a useful basis for the revival of
> such languages at a point in the future... [C]orpus linguistics is faced
> with a spoken language archiving crisis—there are many languages for
> which spoken language corpora need to be generated before it is too late.
> (McEnery and Ostler 2000, 414)

The outlook for Scottish Gaelic (ScG) as a community-based spoken language is far
from promising. Increasingly its fluent, active speakers are growing older and are not
being replaced by a younger generation.[1] Assuming that Gaelic proficiency is related
to age, effectively our best speakers are being lost with each passing year. In the Uists,
a group of islands in the Western Isles of Scotland, ScG has not been spoken naturally
by groups of children in school playgrounds largely since the late 1960s and not at all
since the 1980s.[2] This is reflected in the fact that Gaelic speakers under thirty years of
age almost exclusively use English with their contemporaries. Consequently, when
considering the 2001 census, it must be tempered by considering the substantial
proportion of returns who, regardless of their proficiency in the language, contribute
very little in terms of overall 'Gaelic output'. For instance, although 21.9% of the
Gaelic speakers were under the age of 25, a small proportion of these would be
habitual speakers. Furthermore, the actual language abilities of this English-
dominant group will be substantially different from older Gaelic-dominant
bilinguals. Although rigorous research has yet to be done on the subject, an
unquestionably bleak prognosis is offered by MacKinnon (1998: 55), the most
prominent researcher of Gaelic sociology: "Unless tackled promptly and effectively,
the prospect of Gaelic continuing as a family and a community language is likely to
cease with the present generation."

Language death is a world-wide phenomenon and a high proportion of natural
human languages now face some kind of threat. However, just because Scottish
Gaelic's situation can be duplicated elsewhere does not diminish the seemingly
irrevocable cultural and linguistic tragedy forecast for Britain. It is worth asking, if

---

[1] MacKinnon (1998) reports that, in Scotland, only 8% of the children of Gaelic-speaking
parents surveyed for the Euromosaic survey were able to speak the language themselves. In a
more recent study, MacKinnon (2004b) finds that in only two places surveyed in the Western
Isles was the proportion of Gaelic-speaking children equal to that of Gaelic-speaking adults.
[2] One of the few 'green shoots amongst the gloom' described by MacKinnon (2004a)
concerning the 2001 census was a boost in the numbers of Gaelic speakers in the 5-11 age
range. This was interpreted as a clear effect of Gaelic-medium education. However, even in
these schools, the language of the playground has remained almost exclusively English.

the last fluent, native[3] ScG speaker were to disappear today, what would be lacking from the linguistic record as it stands? Fortunately for future generations and unlike many other of the world's languages, ScG has been fairly well-documented at a number of levels, for instance its dialectology (Ó Dochartaigh 1994-97), phonetics/phonology (see Ternes 1994), and basic grammar (Calder 1923; Lamb 2001). However, there is a conspicuous dearth of linguistic and pedagogical resources focusing on natural, spoken ScG.[4] Almost all of those extant concern, and originate with, the written language.[5] This is an ironic situation, for when one considers overall language production, the habits of its users, and its most influential linguistic domains, Scottish Gaelic is primarily an oral language; our documentation is out of step with its linguistic and cultural reality.

It is an established linguistic fact that spoken and written language differ in terms of communicative goals, context, and linguistic form (Chafe 1982 *inter alia*; Biber 1988; 1995; Halliday 1989 *inter alia*; Biber et al. 1999). In particular, spontaneous conversation has been reported to diverge from other language varieties in certain key linguistic properties, such as proportion of subordinate clauses, having a different and less varied lexicon, and evincing different types of morphosyntactic marking (Greenbaum and Nelson 1995; Greenbaum, Nelson and Weitzman 1996; Miller and Weinert 1998). However, for endangered languages such as Scottish Gaelic, it has been debated whether variation of this type even exists. Dressler (1988) claims that one of the hallmarks of an endangered language is its monostylism; effectively an absence of register variation. However, a recent data-intensive study on Scottish Gaelic register variation (Lamb 2002) demonstrated that, at least in this endangered language, there exists a magnitude of register variation to rival many larger world languages.[6] Most of the eight registers investigated[7] were seen to have distinct linguistic profiles, and the study replicated many key findings from studies such as those above. Indeed, one of the most important results was that conversational Gaelic is in some ways unique, diverging from other registers at all linguistic levels, and especially in its syntax.

Some Characteristics of Spontaneous Spoken Gaelic

Syntactic Properties

One of the basic findings of Lamb (2002) was that ScG conversation tends to spread information out over several clauses, whereas most types of writing and some

---

[3] That is, a speaker whose acquisition of the language was pre-pubescent from close relatives and/or the community.

[4] Like Irish (see Ní Laoire 1993) and Modern Greek (Goutsos et al 1994), there has been almost no linguistic work on spoken Scottish Gaelic above the level of segmental phonology.

[5] On current grammatical descriptions, Macaulay (1979, 28) says: '...pedagogic grammars of Gaelic, and indeed Gaelic pedagogic materials in general, have concentrated on the written language...'.

[6] Cf. Biber 1988.

[7] Four spoken and four written registers were investigated: 1) conversation; 2) traditional narrative; 3) radio interview; 4) sports reportage [SPOKEN REGISTERS]; 5) fiction; 6) academic prose; 7) popular writing; 8) news scripts [WRITTEN REGISTERS].

rehearsed speech tend to prefer tight, lexically rich structures. This has been characterised by some researchers as *fragmentation*. However, the label is not meant to be derogatory; the processing limits on spontaneous speech actually often result in an information structure and syntax that is subtly more complex. While speech can enlist prosodic features such as pitch and amplitude to accomplish certain clausal relations such as foregrounding, writing must use more static lexico-grammatical strategies (e.g. relativisers and complementisers). Although more highly rated by most language users, these highly specified structures can actually be clumsy and infelicitous in some cases with on-line spoken language. This is partly due to the different ways in which typical speech and writing deal with information structure. In unmarked (i.e. asyndetic) clausal juxtaposition, for example, clauses are related semantically but the relations themselves are left unspecified. In other words, despite a clause being semantically dependent upon a previous one—as in the case of a complement—the syntax itself indicates no such relation. Consider the following example:

(1) ¹**chuala mi** ²<u>am boireannach</u> ³bha mi ag ràdh riut an-dè (² ᶜᵒⁿᵗ·)<u>a chunna mi an Griminis an-shiudach</u> ⁴bha i sa *bhunkhouse* againn ⁵thall an-shiudach chunnaic mi i ⁶**tha an càr aice an Griminis fhathast**

Gloss: ¹**I heard** ²<u>the woman</u> ³I was saying to you yesterday (² ᶜᵒⁿᵗ·)<u>that I saw in Griminish there</u> ⁴she was in our bunkhouse ⁵over there I saw her ⁶**her car is in Griminish still**

This is a good example of the gradual build up of information in spontaneous spoken language. (The numbers above refer to distinct clauses. The underlined and bold parts are apparently related, but separated by one or more parenthetical statements.) While clause 2 is a relative clause headed by the noun *am boireannach* 'the woman', the relation between clause 1 and 6 is not overtly marked despite a clear semantic link. In more polished prose, a complement clause would have been employed—*chuala mi gu bheil an càr aice ann an Griminis fhathast* 'I heard that her car is still in Griminish', but this is not what happened. Instead of the dependent clause, using the dependent verbal form *gu bheil*, we have an independent clause (*tha* is the independent form of the present tense verb 'to be'). The relation type existing between the clauses has been left unspecified; they are asyndetically juxtaposed. This is possible, and indeed sometimes preferable, in speech. It minimises parsing difficulties for the listener, and actually leads to a greater dynamism and expressiveness in some cases. If we restructure this example using syntactically-integrated language, the linear syntax necessary results in a change to the basic information structure of the utterance:

(2) ¹Bha mi ag ràdh riut an-dè ²gum faca mi am boireannach ³a bha 'sa *bhunkhouse* againn ann an Griminis. ⁴Chuala mi ⁵gu bheil an càr aice ann an Griminis fhathast.

Gloss: ¹I was saying to you yesterday ²that I saw the woman ³who was in our bunkhouse in Griminish. ⁴I heard ⁵that her car is Griminish still.

We notice that example (2) has a two-sentence structure and three dependent clauses (two complement clauses and a relative clause), while example (1) has only one dependent clause: a relative clause. Although the dependent clauses in example (2) encode a greater semantic specificity, they alter the information structure of the original message. Example (1) offers the new, important information, to which the whole utterance builds—that the woman's car is still (worryingly[8]) in Griminish—as an independent clause. This clause stands apart from the rest of the utterance; the addressee waits for the speaker to provide the semantic object to *chuala mi* and it has finally arrived. Example (2) lacks the dynamic presentation of example ; somehow the independent clause conveys more impact than the complement clause. The written version wins on measures of succinctness, but loses on expressiveness.

Detachment expressions are another type of construction not usually found in written language. They are characterised by the presence of an noun phrase (NP) which is associated with a clause but outside of it, generally before or after. Reference is made to the NP within the clause through a pronoun. Pronouns are informationally light and easier to process than a full NP. Essentially, detachment serves to separate the functions of role and reference in a clause:

REFERENT ROLE [SUBJECT]

(3) an duine aig a' chùl chì e na tha a' tachairt reimhe
'the man at the back he can see all that happens before him'

Similar to asyndetic clausal juxtaposition, detachment acts to spread out information. One of its functions is to introduce heavy NPs in such a way that facilitates both the production process and parsing. One of the findings of Lamb (2002) was that conversation had a strong preference for the introduction of heavy NPs in such extraclausal positions, as opposed to having them occur within the clause.

It is important to note that these two constructions—asyndetic clausal juxtaposition and detachment—show that there are basic syntactic differences between Gaelic conversation and other registers. The general picture is that syntactic relations in conversation are less overtly marked, with more gradual staging of information and generally less subordination. Additionally, clauses are more frequent and smaller. Even the very notion of the 'sentence', so ingrained in most people during grammar school days, does not usually have descriptive validity when examining on-line speech (cf. Miller and Weinert 1998).

Morphological and Lexical Properties

As well as differences at the level of syntax and information structure, there are also lexical and morphological contrasts to be found between conversation and other registers. For a start, conversation was found to have several times more instances of code switching and phonologically unassimilated loans than other registers. The influence of English upon the language has not been studied to any great extent, with some Gaelic academics given to burying their heads in the sand and hoping matters will be alleviated through improved education, legislation, etc. Obviously, for such a ubiquitous phenomenon, much more could be done to understand it. Nancy Dorian

---

[8] She had gone kayaking for the day and had been expected back.

(1994b) found informal Gaelic to have a greater frequency than formal Gaelic of profanity and strong interjections. There has not been any publication dedicated to Gaelic swearing, asseveration or profanity, which is perhaps not surprising given its strong religious culture. However, like the effect of English, such pockmarks are nonetheless a part of linguistic heritage and deserve to be recognised and studied.

The morphological contrasts between conversation and most other registers are many, with perhaps the most notable being case marking. The genitive, especially, was treated differently in conversational texts, with a generally simpler morphological expression of the article, and less suppletion and stem modification in the noun (i.e. less specifically 'genitive' forms). Due to its shared spatio-temporal situation, and common knowledge in the participants, there was also a higher frequency of pronominal forms, fewer full nouns, and more indefinite noun forms (e.g. *rudeigin* 'anything'). Finally, conversation showed fewer complex NPs (those with more than 1 modifier), fewer instances of modifiers such as attributive adjectives and genitives, and smaller words in general.

To sum up, the following differences have been found between informal, spoken Scottish Gaelic and other types of Scottish Gaelic registers:

Syntax	Morphology	Lexicon
• More asyndetic clausal juxtaposition • More detachment expressions • Information is staged, over several clauses • Generally less subordination	• Less 'standard' case marking, esp. of genitives • More pronouns • Fewer full nouns • Simpler NP modification • More indefinite nouns • More unassimilated loans from English	• More code switching • Smaller words • More colourful language, such as swearing

The Primacy of Conversation

An apt metaphor for the situation of informal, on-line speech versus other kinds of language can be found in the differences between improvisational jazz and classical music. Improvisational jazz, like speech, is in many ways a product of the present, with complex motifs arising spontaneously against an often minimally constrained background. Classical music, as often performed, strictly conforms to a pre-determined score evincing all of the highly edited intricacies that are possible in a context of few time constraints. Our current research agenda could be likened to a group of accomplished improvisers who are content to see their Coltrane recordings go to dust on phonographs whilst ensuring that their Bach ones are preserved in a robust, digital medium. Speech and writing are different and we need to understand both if we are to gain the full picture of any human language. Chafe (1992) suggests that primacy, actually, should be given to speech, especially conversation:

It is plausible to suppose that humans are "wired up" to speak and listen, that the evolution of speech was inextricably interwoven with the physical evolution of our species. The same cannot be said of writing ... If speaking has a priority in this sense, we can identify conversational language, as opposed to various manifestations of oral literature, as constituting the most basic kind of speaking ... Conversation can justifiably be taken as the use of language to which humans are best adapted and thus the one that can tell us most directly about inherent properties of language and the mind. (1992: 88-89)

Although natural, spontaneous conversation should be the most esteemed language variety in terms of its linguistic and cultural value, it is the one in Scottish Gaelic for which we have the smallest record and know the least about. Furthermore, as time goes by, our potential data source—linguistically- and socially-competent ScG speakers—is rapidly contracting. This predicament has profound ramifications for the future state and viability of research on the language. In the absence of a dynamic speech community, a myriad of hitherto unexplored topics will be obstructed or precluded. In order to safeguard against this undesirable situation it makes sense to act soon and in response to range of needs. Foremost amongst these is the need to archive the linguistic form and sociological facets of informal, conversational Scottish Gaelic for future generations.

Using widely available computer technology, it is possible to effectively manage and search millions of words of text and audio in the form of a digital database. Such a body of data, when collected for a specific purpose, is termed a 'corpus'. Today, corpora are often 'tagged' to provide useful information about the morphosyntactic features of the lexical items within. With a socio-linguistically informed approach, the development of a large, tagged corpus of ScG conversation would be a virtual panacea for the problems enumerated above. It would provide a snapshot of the ScG speech community while there are still Gaelic-dominant native speakers available to record; enable progress on language teaching materials based upon the spoken language; rescue the potential for a wide range of future linguistic studies on spoken ScG; and offer a means of advancing descriptive and lexicographic resources that are currently lacking for the language.[9]

Before discussing a proposal that could address all of these areas, it is worth taking stock of the small amount of work that has been done to this point in Gaelic corpora.

Gaelic Corpora Construction and Research To Date

Very little empirical, corpus based research has appeared on Scottish Gaelic. Dorian (1994a; 1994b; 1999) collected and transcribed interviews with speakers of the East Sutherland dialect and employed some empirical methodology for their linguistic analysis. Macaulay (1979) notes that he once made surreptitious recordings of Gaelic conversation but did not presented them in his work because he felt that they would

---

[9] Currently, there is no ScG thesaurus, the only Gaelic-Gaelic dictionary (Cox 1991) is aimed at primary school children, and the most useful Gaelic-English dictionary (Dwelly's) is more than a century old.

not be understood.[10]

Currently, two projects are underway to develop Scottish Gaelic corpora. The first, the Scottish Corpus of Texts and Speech, has the wide remit of including many of the languages of Scotland—Scottish Gaelic amongst them—but it is to be mainly oriented towards Scots. It has yet to bear fruits on the side of Gaelic. The second, based at the University of Lancaster, is the development of a 40,000 word corpus of spoken Scottish Gaelic, which will be annotated using EAGLES conformant tags. Neither of these studies will be representative enough, or large enough, to fulfil the necessary goals. However, they may make an important contribution to future corpus development in the language.

Lamb (2002), a study of ScG register variation on a 81,677 word corpus (~42k words of transcribed speech), is currently the only computer-based corpus investigation on the language. Due to its successful use of natural, spontaneous conversations, which were elicited from Gaelic-speaking families, and its development and implementation of an extensive morphosyntactic tag set, it is an ideal pilot for a large corpus of spontaneous spoken Gaelic.

Proposal

It is proposed that a large corpus of conversational Scottish Gaelic be created along the same lines of the British National Corpus (BNC) of English, but tailored to the exigencies and limitations of Gaelic's unique linguistic situation. It is imperative that the corpus is morpho-syntactically tagged, and large and varied enough to inform a wide range of potential interests and applications (e.g. dialectology, pedagogy, phonology, syntax and lexicography). As a benchmark, the BNC had similar motivations (see Crowdy 1993) and achieved 4.2 million words of informal spoken conversation (http://info.ox.ac.uk/bnc/what/balance.html). It would be sensible to collect and transcribe a similar number of words of Scottish Gaelic (4 million or more), with informants equally distributed by gender. However, sampling should probably favour stronger dialects over weaker ones to procure as much as possible a snapshot of a whole language community. Perhaps an argument can also be made for including more older speakers than younger ones, as competency level in ScG tends to positively correlate with age.

Collection and Storage

The BNC team collected its conversation data using a demographic sampling approach, randomly selecting 124 different volunteers to represent a wide range of social, class, and geographic variables. These participants then surreptitiously recorded every conversation that they had over a set period of time (usually 2-3 days) and logged the details of each interaction (setting, etc.) in a notebook. This kind of approach is ideal in many ways, and relatively easy with a language such as English, but it is possibly precluded in Gaelic by its smaller population, bilingualism and cultural differences. Demographic sampling was attempted in a recent corpus

---

[10] Macaulay says: 'I have used a very restricted range of constructed sentences to exhibit the [phonological] tone distinctions, rather than the very heterogeneous material in my actual data texts, which the reader might have found intolerably confusing' (1979: 37).

building venture on spoken Sylheti (Baker et al. 2000) but was unsuccessful for a number of reasons:

1. Self-consciousness of the informant in the presence of the recorder
2. Mistrust of the researchers' aims
3. Problems in using the equipment

The researchers resolved to use radio speech and one-to-one interviews in lieu of this information. Despite the problems that they had, and the likelihood that we would experience similar ones, it is not ideal to resort to this kind of data. Radio speech and one-to-one interviews are both linguistically and contextually different than informal speech. Lamb (2002) achieved its spontaneous spoken sub-corpus by asking families to record themselves at mealtimes or other times when conversation naturally occurred. However, it should also not be ruled out that 'surreptitious roving participants' could be used effectively, perhaps in tandem with more situated recording methods. To decrease the likelihood of negative reactions from surreptitious recording methods, the following steps could be followed:

1. After funding is secured, an initial wave of publicity is released to the local and national papers to generate interest in the project
2. A second wave of publicity is released later, requesting participants in specific locales
3. In the publicity, it is made clear what the recordings are for and why they must be done surreptitiously—to keep them as natural as possible
4. Community coordinators (hereafter 'CC')—natives local to a place—are enlisted to locate willing participants and are the 'go-betweens' for information collection and management
5. Main participants are well paid for their work
6. All informants are fully debriefed about the project and are asked to provide informed consent for the use of the recordings

Certainly, there are potential problems with attempting such an approach with Gaelic. For one, Gaelic will not be the only, nor even main, language used by many of the participants on a day-to-day basis. Those speakers using mainly Gaelic will tend to be older and possibly less able to reliably operate any recording equipment left with them. It may be the case they would be more likely to participate on a 'one-off' or situated (e.g. dinner conversation) basis. Also, the Gaelic proficiency level of each speaker will have to be accounted for, as well as whether they are L1 or L2 speakers of the language. Level of fluency could be judged by CCs on a log sheet using a Likert-type scale (e.g., 1 *highest* - 5 *lowest*). Finally, it will be necessary to decide whether the corpus is to be natural at all costs, with increased code-switching, or weighted towards Gaelic rather than English use. Either way, there are ramifications for the many aspects of the study.

The following list presents a possible collection scenario:

1. A participant contacts the project's base to express interest in the project. After speaking with the community coordinator, s/he decides to take part (*Alternatively* the CC contacts an individual who s/he believes would be likely to take part and

this person agrees[11])
2. The application is reviewed by the committee and the participant is accepted to the project
3. The participant comes to the office and is informed by the CC on how the equipment works and how to complete the conversation logs
4. The participant leaves and records all conversations s/he has over the time period (*or* those which s/he feels are likely to have Gaelic content, if a Gaelic-preferential model is used)
5. The participant returns the equipment after a) a certain number of Gaelic conversations are completed or b) a pre-determined amount of time has passed
6. All participants are debriefed and asked to give informed consent for the use of the recordings in the corpus and for future research

Corpus Transcription, Digitisation and Mark-Up

A number of individuals would need to be hired for the purposes of transcription. These would be part-time positions and the applicants would need to be fluent and literate in the language. They would be trained as necessary in transcription protocols such as the orthographical standards adopted by the Scottish Examination Board. It will be important to decide whether and how the transcription should be different than simple orthographic representation; e.g. pause measures, intonation, or simple phonetic information. In the interests of time, it may suffice to conduct the initial transcription at a purely lexical level.

The audio recordings themselves would be converted to a compressed format,[12] removing frequencies outside of the range of speech, and aligned with the corpus. The finished product would be issued on CD-ROM and allow users to both view and hear each text. Names and places would be removed or altered. Voices could also be digitally masked so that participants remain fully anonymous. A version could be put on the Internet, and the tagger could be made freely available. For instance, Gaelic documents e-mailed to a specific address could be returned in a tagged state.

The mark-up of the corpus—morphosyntactic tags and SGML codes—would need to be directed by a linguist fluent in Gaelic. A computer expert with experience in corpora studies would be needed to develop the software to implement the tag set and ensuring the corpus was conformant with current industry standards (such as those of the Text Encoding Initiative (TEI): see Burnard 1995). Fortunately, two MSc dissertations at the University of Edinburgh's Infomatics Dept. (Kosntantopoulos 1998; Crane 1999) have gone some way towards developing Gaelic corpus tools. Additionally, a tag-counting and concordance package (LinguaStat©) was developed for Lamb (2002) that will be of help in this effort. Early on, it will be necessary to decide whether to use a pre-existing automatic tagger, such as CLAWS (Garside 1995), or go about custom designing one. Fortunately, there has been a great deal of work on this area in a wide variety of languages, some of which—e.g. Greek—present a far more complex morphology than Gaelic. Some taggers are reputed to be 'language-independent' and perhaps one could be readily tailored to Gaelic. On-line

---

[11] Good possibilities would be those persons who are involved in community leadership or Gaelic education. Older crofters and retirees would be the best informants in many ways as they are likely to lead the most Gaelic-oriented lives.
[12] A non-compressed version would be made available for phonological/phonetic interests.

Gaelic lexicons are now in a fairly advanced stage, and it will be possible to convert one or more for use in the study. The end goal would be to develop an interactive tagging programme capable of dealing with both spoken and written texts.

Conclusion

The development of spoken Gaelic corpora is imperative if the language is to have a place in what looks to be our highly technological future:

> Corpora have become the touchstone of credibility ... Access to corpus data will consequently determine whether state-of-the-art reference resources for a language are available or not. Given that access to such resources is a vital component of education in general and language education in particular, access to corpus data is consequently of importance to endangered and less studied languages (Baker et al. 2000: 421).

By providing this basic resource, we will have opened up a number of adjunct possibilities. Of course, linguistic and general interest on Scottish Gaelic will be intensified through the dissemination of information about, and research conducted on, the corpus. More importantly, however, it will provide both the impetus and framework for further computer-based language work and applications, such as concordancers, automatic speech recognition and machine translation. Rhodri Jones poses the question in *The Language Machine* (Atwell 1999), '[in the future] will we still be to learning languages at all?' There is, of course, the possibility that the apparently inexorable trend for endangerment to lead to extinction will continue unabated until we are left with few distinct human tongues. Yet there is the more intriguing possibility that advances in computer technology—specifically automatic machine translation—will make it possible to be a minority language monoglot, but still be able to spontaneously communicate with nearly every other human being on the planet. Such a development would eventually dissolve the monopolies of power currently enjoyed by a small number of languages. With the emergence of a level-playing field of this kind, perhaps Gaelic speakers might one day not fear for the future of their language. However, developing a large, tagged corpus of Scottish Gaelic conversation is the necessary first step before we can even entertain such possibilities.

References

Atwell, Eric (1999) *The Language Machine*, London: The British Council.

Baker, P., Lie, M., McEnery, T. and Sebba, M. (2000) 'The construction of a corpus of spoken Sylheti', *Literary and Linguistic Computing*, 15(4): 421-431.

Biber, D. (1988) *Variation Across Speech and Writing*, Cambridge and New York: CUP.

Biber, D. ed. (1995) *Dimensions of Register Variation: A Cross-linguistic Comparison*, Cambridge: CUP.

Burnard, Lou (1995) 'The Text Encoding Initiative: an overview', in G. Leech, G. Myers and J. Thomas, eds. 69-81.

Calder, G. (1923) *A Gaelic Grammar* (1990 edition), Glasgow: Gairm Publications.

Chafe, Wallace (1982) 'Integration and involvement in speaking, writing and oral literature', in D. Tannen, ed. *Spoken and Written Language: Exploring Orality and Literacy*, 35-53, Norwood, NJ: Ablex.

—— (1985) 'Linguistic differences produced by differences between speaking and writing', in Olson, D.R., Torrence, N., and A. Hildyard, eds. *Literacy, Language, and Learning*, Cambridge: CUP.

—— (1992) 'The importance of corpus linguistics to understanding the nature of language', in Svartvik, J. ed. 79-97.

Chafe, W. and Danielewicz, J. (1987) 'Properties of written and spoken language', in R. Horowitz and S.J. Samuels, eds. *Comprehending Oral and Written Language*, 83-113, New York: Academic Press.

Cox, Richard (1991) *Brìgh nam Facal: Faclair Ùr don Bhun-sgoil*, Glaschu: Oilthigh Ghlaschu.

Crane, Andrew (1999) *A Spell-checker in Scottish Gaelic*, unpublished MSc dissertation, University of Edinburgh.

Crowdy, S. (1993) 'Spoken corpus design', *Literary and Linguistic Computing*, 8(4): 259-65.

Crowdy, S. (1995) 'The BNC spoken corpus', in G. Leech, G. Myers, and J. Thomas, eds. 224-234.

Dorian, Nancy (1994a) 'Stylistic variation in a language restricted to private-sphere use', in D. Biber and E. Finegan, eds. *Sociolinguistics Perspectives on Register*, 217-34, New York: Oxford University Press.

Dorian, Nancy (1994b) 'Varieties of variation in a very small place: Social Homogeneity, prestige norms, and linguistic variation', *Language*, 70 (4): 631-696.

Dorian, Nancy (1999) 'Celebrations: In praise of the particular voices of languages at risk', *Ogmios*, 12: 4-14.

Dressler, Wolfgang U. (1988) 'Language death', in F. Newmeyer, ed. *Linguistics: The Cambridge Survey IV*, 184-192, Cambridge: CUP.

Garside, Roger (1995) 'Grammatical tagging of the spoken part of the British National Corpus: a progress report', in G. Leech, G. Myers and J. Thomas, eds. 161-167.

Goutsos, D., Hatzidaki, O., and King, P. (1994) 'Towards a corpus of spoken modern Greek', *Linguistic and Literary Computing*, 9(3): 215-223.

Greenbaum, S. and Nelson, G. (1995) 'Clause relationships in spoken and written English', *Functions of Language*, 2: 1-21.

Greenbaum, S., Nelson, G. and Weitzman, M. (1996) 'Complement clauses in English', in J. Thomas and M. Short, eds. *Using Corpora for Language Research: Studies in the Honour of Geoffrey Leech*, 76-91.

Halliday, M.A.K. (1987) 'Spoken and written modes of meaning', in Rosalind Horowitz and S. Jay Samuels, eds. *Comprehending Oral and Written Language*, New York: Academic Press.

Halliday, M.A.K. (1989) *Spoken and Written Language*, Oxford: OUP.

Halliday, M.A.K. (1994) *An Introduction to Functional Grammar*, London: Arnold.

Konstantopoulos, Stasinos (1998) *A Morphological Analyser for Scottish Gaelic*, unpublished MSc dissertation, University of Edinburgh.

Lamb, William (1999) 'A diachronic account of Gaelic News-speak: The development and expansion of a register', *Scottish Gaelic Studies*, XIX: 141-171.

Lamb, William (2001) *Scottish Gaelic*, Languages of the World/Materials, München: Lincom Europa.

Lamb, William (2002) *Speech and Writing in Scottish Gaelic: A Study of Register Variation in an Endangered Language*, unpublished PhD thesis, University of Edinburgh.

Leech, G., Myers, G. and J. Thomas, eds. (1995) *Spoken English on Computer: Transcription, Mark-up and Application*, Harlow: Longman.

Macaulay, D. (1979) 'Some functional and distributional aspects of intonation in Scottish Gaelic: A preliminary study of tones', *Occasional Papers in Linguistics and Language Learning*, 6: 27-38.

McEnery, T. and Ostler, N. (2000) 'A new agenda for corpus linguistics—Working with all of the world's languages', *Literary and Linguistic Computing*, 15(1): 403-419.

MacKinnon, Kenneth (1998) 'Gaelic in family, work and community domains: Euromosaic Project 1994/95', *Scottish Language*, 17: 55-69.

MacKinnon, Kenneth (2004a) 'Gaelic in the 2001 census: a few green shoots amongst the gloom', in J.D. McClure, ed. *Doonsin' Emerauds: New Scrieves anent Scots an Gaelic*, Belfast: Cló Ollscoil na Banríona, 24-35.

MacKinnon, Kenneth (2004b) 'Reversing Languge Shift: Gaelic to English – Any Evidence?', talk given at *Rannsachadh na Gàidhlig 2004*, University of Edinburgh.

Miller, J., and Weinert, R. (1998) *Spontaneous Spoken Language*, Oxford: Clarendon.

Ní Laoire, Siobhán (1988) 'Preliminaries to a study of register in Modern Irish', *Language, Culture and Curriculum*, 1(3): 289-301.

Svartvik, J. (1992) *Directions in Corpus Linguistics: Proceedings of Nobel Symposium 82, Stockholm, August 4-8, 1991*. Berlin: Mouton de Gruyter.

Gnéithe d'antraipeolaíocht theangeolaíoch phobal Ros Muc, Co. na Gaillimhe.

Conchúr Ó Giollagáin

1.0 Réamhrá

Scagadh ar thorthaí a bhaineann le tionscadal taighde ar ghnéithe éagsúla de nósmhaireachtaí teanga phobal comhaimseartha Ros Muc (RM) atá san alt seo. Is é an dara halt é i sraith atá á réiteach agam ar antraipeolaíocht theangeolaíoch na Gaeltachta. Leanfar den mhodheolaíocht chéanna anseo is a cuireadh i bhfeidhm ar fhaisnéis an ailt tosaigh ar Ghaeltacht Ráth Cairn (RC)i gContae na Mí[1] agus déanfar iarracht an t-ábhar a leagan amach de réir an mhúnla chéanna a cleachtadh i gcás an tionscadail i RC d'fhonn cur leis an anailís chomparáideach.

Ach an oiread leis an mbunaidhm a bhí taobh thiar den taighde i gcás phobal RC, thug mé faoin tionscadal seo i RM ar mhaithe le teacht ar thuiscint níos fearr ar an imoibriú sochtheangeolaíochta atá mar chrann taca don phobal Gaeilge sa gceantar seachas mioneolas ar an bpobal seo a nochtadh agus a fhógairt don saol mór. Ina cheann sin, tabharfaidh an t-alt seo deis dúinn athmheas a dhéanamh ar chuid de na conclúidí sealadacha a bhí san alt tosaigh ar RC i dtaca leis an saol comhaimseartha Gaeltachta. Tiocfaidh pictiúr níos iomláine chun solais de réir mar a chuirfear ceantair éagsúla isteach sa meá.

Is laistigh de fhráma tagartha na hantraipeolaíochta teangeolaí a leagann béim ar ról na teanga i bpobal mar áis chultúrtha, agus ar réaladh na ngnás éagsúla labhartha i gcás na líonraí coimpléascacha sóisialta a fheidhmítear sa bpobal, a tugadh faoin taighde seo.[2] Tugann an tionscadal seo aghaidh ar anailís a dhéanamh ar theacht chun cinn na gcineálacha éagsúla cainteoirí i bpobal RM agus féachann sé le hiniúchadh a dhéanamh ar na dinimicí sochtheangeolaíochta is bunús leo ag leibhéal an teaghlaigh agus an phobail.

Is éard is ciall le pobal RM, i gcás an taighde seo, an pobal sa gcuid sin de pharóiste RM[3] a bhfuil cónaí orthu sna naoi mbaile fearainn seo a leanas: An Gairfean, An Gort Mór, An Turlach Mór, An Turlach Beag,[4] Cill Bhriocáin, Glinn Chatha, Ros Cíde, Ros Muc agus Snámh Bó. Seo iad na bailte a shíníonn isteach sa leithinis ón bhfearann idir Droichead Inbhir sa Turlach Mór agus Droichead

---

[1] Féach Ó Giollagáin (2002: 25-56) in *The Irish Journal of Anthropology*.

[2] Sainmhíníonn Duranti (1997: 2-3) an antraipeolaíocht theangeolaíoch ar an gcaoi seo a leanas: "...the study of language as a cultural resource and as speaking as a cultural practice... This means that linguistic anthropologists see the subject of their study, that is the speakers, first and above all as social actors, that is, members of particular, interestingly complex, communities, each organized in a variety of social institutions and through a network of intersecting but not necessarily overlapping sets of expectations, beliefs, and moral values about the world."

[3] Thugtaí Paróiste Chill Bhriocáin air tráth (Robinson 1990: 105). Is cuid de pharóiste RM é ceantar Chamuis, ach níl faisnéis Chamuis á cur san áireamh sa taighde seo.

[4] Cloífear anseo leis an nós litrithe a mholann Robinson (1990: 114); deir sé gur *tuar* is bunús leis an logainm maidir leis an Turlach Mór/Beag.

Abhainn na Scríbe i nGlinn Chatha.[5] Is mar seo a aithnítear ceantar RM i RM féin agus i gceantar Chonamara (CN) i gcoitinne.

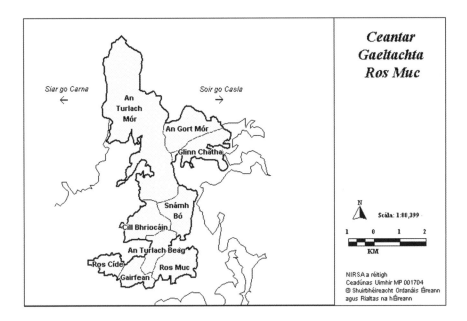

1.1 Cúlra Stairiúil agus Cultúrtha

Is í aidhm na haiste seo trácht a dhéanamh ar ghnéithe den antraipeolaíocht theangeolaíoch chomhaimseartha i RM agus ar na himpleachtaí a bheidh ag na dinimicí teanga reatha sa gceantar don phobal amach anseo. Déanfar plé gairid anseo thíos ar chúlra stairiúil agus cultúrtha an cheantair ar mhaithe le comhthéacs a thabhairt don fhaisnéis atá á cíoradh sa taighde seo. Dar ndóigh, d'fhéadfadh éifeacht láidir a bheith ag claochluithe soch-chultúrtha ar ghnáis teanga pobail agus impleachtaí substaintiúla stairiúla a bheith ann dá réir. Tugann an taighde seo spléachadh tosaigh ar athruithe suntasacha sochtheangeolaíochta agus soch-chultúrtha atá ag teacht chun cinn i RM a mbeidh impleachtaí láidre acu d'fhorás phobal RM mar cheann de shainphobail stairiúla Ghaeilge Iar-Chonnacht. D'fhéadfaí a áiteamh, mar thoradh ar láithriú fhaisnéis an taighde seo, gur cosúil go bhfuil pobal RM ag teannadh le staid chinniúnach agus dhúshlánach maidir lena bhféiniúlacht mar phobal Gaeltachta de réir mar a tuigeadh an fhéiniúlacht sin sa gceantar go nuige seo. Léiríonn na hathruithe teangeolaíochta atá ag teacht i bhfeidhm faoi láthair i RM, mar atá sonraithe anseo i bhfaisnéis nósmhaireachtaí teanga aos óg an cheantair, go bhfuil an chuma ar an scéal go bhfuil pobal RM ar tí dul thar thairseach suntasach stairiúil ó thaobh a n-oidhreachta soch-chultúrtha de.

---

[5] Cloistear go minic an sainiú 'an dá dhroichead' agus 'idir an dá dhroichead' ag daoine san áit le tagairt a dhéanamh don cheantar sa gcuid thuaidh den Turlach Mór, don Ghort Mór agus Glinn Chatha.

Máirtínigh Bhaile na hInse a raibh forlámhas acu mar thiarnaí talúna ar an gceantar i dtréimhse na nua-staire (Mac Aonghusa 1991: 1; Melvin 1996: 348; Robinson 1995: xi). Bhí orthu a n-eastát a dhíol sa naoú haois déag le seanfhiacha a ghlanadh. Aithnítear gur eascair géarchéim airgeadais na Máirtíneach as fiacha troma cearrbhachais, ach is gá ualach trom na bhfiach a chur i gcomhthéacs na laincisí leanúnacha a bhain leis "na heastáit neamhacmhainneacha", a bhí forleathan in iarthar na hÉireann sa naoú haois déag, a chur san áireamh freisin ar mhaithe le teip na Máirtíneach a thuiscint. Ba é Richard Berridge, grúdlannaí de bhunadh Londaineach (Robinson 1995: xi), a ghlac seilbh ar chuid shuntasach d'iareastát na Máirtíneach in 1872. Maíonn Mac Aonghusa (1991: 2) go raibh an-tionchar ag soiscéal Mhichíl Mhic Dháibhéid ar an gceantar i ngeall ar an taithí a bhí ag muintir na háite ar thiarnaí talúna, go háirithe Berridge. Ba i 1914 a cheannaigh Bord na gCeantar gCúng talamh Bherridge i RM agus roinneadh an talamh ar na tionóntaí (Robinson 1990: 105).

Neadaigh raidiceachas eile polaitiúil sa gceantar aimsir na hathbheochana náisiúnta ag tús an fhichiú haois a bhfuil a thionchar le brath ar an gceantar i gcónaí. Cuireadh craobh de Chonradh na Gaeilge ar bun sa gceantar i 1903 agus bunaíodh cathlán d'Óglaigh na hÉireann ann i 1913 a raibh daoine as RM, an Cheathrú Rua agus Ceantar na nOileán páirteach ann agus a raibh Pádraig Mac Piarais ina oifigeach ceannais air. Ba thrí obair an Phiarsaigh le Conradh na Gaeilge sa gceantar roimhe sin a chuir sé aithne ar mhuintir RM. Déanann Mac Aonghusa amach (1991: 8) gur bhunaigh an Piarsach cathlán neamhspleách sa gcuid sin den chontae gan dul i dteagmháil le lucht ceannais Chathlán na Gaillimhe. Rinne an Piarsach é seo sa gcaoi nach mbeadh Béarlóir(í) as áit éigin eile sa gcontae ag glacadh ceannasaíochta ar bhuíon óglach Gaeltachta. Breithiúnas a léirigh tuiscint an-ghrinn ar dhinimící sochtheangeolaíochta ag an am, más fíor. Maíonn Mac Aonghusa (1991: 17) go raibh 38 óglach páirteach i mbuíon RM agus ba é Colm Ó Gaora, a d'fhág cuntas againn ar an tréimhse sin i RM ina dhírbheathnéis, *Mise* (1943), a bhí i gceannas orthu.

I gcás na scríbhneoirí eile a fáisceadh as pobal RM i gcaitheamh an fhichiú haois, ba é Pádraic Ó Conaire agus a shaothar (1882 – 1928) ba mhó a tharraing aitheantas ó thaobh cúrsaí liteartha de. Shaothraigh sé an t-úrscéalaíocht, an ghearrscéalaíocht, an drámaíocht agus an iriseoireacht, agus bhí tionchar nach beag aige ar shaol cultúrtha agus liteartha na Gaeilge lena linn i ngeall ar a chuid ceannródaíochta i réimse na scríbhneoireachta. Scrúdaigh a chuid scríbhinní téamaí a bhain lena shaolré féin agus a nochtaigh an saol, idir thuath agus chathair, dá chuid léitheoirí de réir mhúnlaí reacaireachta a bhí ag teacht leis an réalachas sóisialta.[6] Ba i gcathair na Gaillimhe a tháinig Ó Conaire ar an saol, ach tháinig sé go RM ina dhílleachta i 1893 lena bheirt dearthháir, áit a raibh cónaí orthu lena n-uncail, Pádraic Ó Conaire, a mba leis Bád Chonraí agus Tigh Chonraí ar an nGairfean a mbíodh siopa á reáchtáil ann.

Bhí gaol ag scríbhneoir eile próis as RM, Pádraic Óg Ó Conaire (1893 – 1971), le Sean-Phádraic agus d'fhág sé oidhreacht seacht n-úrscéal agus dhá chnuasach gearrscéalta ina dhiaidh (Ó Conghaile 1988: 19). B'as RM do Chaitlín Maude (1941 – 1982) a shaothraigh an fhilíocht den chuid is mó.[7] Tá mírín spéisiúil staire ó thaobh cúrsaí teanga de i dTuarascáil Choimisiún na Gaeltachta a foilsíodh i 1926 a

---

[6] Féach de Bhaldraithe (1982), Denvir (1983), Ní Chionnaith (1995), Ó Broin (1984) agus Riggs (1994).
[7] Ba é Ciarán Ó Coigligh a chuir cnuasach dá cuid filíochta in eagar tar éis a báis (Maude 1984).

bhaineann le ceantar RM. Foilsíodh dhá shraith léarscálacha in éineacht leis an Tuarascáil a léirigh líon na gcainteoirí Gaeilge de réir toghranna ceantair; tagraíonn léarscáil 1 do thorthaí daonáireamh 1911 agus léarscáil 2 don fhaisnéis teanga a bailíodh chun críche obair Choimisiún na Gaeltachta i 1925. Tugann léarscáil 1 (1911) le fios gurbh ionann líon na gcainteoirí Gaeilge i dtoghroinn cheantair an Turlaigh, a fhreagraíonn cuid mhór do limistéar an tionscadail atá faoi chaibidil san aiste seo, agus 93% de dhaonra an cheantair (1,452 duine). Léiríonn léarscáil 2 gur mhéadaigh a líon do 99.9% den daonra (1,307 duine) tar éis bhunú an Stáit Éireannaigh de réir fhaisnéis Choimisiún na Gaeltachta i 1925.

Leag an Coimisiún céanna critéir chéatadánacha síos d'fhonn sainiú a dhéanamh ar an bhFíor-Ghaeltacht agus ar an mBreac-Ghaeltacht. Aithníodh ceantar mar Fhíor-Ghaeltacht dá mbeadh 80% nó níos mó dá phobal ina gcainteoirí Gaeilge (Tuarascáil Choimisiún na Gaeltachta 1926: 6; Walsh 2002: 12); aitheantas a tugadh *ipso facto* do cheantar RM ag an am, dar ndóigh, agus athdhearbhaíodh an stádas seo nuair a cuireadh forálacha Acht na Gaeltachta i bhfeidhm i 1956.[8]

Bhí ról tábhachtach ag pobal RM i mbunú Raidió na Gaeltachta i ngeall ar an mbaint a bhí acu le bunú Shaor-raidió Chonamara ar craoladh a chéad chlár ar an 28 Márta 1970.[9] Bua cliste bolscaireachta a bhí i mbunú an stáisiúin bhradaigh seo a thug dúshlán an stáit i ngeall ar a chuid faillí ó thaobh na craoltóireachta Gaeilge de. Bhí lámh chinniúnach ag Piaras Ó Gaora san obair seo ar fad agus bhain an feachtas agus an chraoltóireacht bhradach fómhar nuair a ghéill an rialtas dá n-éileamh Raidió na Gaeltachta a bhunú. Ar Dhomhnach Cásca 1972 a chraol Raidió na Gaeltachta don chéad uair.

Cuireadh togra spéisiúil teangeolaíochta ar bun sa gceantar i bhFómhar na bliana 1964 a raibh Hans Hartmann, Ollamh le Teangeolaíocht Chomparáideach in Ollscoil Hamburg, i gceannas air. Ba i bhfoirm gnáthchomhráite a taifeadadh an t-ábhar ó sheachtar de bhunadh na háite. Ba léir go raibh aidhmeanna teangeolaíochta chun tosaigh sa togra seo, is é sin go mbeadh taifead gairmiúil coinnithe ar chaint an cheantair, ach faightear eolas lena chois seo ar stairsheanchas a bhaineann le ceantar RM mar aon le míríní beathaisnéise agus seanchais sa gcuntas tras-scríofa a réitigh Arndt Wigger don chló (Wigger 2004).

1.1.1 Faisnéis Ghinearálta ar RM faoi láthair

Murab ionann agus RC is pobal imeallach tuaithe atá i RM a bhfuil scáth na dífhostaíochta agus sciar suntasach na n-aosach sa bpobal le sonrú go láidir ar phróifíl socheacnamaíochta an cheantair.[10] Níl ach an t-aon togra amháin tionsclaíochta ag feidhmiú sa gceantar, Saotharlann Chonamara Teoranta sa nGort Mór. Is fiontar príobháideach é in earnáil na bithcheimice a fhostaíonn 20 duine (tá fostaíocht

---

[8] Acht na Gaeltachta 1956, Aguisín C (Ordú na Limistéirí Gaeltachta).

[9] Féach Ó Glaisne (1982: 27-9).

[10] Tá an t-imeallú seo a bhfuil pobal RM ag dul i ngleic leis go fóill le sonrú ar fhóras stairiúil an cheantair. Is féidir leanúnachas théama an imeallaithe a rianadh trí ghanntanas an naoú haois déag, na brúnna déimeagrafaíochta agus sóisialta a nochtaíodh le linn thréimhse Bhord na gCeantar gCúng, fhadhb na heisimirce agus tríd an gclamhsán comhaimseartha faoin easpa forbartha tionsclaíochta sa gceantar, féach mar shampla: O'Neill, T.P. (1996); Coimisiún Dudley (1907) agus Mac Aonghusa (2000: 399).

pháirtaimseartha san áireamh sa líon seo) a mbaineann thart ar an gceathrú cuid díobh le ceantar RM. Tá dhá bhunscoil san áit Scoil an Ghoirt Mhóir agus Scoil an Turlaigh Bhig, agus meánscoil amháin, Gairmscoil na bPiarsach. Tá dhá theach tábhairne agus dhá shiopa i RM, a bhfuil Oifig an Phoist i gceann acu. Tá duine fostaithe in oifig a dháileann comhairle agus eolas ar an bpobal áitiúil, Cumas Teoranta, agus is i RM atá oifig an Phléaráca lonnaithe freisin. Eagraíonn Pléaráca Teoranta, i measc dualgas eile, ócáidí cultúrtha agus imeachtaí pobail ar fud Chonamara go háirithe; tá triúr fostaithe ag Pléaráca le plé leis na cúraimí seo. Tá fostaíocht de chineál áirithe i gceist leis na scéimeanna FÁS a reáchtáiltear go háitiúil. Ach an oiread le ceantar ar bith, ní gá gur go háitiúil atá cónaí ar fhostaithe na n-institiúidí agus na dtograí thuas. Bhíodh deichniúr fostaithe áitiúla ag obair i Stáisiún Ginte Leictreachais Scríb (i nGlinn Chatha) agus neart de mhuintir na háite ag saothrú ioncaim éigin ó bheith ag soláthar móna don stáisiún, ach dúnadh an stáisiún ginte ann i 1979 ar chúiseanna airgeadais.

In ainneoin thírdhreach tarraingteach na háite, is beag forbairt i réimse na turasóireachta atá curtha i gcrích i RM, cé is moite de chuairteoirí a thagann chuig an gceantar ar mhaithe le Gaeilge a fhoghlaim, daltaí dara leibhéal den chuid is mó. Eagraíonn Coláiste na bhFiann Teoranta agus Spleodar Teoranta cúrsaí Gaeilge sa samhradh do dhaltaí scoile agus fanann na daltaí le mná tí an cheantair. Tá cúrsaí turasóireachta i RM ag brath go hiomlán beagnach ar acmhainní Gaeilge an phobail.

Déanann an taighde seo amach nach féidir ach 7% de phobal infhostaithe RM a rannú i ngrúpa sochaicmeach a bheadh níos airde ná rannaithe a bhaineann le cúraimí lucht oibre. Léiríonn an fhaisnéis seo go bhfuil 23% de phobal iomlán an cheantair dífhostaithe agus is ionann sin agus 42% de rannóg oibre an phobail, is é sin má bhaintear páistí, pinsinéirí agus daoine atá ag plé le hoideachas lánaimseartha as an gcuntas. Is í an earnáil seirbhísí (siopaí, tithe ósta, tithe banaltrais, srl.) an rannóg fostaíochta is mó a thugann deiseanna oibre do phobal RM, ach tá sciar suntasach d'fhostaithe an cheantair ag obair mar oibrithe tógála, tiomána nó oibrithe de chuid na Comhairle Contae freisin.

Feicfear sa bhfaisnéis thíos go bhfuil pobal RM i bhfad níos aonghnéithí ná pobal RC ó thaobh chúlra na ndaoine agus rannú na gcainteoirí a bhfuil cónaí orthu sa gceantar. Ní údar iontais an méid seo nuair a chuirtear san áireamh gur cuid de phobal orgánach stairiúil Gaeilge Iar-Chonnacht é pobal RM agus gur mar thoradh ar scéim aistrithe ó Chonamara a tháinig pobal Gaeltachta ar an bhfód i RC sa ré chomhaimseartha i gceantar tuaithe in oirthear na tíre a raibh an t-aistriú teanga curtha i gcrích ann roimhe sin.[11]

1.2 Modh Oibre

Idir Fómhar 2002 agus Samhradh 2003 go príomha a tugadh faoi fhaisnéis a chruinniú don taighde seo. D'iarr mé ar chúigear de bhunadh RM a bhfuil cónaí orthu sa gceantar cúnamh a thabhairt dom ar bhealaí éagsúla faisnéis a chruinniú i dtaobh dinimicí éagsúla de shochtheangeolaíocht an phobail i RM. Duine as an gcúigear a roinn formhór an eolais a bhí mé a lorg agus chuidigh an ceathrar eile liom an bunábhar faisnéise a dheimhniú.[12] Murab ionann agus a mhacasamhail den

---

[11] Tá comhthéacs staire an aistrithe go RC pléite in Ó Conghaile (1986) agus Ó Giollagáin (1999).

[12] Gabhaim buíochas ó chroí leis na daoine i RM a thug cúnamh dom an fhaisnéis seo a bhailiú.

taighde i RC, bhí mé ag brath go mór ar an bhfaisnéis a bhí á cur ar fáil dom seachas ar eolas a bhí saothraithe agam féin ar an bpobal in imeacht na mblianta. Tar éis gur chuir mé aithne áirithe ar cheantar agus ar phobal RM den chéad uair i mblianta deireanacha na n-ochtóidí agus mé i mo mhac léinn ollscoile, ní raibh mo dhóthain eolais agam ar an bpobal ann ag leibhéal na sochtheangeolaíochta gan dul i dtuilleamaí ar fhaisnéis a chuirfeadh daoine as an gceantar ar fáil dom. Is léir go músclaíonn sé seo ceisteanna i dtaobh intaofacht agus inchomparáideacht na faisnéise le hais fhaisnéis RC, áit a bhfuil i bhfad níos mó eolais agam ar an bpobal agus ar na dinimicí teanga a bhaineann leis. Is féidir seasamh le torthaí an taighde seo i gcás RM, dar liom, ar na húdair seo a leanas:

- Duine meabhrach cuiditheach atá sa bpríomhfhaisnéiseoir a bhfuil sáreolas aige ar a cheantar agus ar a phobal
- Thuig an príomhfhaisnéiseoir na rannuithe idir na cineálacha éagsúla cainteoirí agus i gcás na gcomhluadar a bhfuil comhthéacs ar leith nó measctha teanga iontu rinneadh mionphlé orthu seo sa gcaoi go mbeadh an bheirt againn ar aon tuiscint amháin fúthu ar deireadh
- Deimhníodh a chuid faisnéise le triúr eile sa gceantar
- Bhí luí aige leis an gcúram a bhí idir lámha againn agus bhraith mé go raibh fonn air cúnamh a thabhairt dom; cheap sé gur mhaith an ní é go ndéanfaí foilsiú ar eolas faoi RM agus go ndéanfaí plé air sa gcaoi go dtabharfaí aird ar an gceantar

Iontráladh an t-ábhar a bailíodh ar dhá bhunachar eolais ríomhairithe, sonraíonn an chéad cheann faisnéis an duine aonair agus tagraíonn an dara ceann d'fhaisnéis na ndaoine as an gcéad bhunachar de réir teaghlaigh/líon tí.[13] Tá iontrálacha a bhaineann le 461 duine curtha san áireamh ar an gcéad bhunachar eolais agus baineann an dara bunachar eolais le sonraí faisnéise 178 teaghlach.

1.3 Bunachar Eolais I (An Duine Aonair)

Roinneadh an fhaisnéis ar an gcéad bhunachar eolais de réir na gcatagóirí seo a leanas:

- Inscne
- Stádas sa teaghlach: athair, máthair, mac, iníon, srl
- Aois
- Baile fearainn
- Scolaíocht i gcás na ngasúr
- Cúlra áitiúil/réigiúnach/cultúrtha
- Cineál cainteora/cúlra teangeolaíoch

1.4 Bunachar Eolais II (An Teaghlach)

Roinneadh an fhaisnéis ar an dara bunachar eolais de réir na gcatagóirí seo a leanas:

---

[13] Is iondúil go n-úsáidtear an téarma teaghlach, seachas líon tí, as seo síos, ach ní ag tagairt d'aon chineál aonaid teaghlaigh ar leith atáthar. Déanfar idirdhealú idir an dá théarma más gá ciall ar leith a léiriú.

- Cineál teaghlaigh/líon tí
- Cúlra áitiúil/réigiúnach/cultúrtha na dtuismitheoirí
- Glúin aoise an teaghlaigh
- Teanga an teaghlaigh (nó gnás teanga an teaghlaigh)
- Gnás teanga na máthar
- Gnás teanga an athar

1.5 Pobal RM – ciall

Freagraíonn an téarma pobal RM do phobal an cheantair limistéaraigh, cé is moite de chorrlíon tí nach de bhunadh na háite iad, a bhfuil tithe saoire acu sa gceantar, agus nach n-áirítear mar chuid den phobal. Ciallaíonn sin go bhfuil faisnéis na ndaoine a bhfuil gnáthchónaí orthu sna naoi mbaile fearainn i gceantar RM, a luadh thuas in alt 1.0, curtha san áireamh sa taighde seo. Ní hionann an cur chuige anseo agus an modh oibre a cleachtadh i gcás taighde RC, áit nach bhfuil an tuiscint faoi phobal an cheantair Ghaeltachta i gcomhréir leis an bpobal limistéarach de réir mar a shaineofaí go hoifigiúil é.[14] Luífeadh sé le réasún nach bhfuil an chastacht chéanna le sonrú ar shainmhíniú a dhéanamh ar an bpobal Gaeltachta i RM i ngeall ar a aonghnéithí is atá sé ó thaobh cúrsaí cúlra de agus gur cuid de cheantar stairiúil Gaeilge Chonamara é RM. Ní fhéadfaí neamhaird a dhéanamh sa gcomhthéacs seo ach an oiread de cheist choibhneasta na hiargúltachta.

1.6 Téarmaíocht – cainteoirí éagsúla[15]

1.6.1 Cainteoir Dúchais

Táthar ag glacadh anseo leis an ngnáththuiscint Ghaeltachta ar céard is cainteoir dúchais Gaeilge (CD) ann: duine de bhunadh Gaeltachta a thógtar le Gaeilge i gceantar Gaeltachta.

1.6.2 Cainteoir Athdhúchais

Is é an éirim a bhaintear as cainteoir athdhúchais Gaeilge (CAD) clann comhchainteoirí Gaeilge a thógtar le Gaeilge nach cainteoirí dúchais iad a dtuismitheoirí.[16]

1.6.3 Cainteoir Leathdhúchais

Baintear feidhm as an téarma cainteoir leathdhúchais (CLD)[17] le cainteoir a thógtar i

---

[14] Tá an pointe seo pléite in Ó Giollagáin (2002: 28-30).

[15] Tabharfar faoi deara go bhfuil an plé anseo athráiteach i bhfianaise a bhfuil scríofa cheana agam faoi RC agus faoi dhinimicí cainteoirí sa nGaeltacht trí chéile (Ó Giollagáin 2002 agus 2004), ach bheartaigh mé na sainmhínithe a thabhairt san alt seo freisin ar mhaithe leis an tsoiléireacht agus mar áis chuidiúleach don léitheoir maidir le faisnéis RM.

[16] D'fhéadfadh clann aontuismitheora a bheith i gceist freisin, dar ndóigh, ach cloífear anseo le húsáid an iolra mar ghnás.

[17] Ní hionann an mheabhair atá á baint anseo as an téarma 'CLD' agus an chiall a bhaineann Fishman (1991: 128) as 'semi-speaker.' Bheadh 'semi-speaker' Fishman ag teacht leis an gciall

gcomhthéacs measctha teanga. Is iomaí gnás teanga is bunús leis seo, ach is iondúil i gcás na Gaeltachta go leantar dhá phatrún: a) cinneann na tuismitheoirí, ar cainteoirí dúchais Gaeilge iad, an mhórtheanga, is é sin an Béarla, a labhairt leis an gclann, ach cloiseann an chlann an Ghaeilge sách rialta i gcomhthéacs caidreamh nó teagmhálacha eile sa gcaoi is go mbíonn deis acu an teanga a shealbhú de réir a chéile ó dhaoine eile, dá easnamhaí é an próiseas sealbhaithe; éiríonn leis na **CLD**-anna óga a gcuid féin a dhéanamh den phróiseas ó bheith ag éisteacht leis an teanga a bheith á labhairt i measc an phobail, nó go deimhin ó bheith ag éisteacht lena dtuismitheoirí ag labhairt eatarthu féin sa teanga a cheileann siad sa gcaidreamh leis an gclann; b) tógtar an chlann leis an mBéarla i ngeall nach bhfuil duine de na tuismitheoirí inniúil ar an nGaeilge, agus déanann an cainteoir dúchais a c(h)uid iarrachtaí féin an Ghaeilge a labhairt leis an gclann mar threisiú ar na comhthéacsanna eile sealbhaithe atá ann ag leibhéal na muintire nó an phobail.

Ach sa dá chás thuas is cainteoirí dúchais Béarla iad na cainteoirí leathdhúchais a shealbhaíonn an Ghaeilge ar bhealach níos coimpléascaí (agus níos achrannaí) nach bhfuil ag brath go hiomlán ar an gcóras scolaíochta nó ar mhodh oibre eile teagaisc mar is gnách leis na comhchainteoirí. Tá úsáid an téarma **CLD** le hidirdhealú ón sainiú a dhéanann Dorian (1981) ar 'semi-speakers' i gcás cainteoirí Gàidhlige in Oirthear Chataibh, Oirthuaisceart na hAlban, sa gcaoi is go bhfuil sealbhú níos cuimsithí déanta ag **CLD**-anna phobal RM ar an nGaeilge seachas mar a rinneadh i gcás na Gàidhlige, mar a thráchtann Dorian uirthi. Murab ionann agus 'semi-speakers' Dorian, is cainteoirí líofa iad **CLD**-anna phobal RM.[18] Níl an gnás sealbhaithe seo coitianta i gcás phobal RM agus níl líon suntasach **CLD**-anna sa bpobal ann dá bharr.

1.6.4 Comhchainteoir

Is é is ciall le comhchainteoir (CC) anseo cainteoir Gaeilge a shealbhaigh an teanga lasmuigh de chomhthéacs bunaidh sealbhaithe an teaghlaigh agus atá in ann páirt ghníomhach a ghlacadh in imeachtaí an phobail i ngeall ar an inniúlacht teanga seo. Ní bhíonn laincisí suntasacha le tabhairt faoi deara ar bhunchumas na gCC-anna a chuirfeadh bac orthu iad féin a chur in iúl i nGaeilge dá nglúin féin go háirithe.[19] Cé is moite de na cainteoirí dúchais, leathdhúchais agus athdhúchais, glactar gur le haicme **CC** a bhaineann gasúir eile na háite i ngeall ar a bhfreastal ar scoileanna

---

atá á samhlú le comhchainteoir leathchumasach anseo. Tá úsáid an téarma 'CLD' bunaithe ar ghné an dúchais agus an phobail a bhaineann le próiseas an tsealbhaithe seachas ar an gcumas teanga a bhfuil Fishman ag trácht air.

[18] Féach Dorian (1981: 106-7): "Unlike the older Gaelic dominant bilinguals, the semi-speakers are not fully proficient in Gaelic. They speak it with varying degrees of less than full fluency, and their grammar (and usually also their phonology) is markedly aberrant in terms of the fluent speaker norm."

[19] Is léir nach mbíonn na CC-anna chomh hinniúil ar an nGaeilge i gcomparáid leis na CD-anna agus go mbeadh réimse cumais níos leithne ag CD-anna ó thaobh stór focal, chruthaitheacht na cainte, agus cruinnis teanga de, ach ní mór cur san áireamh gur minic a bhíonn éifeacht dhiúltach ag na CC-anna ar na CD-anna sa méid is go gcuireann sí srian ar fhorás inniúlachta na gCD-anna. Má tá gnás na comhchainte sách bisiúil i measc an aosa óig, bíonn an chontúirt ann go sealbhóidh na CD-anna nósmhaireachtaí cainte na gCC-anna, seachas na CD-anna a bheith ag saibhriú chumas cainte na gCC-anna.

Gaeltachta an cheantair, in ainneoin go dtógann sé cúpla bliain orthu i mblianta tosaigh na bunscoile an staid sin a bhaint amach. Is iondúil nach mbaineann daltaí scoile sa tsainaicme seo leibhéal cumais na comhchainte amach go dtí go mbíonn siad i rang a haon nó rang a dó sa mbunscoil ar a luaithe.

1.6.5 Béarlóir[20]

Cainteoir Béarla nach bhfuil inniúil ar an nGaeilge a labhairt nó nach bhfuil i mbun iarrachta í a fhoghlaim is ciall le Béarlóir (B) anseo.[21]

2.0 Faisnéis ghinearálta i dtaobh na gcainteoirí

Tugann na léaráidí seo a leanas léargas ginearálta dúinn ar rannú na faisnéise de réir na gcineálacha éagsúla cainteoirí agus de réir chúlra áitiúil agus cultúrtha na gcainteoirí.

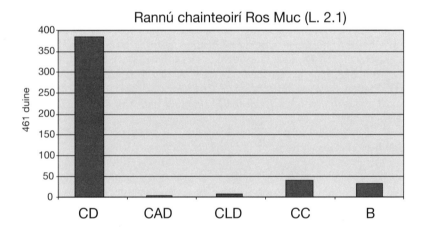

Léaráid 2.1 Rannú na gCainteoirí: Sainaicme Teanga (L. 2.1)

Le céatadáin a dhéanamh d'fhigiúirí na léaraide 2.1 feictear go bhfuil cumas sa nGaeilge ag beagnach 93% de phobal RM, agus gur **CD**-anna iad beagán le cois 82% den phobal. Murab ionann agus an fhaisnéis a bailíodh i RC, ní féidir suntas ar leith a thabhairt do líon na g**CAD**-anna ná na g**CLD**-anna i gcás phobal RM. Léiríonn na staitisticí ina dtaobh, triúr **CAD**-anna (0.7%) agus seisear **CLD**-anna (1.3%) as líon iomlán na ndaoine, nach bhfuil aon bhisiúlacht ag baint leis na gnáis sealbhaithe seo i RM. Is ionann **CC**-anna an cheantair agus 8.7% den phobal agus **B**-anna 7.2% den phobal. De thoradh scagadh tosaigh a dhéanamh ar na figiúirí seo, d'fhéadfaí a áiteamh gur phobal aonghnéitheach den chuid is mó é pobal RM ó thaobh na ngnás sealbhaithe de.

---

[20] Ní bhactar anseo le rannú na comhchainte a chur i bhfeidhm i gcás na mB-anna a fhreastalaíonn ar an naíonra áitiúil.

[21] Ní fhaightear an rannú 'foghlaimeoir' i bpobal RM mar atá sonraithe i gcás RC (féach Ó Giollagáin 2002: 32).

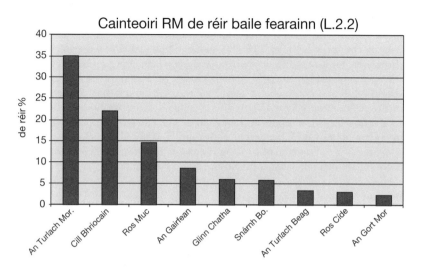

Léaráid 2.2 Cainteoirí de réir baile fearainn (L. 2.2)

Tugann faisnéis chéatadánach L. 2.2 léargas ar an gcaoi a bhfuil daonra an cheantair scaipithe trí na naoi mbaile fearainn i RM. Tá beagnach dhá thrian den phobal ina gcónaí i dtrí cinn de na naoi mbaile fearainn san áit: An Turlach Mór, Cill Bhriocáin agus Ros Muc.[22]

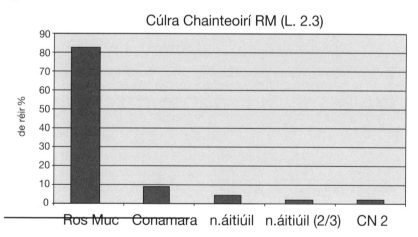

Léaráid 2.3 Cúlra Cultúrtha na gCainteoirí (L. 2.3)

---

[22] Níl an tábhacht chéanna ag baint le cur i láthair na faisnéise faoi na bailte fearainn i RM is atá i gcás RC. I gcás RC ní mór pointe faoi phobal dúchasach na Mí sna bailte fearainn ar imeall theorainn na Gaeltachta agus a gcaidreamh siadsan leis an bpobal Gaeltachta a bhreithniú. Cuireadh faisnéis na mbailte fearainn san áireamh anseo sa gcaoi go bhfreagaródh cur i láthair an dá thionscadal dá chéile.

Feiceann muid arís sa bhfaisnéis i L. 2.3 i dtaobh chúlraí na ndaoine éagsúla sa gceantar an cineál aonghnéitheachta céanna a tugadh chun solais i L. 2.1. Is dúchasaigh de chuid na háite iad 83% (381 duine) de phobal RM; baineann 9% (42 duine) den phobal le ceantair eile de chuid Chonamara; baineann 4% (19 nduine) den phobal le ceantair taobh amuigh de Ghaeltacht Chonamara, is é sin cúlra 'neamháitiúil', agus as an líon seo tá seachtar ina measc a tháinig thar sáile isteach sa gceantar. Is ionann an dara agus an tríú glúin de chúlra neamháitiúil atá á dtógáil i RM agus 2% (deichniúr) den phobal. Baineann an 2% eile (naonúr) den phobal le daoine de bhunadh RM nó Chonamara a tógadh i Sasana nó sna Stáit Aontaithe, 'CN2', a tháinig ar ais chun cónaithe san áit. Léiríonn an fhaisnéis chéatadánach seo go mbaineann 92% den phobal le cúlra áitiúil RM nó Chonamara.

2.4 Rannú dhúchasaigh an cheantair

Má dhéantar mionscagadh ar na figiúir a bhaineann leis an dá rannú RM agus CN thuas, tugtar faoi deara gur **CD**-anna iad beagnach 90% de dhúchasaigh fhadchónaithe an cheantair.[23] Is iad 6%, 3% agus 1% na céatadáin a bhaineann leis an dá rannú seo do na haicmí eile cainte **C, B** agus **CLD** faoi seach.

3.0 Próifíl Teanga na nDaoine

Déantar thíos rannú níos mine ar na gnáis éagsúla chainte i gcomhthéacs phróifíl aoise an cheantair. Tabharfaidh scagadh ar an bhfaisnéis seo deis dúinn teacht ar thuiscint níos soiléire ar bhunús na ndinimicí teanga i RM.

3.1 Próifíl Teanga agus Aoise

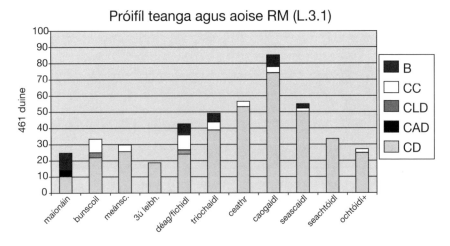

---

[23] Tá faisnéis na ndaoine sa dá rannú, neamháitiúil agus CN2, curtha as an áireamh anseo chun críche an chuntais áirithe seo d'fhonn teacht ar fhaisnéis staitisticiúil a bhaineann leis an mbunphobal dúchasach sa gceantar. Iarracht atá anseo le teacht ar thuiscint ar chomhdhéanamh ghnáis sealbhaithe an phobail sula gcuirtear na castachtaí sochtheangeolaíochta a bhaineann leis na gnáis 'thar teorainn isteach' sa gcuntas.

Léiríonn an fhaisnéis i L. 3.1 ar bhealach lom ualach mór na ndúshlán ar gá don phobal dul i ngleic leo má tá pobal inmharthanach le bheith i RM amach anseo, bíodh sé ina phobal Gaeltachta nó eile. Tá brú déimeagrafaíochta an cheantair le sonrú go láidir má chuirtear na chéad cheithre rannóg aoise, is iad sin rannóga aoise na scolaíochta/an oideachais/na hóige, i gcomparáid le rannóga aoise na glúine roimhe sin. Níl in óige an cheantair (ceithre rannóg tosaigh L. 3.1) ach 23% den phobal iomlán i RM. Ina theannta sin, níl ach mullach amháin faisnéise sa bpróifíl aoise seo agus léiríonn an mullach sin sonraí faisnéise na ndaoine atá in aoisghrúpa na gcaogaidí. Is léir go bhfuil titim shuntasach sa daonra i ndán do cheantar RM má leanann cúrsaí mar atá siad. Is suntasaí fós an titim seo má chuirtear daonra 1911 (1,452 duine)[24] i gcomparáid le daonra reatha na háite atá faoi chaibidil sa taighde seo (461 duine); is é sin titim de 68% i ndaonra an cheantair ó 1911 go dtí an lá atá inniu ann.

I bpobal a mbeadh cúinsí déimeagrafaíochtaí níos socra le sonrú air, bheifí ag súil le dhá mhullach ar an bhfaisnéis aoise: ceann a bhaineann le rannóg aoise na hóige agus ceann eile a bheadh ag freagairt d'aoisghrúpaí na tuismitheoireachta, ó aoisghrúpa na bhfichidí go dtí na caogaidí, cuir i gcás. Dá airde an t-aon mhullach amháin faisnéise i dtéarmaí réimse na n-aoisghrúpaí i bpobal is amhlaidh is géire an éigeandáil déimeagragaíochta a bhfuil an pobal inti.

Tuigtear ón bplé thuas (alt 1.1) go bhféadfaí bunús na ndeacrachtaí déimeagrafaíochta seo i gcás RM a aimsiú i dtranglam coimpléascach de chúinsí cultúrtha, socheacnamaíochta agus tíreolaíochta. Ní mór na laigí déimeagrafaíochta seo a chur san áireamh agus an t-iniúchadh ar antraipeolaíocht theangeolaíoch RM idir lámha againn sa taighde seo. Baineann an pointe seo casadh ar leith as cuma na haonghnéitheachta ó thaobh na ngnás sealbhaithe teanga de sa gceantar, ar tagraíodh thuas di; thabharfadh an chéad amharc dromchlach ar na gnáis sealbhaithe le fios go bhfuil bonn réasúnta téagartha faoi sheachadadh na Gaeilge mar theanga dhúchais i RM. Ach, dar ndóigh, ní fiú tráithnín anailís ar ghnáis teanga mara dtabharfaidh sí aird ar na cúinsí socheacnamaíochta a bhfuil pobal labhartha na teanga sin ag dul i ngleic leo. Fiú, má fhágtar na ceisteanna achrannacha a mhúsclaíonn faisnéis na naíonán i L. 3.1 de leataobh ar feadh meandair, tá laincisí chomh trioblóideach céanna le sárú ag pobal RM i bhfianaise na ndúshlán déimeagrafaíochta atá ann má tá an Ghaeilge le teacht slán mar theanga chumarsáide ag cuid shuntasach den phobal sa gceantar. Is léir, i bhfianaise an chúngaithe shuntasaigh ar dhaonra RM, go mbeidh gá le hiarracht chomhfhiosach ar leith ón bpobal ar mhaithe le cur in aghaidh bhrú méadaithe na mórtheanga.

Tá toradh soiléir diúltach na mbrúnna sochtheangeolaíochta agus déimeagrafaíochta le sonrú go suntasach ar an maide faisnéise a léiríonn gnáis teanga na naíonán (an chéad mhaide faisnéise ar thaobh na láimhe clé i L. 3.1). Léiríonn an taighde seo gurb iad na cainteoirí aonteangacha Béarla (**B**-anna) an grúpa is líonmhaire i measc an aoisghrúpa seo, 44% de na naíonáin sa gceantar. Is iad na **CD**-anna Gaeilge an dara rannú teanga is suntasaí, 40% d'aoisghrúpa na naíonán, agus tá an 16% eile den rannóg aoise seo comhdhéanta de **CLD** amháin agus triúr **CAD**-anna. Léiríonn scagadh ar na trí rannóg aoise is óige a shonraítear anseo, na naíonáin, gasúir in aois na bunscoile agus daltaí meánscoile, dáileadh ar na sainrannuithe éagsúla cainte i measc na n-óg ar an gcaoi seo a leanas: **CD**-anna – 64%; **CC**-anna – 15%; **B**-anna – 13%; **CLD**-anna – 5% agus **CAD**-anna – 3%. Is le rannóg aoise na

---

[24] Tuarascáil C hoimisiún na Gaeltachta 1926: Léarscáil 1.

naíonáin amháin a bhaineann líon na m**B**-anna a shonraítear sa léiriú céatadánach seo.

Coradh cinniúnach i bhforás stairiúil RM mar shaincheantar Gaeltachta atá á léiriú sa bhfaisnéis seo. Léiríonn faisnéis na naíonán go bhfuil athruithe ó bhonn ar tí titim amach ó thaobh na mbunghnásanna seachadta sa gceantar a bhainfidh den choincheap stairiúil traidisiúnta atá ag muintir RM orthu féin mar phobal Gaeltachta, is é sin gur i gcomhthéacs an teaghlaigh a sheachadtar an Ghaeilge ó ghlúin go glúin agus gur ón mbunghnás nádúrach sóisialta seo a chruthaítear an pobal labhartha Gaeilge sa gceantar.[25] Má leanann cúrsaí mar atá siad, is ag dul i ngleic leis na himpleachtaí agus castachtaí sochtheangeolaíochta agus antraipeolaíochta a bhaineann le gnáis mheascta seachadta a bheidh pobal RM feasta má tá an Ghaeilge le bheith ann mar theanga pobail. Ach is léir go bhfuil constaicí móra le sárú ag an bpobal i bhfianaise dhúsláin déimeagrafaíochta agus sóisialta na háite agus na n-athruithe sochtheangeolaíochta atá tagtha chun solais i measc na naíonán.

Tá cainteoirí dúchais Gaeilge á gcruthú i gcónaí i RM, dar ndóigh, ach is léir go mbeidh cibé cén cineál pobail Ghaeilge a bheidh ag teacht chun cinn sa gceantar, dála RC, comhdhéanta de chineálacha éagsúla cainteoirí a mbeidh **CC**-anna nó cainteoirí institiúidithe le sonrú go suntasach ina measc má leantar de na gnáis a bhfuil léargas orthu i bhfaisnéis na n-óg anseo. Tá cineál nua pobal teanga á phréamhú i RM a bheidh bunaithe, ní hamháin ar bhunghnás seachadta an teaghlaigh ach, ar chúnamh institiúideach an chórais oideachais agus ar thacaíocht ó réimsí eile stáit. Dá mhéad a théann an gnás nádúrach seachadta i léig is amhlaidh is mó a bheidh an ceantar ag brath ar thionscnaimh agus scéimeanna tacaíochta ó réimse na pleanála teanga. Is éard atá ag péacadh aníos i dtorthaí an taighde seo ar RM ná Ráth Cairniú na Gaeltachta traidisiúnta. Is iad na ceisteanna is práinní do mhuintir RM a eascraíonn as an gcomhthéacs measctha seo: (i) an gcuirfear na hacmhainní pobail agus tacaíocht institiúideach i bhfearas sách sciobtha le déileáil leis na dúshláin teanga seo a leagfaidh síos buneagar éigin d'úsáid na Gaeilge mar theanga pobail sa gceantar amach anseo?; (ii) an mbeidh fonn ar mhuintir an cheantair comhoibriú leis na hiarrachtaí tacaíochta agus pleanála teanga ag leibhéal an phobail? An mbeadh coiste pobail, cuir i gcás, sásta plé a dhéanamh ar na himpleachtaí a bhaineann le cineálacha éagsúla cainteoirí a bheith sa bpobal agus straitéis a leagan amach nó imeachtaí a eagrú dá réir i gcomhar le múinteoirí, coistí tuismitheoirí, lucht stiúrtha an naíonra, srl., féachaint le modhanna oibre a aimsiú i gcás réimse leathan imeachtaí/ócáidí a chinnteodh go dtabharfaí tús áite d'úsáid na Gaeilge iontu?

Cé go nochtann an fhaisnéis anseo go bhfuil dúshláin sochtheangeolaíochta i ndán do phobal RM, léiríonn na maidí faisnéise a thagraíonn d'aoisghrúpaí an oideachais údar dóchais. D'éirigh le scoileanna an cheantair go nuige seo **CC**-anna a dhéanamh de na **B**-anna aonteangacha naíonda ar fad, chúns nach raibh úsáid an Bhéarla mar ghnás mórlaigh i measc na n-óg, rud a thugann le fios nach gá d'iarrachtaí i réimse na pleanála teanga a bheith ag díriú ar chumas sa nGaeilge a chothú i measc na n-óg. Fágann sin, dar ndóigh, go gcaithfear tabhairt faoi chomhthéacsanna a chruthú i gcónaí a spreagfaidh úsáid na Gaeilge mar ghnás teanga ag leibhéal an phobail. Cúram atá i bhfad níos dúshlánaí ná cruthú an chumais, dar ndóigh, nach féidir a fhágáil mar fhreagracht ag na scoileanna leo féin

---

[25] Tugann Fishman (1991: 112): "intergenerational mother tongue transmission" ar an ngnás bunaidh teangeolaíochta seo.

má tá rath le bheith ar iarrachtaí den chineál seo. Tá buntáiste ag pobal RM ar phobal RC sa gcomhthéacs seo sa méid is go bhfuil cruthú an chumais sa nGaeilge ina ábhar suntasach dúshláin do phobal RC. Léiríonn faisnéis RC go bhfuil cainteoirí aonteangacha Béarla fite fuaite tríd an bpobal agus le sonrú ar gach rannú aoise nach mór (Ó Giollagáin 2002: 37).

An fhaisnéis i bhfoirm staitisticiúil – líon daoine

An fhaisnéis i bhfoirm staitisticiúil – líon daoine

	CD	CAD	CLD	CC	B
Naíonáin	10	3	1	0	11
Bunscoil	22	0	3	9	0
Meán-scoil	26	0	0	4	0
3ú leibh.	19	0	0	0	0
Déaga/20dí	25	0	2	10	7
30dí	39	0	0	5	5
40dí	54	0	0	3	0
50dí	75	0	0	4	7
60dí	51	0	0	2	3
70dí	34	0	0	0	0
80dí+	25	0	0	2	0

Thabharfadh na staitisticí a thagraíonn d'fhaisnéis na naíonán anseo le fios go bhféadfaí dátú a dhéanamh ar an athrú is suntasaí i gcinniúint phobal RM mar phobal Gaeltachta. Is féidir an bhliain 2000 a lua le claochlú shochtheangeolaíoch an cheantair, is é sin an chéad uair nár éirigh le pobal RM móramh de chainteoirí dúchais Gaeilge a chruthú. Ní mór dúinn machnamh a dhéanamh ar a thobainne is a tharla an t-athrú cinniúnach seo i RM agus a bheith san airdeall ar an bpointe seo i gcás a bhfuil i ndán don Ghaeltacht trí chéile.

4.0 An fhaisnéis ag leibhéal an teaghlaigh

Leagann an tsochtheangeolaíocht an-bhéim ar sheachadadh teanga ag leibhéal an teaghlaigh, go háirithe ar anailís shoch-chultúrtha ar an gcomhthéacs ina gcuirtear an próiseas seo as a riocht. Is minic a bhíonn an leagan amach sochtheangeolaíochta atá ag pobal ina chíor thuathail i ngeall nach bhfuil an neart sóisialta ag an bpobal, agus stádas cuí dá réir ag a dteanga, le dul i ngleic leis na brúnna a bhaineann le feidhmiú i sochaí a bhfuil mórtheanga á labhairt inti. Tuigtear freisin gur toradh ar dhinimic choimpléascach shóisialta é an gnás teanga a chleachtar i gcás an teaghlaigh agus breathnaítear go minic ar a théagartha is atá teanga ag an mbunleibhéal seo d'fhonn a seasmhacht mar theanga pobail a thomhais. Le tuiscint níos doimhne a bheith againn ar an bhfaisnéis thíos, ní mór coinneáil i gcuimhne gur ceann scríbe agus pointe tosaigh in éindí é an gnás bunaidh teanga seo: is í an teanga teaghlaigh an bunaonad ginte a thugann gus do theanga ag leibhéal an phobail, ach is scáthán í freisin ar an gcaoi a gcaitear le teanga agus lucht a labhartha ar scála níos leithne na sochaí.

Leagadh neart béime le blianta beaga anuas ar líon na gcainteoirí laethúla Gaeilge le hais líon na gcainteoirí Béarla sa bplé ar chás na Gaeilge, is cruthú ar bhealach eile é an scagadh coibhneasta seo ar ghnás teanga ag leibhéal an teaghlaigh/líon tí ar athruithe suntasacha ar nósmhaireachtaí teanga phobal na Gaeltachta.[26] Féachann an plé thíos le hiniúchadh a dhéanamh ar an gcoibhneas idirtheangach seo i gcás na líonta tí éagsúla i RM.

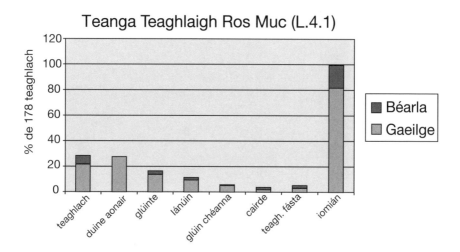

Léaráid 4.1 Teanga Teaghlaigh (L. 4.1)

Bailíodh sonraí 178 teaghlach a chomhlíon critéir an tionscadail seo. Áirítear 82% díobh ina dteaghlaigh labhartha Ghaeilge agus 18% líon tí ina dteaghlaigh Bhéarla. Áireamh a thabharfadh le fios ar an gcéad amharc go bhfuil gnás labhartha na Gaeilge neadaithe go maith sa bpobal i ngeall ar a sheasmhaí is atá an Ghaeilge ag leibhéal an teaghlaigh. Tabharfaidh scagadh níos géire, a dhéanfar thíos, ar ghnáis na dteaghlach óg pictiúr níos iomláine dúinn ar théagar chultúr sochtheangeolaíochta phobal RM faoi láthair.

Tagraíonn an rannú 'teaghlaigh' i léaráid 4.1 do chomhluadair le tuismitheoirí a bhfuil clann in aois na scolaíochta/an oideachais acu. Baineann formhór na líonta tí a shonraítear sa rannú 'glúinte' le teaghlaigh a bhfuil duine/daoine aosta a bhfuil clann fhásta sa teach i gcónaí acu, ach áirítear anseo freisin comhluadair le níos mó ná dhá ghlúin sa teach agus na comhluadair a bhfuil tuismitheoir amháin i mbun chúram na clainne orthu. Is do líon tí a bhfuil daoine fásta muintireacha ann a thagraíonn an rannú 'glúin chéanna.'

Feictear i léaráid 4.1 gurb ionann líon na dteaghlach óg (agus réasúnta óg)

---

[26] Tá gnéithe éagsúla den cheist a bhaineann le líon na gcainteoirí Gaeilge sa nGaeltacht chomhaimseartha pléite in Ó Murchú (2000); i d*Tuarascáil Choimisiún na Gaeltachta* (2002: 21) agus in ailt Dhonncha Uí Éallaithe (1999, 2002, 2003 agus 2004).

Gaeilge agus beagnach 22% (38 teaghlach)[27] de na teaghlaigh i bpobal RM. D'aithin an taighde seo 12 theaghlach óg eile, beagnach 7% de na líonta tí ar fad i RM, a bhféadfaí iad a áireamh ó thaobh gnáis de mar theaghlaigh Bhéarla. Is iad na líonta tí le duine aonair iontu, ar seandaoine a bhformhór mór, an rannú céatadánach is mó i measc na dteaghlach Gaeilge (28% den iomlan nó 50 líon tí).

Má chuirtear san áireamh go bhfuil seandaoine nó daoine meánaosta le sonrú i gcuid mhór de na rannuithe eile a dhéantar ar na líonta tí, is gá téagar coibhneasta na dteaghlach Gaeilge, 82% de na teaghlaigh ar fad, a athmheas i gcomhthéacs a sheasmhaí is atá an dá lucht teanga i bhfianaise an phróifíl aoise agus teaghlaigh atá orthu. Breathnófar a thuilleadh ar an gceist seo i léaráid 4.2, ach is léir go bhfuil an fhaisnéis anseo i dtaobh RM ag teacht le háiteamh Uí Mhurchú (2000: 17) maidir le treise an Bhéarla sa nGaeltacht.[28] Mara dtabharfaí ach aird chéatadánach ar an gcoibhneas i RM idir imoibriú na Gaeilge agus an Bhéarla i gcomhthéacs na dteaghlach (82% : 18%), mhaithfí don té nach ngéillfeadh d'áitimh seo na práinne i gcás inmharthanacht na Gaeltachta i RM. Ach is é an áit agus an chaoi a bhfuil an Béarla préamhaithe i bpobal RM a thabharfadh ábhar imní dóibh siúd ar cás leo a bhfuil i ndán don Ghaeilge agus do lucht a labhartha i RM. I gcás na dteaghlach Béarla, is é rannú na dteaghlach óg an ceann is bisiúla. Míníonn an fhaisnéis seo líon suntasach na mB-anna a shonraítear i rannóg aoise na naíonán i léaráid 3.1. Ar an taobh eile den scéal, is é rannú an 'duine aonair', a chuimsíonn faisnéis na n-aosach den chuid is mó, an ceann is substaintiúla ó thaobh na dteaghlach/líonta tí Gaeilge de. Má dhéantar scagadh céatadánach ar na teaghlaigh Ghaeilge, agus na teaghlaigh Bhéarla a chur de leataobh ó thaobh na staitistíochta de ar feadh meandair, ardaíonn líon na dteaghlach/líonta tí nach bhfuil ach duine aonair iontu go 34% de na teaghlaigh Ghaeilge.[29]

Seo a leanas na staitisticí céatadánacha do na rannuithe eile teaghlaigh, Gaeilge : Béarla faoi seach: glúinte: 13% : 3%; lánúineacha: 10% : 2%; glúinte céanna: 5% : 1%; cairde: 1% : 2%; teaghlaigh fhásta: 3% : 3%.

---

[27] Tá trí theaghlach a bhfuil **CLD**-anna á dtógáil iontu curtha san áireamh sa bhfigiúr seo.

[28] Deir Ó Murchú (2000: 17): "go bhfuil an Béarla lonnaithe go láidir faoin am seo sa Ghaeltacht oifigiúil agus ag síordhul i dtreise. Nuair is teanga thréan dhomhanda í an teanga atá tar éis ionad chomh deimhnitheach seo a fháil i bpobal imeallach lagaithe mionteanga, ní mór a admháil gur staid gháifeach í."

[29] Déanann Ó Murchú (2000: 17) amach ina scagadh ar Dhaonáireamh 1996 gurb ionann líon na dteaghlach le (sean)duine aonair agus 29% de na teaghlaigh Ghaelacha sa nGaeltacht trí chéile. Léiríonn an fhaisnéis anseo ó thaobh na dteaghlach agus phróifíl aoise na háite go bhfuil an coibhneas aoise seo gaibhte in ainseal i gcás RM.

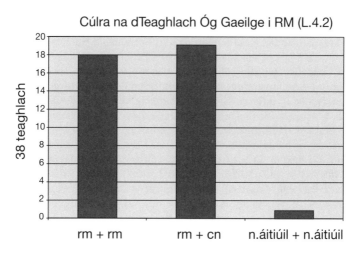

Léaráid 4.2 Cúlra na dTeaghlach Óg Gaeilge (L. 4.2)

Léirítear i léaráid 4.2 comhdhéanamh na lánúine ó thaobh cúlra de i gcás na 38 teaghlach óg Gaeilge a aithníonn an tionscadal seo i bpobal RM. Feictear gur féidir trí rannú a cheapadh le cur síos a dhéanamh ar an ngné seo de phobal RM: beirt dúchasach as RM pósta nó i gcumann lena chéile; dúchasach de chuid RM pósta ar chainteoir dúchais as ceantar éigin eile i gConamara; an bheirt pháirtithe sa lánúin nach de bhunadh RM ná CN iad. Is mar chainteoirí dúchais atá clanna na dteaghlach seo (RM/CN) á dtógáil cé is moite de thrí cinn de theaghlaigh de bhunadh RM agus CN a bhfuil cainteoirí leathdhúchais á dtógáil iontu. Baineann na **CLD**-anna seo le lánúineacha den chomhdhéanamh RM agus CN.[30] Murab ionann agus RC, ní fhéadfaí aon phatrún ar leith inscneach a aithint i gcás chruthú na g**CLD**-anna i

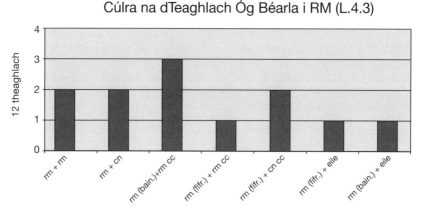

Léaráid 4.3 Cúlra na dTeaghlach Óg Béarla (L. 4.3)

---

[30] Tá comhchainteoir amháin curtha san áireamh agam sa gcuntas seo ar na lánúineacha den chomhdhéanamh RM agus CN.

RM.[31] Níl ach teaghlach amháin i RM a bhfuil **CAD**-anna á dtógáil ann agus, mar is léir ó léaráid 4.2, baineann siad leis an lánúin nach de bhunadh na háite ná de bhunadh Chonamara iad. Tagann an claonadh chun aonghnéitheachta atá mar bhunús leis an bpobal Gaeilge sa gceantar chun solais arís sa bhfaisnéis seo ar chúlra cultúrtha/réigiúnach na dtuismitheoirí sna teaghlaigh Ghaeilge i RM.

I gcodarsnacht le faisnéis L. 4.2 i dtaobh na dteaghlach óg Gaeilge, feictear patrún níos casta i léaráid 4.3 maidir le faisnéis na dteaghlach óg Béarla i RM. Bheifí ag súil ar bhealach leis an gcontrárthacht seo sna gnáis teagmhála sochtheangeolaíochta idir teanga mhionlaithe agus mórtheanga. Is minic a fheidhmíonn na bunghnáis seachadta teanga ar bhealach slán ag leibhéal an teaghlaigh atá chun leas na teanga dúchasaí má bhíonn an dá pháirtí sa lánúin préamhaithe go maith i dtraidisiún sóisialta agus cultúrtha an cheantair. Chonaic muid i léaráid 4.2 go bhfuil mórchuid shuntasach de na teaghlaigh óga Ghaeilge i RM comhdhéanta de lánúineacha cainteoirí dúchais de bhunadh RM/CN, is é sin gur den dúchas céanna réigiúnach agus teangeolaíoch iad beirt. Léiríonn an fhaisnéis i léaráid 4.3 leochaileacht na ngnás seachadta más gá don lánúin déileáil le haon chastacht sochtheangeolaíochta atá níos coimpléacsaí ná bunghnáis sealbhaithe na gcainteoirí dúchais. Tugtar faoi deara i L. 4.3 go bhfuil cumas sa nGaeilge ag beirt pháirtithe na lánúine i gcás na dteaghlach óg Béarla i RM i gcás 10 dteaghlach as an 12 cheann a bhfuil a gcuid faisnéise á cíoradh i L. 4.3. Tugann torthaí an taighde seo le fios go bhfuil sé cinn de theaghlaigh, a bhfuil **CC** i gcumann le **CD** agus an dá pháirtí den dúchas réigiúnach céanna, RM/CN, i mbun na gclann a thógáil le Béarla. D'fhéadfaí a mhaíomh go dtacaíonn an fhianaise sa tionscadal seo ar RM leis an áiteamh a rinneadh i gcás taighde eile go bhfuil bisiúlacht sochtheangeolaíochta na gCC-anna teoranta do **CC**-anna a chur ar fáil.[32]

Sonraíonn fianaise na léaráide seo (L. 4.3) go bhfuil a gclann á dtógáil le Béarla ag ceithre lánúin sa gceantar in ainneoin cumas **CD** sa nGaeilge a bheith ag an dá pháirtí sa lánúin agus gur daoine de bhunadh na háite iad. Ní mór a aithint gur léiriú ar ghnás mionlaigh atá i bhfaisnéis na dteaghlach seo, go háirithe, má chuirtear an gnás seo i gcomparáid leis an bpatrún bunaidh seachadta a bhfaightear spléachadh air i L. 4.2 i dtaobh na dteaghlach óg Gaeilge. Ach, léiriú atá sa bhforás áirithe teanga seo, dá theoranta é, ar amhras cuid den phobal i leith luach a n-oidhreachta stairiúla soch-chultúrtha agus faoi chumas a bpobail dul i ngleic le brúnna sochtheangeolaíochta agus eile a bhaineann le uileláithreacht an mhórchultúir Bhéarla. Feicfear a bhisiúla is atá na gnáis teanga a bhfuil an Béarla ceannasach iontu má dhéantar iniúchadh ar ghnáis teanga an dá theaghlach déag a léirítear i L. 4.3. i gcomhthéacs líon céatadánach na gcainteoirí aonteangacha Béarla agus líon na gCC-anna i measc aosa óig go ginearálta, agus líon teoranta na gCLD-anna sna teaghlaigh a bhfuil comhthéacs measctha teanga i gceist leo.

5.0 Conclúidí agus Impleachtaí

Cuireann an taighde seo leis an scagadh atá á dhéanamh ar ghnéithe den antraipeolaíocht theangeolaíoch sa nGaeltacht chomhaimseartha. Féachadh le córas rannaithe a chur ar fáil agus a chur i bhfeidhm ar na hidirdhealuithe éagsúla a fhaightear i measc cainteoirí comhaimseartha i nGaeltacht RM agus le faisnéis a chur

[31] Féach Ó Giollagáin (2002: 48).
[32] Féach Edwards (1985: 72), Fishman (1991: 128), Hindley (1990: 142), Jones (1998: 235) agus Ó Giollagáin (2004).

ar fáil a chuirfeadh comhthéacs comparáideach ar fáil do na torthaí taighde a d'eascair as a mhacasamhail de thionscadal i RC. Bheifí ag súil go gcuideodh léargais na dtionscadal seo le fráma tagartha níos leithne a sholáthar don chur is cúiteamh atá á dhéanamh faoina a bhfuil i ndán don Ghaeltacht trí chéile. Má tá an Ghaeltacht le teacht slán mar shaincheantar teanga agus cultúrtha, ní mór na nósmhaireachtaí teanga a chleachtar sna Gaeltachtaí ag leibhéal an teaghlaigh agus an phobail a thuiscint i dtosach báire agus modhanna oibre a aimsiú ina dhiaidh sin a chothaíonn na gnáis seachadta is feiliúnaí a thabharfaidh aghaidh éifeachtach ar chomhthéacs mionlaithe na Gaeilge. Ba ghá freisin cleachtais a cheapadh le dul i ngleic leis na laincísí soch-chultúrtha a spreagann an neamhbhisiúlacht teanga sa gcaidreamh idirghlúineach i gcomhthéacsanna measctha sochtheangeolaíochta. Aithním, i measc na laincísí seo, an doicheall roimh phlé oscailte a dhéanamh ar cheisteanna íogair a bhaineann le cúinsí teanga den aitheantas Gaeltachta, an easpa pleanála ag leibhéal an phobail le déileáil le deacrachtaí sochtheangeolaíochta, an easpa comhordaithe idir institiúidithe áitiúla agus an pobal le díriú ar chúinsí teanga, agus an dearcadh fulangach gur fhorás dosheachanta de chuid an tsaoil é an t-aistriú teanga ó Ghaeilge go Béarla.

Cheadódh iniúchadh ar thorthaí an taighde seo na háitimh seo a leanas i gcás phobal RM:

(a) is gnáthaí go dtagann gnás seachadadh teanga na Gaeltachta traidisiúnta slán i gcás na dteaghlach óg más beirt chainteoirí dúchais Gaeltachta atá sa lánúin;

(b) tá laincísí achrannacha sóisialta agus déimeagrafaíochta le sárú ag pobal RM a mbeidh impleachtaí láidre teanga ag baint leo;

(c) in ainneoin a aonghnéithí is atá pobal RM tá amhras ag teacht ar chuid den phobal maidir leis an luach a chuirfidís lena n-oidhreacht chultúrtha agus teanga sa saol comhaimhseartha;

(d) tá leochaileacht le brath ar acmhainní teanga an phobail má théitear i ngleic le comhthéacs sochtheangeolaíochta atá níos casta ná na gnáis bhunaidh thraidisiúnta seachadta;

(e) murab ionann agus RC níl líon suntasach ag baint le líon na g**CLD**-anna agus g**CAD**-anna;

(f) murab ionann agus RC níl gné inscneach le tabhairt faoi deara i gcás cruthú cineálacha éagsúla cainteoirí;

(g) léiríonn líon na m**B**-anna i measc na naíonán agus teacht chun cinn na g**CC**-anna i measc na n-óg gur ré chinniúnach teangeolaíochta atá buailte le pobal RM;

(h) is féidir an bhliain 2000 a lua leis an ré nua teangeolaíochta;

(i) tá an ráta fáis a bhaineann le líon na gcainteoirí Gaeilge a shealbhaigh an teanga le cúnamh institiúideach na scoile(anna) (**CC**-anna) ag méadú;

(j) bíonn éifeacht dhiúltach ar an nGaeilge nach bhfuil i gcoibhneas lena líon ag **CC**-anna óga an cheantair ar nósmhaireachtaí teanga an aosa óig i RM (féach 5.2 thíos).

Thabharfadh faisnéis an tionscadail seo le fios gurb iad na laincísí a bhaineann le deacrachtaí sóisialta agus déimeagrafaíochta mar aon le nósmhaireachtaí teanga an aosa óig na dúshláin teangeolaíochta is mó atá le sárú ag pobal RM má tá an pobal ann le teacht slán mar phobal Gaeltachta. Tá an chuma ar an scéal go bhfuil líon na g**CD**-anna agus an coibhneas idir líon na dteaghlach óg Gaeilge agus líon na dteaghlach óg Béarla réasúnta sláintiúil (69% le hais 31%) go céatadánach. Ní mór aird a thabhairt, áfach, ar éifeacht an lín seachas ar a dtéagar staitisticiúil le hais sainrannuithe teangeolaíochta eile (líon na gCC-anna, cuir i gcás) ar mhaithe le tuiscint a fháil ar thionchar an choibhnis seo ar nósmhaireachtaí teanga an phobail agus an teaghlaigh.

5.1 An Teaghlach

Is líonmhaire i bhfad na teaghlaigh óga Ghaeilge (38) seachas teaghlaigh san aoisghrúpa seo a thógann a gclann féin le Béarla (12) i RM. Tugann faisnéis na dteaghlach Béarla seo le fios go bhfuil brú stádas mionlaithe na Gaeilge ag teacht i bhfeidhm diaidh ar ndiaidh ar nósmhaireachtaí teanga phobal RM. Tá leochaileacht teangeolaíochta le sonrú ar na teaghlaigh Bhéarla sa méid is gur cainteoirí inniúla Gaeilge atá sa dá pháirtí sa lánúin i gcás breis is trí cheathrú díobh, agus i gcás trian (4 theaghlach) den iomlán is **CD**-anna iad an dá pháirtí. D'fhéadfaí a mhaíomh go léiríonn faisnéis den chineál seo go bhfuil muinín á cailleadh as an nGaeilge mar theanga phobail i RM agus go bhfuil fáinne fiaigh teangeolaíochta á neadú sa bpobal ann. I gcás lánúine i RM nár tógadh an dá pháirtí inti de réir bungnás dúchasach seachadta na Gaeltachta, is é an claonadh sochtheangeolaíochta is bisiúla Béarla a thabhairt dá gclann sa mbaile agus cúram na Gaeilge a fhágáil faoi institiúidí oideachais. Fágann sin go bhfuil cainteoirí dúchais Béarla agus Gaeilge an cheantair á sóisialú i dteannta a chéile i gcomhthéacs an choibhnis idir mórtheanga agus teanga mhionlaithe. Is léir go bhfuil claonadh láidir in imreas sóisialta ar bith idir mionlach agus mórlach géilleadh do ghnás an mhórlaigh agus is amhlaidh atá na cúrsaí seo ó thaobh nósmhaireachtaí teanga aos óg an cheantair. In ainneoin gur nós mionlaigh sa gceantar trí chéile gasúir a bheith á dtógáil le Béarla, is léir go bhfuil imoibriú sochtheangeolaíochta na ngnás teanga seo i RM á mhunlú ag dioscúrsa teanga atá i bhfad níos leithne ná teorainneacha RM ná, go deimhin, na hÉireann féin. Tá fianaise láidir á nochtadh i dtorthaí an taighde seo go bhfuil patrún comhaimseartha teangeolaíochta RM á leagan síos de réir cúinsí a bhaineann leis an gcoibhneas idir an Ghaeilge agus an Béarla ag leibhéal os cionn an aitheantais áitiúil nó réigiúnaigh, bíodh sin ag leibhéal náisiúnta nó iarnáisiúnta na cumarsáide domhanda a bhfuil forlámhas ag an mBéarla uirthi.[33]

Léiríonn líon íseal na gCAD-anna nach féidir le pobal RM a bheith ag brath ar áitritheoirí nua sa gceantar, ar cainteoirí bisiúla Gaeilge iad, murab ionann agus pobal RC, le tacaíocht a thabhairt do staid na Gaeilge sa bpobal. Dar ndóigh, is túisce a luafaí an iargúil le RM seachas le RC in ainneoin an dá cheantar a bheith chomh fada céanna ó chathair mhór, ach is gaire RC do bhailte (Áth Buí agus Áth Troim, cuir i gcás) a bhfuil réimse leathan seirbhísí ar fáil iontu. Tá ceantar mór Gaeltachta idir RM agus cathair na Gaillimhe a bheadh níos tarraingtí ó thaobh áiseanna, soláthar seirbhísí agus cúrsaí taistil de d'áitritheoirí nua Gaeilge le hais cheantar RM.

---

[33] Tá cumhacht an Bhéarla i saol cultúrtha an domhain chomhaimseartha pléite ag Crystal (2000: viii), Krauss (1992: 5) agus McCloskey (2001: 21). Is i gcomhthéacs éigeandála a thráchtann Krauss ar fhadhb idirnáisiúnta an aistrithe teanga agus leagann sé an-bhéim ar ról na teilifíse sa ngéarchéim teangeolaíochta seo: "The circumstances that have led to the present language mortality known to us range from outright genocide, social or economic or habitat destruction, displacement, demographic submersion, language suppression in forced assimilation or assimilatory education, to electronic bombardment, especially television, an incalculably lethal new weapon (which I have called 'cultural nerve gas')." Krauss (1992: 6).

5.2 Nósmhaireacht an Aosa Óig

Tá macallaí ar nósmhaireachtaí na lánúineacha measctha ó thaobh na teangeolaíochta de le brath ar na gnáis teanga a chleachtann daoine óga a shealbhaigh an Ghaeilge ar bhealaí éagsúla. Sa rianadh siar a rinneadh in imeacht an taighde seo ar fhaisnéis na ndaoine óga tugadh faoi deara go raibh dlúthcheangal idir na nósmhaireachtaí teanga i measc an aosa óig i RM agus an bunghnás sealbhaithe ag leibhéal an teaghlaigh. Is é préamhú dúchasach na teanga an ghné is tábhachtaí sa rogha a dhéanfaidh daoine óga an cheantair maidir le cé acu an Ghaeilge nó an Béarla a bheidh mar theanga chumarsáide eatarthu. Sa gcíoradh a rinne mé ar an gceist seo le cuid de dhéagóirí agus de dhaoine sna fichidí i RM i dtaobh líonraí CLDsóisialta a lucht aitheantais, dearbhaíodh gurb iondúil go mbunaíonn daoine a shealbhaigh an Ghaeilge de réir bhunghnáis an teaghlaigh, is é sin **CD**-anna, a gcuid caidreamh trí mheán na Gaeilge agus gur cumarsáid i mBéarla atá le sonrú ar chaidrimh idir **CD**-anna agus **CC**-anna. Is í an loighic teangeolaíochta atá leis na nósanna teanga seo go dtiocfaidh cúngú ar na líonraí sóisialta Gaeilge de réir mar a thagann méadú ar líon na g**CC**-anna i gcoibhneas le líon na g**CD**-anna. Tá teorainn shoiléir bisiúlachta le brath ar chainteoirí Gaeilge nár shealbhaigh an Ghaeilge mar **CD**-anna i gcás phobal RM. Léiríonn an taighde seo nach bhfuil úsáid na Gaeilge i measc na g**CC**-anna le sonrú ar aon bhealach rathúil ag leibhéal an teaghlaigh ná i gcomhthéacs an phobail taobh amuigh de chúraimí agus imeachtaí oideachais.

Caithfear cur san áireamh freisin nach gcloíonn líonraí sóisialta na n-óg le sainaicmí éagsúla teanga ar leith agus go bhfaighfí cineálacha éagsúla cainteoirí i líonraí ar leith. Bunaítear dinimicí teanga in imeacht aimsire i ngeall ar chúinsí éagsúla sóisialta agus pearsanta agus i gcomhthéacs imreas níos leithne teangeolaíochta a bhaineann le stádas na Gaeilge le hais an Bhéarla ag leibhéal os cionn an tsainaitheantas réigiúnaigh. Is minic i mhúnlaíonn na pearsantachtaí ceannasacha in aon líonra na dinimicí teanga a chleachtar i gcaidrimh choiteanna an líonra sin. Is léir go bhfuil líonraí Gaeilge an aosa óig ag brath ar théagar choibhneasta líon na g**CD**-anna agus ar phearsantachtaí ceannasacha, ar **CD**-anna iad, a bheith iontu.

Tá naíonra agus scoileanna an cheantair ag iarraidh dul i ngleic le comhthéacs measctha an tsealbhaithe agus ag féachaint le polasaithe a fhorbairt a thabharfaidh cúnamh do ghasúir feidhmiú i gcomhréir le haidhmeanna teanga na n-institiúidí éagsúla oideachais i RM, ach tugann an scagadh seo ar líonraí sóisialta éagsúla na n-óg i RM le fios gur cainteoirí institiúidithe formhór mór de **CC**-anna RM agus RC. Éiríonn leis na scoileanna cainteoirí cumasacha Gaeilge a chruthú, i gcás na ndaoine nár tógadh le Gaeilge, ach tá léiriú agus úsáid an chumais sin teoranta d'imeachtaí agus ghníomhaíochtaí a bhaineann le húsáid na teanga i gcomhthéacs institiúideach. Dearbhaíonn torthaí an taighde an tábhacht lárnach a bhaineann le húsáid nádúrtha na teanga ag leibhéal an teaghlaigh agus an tionchar a imríonn an nósmhaireacht seo ar úsáid na Gaeilge sa bpobal trí chéile.

Ceangal

Is é an pointe is sonraithí atá curtha i láthair san aiste seo go bhfuil pobal RM ag crosbhóthar teangeolaíochta. Tá na gnáis seachadta dúchais ar marthain i gcónaí sa gceantar agus réasúnta bisiúil fós, ach tá líon na ngasúr atá ag brath ar chomhthéacs institiúideach na comhchainte le hinniúlacht sa nGaeilge a fháil ag dul i méad i gcoibhneas le líonmhaireacht na gCD-anna i measc an aosa óig. Tá níos mó Béarlóirí ná cainteoirí dúchais Gaeilge i measc na naíonán agus tugann an fhíric lom seo le fios go bhfuil géarghá le straitéis dhearfach agus céimeanna misniúla pobail má tá an ghoimh le baint as an bpointe suntasach i dtreo an bháis. Tá impleachtaí stairiúla ó thaobh na teangeolaíochta le n-aimsiú sa bhforás soch-chultúrtha seo don fhéiniúlacht Ghaeltachta i RM. De réir mar a thagann gnás na comhchainte chun cinn, is amhlaidh is mó a chothaítear an chontúirt teangeolaíochta d'fhéiniúlacht Ghaeltachta RM gur i mBéarla a bheidh dinimicí teanga líonraí sóisialta an aosa óig as seo amach.

Mara n-éiríonn leis an bpobal i RM borradh a chur faoi na gnáis dhúchasacha seachadta an athuair, beidh ar an bpobal ann bóthar na pleanála teanga a thabhairt orthu féin ar bhealach níos treallúsaí. Ach dá fheabhas iad na straitéisí pleanála, ba dheacair maolú a dhéanamh ar na laincisí sochtheangeolaíocha a chothaíonn fás ghnáis na comhchainte i measc an phobail, an Béarla ag glacadh áit na Gaeilge de réir a chéile i líonraí sóisialta na n-óg, mara mbeidh bunchloch sách daingin ag nósmhaireachtaí Gaeilge an teaghlaigh i RM le pleananna teanga a thógáil orthu. Is léir nach féidir tógáil ar nós nach gcothaítear.[34]

Is léir go bhfuil lagbhrí shóisialta agus eacnamaíochta le brath go forleathan i measc phobal an cheantair. Níor ródhána an mhaise d'údar na haiste seo dá maífeadh conclúidí an tionscadail seo gur athnuachan thar réimse leathan saoil atá de dhíth ar phobal RM. Laghdófar ar éifeacht agus ar dhinimiciúlacht straitéisí teanga a d'fhéadfaí a chur ar bun sa gceantar mara dtabharfaidh siad aghaidh ar an gcúlra socheacnamaíochta atá mar bhonn leis an gcoibhneas idir úsáid na Gaeilge agus an Bhéarla i measc phobal an cheantair.

Tá teorainn shoiléir leis an méid is féidir le hinstitiúidí áitiúla, fiú le tacaíocht fhial dhearfach áisíneachtaí seachtracha stáit agus réigiúnacha, i réimse na pleanála teanga a dhéanamh, mara bhfeicfidh an pobal an riachtanas a bhaineann le bheith páirteach in iarrachtaí pleanáilte le gnéithe éagsúla teaghlaigh agus pobail de chinniúint na Gaeilge a fhorbairt. B'fhánach an mhaise d'institiúid ar bith a cheapadh go bhféadfadh sí straitéis a chur i bhfeidhm a mbeadh rath uirthi murar múnlaíodh an fhealsúnacht atá mar bhunús léi as cur is cúiteamh ag leibhéal an phobail agus as comhthuiscint ar chaidreamh na hinstitiúide leis an bpobal. Dá fhorbartha is atá acmhainní cumarsáide dioscúrsúla ag bunleibhéal an phobail is amhlaidh is fearr a thiocfaidh borradh ar mhuinín phobal an cheantair le dul i ngleic leis an staid chinniúnach teangeolaíochta atá i RM.

Thabharfadh cuid den fhaisnéis anseo a bhaineann leis na teaghlaigh óga agus nósmhaireachtaí teanga an aosa óig le fios go bhfuil dearcadh *laissez-faire* ag eilimintí den phobal i RM i leith chinniúint na teanga sa gceantar.[35] Is éasca ceann scríbe soiléir a aithint i gcás na Gaeilge i RM má éiríonn leis an dearcadh seo cos a chur i dtaca sa bpobal trí chéile. Ní theastaíonn aon saineolas ar leith teangeolaíochta le teacht ar an

---

[34] Deir Fishman (1991: 113) ina chuid anailíse i dtaobh iarrachtaí buanaithe teanga nach dtugann aird shuntasach ar an ngné chinniúnach a bhaineann le seachadadh na teanga i gcomhthéacs an teaghlaigh: "That which is not transmitted cannot be maintained."

[35] Léiriú é seo freisin, dar liom, ar mhaolú ar ghné na heitniúlachta teanga den fhéiniúlacht Ghaeltachta agus ar an tuiscint choiteann ar ról na Gaeilge sa bhféiniúlacht sin. Maíonn Fishman (1989: 24) ag leibhéal níos leithne na heitniúlachta: "Ethnicity is rightly understood as an aspect of a collectivity's self-recognition as well as an aspect of its recognition in the eyes of outsiders."

tuiscint go bhfaighidh gnáis teanga an mhórlaigh an ceann is fearr ar ghnáis an mhionlaigh más dearcadh *laissez-faire* atá i réim i measc an mhionlaigh. Is achrannach an cúram é ar aon chaoi cúrsa a stiúradh trí thranglam na ndinimicí idirtheangacha mionlaigh/mórlaigh, ach is féidir a bheith cinnte gur aistriú teanga atá ar na bacáin do phobal RM mara dtiocfaidh fealsúnacht, idé-eolaíocht nó tuiscint choiteann éigin chun tosaigh ar luach a gcuid acmhainní soch-chultúrtha agus oidhreachta i dtosach báire agus fonn gníomhú dá réir ina dhiaidh sin le cosaint a thabhairt dóibh. Ach an oiread le dúshlán nua ar bith, is le coiscéim amháin a thosaítear gach aistear. Is léir go bhfuil dúshláin mhóra le tabhairt ar nósmhaireachtaí éagsúla teanga agus sóisialta atá ina mbagairtí d'inmharthanacht na Gaeilge mar theanga teaghlaigh agus pobail. Ní fhéadfaí a mhaíomh ach an oiread gur sampla aonaránach é pobal RM i gcás chinniúint na Gaeltachta comhaimseartha.

Noda

B	béarlóir
CAD	cainteoir athdhúchais
CD	cainteoir dúchais
CLD	cainteoir leathdhúchais
CC	comhchainteoir
CN	Conamara
CN2	clann daoine as Conamara a tógadh thar sáile
L	léaráid(í)
n.áitiúil	neamháitiúil
RC	Ráth Cairn, Co. na Mí
RM	Ros Muc, Co. na Gaillimhe

B-anna	béarlóirí
CAD-anna	cainteoirí athdhúchais
CD-anna	cainteoirí dúchais
CLD-anna	cainteoirí leathdhúchais
CC-anna	comhchainteoirí

Tagairtí

Crystal, D. 2000. *Language Death*, Cambridge University Press, Cambridge.
de Bhaldraithe, T. (Eag.) 1982. *Pádraic Ó Conaire: Clocha ar a Charn*, An Clóchomhar, BÁC.
Denvir, G. (Eag.) 1983. *Pádraic Ó Conaire: Léachtaí Cuimhneacháin*, Cló Chonamara, Indreabhán.
Dorian, N. 1981. *Language Death: The Life Cycle of a Scottish Gaelic Dialect*, University of Pennsylvania Press, Philadelphia.
Duranti, A. 1997. *Linguistic Anthropology*, Cambridge University Press, Cambridge.
Edwards, J. 1985. *Language, Society and Identity*, Blackwell, Oxford.
Fishman, J. 1989. *Language and Ethnicity in Minority Sociolinguistic Perspective*, Multilingual Matters 45, Philadelphia.
Fishman, J. 1991. *Reversing Language Shift*, Multilingual Matters 76, Clevedon.

Hindley, R. 1990. *The Death of the Irish Language*, Routledge, Londain.

Jones, M. C. 1998. *Language Obsolescence and Revitalization: Linguistic Change in Two Sociolinguistically Contrasting Welsh Communities*, Clarendon, Oxford.

Krauss, M. 1992. "The world languages in crisis," in *Language*, Iml. 8, Uimh. 1: 4-24.

Maude, C. 1984. *Caitlín Maude: Dánta* (Eag. Ciarán Ó Coigligh), Coiscéim, BÁC.

Mac Aonghusa, P. 1991. *Ros Muc agus Cogadh na Saoirse*, Conradh na Gaeilge, BÁC.

Mac Aonghusa, P. 2000. "Ros Muc," in Ó Tuathaigh et al. 2000: 396-408.

Mac Mathúna, L., Mac Murchaidh, C., agus Nic Eoin, M. (Eag.), 2000. *Teanga, Pobal agus Réigiún: Aistí ar Chultúr na Gaeltachta Inniu*, Coiscéim, BÁC.

McCloskey, J. 2001. *Guthanna in Éag: an mairfidh an Ghaeilge beo?*, Cois Life, BÁC.

Melvin, P. 1996. "The Galway Tribes as Landowners and Gentry," in Moran 1996: 319-74.

Moran, G. (Eag.) 1996. *Galway history and society : interdisciplinary essays on the history of an Irish County*, Geography Publications, BÁC.

Ní Chionnaith, E. 1995. *Pádraic Ó Conaire: Scéal a bheatha*, Cló Iar-Chonnachta, Conamara.

Ó Broin, T. 1984. *Saoirse Anama Uí Chonaire: compánach d'úrscéal fiontrach, 'Deoraíocht'*, Officina Typographica, Gaillimh.

Ó Conaire, B. (Eag.) 2004, *Aistí ag Iompar Scéil: In ómós do Shéamus Ó Mórdha*, An Clóchomhar, BÁC.

Ó Conghaile, M. (Eag.) 1986. *Gaeltacht Ráth Cairn*. Cló Iar-Chonnachta, Conamara.

Ó Conghaile, M. 1988. *Conamara agus Árainn 1880-1980: Gnéithe den Stair Shóisialta*, Cló Iar-Chonnachta, Conamara.

Ó Gaora, C. 1943. *Mise*, Oifig an tSoláthair, BÁC.

Ó Giollagáin, C. (Eag.) 1999. *Ón Máimín go Ráth Chairn: Stairsheanchas Mhicil Chonraí*, Cló Iar-Chonnachta, Conamara.

Ó Giollagáin, C. 2002. "Scagadh ar rannú cainteoirí comhaimseartha Gaeltachta: gnéithe d'antraipeolaíocht teangeolaíochta phobal Ráth Cairn," in *The Irish Journal of Anthropology*, Iml. 6, 2002: 25-56, Ollscoil na hÉireann, Má Nuad.

Ó Giollagáin, C. 2004. "Ár scéal féin inár dteanga féin: Dinimicí teanga Ghaeltacht ár linne," in Ó Conaire 2004: 153-70.

Ó Glaisne, R. 1982. *Raidió na Gaeltachta*, Cló Chois Fharraige, Conamara.

Ó hÉallaithe, D. 1999. "Uair na Cinniúna don Ghaeltacht," *Cuisle*, Imleabhar 5: 10-13, Feabhra 1999.

Ó hÉallaithe, D. 2002. "Todhchaí na Gaeltachta," *Foinse*, 19 Bealtaine 2002: 10-12.

Ó hÉallaithe, D. 2003. "Scéim Labhairt na Gaeilge: Anailís ar fhigiúirí 2001/02," *Foinse*, 5 Eanair 2003: 8-10.

Ó hÉallaithe, D. 2004. "Cé mhéad a labhrann Gaeilge?" *Foinse*, 4 Aibreán 2004, Faobhar 6: 20-21.

Ó Murchú, M. 2000. "An Ghaeltacht mar Réigiún Cultúrtha: Léargas Teangeolaíoch," in Mac Mathúna et al. 2000: 9-20.

O'Neill, T.P. 1996. "Minor Famines and Relief in County Galway, 1815-1925," in Moran 1996: 445-86.

Ó Tuathaigh G., Ó Laoire, L. agus Ua Súilleabháin, S. 2000. *Pobal na Gaeltachta: a scéal agus a dhán*, Cló Iar-Chonnachta, Conamara.

Rialtas na hÉireann, 1926. *Gaeltacht Commission: Report,* Oifig an tSoláthair, BÁC.

Rialtas na hÉireann, 1926. *Gaeltacht Commission: Report – Léarscáil 1 agus 2,* Oifig an tSoláthair, BÁC.

Rialtas na hÉireann, 2002. *Tuarascáil Choimisiún na Gaeltachta,* BÁC.
Rialtas na hÉireann, Acht na Gaeltachta 1956, Aguisín C (Ordú na Limistéirí Gaeltachta).
Riggs, P. 1994. *Pádraic Ó Conaire: deoraí,* An Clóchomhar, BÁC.
Robinson, T 1990. *Connemara: Part 1,* Folding Landscapes, BÁC.
Robinson, T (Eag.) 1995. *Connemara after the famine: journal of a survey of the Martin estate by Thomas Colville Scott,* Lilliput Press, BÁC.
Tuarascáil Choimisiún Dudley (Royal Commission on Congestion in Ireland) 1907, Iml 1-10.
Walsh, J. 2002. *Díchoimisiúnú Teanga: Coimisiún na Gaeltachta 1926,* Cois Life, BÁC.
Wigger, A. (Eag.) 2004. *Caint Ros Muc,* Iml. 1+2, Institiúid Ard-Léinn Bhaile Átha Cliath, BÁC.

Achoimre/Abstract

Aspects of the Linguistic Anthropology of the Ros Muc Community, County Galway

This paper presents an analysis of the linguistic anthropology which underpins the language dynamics of the Gaeltacht (Irish-speaking) community of Ros Muc in Conamara, Co. Galway. The research underpinning the analysis presented here was carried out in the area during 2002/3. Its aim was to gather data on the various types of speakers in a contemporary Gaeltacht community in order to gain a deeper understanding of the language use patterns operating in the various generations. This research seeks to explain how these different types of speakers have emerged in the community and to demonstrate how they interact with each other on a sociolinguistic basis.

The findings of the project indicate that the Ros Muc community has reached a critical linguistic juncture and that the productive family-based transmission of Irish from one generation to the next is coming under increasing pressure. The language dynamics emerging in this context are raising significant issues in relation to the linguistic vitality of Ros Muc as an Irish-speaking community. A commentary on both the historical sociolinguistic context and the contemporary challenging socio-economic climate in which these sociolinguistic pressures have emerged is also included in the order to highlight the extent of the challenge faced by the Ros Muc community if it is to remain an Irish-speaking community.

Kashubian as a Regional Language

Tomasz Wicherkiewicz

The problem of lesser-used languages is complex and quite extensive, and yet, it has interested politicians only during recent decades. Moreover, in most large European countries, there is a tendency to consider solely the national languages: in Germany one speaks German, in France – French, in Poland – Polish. Admittedly, it is known, that there are bilingual nations, or that historical events have left speakers of a language on the other side of state borders – speakers who are considered to be poor fellow-citizens lost on a foreign territory. Besides, the superposition between language and nationality has been a source of some important conflicts, even if the will of coincidence has not always been the real cause of these conflicts; it has often served as a pretext.

When we investigate various idioms which do not correspond with the easy superposition language/nation-state, we realize that we can group them in three categories:

a. Languages of nation-states used by a minority of speakers in another nation-state

Languages of nation-states used by a minority of speakers in another nation-state are a very frequent case in Europe, resulting not necessarily from migration processes, but more from historical and geographical circumstances. This is the case of German-speaking minorities in Belgium, Denmark, France and Italy, speakers of Swedish in Finland, Slovene-speaking minorities in Italy and Austria.

Generally, these minorities are well protected and receive often a double support: from the nation-state where their language is dominant, and from the nation-state where it is spoken as a minority language and, because of democratic principles there is a will to protect it. Certainly, it is the first state that exercises its power, and the second one tends to respect the rights of minorities. This leads often to some subtle "bargains" – like in the case of protection of the Danish-speaking minority in Germany, which was simultaneously negotiated with the German-speaking minority in Denmark. One could quote similar cases between Finland and Sweden, or between Greece and Turkey. Another problem concerns language varieties which are really only spoken by a minority group. Do the German-speakers from Italian Tyrol speak *Hochdeutsch* or rather a Germanic (Allemanic) variety? Do the inhabitants of Val-d'Aosta speak French or Franco-Provencal? Do the Alsatians speak German or a variety of Franconian or Allemanic? Do the Belorussians in Poland speak Belorussian or rather a transitional dialect of Ukrainian, Belorussian and Polish? In such cases, two tendencies arising from a certain form of linguistic imperialism can be observed.

b. Languages not related to a language of a nation-state

Languages not related to a language of a nation-state are certainly the case of Basque, Breton, the Sámi language group, most of the Celtic languages, or Livonian in Latvia (the latter spoken actually by less than nine people!); to some extent obviously also Frisian or Catalan. We face here quite different situations. Can Catalan be considered a minority language? It is certainly not a vehicle of a nation-state, but it has more speakers than e.g. Danish, Czech, Slovak, or Lithuanian, Latvian and Estonian together, and enjoys an unconditional support from powerful regional authorities. On the other hand, what should we say of Cornish with its several hundreds of speakers, or Saami, which is spoken by a less numerous population, but inhabits an immense territory, split among four countries? Moreover, we could include into this category the languages which do not have any territorial structure: Yiddish, Judeo-Español, the ancient Turkic language of Karaims in Poland and Lithuania (less than 50 speakers), the Armenian language(s) in Eastern Europe, and a range of Roma vernaculars.

c. Languages related linguistically to a language of a nation-state (regional or collateral languages)

With languages related linguistically to a language of a nation-state (regional or collateral languages), we are dealing with a group of languages with equal problems as the previous case; the main difficulty resulting, however, from the label which comes to be attached: "language" or "dialect". This is the case of Scots in relation to English, Low German in Germany and Low Saxon in the Netherlands in relation to (High) German, Asturian and Aragonese in relation to Spanish, Sicilian, Piemontese or Venetian in relation to Italian, Occitan and the Oïl languages in relation to French, Limburgian in relation to Dutch, Kashubian in relation to Polish, Latgalian in relation to Latvian, Samogitian (Žemaitian) in relation to Lithuanian, Võro in relation to Estonian, Ruthenian in relation to Ukrainian, or – only recently starting to stress their independence - Silesian in relation to Polish, Moravian in relation to Czech, Eastern Slovak in relation to standard Slovak or Polesian in relation to Belorussian and Ukrainian.

Their collateral aspect has often resulted in their assimilation into simple local or regional varieties of nation-state languages, into dialects, or even patois.

Problems of terminology: regional or collateral language versus dialect

First of all, it was linguists who during the nineteenth century were interested in the collateral vernaculars and developed consistently a new discipline – dialectology. Dialectology has achieved remarkable scholarly results, but, from the sociological point of view, it has also had harmful consequences. Actually, this field deals with studies of linguistic factors without caring about their status – referring them to as "dialects" brings detrimental consequences to their speakers. Without entering into a semantic discourse, we could nevertheless consider the term "dialect", the polysemy of which is particularly remarkable and generates never-ending discussions; it seems useful to bring here a few lexical details. In its general meaning, used more in Anglo-Saxon linguistics, a dialect is a geographical variety of a language: French of Liège, English of Liverpool, Chilean Spanish or Polish of Cracow – linguists speak there of "regiolects". Possible in that respect is also consideration of complementary social diversification: Black English Vernacular, Polish spoken by illegal workers in London, etc. – "sociolects" in linguistic terms. In France, in order to comply with the geographical meaning of the term "dialect", the adjective "regional" is often used. At the same time, because of political provisions, the same adjective is applied in relation to actually all languages

We could hold the same discourse in case of all above-mentioned collateral languages; numerous specialists on these idioms have abandoned the usage of the term "dialect" in favour of the expression: "regional endogenous language" (cf. Fauconnier 2004).

A terminological problem of great importance

The report *Euromosaic*, subsidized by the European Commission, and launched in order to describe the mosaic of regional and minority languages in Europe, has hardly dealt with collateral languages, considering them to be linguistic varieties not deserving the status of language. Moreover, the newest version of the *Euromosaic*, which was to envisage the recent extension of the European Union, continues this tendency (with one exception – Kashubian in Poland). The *European Charter on Regional or Minority Languages* itself does not include dialects, or migrants' languages, and it leaves to the member states the decision about what is a language or a dialect. The Charter is not concerned with local varieties or various dialects of the same language. However, it does not express any opinion on the often controversial question when linguistic varieties constitute separate languages. This question depends not only on purely linguistic deliberations, but also on the psycho-sociological and political factors that can lead to a different answer in each case. It remains also within the competence of each state's proper authorities, within the framework of suitable democratic processes, to determine when a linguistic variety constitutes a distinctive language. Therefore, it is sufficient for a state to decide whether a particular variety is a dialect, even without a linguistic justification, thereby excluding it from the profits provided by the *Charter*.

The first precedent of consistent use of the term *regional* in relation to such a collateral language was made by German legislators, when ratifying the Charter in relation to Germany's minority languages (*Minderheitensprachen*: Danish, Upper and Lower Sorbian, Frisian, Yiddish and Romany) and the *Regionalsprache Niederdeutsch* (Low German). In Central and Eastern Europe this problem is also of political, historical and terminological significance: since the minorities are traditionally classified as national minorities or ethnic minorities (with or without a kin-state), some groups with a strong feeling of *Heimatidentität* and *linguistic regionalism* are now developing into such regional language groups. This process has also been influenced by an imminent unification of dialectal varieties, often caused by enormous migrations of population after the World War II.

Regional languages throughout Europe: what do they have in common?

All of the languages mentioned earlier have some common features, as they generally fit the criteria of what is called *langues collatérales* in the French tradition (cf. Eloy 2004) or *Ausbausprachen* in Heinz Kloss's typology (cf. Kloss 1967). These features include:

- close genetic relationship to the corresponding majority language of the state; regiolects are often regarded as being "only" dialects of a majority/state language;
- relatively long history of common development, especially sociopolitical, of the regional and the corresponding majority language;
- lacking or not fully shaped feeling of national separateness within the group of speakers; however, strong regional and/or ethnic identity, with the language

constituting the main constituent of the identity/regional ethnicity;
- high dialectal differentiation within the regiolects, often classified as dialect clusters or L-complexes;
- lacking an adopted uniform literary standard or literary norm, or the standard being *in statu nascendi*;
- rich, often very ancient literary tradition of dialectal/regional literature;
- relatively low social prestige of a regiolect, often lower than in the past;
- underdeveloped status language planning methods;
- opposition within the group against being perceived and officially treated as national minority group, often a paradoxical resistance against being seen as minority group at all; and a specific "embedded" national and/or linguistic identity. (cf. Wicherkiewicz 2003)

Kashubian

Language
Kashubian is a West-Slavic language, spoken in northern Poland, in the province of Pomerania, mainly in its 9 central northern counties. The Kashubian-Pomeranian Association and some regional politicians strive for a change of the Province's official name into "Kashubian-Pomeranian".

The Kashubs inhabit an area of some 6,000 square kilometers on the southern coast of the Baltic Sea – a tetragonal of ca. 130 kms long and 50 kms wide.

Historically and paleoethnologically, the Kashubs are said to be direct descendants of the Pomeranians, a Slavic people that inhabited the Baltic coast between the Vistula (*Wisła*) nad the Oder (*Odra*) rivers, perhaps even as far westward as the Elbe, in the early Middle Ages, and who long constituted a serious threat to the Lekhits – the ancestors of what later became the Polish nation. The modern history of Kashubian began in the mid-19th century, with ideas brought by the Spring of Nations and the pan-Slavic movement. Since then, the sense of ethnic, regional and language identity has been strengthened by the efforts of Kashubian writers: Florian Ceynowa, Hieronim Derdowski, Aleksander Majkowski, Jan Karnowski, Aleksander Labuda and Jan Trepczyk.

The Kashubian language area is nowadays situated within the Polish state and simultaneously on the Polish linguistic area. It is its geographic location that has determined the history, political and social conditions of the existence of its population, mostly rural with agriculture and fishing as main occupations, as well as the development of Kashubian and its linguistic contacts with Polish (standard and dialectal) and German (standard High German and Low German dialects) in the past (cf. Zieniukowa 1997).

Kashubian is entirely diversified into local dialects, the number of which is estimated by some dialectologists at over 50; they can, however, be divided into three main groups: northern, central, and southern (cf. Stone 1993, Wicherkiewicz 2000).

Population
The area inhabited by the Kashubs has diminished significantly over the centuries. The dawn of Kashubian as an ethnic group may be looked for among Pomeranians (cf. above). Under the pressure of German colonization, the Pomeranians moved eastward, and the Slavic elements east of the Oder river disappeared. Since the eighteenth century, the Kashubian territory has not changed significantly, except for

certain losses in the western part inhabited earlier by Protestant Kashubs and their linguistic sub-group – Slovincians. Periods of Germanization alternated with waves of Polonization. As the Kashubs were traditionally Catholic, their nobility and middle classes easily assimilated with the Polish majority (cf. Treder 1997).

During the twentieth century, the population of Kashubs was estimated at various times as follows:

* 1900: 102,000
* 1910: 111,000
* 1926: 155,000
* 1968: 140,000–150,000
* 1975: 150,000–220,000 with ca. 4,500 speakers of Kashubian.

According to the results of the first ever sociodemographic and sociolinguistic research in the late 1980s, the number of Kashubs (i.e. persons who regard themselves as Kashubs or "half-Kashubs") has been estimated at 350,000 to 500,000, including 150,000–250,000 of those who knew or could speak Kashubian to some degree. The region of Kashubia is inhabited by 1.5 million people altogether.

The population Census of 2002, the first since 1931, contained two questions dealing with the questions of "nationality" and "home language":

1. *Among which nationality do you rank yourself?*
2. *Which language(s) do you speak the most often at home?*

The definition of "nationality" was provided: Nationality is everybody's declarative (i.e. based on subjective feeling) individual feature which expresses one's emotional, cultural or genealogical affiliation with a specific nation.

The answer "Kashubian" to the former question has been given by 5,062 persons (5,053 of them were Polish citizens). The absolute majority of them inhabit the Province of Pomerania (4,897); the remaining persons live in the Provinces of Silesia (46), Mazovia (31), Kuiavia-Pomerania (29), Great Poland and Western Pomerania (11 each), Lower Silesia (9) and Varmia-Mazuria (8). The latter question has been answered: "Kashubian", "Kashubian and Polish" or "Polish and Kashubian" (no distinct data have been published) by 52,665 persons (52,567 were Polish citizens).

The Census included a grand total of 38,230,080 inhabitants of the country, in this number, there were 37,529,751 Polish citizens, of whom 492,176 declared a non-Polish language as one of most often used home languages, and of whom 46,559 declared a non-Polish language to be the only used home-language.

Several thousand Kashubs live abroad; worth mentioning are Kashubian enclaves in Ontario/Canada.

Language status
Until the 1990s, according to most of linguistic sources, Kashubian had been regarded as the most distinct or one of the most distinct dialects of Polish (contemporary Polish is traditionally divided into Great-Polish, Little-Polish, Mazovian, Silesian +/- Kashubian dialects). Those who regard Kashubian to be a separate language classify it as one of West-Slavic languages (together with Polish, Upper and Lower Sorbian, Czech and Slovak), forming with Polish and extinct Polabian a separate sub-group of so-called Lekhitic languages. Because of numerous West-Slavic archaic features, one of the most eminent 19th-century Slavists J. Baudouin de Courtenay stated even that *Le cachoubien est plus polonais que le polonais*

même ...

Until 1989, it was prohibited by the Communist censorship to use the noun *język* (Polish for "language") in relation to Kashubian. Therefore, the Kashubian scholars, writers and activists used to call their ethnolect *kaszubszczyzna* ("Kashubianness") or *mowa kaszubska* ("Kashubian speech").

Since 1989, Kashubian has significantly upgraded its linguistic status. The most important factors that contributed to its present position have been:

• activities of the pan-Kashubian association Zrzeszenie Kaszubsko-Pomorskie, founded in 1956
• translation of the New Testament – *Kaszëbskô Biblëjô* (1992) by Franciszek Grucza and *Swięté Pismiona Nowégo Testamentu* (1993) by Eugeniusz Gołąbk
• agreement concerning the unified spelling system for literary Kashubian; before 1996 two competitive systems had been used
• continuous efforts of the Kashubian activists to include the language in all legal acts pertaining to minority issues and official nomenclature – the Kashubs have successfully applied for recognition as "ethnic minority"
• organization of the 39th Congress of the Federal Union of European Nationalities in Gdansk in 1994
• organization of the 6th International Conference on Minority Languages in Gdansk in 1996
• establishment of the Polish Bureau for Lesser Used-Languages (PolBLUL) in 2003.

The 1997 *Constitution of the Republic of Poland* contains two articles, which appertain directly to minority rights, including their linguistic rights:

Art. 27.
Polish shall be the official language in the Republic of Poland. This provision shall not infringe upon national minority rights resulting from ratified international agreements.
Art. 35.
1. The Republic of Poland shall ensure Polish citizens belonging to national or ethnic minorities the freedom to maintain and develop their own language, to maintain customs and traditions, and to develop their own culture.
2. National and ethnic minorities shall have the right to establish educational and cultural institutions and institutions designed to protect their religious identity, as well as to participate in the resolution of matters connected with their cultural identity.

The 1999 *Bill on the Polish Language* provides, among others, for a possibility of introducing a minority language as an "auxiliary" language in the areas with a "considerable share of non-Polish population", where minority languages could be used in bilingual place-names, in personal first names and surnames, and occasionally in local administration. The Bill lacks, however, proper executive regulations, nor does it contain any provisions for usage of minority languages in jurisdiction or state/central administration.

The *Framework Convention for the Protection of National Minorities* was signed by Poland in 1995 and ratified in 2000. It has, however, no impact on the legal situation of the Kashubian language, since the (majority of) Kashubs are neither regarded – nor regard themselves – as *national minority*.

In 2003, the government of the Republic of Poland signed the *European Charter for Regional or Minority Languages*; its ratification will probably follow the adoption of *Bill on National and Ethnic Minorities and on the Regional Language* by the Polish Parliament. Chapter 4 (Art. 17 and 18) of the most recent project of the latter contains the following provisions:

Art. 17.
The regional language as understood by the Bill is the Kashubian language. The regulations of articles 7-14 will be applied respectively. the mentioned articles 7-14 of the Bill pertain to the usage of minority languages in:
- spelling of Christian names and family names,
- private and public life,
- official sphere as auxiliary languages,
- information,
- geographical names, names of streets, names of offices and institutions.

Art. 18.
1. The educational rights of persons, who speak the language mentioned in the art.17, will be exercised on the base of art. 15. (Article 15 pertains to the rights of persons belonging to minorities to be taught their minority language and/or in a minority language, as well as history and culture of the minority group).
2. The persons, who speak the language mentioned in the art. 17, have the right to found and run schools and educational institutions that enable teaching of or in the language, based on the general regulations.
3. The public authorities are obliged to undertake appropriate measures in order to support all activities which aim at preservation and development of the language mentioned in the art. 17, based on the general regulations.
4. The measures mentioned in the §3 may be granted from the budget of a territorial self-government unit to organizations and institutions that fulfill the tasks aiming at preservation and development of the language mentioned in the art. 17.

Status of language education
Crucial for the status of education about and in minority languages in Poland are the following legal acts:
- *Bill on the system of education* of 1991, which grants the pupils right to maintain their national, ethnic, religious and linguistic identity, and particularly to be given classes in/of their mother tongue, as well as their history and culture;
- *Decree of the Minister of Education and Sport on conditions and methods of enabling pupils belonging to national minorities and ethnic groups to maintain their national, ethnic and linguistic identity* of 2002 (substituting the previous one issued in 1992, which pertained solely to "national minorities"; the former decree was applied also in relation to the Kashubian language group on the basis of an … internal amendment by the then in-office Minister of Education).

Private and public education
In general, Polish educational institutions can act as public, community and private establishments. By now, there are no private schools providing education about or in Kashubian. The existing schools are predominantly public or community ones.

Bilingual education forms
In the 1990s, only one primary school provided bilingual education to ca. 20 children. Due to financial and educational problems, the school has been transformed into a school with additional (although compulsory) education of Kashubian language (3 hours a week).

Teachers' training
In December 2002, the second edition of a "Qualification course for teachers of Kashubian language and regional culture" was launched at the University of Gdańsk, in cooperation with the Section for Education of the Kashubian-Pomeranian Association. Each course has been planned for 1.5 years (3 semesters). 41 persons completed the first edition (in 2002); the second one is attended by 51 teachers and will finish in May 2004.

At present there are 25 qualified teachers of Kashubian, 41 graduates from the first edition of the course for teachers and 51 students of the second edition (in total 117 teachers).

Pre-school education
Kashubian is used during pre-school education in only two private kindergartens. An early-immersion language program, based on the experiences of similar programs in Wales, Brittany and Lusatia is planned to start in 2005, probably under the name *Pùfôtk* (Kashubian for "Winnie the Pooh").

Primary and middle education
The State provides funds for teaching of Kashubian if its weekly provision amounts to three hours of classes. The subvention rate for schools providing education about or in minority languages amounts to 120% of the rate for other schools. If the number of pupils in such a school does not exceed 42, the rate amounts to 150%. The funds for the first four months of language teaching must be laid out by the commune. In some cases, this sum may also be paid out by the Ministry of Education and Sport at the beginning of the school year.

The teaching programs for primary and middle schools providing education of Kashubian were accepted by the Ministry of Education in Sport in 2002.

Language use
The respective subjects are labeled: "Kashubian language", "Kashubian language with elements of regional culture", and "Regional education with elements of Kashubian language" and are taught for one, two or three hours a week.

The Handbooks of Kashubian that have been published in the last years include a primer, a primary school dictionary, a language course-book for primary schools and for middle schools, as well as materials for language teachers.

Statistics

In 2002–03, 71 primary schools provided classes of Kashubian language and/or regional education with elements of Kashubian for 4,667 pupils. 14 middle schools provided such education for 446 pupils. Only three secondary schools and one vocational school provided education of Kashubian in any form and the classes were attended by 338 pupils.

Higher education

Since 1992 Kashubian has been taught at a language course at the University of Gdańsk, as an optional specialization for students of Polish language and literature.

At the Dioecesal Seminary in Pelplin, Kashubian is taught two hours a week every year as a language course to some 15 seminarists.

The so-called "Kashubian Folk Universities" in Wieżyca and Starbienino do not organize any language courses.

The only language course-book for university students was published by in 1992. And here we have also a bilingual handbook on the Kashubian history, geography, language and literature.

In 2002–03, courses of Kashubian language and culture for adults were organized in three centers and attended by 46 participants. (cf. Majewicz and Wicherkiewicz 1990, Wicherkiewicz 2004).

Prospects

Recent research has provided some reliable data on the situation of Kashubian. The results of the 2002 population census could be disappointing in that respect, but taking into consideration its pioneering character, unclear criteria and certain lack of confidence as far as all national and/or ethnic question are concerned, the number of 52,665 persons declaring Kashubian to be their home language is undoubtedly an important indicator for language planners and educational activists.

Bearing in mind that Kashubian was introduced (in a very modest way and dimension) as late as in 1991, the total number of 5,451 pupils taught Kashubian (in any form) by 117 teachers seems quite impressive. During the recent 13 years the most important obstruction in the education about and in Kashubian has been abolished – namely the traditional school system. It was the school that imposed the conviction of the superiority of "urban Polish" culture over "rural Kashubian". The pupils and parents were mentally accused of the "backwardness" of Kashubian with its poor career possibilities for their children. This mental attitude has certainly been reversed.

Further development of Kashubian education is undoubtedly conditioned on efforts of regional activists and further training of qualified teachers. Crucial in that respect will be also the ratification of the *European Charter for Regional or Minority Languages* by Poland, preceded by the internal *Bill on national and ethnic minorities and on the regional language*.

References

Eloy, Jean-Michel 2004. *Des langues collatérales*. Paris: L'Harmattan.

Fauconnier, Jean-Luc 2004. "Les langues d'oïl, des idiomes en voie de reconnaissance", in: Wicherkiewicz et al. (eds.) 2004: 22-31.

Kloss, Heinz 1967. "*Abstand* Languages and *Ausbau* Languages". *Anthropological Linguistics* 9 (7): 29-41.

Majewicz, Alfred F. and Tomasz Wicherkiewicz 1990. "National Minority Languages in Media and Education in Poland", in: D. Gorter et al. (eds.) *Fourth International Conference on Minority Languages*. Vol. II. *Western and Eastern European Papers*. Clevedon and Philadelphia: Multilingual Matters. 149-174.

Stone, Gerald 1993. "Cassubian", in: B. Comrie and G.G. Corbets (eds.) *The Slavonic Languages*. London and New York: Routledge. 759-794

Synak, Brunon 1995. "The Kashubs' Ethnic Identity: Continuity and Change", in: B. Synak (ed.) *The Ethnic Identities of European Minorities*. Gdańsk: Uniwersytet Gdański. 155-166.

Synak, Brunon and Tomasz Wicherkiewicz (eds.) 1997. *Language Minorities and Minority Languages in the Changing Europe*. Gdańsk: Uniwersytet Gdański.

Treder, Jerzy 1997. "Polish-Kashubian". in: H. Goebl et al. (eds.) *Kontaktlinguistik. Contact Linguistics. Linguistique de contact*. Vol. 2. Berlin and New York: Walter de Gruyter, 1600-1606.

Wicherkiewicz, Tomasz 2000. "Kashubian", in: Jan Wirrer (ed.) *Minderheiten- und Regionalsprachen in Europa*. Wiesbaden: Westdeutscher Verlag. 213-222.

Wicherkiewicz, Tomasz 2003. "Becoming a regional language – a method in language status planning?", in: *Actes del 2n Congrés Europeu sobre Planificació Lingüística. Andorra la Vella 14-16 noviembre de 2001*. Barcelona: Generalitat de Catalunya, Departament de Cultura. 473-477.

Wicherkiewicz, Tomasz 2004. *The Kashubian in education in Poland*. Regional dossiers. Ljouwert: Mercator Education.

Wicherkiewicz, Tomasz [Viherkevičs, Tomašs] et al. (eds.) 2004. *Regional Languages in the New Europe. Reģionālās valodas musdienu Eiropā. Regionaluos volūdys myusdinu Eiropā – Proceedings of the International Conference 20-23 May 2004.* Rēzekne: Rēzeknes Augstskola [Latvia].

Zieniukowa, Jadwiga 1997. "On the Languages of Small Ethnic Groups – the Case of Sorbian and Kashubian", in: Synak and Wicherkiewicz 1997: 311-316.

An Eastern Slavonic Perspective on Scots

Alexander Pavlenko

Comparing the linguistic situation formed by Scots and English in Lowland Scotland with other situations constituted by pairs of closely cognate languages has become a popular approach in the field of Scots studies. It is easy to recall quite a number of examples of linguistic situations in Europe that are characterized by co-existence of dominating state languages with cognate or non-cognate regional or minority languages. This approach can help in obtaining valuable data necessary for language planning.

In the recent decades when the attitudes towards regional and minority languages have undergone dramatic changes, there have appeared a number of works comparing the social history and the status of Scots with such languages as Low German, Flemish, Provençal, Catalan and others. Not only the material of lesser-used languages can be attracted in this context but also that of official languages as it can be equally valuable. No Slavonic languages have been chosen for a detailed comparison like that so far, to say nothing of mentioning some typologically close situations (e.g. Czech - Slovak in Kloss 1968, Serbian - Croatian in Görlach 2000, etc. In this respect, an abundant material can be provided by Eastern-Slavonic languages, i.e. Russian, Ukrainian and Byelorussian, which are very closely cognate. It is their closeness manifested by mutual intelligibility as well as the closeness of their fortunes that make Eastern-Slavonic languages quite appropriate for comparing them with English and Scots.

Further, I propose to dwell on some historical and sociolinguistic parallels between Scots and the Ukrainian language and to compare the key stages and trends of their social history proceeding from the seventeenth century. to the present day. For all the structural and functional dissimilarity and geographical remoteness of Scots and Ukrainian from each other, we can make some interesting observations regarding the social history of these languages.The most important socio-cultural circumstance that has affected the development of the indigenous languages in Scotland and in Ukraine was the union with a larger neighbouring state – England and Russia respectively. Both in Scotland and in Ukraine such unions that took place in the seventeenth century and had a voluntary character, led to similar after-effects as regards linguistic situation. The indigenous languages, i.e. Scots and Ukrainian, were soon forced out of the register of formal communication, while in all the other fields, including literature, their use was shrinking rapidly. However, this process was proceeding in different ways in the two countries. In Scotland, a kind of voluntary "giving up" of the indigenous language took place along with a "peaceful" supplanting of it by southern English, whereas in Ukraine the major factor of supplanting Ukrainian by Russian was the purposeful official policy of Russification.

It was in the eighteenth century when both Ukrainian and Scots were being most intensively drawn into the systems of the dominating cognate languages. In both cases this process started in urban communities while the native speech was conserved in the rural areas. The process of Anglicization of Scots and Russification of Ukrainian had gone quite far in both countries by the mid eighteenth century and brought about very similar linguistic situations whose main feature was a bipolar dialect continuum that has existed in both countries since that time.

As the present, distinguished audience is very well acquainted with the main stages of the history of Scots, I shall permit myself only to name some relevant events in the history of Ukrainian and then point out some important similarities and differences in the histories of the both languages.

The war of liberation from the Polish rule (1648-1654) led the bigger part of the Ukrainian lands to the Union with Russia in 1654 that was concluded on the terms of preservation of self-determination and the right to elect military and civil officials. However, gradually the Russian authorities (especially after Peter I's reign) started to restrict the rights and privileges of Ukraine. Eventually the Ukrainian self-determination was abolished between 1764 and 1782 when all-Russian institutions, serfdom and administrative division were introduced. Total Russification of cities and boroughs, the introduction of Russian in official sphere and the switch-over of most Cossack nobles from Ukrainian to Russian - all that made the Old Ukrainian literary language, having little in common with the inhabitants of Eastern Ukraine, quite useless and from the second half of the eighteenth Old literary Ukrainian was being on the decline. By the end of the century it had collapsed and practically got out of use. That provoked an interruption of the Old Ukrainian literary tradition in the Eastern regions of the country and thus the main part of the Ukrainian people lost their literary language altogether for a considerable period (cf. Zhilko 1962: 107). However from the end of the eighteenth a new literary language was already forming on the basis of the mid-Dnieper and south-eastern dialects. For a vast historical period the principal role in the development of Ukrainian was played by the rural dialects, as the speech of the urban centres was completely dominated first by the Polish language and from the eighteenth on by Russian.

After a considerable period of suppression and persecution, which fell on early nineteenth century, the 1840s saw the rise of Ukrainian nationalism. The periods of relative tolerance alternated with severe reaction. Thus, in 1863, the Russian authorities banned publication of academic and ecclesiastic literature in Ukrainian. Only fiction was allowed. In 1876, it was prohibited to use Ukrainian in the theatre. Of course, no teaching in Ukrainian was available in the lands subordinate to Moscow. However, despite all these restrictions, the 1870s saw the successful launch of a nationalistic Ukrainian literary periodical entitled "Kiev Antiquity". After the revolution of 1905 all the formal restrictions on using languages other than Russian were abolished in the Russian Empire. This democratization led to quick rise of publishing and teaching in Ukrainian.

After 1917, or rather after the civil war which had come to an end in 1920 and with the creation of the USSR in 1924, Ukraine acquired the status of a Union republic and later (after WWII) even participated in the United Nations as a member with full rights. The new literary language, which started to develop as far as late eighteenth century, in the times of the Soviet Regime finally became the language of all the Ukrainian people. This variety based on south-eastern dialects also borrowed some western-Ukrainian features. It was the reunification of the Ukrainian lands by mid twentieth century. which made it possible to develop the national spoken standard which did not exist before. It can be stated that despite the contradictory character of language development under the Soviet regime it was this period when Ukrainian finally elaborated its stylistic and genre system.

The attitudes of the Soviet state towards Ukrainian and other ethnic languages were subject to dramatic changes following the changes of the internal policy. They fluctuated from all possible assistance to neglect or ousting. As an example of

Figure 1: Map of Ukraine

support for the Ukrainian language, I can mention the plans of complete Ukrainization of Krasnodar teacher training institute in late 1920s in view of numerous Ukrainian-speakers in Krasnodar region of the Russian Federation. If those plans had been successfully completed, it would have been an interesting example of language support outside its historical area.

After a period of advancing although contradictory language development by mid 1930s, the turn to promotion of Russian in both union and autonomous republics began to show. This trend manifested itself first of all in teaching and finally got outlined after WWII due to hypercentralization of the USSR.

In 1958, parents were permitted to choose schools for their children according to language preferences what made most families choose Russian schools which in common understanding provided better career opportunities (cf. the attitudes characteristic of the Lowlanders after the union of the Crowns as regards the choice between Scots and English). Thus the number of Russian schools in the Ukraine had outnumbered that of Ukrainian schools by mid 1970s. In Ukraine the Ukrainian language was being forced out intensively in teaching, mass communication and administrative sphere by local varieties of Russian. At the same time the structure of the Ukrainian language was being affected by that of Russian.

It would be true to say that the process of supplanting of Ukrainian by Russian was a slow natural retreat of the former and the state did not have any aggressive plans of exterminating Ukrainian altogether. It was rather not a deliberate Russification but a natural process of spreading a dominating language within a large multicultural country.

Since Ukraine finally obtained its independence in 1991 after the collapse of the Soviet Union, the Ukrainian language has enjoyed maximum support on behalf of the state. The Ukrainian language has always been an important symbol of identity in the local nationalist doctrine, which is the basis of today's Ukrainian state ideology. So, no matter how radical a government might be, the native language is sure to gain maximum support even at the expense of the other languages spoken in Ukraine (I mean first and foremost Russian).

According to the official data of the census of 2001, 67.5% of the Ukrainian population consider Ukrainian as their native language and only 29.6% are Russian native speakers. However, it is difficult to admit unreservedly this statistics as such because it is common knowledge that vast and densely populated areas of Ukraine – especially eastern and southern ones – are mostly Russian speaking (see Figure 1). Besides Kiev authorities are sure to be biased and may deliberately diminish the amount of the speakers of Russian. The biggest cities including Kiev, the capital of the country, are mostly Russian speaking, varieties of Russian being the principal means of home and business communication. According to some independent estimations the share of the speakers of Russian is not less than 51% (see Tolochko 1999: 17).

Further, I am going to point out some sociolinguistic parallels between Ukrainian as spoken before 1905 (i.e. the starting point of wide democratization in the Russian Empire) and the present day Scots. First come some most obvious similarities. Thus:

a. Both Ukrainian and Scots used to exist as dialect groups of mainly rural character although having prestigeous literary traditions and vast corpuses of texts (old and new).

b. Ukrainian used to be treated both by Russian philologists and authorities as a dialect group of the so called Great Russian language like until quite recently it was characteristic of the attitudes towards Scots and English in Lowland Scotland.

c. Neither Ukrainian nor Scots used to have any legal status and therefore they were not present in either educational system or administrative sphere.

d. Both Ukrainian and Scots were associated with lower classes.

e. Being the systems suppressed by other languages enjoing all the advantages of state support and promotion the status of both Ukrainian and Scots could be characterized as threatened.

As to differences characteristic of the two languages I can mention the following:

a. Unlike Scots the Ukrainian language has always been spoken outside the political borders of Ukraine (which used to change very often) and although no variety of it has ever had a high status abroad, there have developed several important literary traditions that could affect the development of the mainstream.

b. Despite the traditionally strong position of Russian diluting Ukrainian in many parts of the country there have always been mostly Ukrainian speaking areas whose population is aware of its speech and has highly positive attitudes towards it.

c. Unlike Scots modern Ukrainian can hardly be characterized as an endangered language as it seems to have passed its worst times.

The comparison with Scots and English brings about some other observations among which are the following:

1. As is known adoption of an alien language and the giving up of a native one can sometimes be promoted by the lack of a considerable cultural gap between the contacting language communities. On the contrary, the existence of deep difference may sometimes hinder such language change. There was no such dramatically deep difference in cultural paradigm between Lowlands and England by the time of the Union in 1603 as that between Ukraine and Russia in 1654. This circumstance would not favour the conservation of Scots but made it easier for Scotland to transfer from Scots to English. On the contrary, the fact that Ukraine came into contact with the western Enlightenment earlier than Muscovite Rus' did and that the Ukrainian culture was more advanced by the time of the Russian-Ukrainian Union in 1654 (cf. Trubetskoy 1991: 246) is very likely to have strengthened the determination of the Ukrainians to protect and develop the language and literature of the country as early as late eighteenth century.

2. Unlike the situation in Lowland Scotland, language has always occupied an essential place in the ideology of the Ukrainian nationalism. After the tsarist regime had suppressed the rising liberation movement in the late eighteenth - early nineteenthth cc. the partisans of the latter turned their efforts to the development of the Ukrainian culture, especially the Ukrainian literature and language. The decline of the Old Ukrainian literary language did not cause a complete break of the literary tradition in general. Language has always remained an important element of the identity of the nation and provided the preservation of the spiritual links among the disintegrated Ukrainian territories.

The Ukrainian nationalistic movement started to develop not only in the Russian empire but also in Austria-Hungary and in both countries its main achievements were limited mainly to protecting the indigenous language, literature and culture of the Ukrainian people. The main figures of the Ukrainian nationalism of the nineteenth century were first and foremost several eminent authors among them Kotliarevskiy, Gulak-Artemovskiy, Kvitka, Shevchenko, Kulish, and Kostomarov. Because of political repression their efforts were restricted to creating a literary register of the language, participating in and facilitating the literary process. In the times of domination first of the Polish and later of the Russian speech in urban communities the Ukrainian language continued to exist in the form of rural dialects and it was the very vernacular that was used by the Ukrainian authors to elaborate a new literary standard. The adherence to the indigenous language of the Ukrainian intellectuals unlike the relative lack of it with their Scottish contemporaries could have resulted from:

1. the reaction on the persecution that the Ukrainian language and literature underwent first under the Polish rule and later within the bounds of the Russian empire;

2. the recognition of cultural self-sufficiency and autonomy of Ukraine caused by its "intermediate" position between the European West and Muscovite Rus' and reluctance to identify themselves with the Russian culture along with the historical impossibility of complete joining the European one.

3. In the twentieth century, the principal changes of the status of the Ukrainian

language resulted from the political changes first in the Russian Empire and further in the Soviet Union. The disintegration of the empire was used by the nationalistic forces, language being one of the powerful instruments in achieving their goals.

Conclusion

To sum up, I shall mention again that the main similarities between Ukrainian and Scots are the strong diluting influence on behalf of a closely cognate languages and the formation of a speech continuum.

The principal difference is rooted in the fact that an awareness of and positive attitudes towards Ukrainian are spreading even among the speakers of Russian in modern Ukraine what is supported by the current language policy. On the contrary in the Lowlands we find the lack of awareness of Scots and the scarecity of positive attitudes towards it.

Ukrainian can be considered as a happy example of a language which is doomed to further positive development, first because despite all the ups and downs it was able to retain a big community of speakers who are quite aware of their means of communication. As important is the fact that the new Ukrainian authorities believe that it pays to support the indigenous language.

It might also be interesting to compare the Ukrainian situation with that in the Republic of Ireland where the community of speakers of Irish has been shrinking until recently despite energetic state support. The comparison above underlines once again the role of prestige characteristic of a once dominating language (in our case Russian and English respectively) in the development of the subordinate languages within the given situation. It is a kind of lingua-cultural competition which, as is known, may have very unlike results.

References

Görlach, M., 2000. 'Ulster Scots: A language?' In: *Language and Politics: Northern Ireland, the Republic of Ireland, and Scotland*. Eds. John M. Kirk, Dónall P. Ó Baoill. Belfast: Cló Ollscoil na Banríona. 2000, 13-31. Belfast Studies in Language, Culture and Politics 1.

Kloss, H. 1968. *Die Entwicklung neuer germanischer Kultursprachen seit 1800*. Düsseldorf: Bagel. Second Edition.

Tolochko, P.P., 1999. 'Chto ili kto ugrozhaet ukrainskomu yazyku?' *Zaporozhye*. [in Russian]

Trubetskoy, N.S., 1991. 'The legacy of Genghis Khan and other essays on Russia's identity.' In: *Michigan Slavic Materials*, 33. Ed. A. Liberman. Ann Arbor. 245-267.

Zhilko, F.T., 1962. 'Nekotoryye osobennosti razvitiya ukrainskogo natsional'nogo yazyka.' In: *Voprosy obrazovaniya vostochnoslavianskikh natsional'nykh yazykov*. Collection of works. Moskva, 102-109. [in Russian]

The Making of the Maltese Language

Joe Zammit-Ciantar

Introduction

The Maltese language is the national language of Malta. It is a living national heritage. It is a mixed language; this is a reflection of the colourful history, and the result of the vicissitudes the inhabitants and the language they used experienced through time. Moreover, the geographical size and position of the Maltese archipelago itself, far from the European mainland in the north, but particularly from the Arabic speakers of North Africa in the south, have helped in the eventual emergence, or perhaps more appropriately, the transformation and making, of the Maltese language from an Arabic dialect into a language by itself. This paper gives a general idea of the political, historical, and linguistic background which helped this process, especially along the last millennium.

The Maltese islands

The Maltese archipelago[1] is situated about 96 km (60 miles) south of Sicily and 295 km (180 miles) north of the African coast. Malta is the largest island with a surface area of *c.* 246 square km (95 square miles), and Gozo,[2] the second larger island, situated about 9 km (5 miles) north-west of Malta, with a surface area of *c.* 67 square km (26 square miles). Both are densely built and inhabited by a population of *c.* 400,000. The smaller islands[3] are not inhabited. The language used by almost all of the inhabitants is Maltese.

Historical background

The fate of the inhabitants – and that of the language they used – depended on the powers which ruled over the Maltese islands from time to time in the last three millennia. These were: the Phoenicians (*c.* 800 BC – *c.* 600 BC), the Carthaginians (*c.* 600 BC– 218 BC), the Romans (218 BC – *c.* AD 530), the Byzantines (*c.* 536-870), the Arabs (870-1091), the Normans, Swabians, Angevins, and Aragonese (1091-1530), the Order of the Knights of St John of Jerusalem (1530-1798), the French (1798-1800), and the British (1800-1964).

The roots of the language

Nothing is known about the language which was used by the people who built the megalithic temples in the period 4000-1500 BC. However, from the artefacts they left,

---

[1] The extreme points of these islands fall within the following position: North – 36° 57' Latitude, South – 35° 48' Latitude, East – 14° 35' Longitude, West – 14° 11' Longitude. Cf. Neville Ransley and Anton Azzopardi, *A Geography of the Maltese Islands*, 4th and enlarged ed., Malta 1988, p. 1.

[2] Malta has a maximum length of 27.3 km (17 miles) and a maximum width of 14.5 km (9 miles), and Gozo, a maximum length of 14 km (8.75 miles) and a maximum width of 7 km (4.3 miles).

[3] These are: **Kemmuna** (Comino), **Kemmunett** (Cominotto), **Il-Gżira** (popularly known as Manoel Island), **Filfla**, and **Il-ġebla tal-ġeneral** (literally 'the general's stone/rock', popularly known as Fungus Rock).

but decidedly from the designs in red ochre and in stone, from the sculptures, and particularly from the architecture and construction of the megalithic temples themselves, one may presume they enjoyed an established level of culture, and surely possessed a sophisticated spoken medium for communication.

It is assumed that the parlance used on Maltese soil during the time of the Phoenicians was Phoenician, itself a north-west Semitic language. Hence, we may assume that the first language our forefathers used and we know of was Phoenician. This might have undergone some transformation during the centuries of Carthaginian colonization, and surely began to be influenced by Latin after Malta was taken over by the Romans. It must be observed, however, that in AD 60 the inhabitants must have still used a dominantly Semitic vernacular, as observed by St Luke in the *Acts of the Apostles* 28, lines 1-2, where he stated that the island where St Paul and those shipwrecked with him landed, was Malta, and that the inhabitants were βάρβαροι (*Barbaroi*);[4] they spoke neither Greek nor Latin and must have still been using Punic.

It might be conjectured that during this period, through social contact, and surely as a result of mixed marriages, that the everyday speech began to eventually pick up from Latin used by Roman soldiers brought over to help in the administration of the islands, and together with Greek, was the language of the administration, and the Latinization of certain names like Phoenician Malta > *Melita*, and GWL > *Gaulos* and *Gaudos* (which later on > *Gozzo* > *Gozo* and > *Għawdex*) was a natural process. Still, although some Maltese words in today's language like **qattus** 'cat', **gawwija** 'sea-gull', **fellus** 'chicken', **forn** 'oven', **Pwales**,[5] and **-skala**,[6] are traceable to Latin *cattus, gavia, pullus, furnus, palude* 'swamp', and *scala* 'landing place', respectively,[7] they may not automatically prove a direct descent from this period; the lexemes could have formed part of an already-established Sicilian, or perhaps North African

---

[4] In *Acts of the Apostles* 27, and 28, 1-13, Luke is describing the shipwreck of St Paul on the shores of Malta, and the three months he and the other 276 men stayed on the island before sailing on for Rome. Luke wrote: 'The natives showed us no ordinary kindness; for they lit a fire and welcomed us all to it, because it was raining, and because of the cold.' *Acts* 28, 1-2. with which cp. 'et cum evasissemus tunc cognovimus quia Militene insula vocatur barbari vero praestabant non modicam humanitatem nobis: accensa enim pyra, reficiebant nos omnes, propter imbrem qui inminebat, et frigus [...]', *Biblia Sacra Juxta Vulgatam Clementinam,* [Desclee], Tournai 1947, Cap. XXVIII, 2; pp. 160-1. Cf. '[...] "natives", *lit.* βάρβαροι; but this only meant that they did not speak Greek, and the term could easily be used by anyone who had such entire facility in Greek as St. Luke. The word is probably onomatopoeic in origin, meaning those whose speech was mere "bar-bar" to the Greeks. The more educated among the Maltese, however, would doubtless speak Greek, or Latin, or both.' Cuthbert Luttey and Joseph Keating, (eds.), *The Westminster Version of the Sacred Scriptures – The New Testament,* Vol. II, 1936, p. 312, n. 2. Today, the biblical βάρβαροι is interpreted to refer to 'people who spoke neither Latin nor Greek'.

[5] **Pwales** is a place-name and has no direct meaning in Maltese.

[6] **-skala** is part of the composite place-name **Marsaskala**, originally Arbic *marsa* ('place good for anchorage') + Italian *scala* ('landing place'); in Maltese **skala** does not survive by itself, and has no immediate meaning.

[7] Cf. P.P. Saydon, 'VII. Lexicologie – The Pre-Arabic Latin Element in Maltese Toponymy', *Orbis,* Vol. V, No. 1, Nuneaton 1956, pp. 191-7.

Arabic, and were brought to Malta centuries later.[8] Maltese religious vocabulary like **ġenna** 'heaven', **isqof** 'bishop', **knisja** 'church', **magħmudija** 'baptism', **qassis** 'priest', **qrar** 'confession', **quddiesa** 'mass', **sawm** 'fasting', **tewba** 'penance', and **tqarbin** 'Holy Communion',[9] may suggest an eastern Christian influence during the Byzantine period. These words are traceable to Semitic Syrian.[10] However, it is most probable that these words 'were introduced into Malta by Arab Christians some of whom might have belonged to the Maronite Order'[11] from the Levant, or by Basilian monks from the east by way of Sicily.[12] It is presumed that the language our forefathers kept using until the Arabs' invasion in 870 could have been Greek,[13] but more probably Late Punic.

This could, or would have been transformed by the Arabs who ruled over the islands for more than two centuries between 870 and 1091, and by those who were allowed to stay on even though Malta was won over by the Normans, until their expulsion from the islands between 1222 and 1249.[14] This was the most acclaimed and accepted hypothesis until the very last decade of the twentieth century. Yet, since the rediscovery[15] of Al Himyari's historical account which speaks of an Islamic violent attack on the Maltese islands in *c.* 870, we now know that the islands 'remained uninhabited ruin'[16] for almost 180 years.[17] This automatically rules out the theory that the Late Punic used before lingered on and was transformed by the new rulers. The islands were eventually repopulated in 1049, with a community of about 5,000 people[18] from Sicily, who already spoke Sicilian Arabic – very probably a Maghrebine Arabic dialect. Al-Himyari's historical information seems to be very reliable. The abrupt change of language in Malta, and the lack of a Punic linguistic substratum in

---

[8] Cf. Joseph Aquilina, *Papers in Maltese Linguistics*, Malta 1961, p. 7.

[9] Cf. ibid., pp. 21 and 46. Cf. also '*ḳnisja, qassis, qaddis, qaddisa, nisrani* are attested in the Greek-Arabic.' Joseph M. Brincat, *Malta 870-1054 – Al-Himyari's Account and its Linguistic Implications*, Malta 1995, p. 24.

[10] Cf. 'As a matter of fact, in the Maltese vocabulary […] we have quite a number of Christian words which we share with our co-religionists of Syria.' *Papers in Maltese Linguistics*, p. 46.

[11] Cf. Joseph Aquilina, 'Maltese Christian Words of Arabic Origin' in *Actes du 1er Congrès d'etudes des cultures méditerraneennes d'influence arabo-berbère*, Alger 1973, p. 74.

[12] Mario Buhagiar, 'The re-Christianisation of Malta: Siculo-Greek Monasticism, Dejr toponyms, and Rock-cut Churches', *Melita Historica*, Vol. XIII, No. 3, Malta 2002, pp. 255-7.

[13] Alexander Borg states that even Greek could have been used. Cf. Id. 'Language' in *Malta – Culture and Identity*, (eds. Henry Frendo and Oliver Friggieri), Malta 1994, p. 34. Borg states that the place-name Xlendi, for an inlet in Gozo, could be a residue of this period; it is traceable to Greek χελαυδιου meaning '*bateaux legers* of the Byzantine navy'. Ibid., pp. 33-4.

[14] Cf. *Malta 870-1054 – Al-Himyari's Account and its Linguistic Implications*, p. 26.

[15] The text on Malta by Al-Himyari was published in a geographical dictionary by Ihsân 'Abbâs, in Beirut, in 1975. However, it was Professor Joseph M. Brincat of the University of Malta who has rediscovered the text (especially for the attention of the Maltese scholars), and eventually published studies on the contents which throw new light on the darkest age in Malta's history. Cf. among these: J.M. Brincat, *Malta 870-1054 – Al-Himyari's Account*, Malta 1991, and id., *Malta 870-1054 – Al-Himyari's Account and its Linguistic Implications*, Malta 1995.

[16] Cf. ibid., p. 11.

[17] Cf. ibid., p. 18.

[18] Cf. ibid., p. 20.

the Maltese language itself, are supporting proof. 'The historical and geographical factors now decidedly point to Sicilian Arabic as the basic source of the Maltese language'[19] still used today, and there seems to be little hope of anybody delving in the possibility of tracing any Punic or Phoenician linguistic remains in it.[20]

With the coming of the Normans in 1091 the islands became a dependency of the Sicilian Crown, and the language used by the inhabitants started a new life. First it came in direct contact with Sicilian and Latin, then with Tuscan Italian brought over and used by the Knights of St John both as a means of communication among themselves and as the language of administration, and later on, eventually, with English – the language of the rulers after 1800.

The natural evolution of Maltese

The basis of the Maltese language, hence, must have been established some one thousand years ago.[21] However, like any other living language, it continued to foster, evolve, and grow, borrowing, and eventually adopting linguistic material from the languages it was continuously in contact with along the centuries later.

When the last Muslims were expelled from the Maltese islands in 1249, the Sicilian Arabic used by the inhabitants lost contact with the 'mother' Maghrebin Arabic dialect, and had to survive on its own. The languages used by the people who came over in the centuries that followed became the sources from which the Maltese started and kept borrowing and adopting the linguistic material needed to make the language meaningful and rich enough to help them express themselves in all the aspects of every human activity. Insularity is the very important element which helped to preserve the secluded vernacular develop into a distinct language. On the other hand, flexibility and adaptability are the main characteristics that have helped keep Maltese a living and effective language.

Some of the process of the evolution of the language may be observed in the sporadic writings which register the use of Maltese words and phrases used in different epochs of the remote past, the various phonological, morphological, and semantic changes that have taken place in certain adaptations in the Maltese language, the adoption of a Roman alphabet, and the present structure of the Maltese language.

---

[19] Cf. ibid., p. 27.

[20] This subject has been dealt with by many a scholar of Maltese. Among these one may refer to Gozitan scholar Gio: Pietro Francesco Agius de Soldanis, *Della Lingua Punica presentemente usata da Maltesi &c. ovvero Nuovi Documenti, li quali possono servire di lume all'antica lingua Etrusca; stesi in Due Dissertazioni &c.*, Rome MDCCL [1750]; Michaelis Antonii Vassalli, *Mylsen* Phoenico-Punicum *sive Grammatica Melitensis*, Rome 1791; and more recently, S.M. Zarb, 'The Maltese Language – Aryan or Semitic?' in *Scientia*, Vol. IX, No. 1, Malta 1942, 35-44; id., 'The Maltese Language – Phoenician or Arabic?' in *Scientia*, Vol. X, No. 4, Malta 1943, pp. 185-90; and P. Grech, 'Are there any traces of Punic in Maltese?', *Journal of Maltese Studies*, No. 1, Malta 1961, pp. 130-8. The scholarly debate on the nature of Maltese must have been sealed long ago, but definitely by the scholarly publication of Joseph Aquilina, *Maltese-Arabic Comparative Grammar*, Malta 1979.

[21] Cf. Joseph M. Brincat, *Il-Malti – Elf Sena ta' Storja* [Maltese – One Thousand Years of History], Malta 2000.

The earliest written Maltese

The earliest samples of 'Maltese' are Maltese and Gozitan nicknames and names of places used by notaries in deeds and contracts written in either Sicilian or Latin.[22] There are hundreds of these, and the earliest date back to the early fourteenth century. In the notarial deeds and in other manuscript material, we also find some Maltese phrases.[23] But the earliest extensive written work in Maltese is the 'Cantilena' by Pietro Caxaro which was composed between 1465 and 1480.[24]

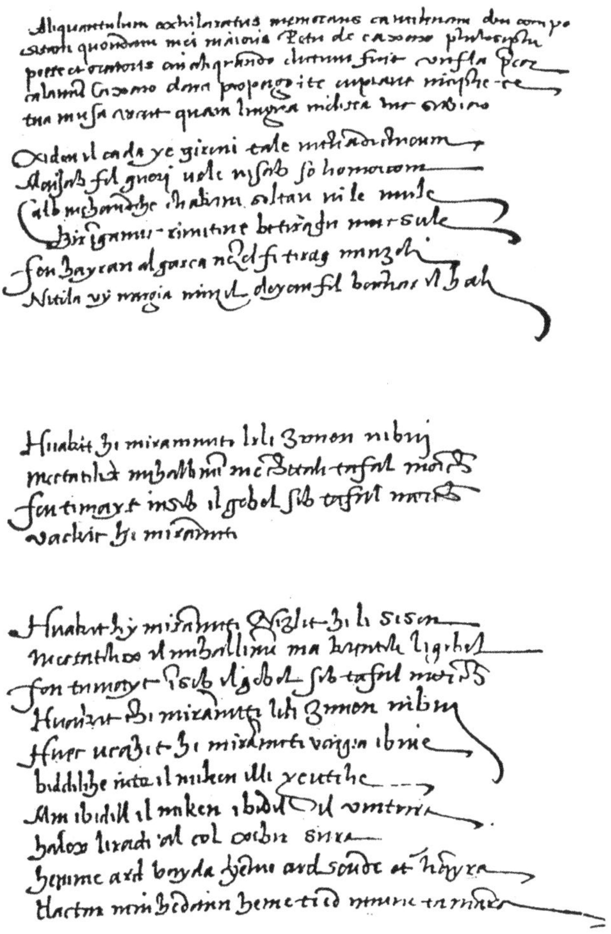

Figure 1: Facsimile of the poem in Mediaeval Maltese 'Cantilena'

---

[22] For a study on the Maltese place-names documented in Maltese notarial deeds going back to the fourteenth century, cf. Godfrey Wettinger, *Place-Names of the Maltese Islands, ca. 1300-1800*, Malta 2000.

[23] Cf. Stanley Fiorini, 'Ut Vulgo Dicitur: Pre-1600 Materials for a Documented Etymology of Maltese', in *Karissime Gotifride* (ed. Paul Xuereb), Malta 1999, pp. 161-76.

[24] Cf. Godfrey Wettinger and Michael Fsadni, *Peter Caxaro's Cantilena*, Malta 1966.

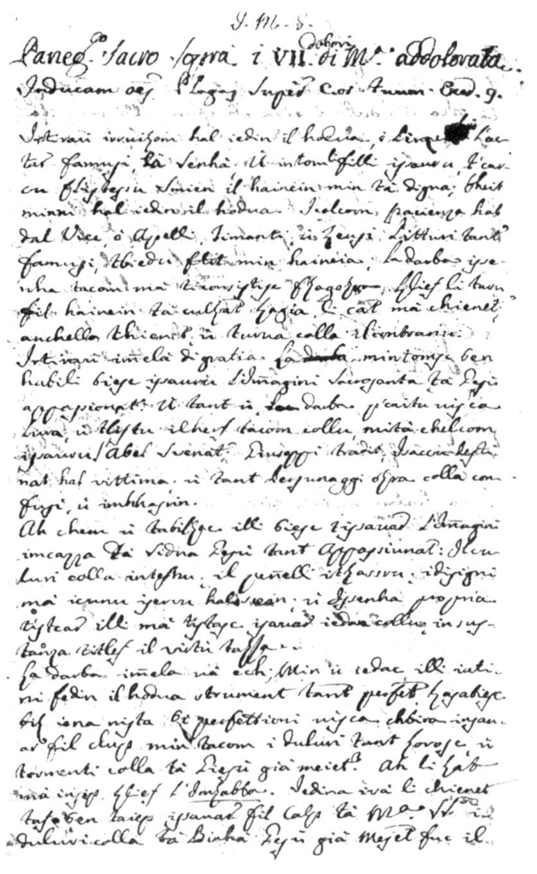

Figure 2: Facsimile of a page from the eighteenth-century manuscript-sermons by Iganzio Saverio Mifsud (National Library of Malta, Library MS. No. 48, p. 3.)

This is a medieval poem in which the vocabulary used is Semitic, and the only loanwords we come across with in the 20-line composition are Romance vintura ('adventure'), and the Latin conjunction **et**. Then, the earliest voluminous prose we know of, yet, consists of hundreds of pages of manuscript sermons in Maltese – abounding with Sicilian and Italian loanwords in the process of being adopted and used harmoniously side by side with the Semitic stock – written down in preparation for their being presented in various churches in Malta, by Maltese *chierico*[25] Ignazio Saverio Mifsud, between 1739 and 1746. The eighteenth-century homilitic material

---

[25] Almost all of the *c.* 43 sermons – the majority of which in Maltese – composed by Ignazio Saverio Mifsud (1722-1773), were presented in various churches in Malta when he was still a seminarian; some of these were delivered even before he was ordained deacon. The only sermons he wrote and presented later on in life – in 1754, when he was an ordained priest – are three: one in Maltese, the other two in Italian.

is by itself concrete evidence of the great number of words the Maltese language had to borrow to help the users keep abreast with the times they were living in. They are also a tangible proof of the very important part played by the Catholic clergy in helping to establish and diffuse an idiom otherwise lacking the necessary expressive lexical terms in the vernacular of the unquestionably Catholic peasant inhabitants.[26] Later still, during the British rule, the inhabitants started encountering and quickly adopting English words for new ideas either the British brought over with them or which were cropping up from time to time.[27]

Phonological, morphological, and semantic changes

Some original Arabic emphatic sounds that came in with the dialect used by the community sent to Malta in the middle of the eleventh century, have by time melted down, and from various emphatic phonemes Maltese retained only one of each respectively. Besides, the Latin phonemes missing in Arabic, and long in use over the island, have infiltrated and today form part of the Maltese alphabet.

The nouns **mughallimin, mirammiti,** and **miken** found among the vocabulary of the 'Cantilena' just referred to above, like many another vocabulary, have experienced a modification; today they have a syllable less: **mghallmin** ('master masons'), **mrammti** ('my house'), and **mkien** ('place'). If we compare many a Semitic lexemes which are used in the local vernacular with their original counterparts in Arabic, we would immediately realize that this phenomenon has become part and parcel of the borrowing and adopting process in the language. Original Arabic nouns **maratun** and **raġulun** are **mara** ('woman') and **raġel** ('man') in today's Maltese; these are only two examples out of hundreds of Semitic lexical terms that have experienced the same development. Moreover, this phenomenon has been taking place also in the adoption of Romance vocabulary as may be confirmed in Italian *pulpito* ('pulpit') > Sicilian *pulpitu* > Maltese **pulptu;** *predica* ('sermon') > **priedka;** *musica* ('music') > **mużga;** *sicuro* ('sure') > **żgur;** etc.

The Maltese language has retained much of the classical Arabic morphology. However, it lost some of the Forms of the verb – Maltese has ten, while Arabic has **fourteen.** Some of the vocabulary has lost the original Arabic plural, diminutive, and other forms. In the meantime some Romance morphological aspects have been adopted by Maltese too; these include the plural morpheme *-i* and several prefixes and suffixes characteristic of the Italian language. Furthermore, some Romance loanwords have adopted Semitic forms too; Italian *bandiera* ('flag') > Maltese *bandiera* > Semitic broken plural **bnadar,** *tappeto* ('carpet') > **tapit** > Romance plural **tapiti**

---

[26] Cf. 'Eoin Mac Neill, one of the future leaders of the revival, pleaded with the Catholic clergy to promote the language (Irish).' In Liam S. Andrews, 'Northern Nationalists and the Politics of the Irish Language: The Historical Background' in *Language and Politics – Northern Ireland, the Republic of Ireland, and Scotland,* (eds. John M. Kirk and Dónall P. Ó Baoill), Belfast 2000, p. 50. It is to be remarked that in Malta nobody needed to ask the clergy to promote the vernacular; they were using it in the most natural way. The inhabitants – all of whom were Catholics – would not have been able to follow the Italian, and moreover Latin, used by the literate and the administrators.

[27] Maltese **kitla** and **kejk** < English *kettle* and *cake* respectively, are examples of the first process, **destrojer, xelter, ħelikopter, parking, fajjar, stering,** < English *destroyer, shelter, helicopter, parking, to fire, steering* respectively, are among the many examples of the second.

or Semitic broken plural **twapet,** *abito* ('dress') > Maltese **labtu** ('scapular') > Semitic plural **labtijiet.** The English adoptions include the plural -*s* morpheme, and hundreds of lexemes, some of which have adapted to the Semitic morphology like 'kettle' > Maltese **kitla** > Semitic broken plural **ktieli,** and 'cake' > Maltese *kejk* > Semitic plural **kejkijiet,** 'team' > **tim** > Semitic plural **timijiet.**

There are also a great number of Semitic words that have experienced a semantic change and in today's Maltese express a shade of meaning which is sometimes quite different from the original they still have in Arabic.

A Latin alphabet

The letter-characters of the Roman alphabet had been in use in inscriptions in public places in both Malta and Gozo, right from the second century BC. It was after more than one thousand years in contact with this alphabet that the inhabitants came in contact with Arabic characters and symbols – a period which, politically, lasted only two hundred and twenty years.

After 1091, the Maltese inhabitants came in contact, and continued to be, with the Latin alphabet of the rulers that came from the north, from continental Europe, after.

This is the reason why the Maltese alphabet has a long history.

Men of letters who endeavoured to write something in Maltese must have been always conscious of, and found it difficult to represent, the Semitic sounds otherwise lacking representation in the Latin and Italian alphabets they had known and perhaps used for many years. In the medieval deeds written in either of these languages, notaries always rendered Maltese place-names using the Roman characters they felt expressive of the sounds they themselves used or heard articulated by their clients; the phonetic representation of the language used in the *Cantilena* is a classical example. Notwithstanding this, some writers have dared using a mixed alphabet by including Arabic characters in the Roman alphabet, too. However, contact with Italian, which was the official language of the Knights of St John for more than two-and-a-half centuries, the language of the administration until late in the nineteenth and early twentieth century, the language which the Maltese clergy and literate men studied, learnt, and used when reading most of the printed material available – among themselves, and to further on their studies at home, but especially in universities in Sicily and Italy – played a very important role on the use of a Latin alphabet, with various letters including diacritical modifications, between the sixteenth and the nineteenth centuries.[28] These were times when the Italian language had become the established language of culture, a status it continued to enjoy by most of the intellectuals until late in 1930s.

The Maltese language today

The two main basic elements that make up the language used today are Semitic and Romance. The Semitic element constitutes the very basic foundation of the language. It manifests itself in about half of the vocabulary of the language, and almost in all of its morphological aspects. The grammar was eventually supplemented by Romance

---

[28] A list of various graphemes proposed and used for Arabic sounds was collected and published by Joseph Aquilina, in his 'Systems of Maltese Orthography' in *Papers in Maltese Linguistics*, pp. 75-101b, and folding table facing p. 90.

and English morphology too. The Romance element – made up mainly of a very few French words, a multitude of Sicilian and Italian lexical terms, and idiomatic and proverbial concepts – constitutes the complementary stock of the language. English came in contact with the Maltese language after 1800. No sooner had the British took over the government of the islands than they introduced the teaching of English in education. It was first used by the people who worked in the Malta Dockyards. However, the widest and more effective contacts were brought about by the Second World War when English and Maltese soldiers fought the enemy side by side. English eventually became the source for borrowing too; today Maltese is continuously borrowing and adopting particularly the modern technical and scientific vocabulary, otherwise lacking in the language.

A Maltese alphabet and a Maltese grammar

The Maltese Alphabet

The Maltese alphabet consists of 30 letters; 6 vowels and 24 consonants

Grapheme	IPA phoneme	Name of letter	English phoneme
A, a	/a/	a	car
B, b	/b/	be	bar
Ċ, ċ	/tʃ/	ċe	church
D, d	/d/	de	do
E, e	/e/	e	elm
F, f	/f/	fe	far
Ġ, ġ	/dʒ/	ġe	germ
G, g	/g/	ge	guard
GĦ, Għ, għ	//gh//	għajn	-
H, h	//h//	akka	-
Ħ, ħ	//ħ//	he	hotel
I, I	/i/	i	him
IE, Ie, ie	/iə/	ie	year
J, j	/y/	je	pay
K, k	/k/	ke	kin
L, l	/l/	le	lard
M, m	/m/	me	mark
N, n	/n/	ne	no
O, o	/o/	o	doll
P, p	/p/	pe	part
Q, q	/ʔ/	qe	-
R, r	/r/	re	roll
S, s	/s/	se	sit
T, t	/t/	te	top
U, u	/u/	u	bull
V, v	/v/	ve	vest
W, w	/w/	we	wow
X, x	/ʃ/ or /ʒ/	xe	shut *and* vision
Ż, ż	/z/	że	cosy
Z, z	/tz/ or /dz/	ze	pizza *and* gazette

Until 1934 the language of the administration was always that of the rulers. But, it may be ascertained that in their daily interactions the inhabitants always kept using the vernacular as a means of communication.[29] As a written language, however, it remained unused, uncared for, unguided, and uncultivated. Very often it was looked down upon as the vulgar tongue of the peasant folk, or as the idiom 'used in the kitchen'. It was after long years of various individual efforts to sort out a standard organized system for writing that some Maltese started to care about their language.

The solution and eventual standardization of a Maltese alphabet and grammar were decided upon in 1924. In the beginning of the twentieth century budding and established Maltese authors who used to write and publish in both Italian and Maltese, accepted a public invitation to come together and eventually unite in what was then called **L-Għaqda tal-Malti** ('The Society for the Maltese [language]'), with the aim of deciding upon and establishing a phonetic Roman alphabet – thus making Maltese the only Semitic language written with a Roman alphabet – and standardizing a Maltese grammar. With regards to the alphabet, it was decided which practical graphemes should represent the twenty-four consonantal phonemes and the five[30] vocalic phonemes of the language.

The difficulty which could have once arisen in the presentation of the original Arabic emphatic sounds had by then disappeared since from three 't' (ت, ث, and ط), three 'd' (د, ذ, and ض), two 'h' (ح and خ), two 's' (س and ص), and two '*ain*' (ع and غ) phonemes Maltese retained only one of each.

The Latin letters long in use for Romance phonemes /c/ (/ch/ in *church*), /g/ (in *garden*), /p/, and /z/ (in *pizza*), had been in use in whatever was written in Maltese for quite a long time, and hence met with no difficulty to be included. The semi-consonants 'j' and 'w' – although with some controversy by the supporters of an 'Italian alphabet' where they are absent – were introduced to represent their counterpart phonemes (ي and و) in Arabic. Diacritical marks helped solve the differences that should distinguish between the graphemes for phonemes /g/ (in *ground*) and /ġ/ (in *gender*), between etymological zero phoneme /h/ and the aspirated /ħ/ (in *hotel*), and between /ż/ (in *żig-żag*) and /z/ (in *pizza*). It was decided that the digrh 'għ' was to represent both of the etymological Arabic '*ain's*. The dot on the only 'ċ' character (for the 'ch' phoneme in *church*) in the Maltese alphabet is today considered as 'historical'; it was introduced to settle down once and forever a Maltese phoneme as against the /c/'s double phonemic value in Italian. The result of these decisions brought to light the first scientific Maltese grammar: *Tagħrif fuq il-Kitba Maltija* (Malta 1924), ('Information about Writing Maltese'), which proved to be a success, and with very little changes since then, saw Maltese accepted as an official language (second to English) in 1934, entrenched in the Independence Constitution as the national language and the first official language of Independent Malta 30 years later; and, very recently accepted as one of the working languages of the European Union, after Malta was confirmed member on 1 May 2004.

---

[29] Compare with 'Italian being spoken in the cities, while that spoken by the countryfolk is an admixture of words and forms of Arabic, [...], and Italian.' J.S. Vater, as quoted in *Il-Malti – Elf Sena ta' Storja*, p. 155.

[30] Today, Maltese has six vowels. The decision to include the 'ie' vocalic phoneme as the sixth vowel was taken by the Akkademja tal-Malti (Academy for Maltese) in 1994.

The Bible and other material in Maltese

Among the first publications to be printed using the new alphabet and grammar were the literary association's quarterly journal *Il-Malti* still published to date[31] – and the books of the Bible,[32] translated from the original in Hebrew and Greek by Maltese Classicist and Orientalist Mgr P.P. Saydon who dared even scholarly coin some vocabulary to make the translation as Semitic in character as possible.[33] It must be noted, however, that books from the Bible had been published in Maltese as early as 1829,[34] and many prayer books of all kinds – some in Maltese side by side with either Latin, or Italian texts – and other biblical material were published even much earlier, before.

The Administration

The alphabet and grammar, however, were officially recognized by the administration of the country, ten years later – in 1924. And when this took place it was realized that although some books in Maltese had already seen light long before, literary material written with the new system, especially for use in schools, was lacking. In 1935 the authorities launched a literary prize which would provide such books.

Maltese in the Law Courts

Until 1932, the language used in the courts was Italian. The use of the Maltese language was introduced in that year by Ordinance No. XVI of 1932 (His Majesty's Letters Patent dated 14 April 1932). The use of Maltese as the official language of the Maltese courts, was then enacted by Ordinance No. XXX of 1934: '495a. (a) Subject to the ensuing provisions of this article, the Maltese language shall be the official language of the Court.' (His Majesty's Letters Patent dated 14 April 1934).

Up to 1934 *The Malta Government Gazette* was still printed in English and Italian. In that same year the administration's official gazette started being printed in English and Maltese, automatically recognizing Maltese as one of the two official languages of Malta, second to English.

---

[31] The first issue was published in January 1924.

[32] The books were published one by one from time to time. The first book, *Il-Ġenesi (Genesis)*, was published in 1929, while the last one, *L-Apokalissi* (the *Apocalypse*), was published in 1959.

[33] This fact later on prevented this Bible from being accepted by the Church for use during Mass in Maltese, from 1964 onwards, for the simple reason that it did not present an immediate rendering to the faithful. For this reason, then the Għaqda Biblika Maltija (Maltese Biblical Society), set on a new 'practical' and in a certain way 'popular' translation which is still the only one in use today.

[34] In the early years of the nineteenth century, a certain William Jowett established the Malta Bible Society (later known as the Bible Society in Malta) with the aim of producing a translation of the Bible in Maltese. The society had to work on a Maltese alphabet, and establish a system of Maltese orthography and grammar. However, Jowett met and commissioned Michael Anton Vassalli – who had already published a Maltese grammar (1792) and a Maltese-Italian-Latin lexicon (1796) – to work on the translation of the Gospels and the Acts of the Apostles. These were eventually published in one volume posthumously in 1829.

The Holy Mass in Maltese

Among other recommendations, Vatican Council II proposed that Holy Mass should be said in the language of the people; this happened in 1964.[35] Until then, as part of the unifying universality concept of the Church, Holy Mass used to be said in Latin; the celebrant used to deliver a homily in which he would explain the readings and expand on them in the vernacular of the congregation. With the new resolution, Maltese became the language of the Mass, and the readings – now taken from a new more popular translation of the Bible – and the liturgy became an important communicative aspect of the use of Maltese.

Maltese in the Constitution of Malta

Malta achieved political independence in 1964. Since then, Maltese has always been entrenched as the recognized and accepted national language of the Maltese. 'The national language is of course Maltese. But both Maltese and English are stated to be official languages.'[36] This has been endorsed also in the constitution when Malta was declared a Republic, in 1974, wherein[37] Section 5 states:

5. (1) The National language of Malta is the Maltese language.
  (2) The Maltese and the English languages and such other language as may be prescribed by Parliament (by a law passed by not less than two-thirds of all the members of the House of Representatives) shall be the official languages of Malta and the Administration may for all official purposes use any of such languages:
   Provided that any person may address the Administration in any of the official languages and the reply of the Administration thereto shall be in such language.
  (3) The language of the Courts shall be the Maltese language:
   Provided that Parliament may make such provision for the use of the English language in such cases and under such conditions as it may prescribe.
  (4) The House of Representatives may, in regulating its own procedure, determine the language or languages that shall be used in Parliamentary proceedings and records.

Maltese in Education

Since the establishment of compulsory education in 1946, Maltese has been taught, side by side with English, in all State schools. Today, both languages are taught in all State, Private, and Church schools from the very first years in primary classes. The teaching of their use in speech, reading, and writing takes place at all levels of Education. This is made compulsory by the 'Education Act',[38] enacted law in 1989.

---

[35] Cf. Circular No. 285 issued form the Archbishop's Curia in Malta, on 21 November, 1964.

[36] Cf. J. J. Cremona, *The Maltese Constitution and Constitutional History since 1813*, Malta 1994, p. 78.

[37] Cf. Constitution of Malta, Chapter I – The Republic of Malta.

[38] The text of the 'Education Act' may be consulted in Joe Zammit-Ciantar, *Education in Malta – a handbook*, (2nd ed.), Malta 1996, pp. 42-82.

The Primary Schools Syllabus

With regards to the teaching of languages in primary education, the 'Education Act' states that children should learn the Maltese and English languages, in the spoken, read, and written forms.[39]

The Secondary Schools Syllabus

The 'Education Act' provides the further teaching of the Maltese and English languages in secondary education too.[40] The students have three hours per week for Maltese, and three hours and forty-five minutes for English and other foreign languages.

The use of Maltese in Tertiary Education

There is no steadfast rule with regards to the delivery of academic information in the tertiary level. However, passes at 'O' Level in both Maltese and English are compulsory for entry into any of the Higher Secondary Schools, or into the University of Malta Junior College, where students are prepared for the 'A' Levels which enable them to proceed to the University. Still, the National Minimum Curriculum for post-secondary education[41] requires that 'An emphasis [be made] on the necessity of effective communication in both the verbal and the written media.' This may be interpreted as 'understood' reference to the use of Maltese, and perhaps especially English, which would be extremely helpful and surely indispensable in graduate courses taken up at the University.

Ordinary Level Examination papers set by the University of Malta Secondary Education Certificate Board are set only in Maltese for the Maltese language and literature, in both Maltese and English for Religious Studies, Social Studies, and Environmental Studies, and only in English for all the other subjects. Advanced Level Examination papers are set only in Maltese for Maltese Language and Literature, again bilingual for Religious Studies and Systems of Knowledge, and only in English for all the other subjects. Passes in Maltese and/or English at Intermediate or Advanced Level are required for certain courses leading to particular degrees at the University of Malta.[42]

---

[39] Section A, 2(a), of Clause 6.3 of the National Minimum Curriculum – Primary Level (Legal Notice 73 of 1989), of the Education Act states: 'At this level teaching should start to be formal and should be intended to achieve … [the] acquisition of the tools of knowledge and expression by the teaching of … the Maltese and English languages, in the spoken, read, and written forms.'

[40] Together with Mathematics, they form part of the 'communicative core': Section 4, B, of Clause 6.4 of the National Minimum Curriculum – Secondary Level (Legal Notice 103 of 1990), of the Education Act. This clause further states that: 'Another language at first year from those offered (Italian, French, German, and Arabic), and yet another language at third year from a wider choice which would also include Latin, Spanish, and Russian,' and 'particular courses in trade schools might opt for technical English in lieu of a third foreign language.'

[41] Cf. Section 2 of the 'Content' of Clause 6.5 of the National Minimum Curriculum – Post-Secondary Level (Legal Notice 56 of 1991).

[42] The passes needed for the particular courses, which may be taken up at the University of

Maltese and English at the University

The languages of the University are Maltese and English.

Maltese in the media

Newspapers in Maltese are very popular, and very widely read. These include the dailies *In-Nazzjon* and *L-Orizzont*, the weekly *Il-Ġens,* and the Sunday *It-Torċa, KullĦadd*, and *Il-Mument.* It is to be noted that although all the news and articles are written in Maltese, whole pages with financial reports, and a great number of both small and large commercial adverts in English are common daily inclusions, too. The dailies *The Malta Independent* and *The Times [of Malta]*, and *The Malta Independent on Sunday*, *Malta Today*, and *The Sunday Times [of Malta]* in English, enjoy extensive readership as well.

In Malta there are several radio and T.V. stations; these include the State owned Public Broadcasting Corporation, and those owned by the political parties: NET and Super ONE. They all use the Maltese language for most of the time; only one radio station broadcasts in English. Again, the airing or transmission of commercial adverts in English, even during programmes in Maltese, is a very familiar accepted norm. All cultural programmes produced locally are in Maltese. However cultural programmes and films in English 'rented' or 'bought' for airing on local T.V. stations are never translated into Maltese and are transmitted without any sort of dubbing.

Maltese in street-names

Until the very recent past, Maltese paper money used to carry all the wording on them in Maltese on one side, and in English on the other; today this is done only in Maltese. Up to some years ago, the names of streets were affixed in both English and Maltese too, but lately, there has been an emphasis on presenting them only in Maltese. The decision has never been opposed and today, all the names of the streets in Malta and Gozo are in Maltese, and so they appear in the telephone directory, and the electoral register.

Maltese in the book market

The Maltese language is used profusely by every Maltese writer. Maltese is used in writing and printing of all sorts of circulars, pamphlets, magazines, and books; every year, quite a number of books are published in Maltese. The run would be in the limits of 1,000 to 3,000. The novel is perhaps the most popular and widely read by both young and old. However, when it comes to specific studies, especially those involving researched works which deal with Maltese politics, history, archaeology, and the Maltese language, scholars prefer to publish in English. Such publications would not enjoy a good market at home; they would, however, appeal to a wider English-speaking audience which includes tourists, and help placing Malta, and its language on the world map.

Malta, may be consulted in the 'University of Malta Special Course Requirements for Undergraduate Courses', which is published by the University of Malta, around May every year. For those for entry into the University of Malta in 2005, cf. *Look ... before you leap*, Malta 2003, pp. 45-55.

Figure 3: A page from the Sunday newspaper *Il-Mument*, wherein articles included are in Maltese, and the accompanying advert is in English.[43]

Maltese a working language in the European Union

Maltese is a living national language.[44] Because of this status, in the accession negotiations Malta has asked that the Maltese language be included as a legal working language – together with those of other member countries – of the

---

[43] This page from the Sunday newspaper, *Il-Mument*, wherein articles included are in Maltese, and the accompanying advert is in English, is reproduced by courtesy of and with the kind permission of the Editor, Mr. Victor Camilleri.

[44] Maltese is used by small Maltese communities who, over the last two centuries, have settled

European Union.[45] The text in the Accession Treaty wherein the Maltese Language is included, states:

> **Institutions:** Article 1
> The official languages and the working languages of the institutions of the Union shall be Czech, Danish, Dutch, English, Estonian, Finnish, French, German, Greek, Hungarian, Italian, Latvian, Lithuanian, Maltese, Polish, Portuguese, Slovak, Slovenian, Spanish and Swedish.

Although with some teething problems with Maltese translators and interpreters, the Maltese language is already being used by Maltese official representatives, and the five Maltese members of the European Parliament participating in European Union meetings in Brussels.

Conclusion

As has been shown in this paper, Maltese is relatively a young language. It is still developing and there are times when translators, interpreters, and authors yet meet with difficulties especially when trying to express new ideas, and use technical terms in Maltese. The globalization, which is fast influencing the economy of countries all over the world, is impinging on the Maltese language too. The hopes of one and all interested in the use of the language in the local educational programmes, and especially in harmonizing the EU laws for use by the Maltese citizens in their own national language, now lies in the hands of all involved in the education of our future citizens. Professional and academically-prepared people working on the translation of EU literature are doing their best to help establish terms and vocabulary, otherwise lacking in the Maltese language. The establishment of a National Council for the Maltese Language, by a bill[46] recently passed in Parliament, aims 'to promote the National Language of Malta and to provide the necessary means to achieve this aim'. However, the use of the language by the inhabitants is the reassuring guarantee that Maltese will live on, adopting and integrating, and growing into an ever living effective national language.

---

in Canada and Australia. Although some Maltese who emigrated to, and settled in, the USA and England are found to have, to a certain extent, preserved their mother tongue, they rarely use it outside their homes unless with fellow Maltese migrants.

[45] With regards to the Maltese language becoming one of the working languages of the European Union, on 12 May 2002, the Malta Government Information Office issued a press release, in Maltese and English which included the following information:

> **Maltese to be EU official language**
> The Maltese Government has been informed that the Committee of Permanent Representatives (COREPER) at the Council of Ministers in the European Union had accepted the recommendation made by the European Commission for the Maltese language to become one of the EU's official languages on Malta's accession.

[46] Bill No. 18, published in Maltese and English in *The Malta Government Gazette – supplement*, No. 17,504, Malta 18.xi.2003.

Irish and Scottish Studies

Peter Gregson

Well good evening ladies and gentlemen. After that introduction, I think it's important to add that of course things aren't quite like that nowadays. Only last year we had to lead ourselves through an institutional audit at Southampton and I've just come here in time to pick up Queen's institutional audit in November. So I've no doubt that we'll be discussing those sorts of topics a bit later next month. Can I first of all say, welcome here, welcome to members of Queen's, welcome especially to our guests. Welcome to this wonderful hall and excellent dinner provided by Queen's outstanding catering services, a fitting occasion to the conclusion of what I understand has been a very enlightening symposium. Certainly by the discussions and the noise level already this evening, I can tell that you've had an enlightening and inspiring time, and I'm sure that some of those discussions will continue this evening and also tomorrow, when I know that some of you have got a very interesting occasion with the launch of a new Irish Bible.

So, what about the symposium tonight? Well it's special for me to be here with you and it's special, I think, at the end of this week because I'm enjoying something of a cultural feast. Only last night, I was sharing the stage at the Queen's Alumni Association in Scotland with Professor Tom Devine. He was talking to us then about Scottish history and the Ulster connection. I have an interest because I was born in Scotland in Dunfermline but, as you've probably realised from my accent, I left there after six months and haven't returned, regrettably. However, I'm beginning to get a greater affinity with the cultures and the connections between *this* great place and our deep associations in Scotland. So this cultural feast, for me, goes on this evening and I'm really looking forward to listening and learning from our two guest speakers this evening, Professors Edna Longley and George Watson. Thank *you* for being here, and I look forward to being a lot wiser at the end of the evening than I am now.

In thinking about this evening and language, it dawned on me that although I've only been here in Northern Ireland for just over three weeks now, I've already become aware that language is a very hot topic here for a number of reasons. And that that's obviously completely right. Language gets to the very heart of cultural identity and it's absolutely right and proper that where we have cultural identities that we celebrate, there, too, we should discuss the nature of language and debate the details of language and how we use it. I think one of my observations is that it's important that we don't think that the debate here in Northern Ireland is unique to Northern Ireland, and one of the things that I was especially impressed by in skimming through some of your previous symposia proceedings was the fact that clearly, over the years, you've looked at some of the issues and the parallels that can be drawn beyond these islands and beyond these shores. And I've been fascinated by some of the papers that I've read in those proceedings. So thank you for sending me those, John, in advance of this meeting. I've also learnt, from speaking to one or two of you, that your proceedings are often not without controversy. I guess that comes to the heart of why you've come. You've come hopefully to indulge in academic discussion and debate, friendly and challenging. Of course, that really gets to the heart of what a university is about, providing we ensure that these rigorous discussions are respectful of academic freedom and respectful of other people's opinions. So I'm really delighted that you've had such a stimulating meeting here, and I look forward to seeing the proceedings when they're published. I really do believe that your field of study is very important. The output of your discussions and your influence on others are going to shape the future relationships both within and between these islands to which we all belong. And I think that Queen's is very proud of the fact that we have a leading research activity in this area. It really is contributing so importantly to the cultural and the social development of this part of Ireland that we're here to serve.

Now, as the incoming Vice-Chancellor here, one of the things that is especially important to me is that in a generation when knowledge knows no bounds and in a generation where different strengths reside in different institutions, we develop strong academic collaborations. And what you've arranged today is witness to the fact that you, too, want to deepen the research base here at Queen's and with the other academic establishments that we're partnering. So it's really great to see this partnership between Aberdeen, who lead it through their AHRB centre, Trinity College Dublin, and ourselves here at Queen's. I believe that you're developing a very strong foundation in an important research area and I'm sure that that will strengthen the overall collaboration between those three very strong institutions.

I'm grateful on behalf of Queen's for John and his colleagues in organising this symposium; I'm really pleased to see such an active partnership between those three universities, and I look forward over the years ahead to see this partnership grow and develop, and the research become even more stimulating in the years ahead. I hope you all enjoy the evening and, as I said earlier, I'm especially looking forward to the contributions from our guest speakers, Edna and George. Thank you very much indeed, and bon appétit.

Irish and Scottish Studies

Edna Longley

This remarkably successful series of Language and Politics symposia belongs to the wider success of Irish-Scottish studies during the last ten years – even the last ten days. I was in Edinburgh last week for the extremely lively conference of the Irish-Scottish Academic Initiative. There are different views on how to pronounce the acronym, ISAI, but I prefer 'Isaiah', with its prophetic ring. ISAI was originally dreamed up on a convivial evening like this, by the then heads of Aberdeen University, Strathclyde and Trinity College Dublin. So vice-chancellors do conceive and sponsor new directions in the humanities. Queen's joined ISAI a little later and Edinburgh University joined two years ago. As most of you know, ISAI promotes Irish-Scottish studies in literature, language, history and politics. Its spirit is inter-disciplinary, as well as inter-national in more senses than one. It also highlights creative exchange between Ireland and Scotland, literary cross-fertilisation, the song traditions that Len Graham and Pádraigín Ní Uallacháin make so wonderfully available through their research and performances. And further, as this annual symposium continually proves, Irish-Scottish studies intersect with the public world of devolution and the Peace Process, with events in Leeds Castle. Here, academic debates are not above the fray, but in it, sometimes bruisingly so. At the ISAI conference we ran at Queen's two years ago, when a unionist crisis – I suppose there's always one – prevented David Trimble from speaking at the dinner. Graham Walker said, "Our lines of scholarly enquiry should lead into some awkward, twisting, and perhaps unattractive landscapes, as we probe the complexities which lie at the heart of our enterprise."

These complexities are not only of parochial interest. At that Belfast conference, a key theme was what has been variously called 'British Isles history', 'the new British history', and 'archipelagic history', the term I use. Here again, there is a vigorous debate, since academic paradigms too are intertwined with politics, and national frameworks can be powerfully defended. Yet, archipelagic history does not necessarily replace, but complements or complicates, national history. That includes national literary history. In Edinburgh last week, one speaker said that Irish-Scottish studies had now made it impossible to write Scottish literary history without mentioning Ireland, and vice-versa. So, both Irish studies and Scottish studies are acquiring new dimensions, whether they are conducted comparatively or proximately. Similarly, an Irish-Scottish axis of enquiry brings much academic anglo-centrism into question, as it also does any exclusive concentration on relations between Scotland and England, or Ireland and England.

In 2002, to mark its centenary, the British Academy organised eight lectures around the UK. These have just been published in a book called *The Promotion of Knowledge*, edited by John Morrill. One lecture took place in Aberdeen under the auspices of the Research Institute and AHRB Centre for Irish and Scottish Studies, a lecture given by the historian Keith Robbins titled, 'Location and Dislocation: Ireland, Scotland and Wales in their Insular Alignment'. There were four responses to that lecture, the only formal responses included in the British Academy centenary volume. One response was from myself, representing Northern Ireland, so to speak, another from Cairns Craig of Edinburgh University. Speaking from a Scottish perspective, Cairns Craig found Keith Robbins's assumptions unduly anglo-centric. I think he thought England had a more insular alignment in another sense. Professor Craig deconstructed 'British' in the Academy's title, and asked what this designation might now mean for literary and cultural studies. He argued, "Some of the key developments in the culture of the archipelago over the past three hundred years do not involve relationships between Ireland, Scotland and Wales on the one side and England on the other, but depend on interactions which go round the peripheries." For instance Francis Hutcheson, Bishop Berkeley and David Hume in Philosophy; Maria Edgeworth and Walter Scott in the novel. So, Cairns Craig was suggesting, and so would I, that England too is implicated in the new understandings generated by Irish-Scottish studies.

Self-quotation is probably a bad habit, but my own perspective was and is that Northern Ireland, or whatever we want to call this area, and contested terms are again part of the picture, constitutes not only a crucial focus for studying archipelagic interaction but a crucial vantage point from which to pursue such study. Here, most of the cultural strands intertwine and snag; here, the historical politics of these islands thicken, and sometimes sicken. To give one example from history: the historian, Jane Dawson, has said of events in Ulster in the late 1590s that they were "of major importance within European politics and dominated the policy-making of the English queen and the Scottish king". Or, to come rapidly up-to-date, and to refer to literature, the founding of the Seamus Heaney Centre for Poetry reflects the current high profile and influence of Northern Irish poetry in the archipelago and beyond. And in this connection Irish-Scottish relations, Irish-Scottish similarities and differences are proving a hugely significant ground for studying the traditions, genres and forms of modern poetry. So, for me, to think *from* Northern Ireland as well as *about* Northern Ireland, seems integral to the developing rationale or paradigm of Irish-Scottish studies. Our double horizon across the border and the Irish Sea can make mutual complexities of language, religion, migration, colonisation and empire uniquely visible. Tomorrow's focus on language and religion is a case in point. But of course, as in this symposium, the chemistry between scholars looking from different points of the archipelagic and European map is what makes the whole field so vibrant and gives it such potential to change disciplinary as well as cultural parameters.

Yesterday, the proceedings of the Cross-currents graduate students' conference were published. One of the exciting things for me at the ISAI conference last week was the way in which young scholars were already challenging their elders and opening up the future. The main organiser of the Edinburgh conference was Aaron Kelly, a graduate in English of this university, where he also took his doctorate. Aaron then became a post-doctoral fellow at Edinburgh University for a three year Leverhulme project in Irish-Scottish literary studies. He now has a lecturing post in Edinburgh University and is busy publishing books on Irish literature, Scottish literature and both together. So I think he's a model of what we're about. But another model, in many respects, has been the language studies in which you're all engaged; in some respects language studies have led the way. And I think it's obvious to everybody here that John Kirk and Dónall Ó Baoill have facilitated a set of dialogues and an intellectual database to which Irish-Scottish studies will forever be indebted.

Irish and Scottish Studies

George Watson

Distinguished guests, Vice-Chancellor, ladies and gentlemen, as John has just said, I am an alumnus of this university, and am very pleased to be so, because I think it is one of the great universities in what we've learned to call 'these islands'. It's a bit like looking up the football results, you know – you always want to see, "How's Queen's doing?" And it's doing very well. And I do want to wish Vice-Chancellor Gregson all the best for the future. I'm sure that he will do a job that will keep this university at the forefront of things, and I wish you well on that.

I just want to explain something that is slightly complicated. As director of the Research Institute of Irish and Scottish Studies in Aberdeen University, I want to explain briefly the relationship between the Institute and the AHRB Centre (Arts and Humanities Research Board Centre), in which, along with Aberdeen and Trinity College Dublin, Queen's is such a significant force. The Research Institute of Irish and Scottish Studies was inaugurated by the President of Ireland [Mary McAleese], in the presence of the then Secretary of State for Scotland [John Reid], on St. Andrew's Day in 1999. And then, in 2001, largely as a result of the excellent, co-operative, academic and intellectual links we had forged with Queen's University and with Trinity College Dublin, we had the glad tidings that the Arts and Humanities Research Board had decided to create one of their new centres in Aberdeen, which is located in the Research Institute of Irish and Scottish Studies. So, this is my only and best way of putting it: the Arts and Humanities Research Board laid a huge egg, £870,000 in the Research Institute of Irish and Scottish Studies. But they wouldn't have laid that egg unless we had this superb relationship with Queen's and Trinity, and we were very lucky to have those, though we had worked on it to make sure it happened.

Edna, Professor Longley, has eloquently demonstrated the compelling intellectual, cultural and political reasons why comparative studies of the histories, literatures and languages of Ireland and Scotland are so vital - vital' in both senses of the word: 'vital' in terms of 'lively', 'alive', and 'vital' also as 'crucial'. And I want to stress how favourably our funding masters look on co-operative, collaborative research, and therefore you must decide now, Vice-Chancellor Gregson, to keep continuing this wonderful input. I see him nod, and I'm lying but never mind. The Arts and Humanities Research Board gave us £870,000 over a five year period. It is quite certain that they would not have done this unless there had been firm links between Aberdeen, Trinity College Dublin and Queen's University Belfast. These links had been established, as Edna was saying, through the Irish-Scottish Academic Initiative, which had been set up in 1995, and it promoted inter-university scholarship and research programmes of Irish and Scottish studies. It's very important and really made a huge impact on our success in getting the AHRB funding. That funding and the AHRB centre that was established – and I stress again, the AHRB centre in Aberdeen is inseparable from Queen's University Belfast and Trinity in Dublin– that has made possible fourteen research projects in the histories, literatures and languages of the two countries. And it would be tedious for you, very tedious at this time of night, if I were to go through them all, so I won't. I'll just mention that one could illustrate how Queen's benefits directly and tangibly from this collaboration. We funded a large project based in Queen's on 20th-century diasporas, emigration from Scotland and Ireland between 1921-2001, and, more pertinent to this particular occasion, the AHRB centre has funded the research in the languages and politics of Scotland and Ireland, which has been led by Dr. John Kirk and Professor Dónall Ó Baoill. And this has developed specific research on Ulster Scots, brought an inter-disciplinary dimension to the hitherto narrowly focused subject-specific approach to English, Scots and Gaelic, Scotland and Ulster, and through international conferences it has generated copious and significant publications under the indefatigable stewardship of Dr. Kirk and Professor Ó Baoill. I mean, anyone who's been at the conference today will have seen in the number and range of their of publications - it's fantastic, amazing, great!

Also, we have always thought that it was very important to help young scholars, and therefore postgraduate students and the whole postgraduate training of students has been a major part of our activity. And so we've had three Cross-currents conferences: one in Aberdeen, one very successful one here and one in Dublin. And these postgraduate students get a chance to meet each other, working in this field, and that's really great! And as you know from yesterday – I'm sorry I couldn't be here – but those of you who were here will have seen an excellent launch of the publication of essays by these postgraduate students.

However, I want to finish off with some exciting news: we're on the cusp here. The Arts and Humanities Research Board has suggested that there would be a phase two programme, which means that, if we're successful, we'll get £1.25 million, which for engineers or medical people, is a mere flea-bite, but for Arts is fantastic! If we get £1.25 million, and I think we have a reasonable expectation of success, then we'd be able to continue the funding of the language and politics programme here at Queen's, which John and Professor Ó Baoill have done so well. We want to continue that. We'll also be able to fund a project that comes from Dr. Fran Brearton and Professor Longley on Irish and Scottish poetry from 1890 to the present. And I think we also will be funding two other projects, one of which is involved with Trinity College Dublin. The main thing is simply to say that we cannot over-emphasise the importance of Queen's, and for that matter, Trinity, but Queen's certainly in this whole exercise, and this is where your new Vice-Chancellor will feel his left ear being bitten severely. The institutional commitment in Aberdeen University has guaranteed, if this thing goes ahead, £710,000, and committed certain strategic plans to making Irish and Scottish studies a research priority in the new college of Arts and Social Sciences. We've actually started poaching some of your major people. In Trinity College, the Centre for Irish and Scottish Studies has been set up, and they've got a research grant award of £IR430,000. That happened in 1999. But in Queen's here, as you'll know, the commitment to Irish and Scottish Studies has been very intense. The strategic plan of the Faculty of Humanities for Research 2000-2005 identifies the development of the new areas of research involving inter-disciplinary, cross-university and inter-university focus groups, as well as seven key objectives. When Queen's joined our work in 1999, four academic appointments that were relevant to the year were made in Celtic Studies and English and in Modern History. And in addition and most importantly, Queen's hosts the well-established Institute of Irish Studies and the Seamus Heaney Centre for Poetry, which confirms its long-term commitment to advance the scholarship of the general area for Irish and Scottish studies.

So, I'll stop there, and I'm sorry for going on so long. I just want to say thanks to the Vice-Chancellor. We wish you well. We wish you very well. You've a precious jewel in Irish and Scottish studies. Nurture it, and you can be assured that we, for our part, will do everything to make it the most successful part of your Humanities operation. Thank you.

202